GLOBAL NEOLIBERAL CAPITALISM AND THE ALTERNATIVES

From Social Democracy to State Capitalisms

David Lane

BRISTOL
UNIVERSITY
PRESS

First published in Great Britain in 2024 by

Bristol University Press
University of Bristol
1-9 Old Park Hill
Bristol
BS2 8BB
UK
t: +44 (0)117 374 6645
e: bup-info@bristol.ac.uk

Details of international sales and distribution partners are available at bristoluniversitypress.co.uk

British Library Cataloguing in Publication Data
A catalogue record for this book is available from the British Library

ISBN 978-1-5292-2090-2 hardcover
ISBN 978-1-5292-2091-9 paperback
ISBN 978-1-5292-2092-6 ePub
ISBN 978-1-5292-2093-3 ePdf

Cover design: Nicky Borowiec
Front cover image: AdobeStock/main image & hand with figure © Hurca!;

FSC
www.fsc.org
MIX
Paper | Supporting
responsible forestry
FSC® C013604

Contents

List of Figures, Tables and Boxes

Figures

Tables

Box

About the Author

David Lane is Emeritus Professor of Sociology at the University of Cambridge and Emeritus Fellow of Emmanuel College. He is a Fellow of the Academy of Social Sciences (UK). He has been a visiting professor at the following universities: Peking, Harvard, Cornell, Odense, Kharkov, Sabanci (Istanbul), Shandong and Graz. His books include:

- *Changing Regional Alliances for China and the West* (2018, ed, with Guichang Zhu)
- *The Eurasian Project in Global Perspective* (2018, ed)
- *The Eurasian Project and Europe* (2015, ed, with Vsevolod Samokhvalov)
- *The Capitalist Transformation of State Socialism* (2014)
- *Elites and Classes in the Transformation of State Socialism* (2011)
- *Rethinking the 'Coloured Revolutions'* (2010, ed, with Stephen White)
- *The European Union and World Politics* (2009, ed, with Andrew Gamble)
- *Varieties of Capitalism in Post-Communist Countries* (2007, ed, with Martin Myant)
- *The Transformation of State Socialism: System Change, Capitalism or Something Else?* (2007, ed)

Acknowledgements

Many people and institutions have assisted me in the preparation of this book. Some chapters originated as lectures given to my MPhil option at the University of Cambridge, and to students and staff members of Peking University, Shandong University and Kharkov National University. I am also indebted to Sergei Bodrunov and to Aleksandr Buzgalin for invitations to their many conferences, and for publication of some related papers in their journals. I would like to thank four referees for their encouraging suggestions and Jacob Zayshley for comments on Chapter 16. I have to thank Christel Lane for her many detailed comments, which have greatly improved the book. I acknowledge the journal, *Eszmele* (Budapest), which published earlier sections of Chapter 15.

1

Introduction

To varying degrees, neoliberal global capitalism shapes modern life not only in Western capitalist societies but also in the rising powers of Asia and Latin America. Its component parts are corporate ownership of assets, free competitive markets, advanced technology, competitive electoral politics, and international forms of interaction and exchange. Its achievements, failures and contradictions are markers that divide human beings at all levels. Defenders of capitalism argue that it is basically sound, it has promoted human freedom, secured human development and achieved significant scientific advances. Even its critics concede that, on a world scale, material conditions have significantly improved. People are living longer and enjoy better health. Consumption of commodities and exposure to a globalised culture are growing at an exponential rate. A world-wide achievement of modern science and a technologically based society has been the enhancement of human well-being. In the late twentieth century, the social dispositions of people have changed. There is a universal expectation for greater equality between sexes, ethnic groups and classes. Not all these developments, however, can be attributed to the capitalist form of economic organisation, let alone its neoliberal variety. Developments in scientific knowledge, bio-technology, the spread of high technology underlying globalisation and the advent of robotisation in manufacture, design and distribution, have also had important positive effects on living standards and modern life.

There are political arguments advanced in favour of capitalism in its contemporary liberal form. Capitalism is contained in a democratic liberal shell, which, it is contended, has prevented the outbreak of wars between democratic countries for the past 75 years. Global capitalism is said to have advanced liberty and peace. Neoliberalism has become the 'common sense' of economic and social policy. When economic policies do not work, the errors are attributed to faulty application rather than to the underlying ideological assumptions on which institutions and policies are based. In

1

the late twentieth century, major influential powers have worked within a neoliberal world view and criticism has been muted.

However, since the beginning of the twenty-first century, neoliberal globalisation, as a theory of how things should be done and a political praxis of how things were being done, has been brought into question. In September 2007, the British bank Northern Rock was unable to meet withdrawals from its customers. It was rescued by the Bank of England, then nationalised by the British government. It was followed by the bankruptcy of the American financial services company Lehman Brothers. In 2008, a global economic crisis had arrived followed by international economic recession. These events brought to a head the uncertainty and insecurity caused by globalised neoliberalism. Despite the advances of the consumer society, many in the advanced Western states had become disillusioned with the consequences of American-led interventions to promote democracy and free markets. Others, in the post-socialist societies of central and Eastern Europe, had become disenchanted by the failure to fulfil the democratic and economic promise of transformation. On a world scale, the disruptive consequences of economic crisis following the financial collapse of 2007–08, led to despair.

The global economic recession raised questions in the public realm about the economic, political and moral foundations of liberal capitalism and its global expression. While capitalism over several centuries has led to an unprecedented rise in living standards, human development has coexisted with very uneven economic development and unjustifiable inequality. Within the core capitalist countries, the export of capital, coupled to technological advance, brought about changes in employment and for many even a decline in living standards. States suffered a significant loss of power and 'shared sovereignty' did not mean equal shares. The movement of capital to areas of low-cost labour production and the promotion of liberal policies by Western regional alliances and international institutions were widely regarded as maintaining the hegemony of Western neoliberal interests. The growth in wealth and income, promised by economic commentators and politicians, has resulted in a very uneven distribution both within countries and between them. Such polarisation has led to instability in the advanced countries. The free movement of people and capital, products and services, strengthened a hegemonic core of the leading Western countries, whereas the post-socialist societies and the South failed to close the economic gap. Globalisation maintained the power of the core states and dependency for others. That is one side of the equation; on the other side has been a remarkable economic development in a number of 'rising states'.

The rising states from the former semi-periphery have not become part of a unitary world system. A consequence of the upsurge of China as an industrial and political power has been the formation of a counterpower to the core states. The shift of industrialisation to the emerging states has led to a massive increase there of a manual working class and the rise of a prosperous middle class including a smaller class of petty bourgeois capitalists. In all the Western post-industrial societies, globalisation had facilitated the transfer of well-paid manual and non-manual jobs to geographical areas of low production costs. To the core post-industrial societies, globalisation supplied cheaper manufactures from the rising states at the cost of significant job losses consequent on outsourcing. Major social changes have occurred consequent on technical advance and computerisation.

Critiques of global capitalism

Political elites adopted neoliberal values and accepted the domestic social costs of the flight of production to the global South, which they believed were outweighed by the positive effects of globalisation. However, the 2007 economic crisis brought to a head many social, political and economic problems. Financialisation, a key component of neoliberalism, heightened levels of public risk, which concurrently promoted unjustifiable rises in differentials of wealth. Critics contended that conflict, domination and exploitation between social groups and also between states are consequences of capitalist competition, of economies based on corporate property driven by dominant global and national capitalist classes. While the positive changes that have taken place under globalised neoliberalism are not denied, I suggest seven major structural problems of contemporary societies that underpin calls for reform:

- Recurring economic crises of capitalism leading to underutilisation of capital (slumps) and labour (under- and unemployment).
- Unjustifiable unequal levels of wealth and income constituted by narrow ownership of wealth.
- Severe social disruption caused by insecure employment and migration. The former being the consequence of technological change, which replaced industrial manual, then non-manual labour with machines; and concurrently, mass migration, being the result of the flight from underdevelopment and poverty. High levels of insecurity and social stress have resulted for the affected social strata.
- Systemic inadequacies of democratic government have given rise to a political legitimacy deficit. Political elites have become 'de-coupled' from social classes. Ruling elites have dominated politics, and political parties have been unable to respond positively to public demands.
- Systemic inequalities between the countries of the core/semi-core/periphery of the world system. Despite the significant rise in living standards, rising levels of education and a decline in mortality rates, not

all have benefitted to the same degree. And unjustifiable inequalities have risen within states creating psychological stress and unfulfilled needs causing ill-health, crime and premature death.

- Unregulated profit driven development involves social costs and environmental damage and contributes to ecological destruction. A limit may be reached to the availability of natural resources, thus ending consumerism and the capitalism necessary to maintain it.

- The threat of war between the industrialised states at the core of the world system (particularly the USA and the UK) and others in the semi-core and periphery has not abated. While democratic states do not fight each other, they regularly go to war with other, what they define as, autocratic non-democratic states.

Many of the dilemmas described existed before or are independent of neoliberalism or globalisation, and it is important to distinguish between them. It is essential not to conflate all problems of the world and to attribute them to one single cause – 'neoliberal capitalism'. As Karl Polanyi has emphasised, capitalism is embedded in historically and socially constituted institutions,[1] which also contribute to social life.

Contemporary critics[2] in the social sciences persist in predicting the 'end of capitalism'. They contend that crises give rise not just to instability but to contradictions that lead to collapse and replacement by something else. Such crises include: inflation of the 1970s, explosion of public debt in the 1980s, rapid rising private indebtedness of the 1990s, the collapse of financial markets in 2008 and the ensuing world economic crisis, the crisis of climate change and ecological unsustainability, the expansion of capitalism generating war, the energy crisis of 2022 and the Russian–Ukrainian war, and rising inequalities that destroy social cohesion.[3] I return to other literature later, but the articles collected by Craig Calhoun and Georgi Derluguian summarise current critical thinking in the social sciences. The contributors to these volumes emphasise the ways that 'neoliberalism' exacerbates capitalism's contradictions and leads to deleterious outcomes.

---

[1] Karl Polanyi, *The Great Transformation: The Political and Economic Origins of Our Time.* Boston: Beacon Press, 1957 (originally published 1944).

[2] Three early twenty-first-century academic collections (one being in three volumes) dwell on the recent crises of capitalism and its impending implosion. Craig Calhoun and Georgi Derluguian, *Business as Usual: The Roots of the Global Financial Meltdown* (Vol 1); *The Deepening Crisis: Governance, Challenges After Neoliberalism* (Vol 2); *The Aftermath: A New Global Economic Order* (Vol 3). New York and London: New York University Press, 2011; I. Wallerstein et al, *Does Capitalism Have a Future?*. Oxford University Press, 2013; Wolfgang Streeck, *How Will Capitalism End?*. London: Verso, 2016. Other books are listed later in this book.

[3] See discussion in Streeck, *How Will Capitalism End?*, p 16.

Currently, there are three sets of broad proposals addressing these ills. First, that there will be a spontaneous collapse of capitalism with an unknown replacement. Second, that neoliberal globalised capitalism can be reformed or replaced by another more acceptable variety of liberal capitalism, or by state capitalism. (By state capitalism, I mean an economy in which the state plays the major role in economic coordination and control, by state-capitalism – with a hyphen – I mean a system in which the state owns and controls economic assets and extraction of profit takes place to the benefit of state functionaries). Third, that capitalism will be transcended by a different form of economy and society – a superior form of economic and social organisation; of those taking this position, some variety of socialism is the most preferred. Most of the influential thinkers contend that neoliberal capitalism can be modified but not transcended. Capitalism has emerged modified but intact from the crises described previously.

Those who predict spontaneous collapse, detect self-destructive tendencies as well as the rise of political movements to control and/or to replace capitalism. Self-destructive tendencies were observed by Karl Marx and Friedrich Engels to follow from the economic exploitation of labour, which led to overproduction, the rate of profit to fall on the one side and growing unemployment and poverty on the other. Concurrently, the massive development of the productive forces would lead to the replacement of labour by machines capable of creating a world of plenty, thus introducing communism. This line of thinking is developed by writers such as Nick Srnicek and Alex Williams.[4] In the 1930s, Maynard Keynes argued that it was the fall in production caused by lack of demand that would lead to a self-induced crisis. J.K. Galbraith, Daniel Bell and Joseph Schumpeter have argued that the development of industrial society would lead to the rise of a technologically based class structure and to the growth of the state thus diminishing the bourgeois class and its propensity for entrepreneurship. In this case, statism, which could take a socialist form, would replace capitalism. In the twenty-first century, writers such as the Russian scholars Alexander Buzgalin and Andrey Kolganov contend that capitalism has reached a 'post-market' form embodying socialistic elements.[5]

These destabilising systemic developments, which, if unattended, are predicted lead to the disintegration, collapse and eventually the replacement of capitalism by some other often undefined social formation. Immanuel

---

[4]   N. Srnicek and A. Williams, *Inventing the Future*. London: Verso, 2015.

[5]   A. Buzgalin and A. Kolganov, *Twenty-first-century Capital*. Manchester: Manchester University Press, 2021. They refer to the economic role of the state, the planning of large business corporations, the rise of 'socially responsible business and non-profit production, the growth of publicly accessible goods which are not privately owned or controlled. See pp 192–3. I return to these discussions in Chapter 11.

Wallerstein declared that capitalism is 'no longer viable'.[6] Following Marx, he believed that it no longer offers capitalists the opportunity to pursue the accumulation of capital. He contemplates a 'confusing situation ... intellectually, morally, and politically' with an outcome that is 'fundamentally unpredictable and uncertain'. Other writers, such as Michael Mann, point to the possibilities of nuclear war and ecological catastrophes resulting from 'escalating climate change' and the unsustainability of the current culture of consumption.[7] Discourse by left-wing writers consistently predicts that capitalism cannot escape its permanent crisis. Samir Amin asserts that 'the reality of contemporary globalised-monopoly capitalism ... [is] that this system cannot survive and that its now ongoing implosion is an inevitability'.[8]

Unlike the collection of Immanuel Wallerstein et al, contributors to the Craig Calhoun and Georgi Derluguian volumes include those who not only condemn the conditions that led to the financial bubbles but also seek changes in the national economic and financial mechanisms to achieve a stable financial order. Some view current economic (and particularly monetary) institutions to be unsuitable in the context of a globalised and globalising economy and seek solutions in new economic and financial architecture. The proposals here are in the second category of the reform of capitalism as mentioned previously and call for reforms of the institutions of global capitalism, such as the World Trade Organization (WTO), the World Bank and the International Monetary Fund (IMF). Those who campaign for reform of globalised capitalism are to be found among elites, not only in politics but also in the media, the economy and academia. Their emphasis is on modifying or controlling neoliberal forms of globalisation within the existing capitalist framework.

It is premature to dismiss such reforms, as advocated by Randall Collins who considers that there are no longer any pathways for capitalism to 'escape' its terminal fate. Many, like him, contend that technology can no longer create new jobs, that there is no room for geographical expansion of markets, that enlarging the financial sector cannot provide a source of labour, that government employment and investment will not solve unemployment.[9] This approach is over-determined. A set of possible remedies would be to reduce the length of the working day, to make the state the employer of last resort and to pay all citizens a living wage.[10]

---

[6]   I. Wallerstein, Dynamics of (unresolved) global crisis, in Calhoun and Derluguian, *The Deepening Crisis*, pp 69–88, quotation p 84.

[7]   Michael Mann, The end may be neigh, but for whom, in Wallerstein et al, *Does Capitalism Have a Future?*, pp 71–98, quotations pp 86–7, 97.

[8]   Samir Amin, *The Implosion of Capitalism*. London: Pluto Press, 2014, p 155.

[9]   Randall Collins, The end of middle-class work, in Wallerstein et al, *Does Capitalism Have a Future?*, pp 39–56.

[10]   Srnicek and Williams, *Inventing the Future*.

International organisations are capable of reform. The balance of controlling states on the board of the IMF, for example, could be changed in favour of rising countries.

Sceptics, however, doubt the possibilities of any significant reform of the global system. As Ha-Joon Chang puts it: 'there is simply too much money, too much power and too much intellectual prestige at stake for the neoliberal regimes to go quietly'.[11] Wolfgang Streeck sums up the current intellectual ethos when he concludes that capitalism 'is vanishing on its own, collapsing from internal contradictions ... what comes after capitalism ... is ... not socialism or some other defined social order, but a lasting *interregnum* ... a period of uncertainty and indeterminacy'.[12] In contrast to twentieth century critics who saw socialism as the antidote, current social scientists' envision the end of neoliberal capitalism as a prolonged period of uncertainty and social 'disorder'.

An important response is articulated by those who reject the basic tenets of modern civilisation predicated on economic growth and an urban industrial form of society. This line of thinking is articulated by J.K. Gibson-Graham,[13] proposing alternative localised communal cooperative autonomous forms of society – the third approach described previously. Such social movements call for greater social autonomy and de-globalisation. There are different groups here formed by people seeking more democratic and autonomous forms of association, 'alternative' types of local self-governing and self-sustaining economies. Their major objective is to institute alternative autonomous forms of economic coordination co-existing with global capitalism. Some already see capitalism as being superseded by post-capitalist forms of production and consumption undermining the capitalist mode of production. These movements are particularly important as counters to the drive for economic growth and development that underpin the consumption economy. Ecological security and safeguarding of nature are major policy objectives. Others are declamatory and consciousness raising – the 'anti-capitalism' and 'anti-Wall St' activists – whose objectives are to expose different forms of domination and injustice.

Here we also find populist political movements seeking to strengthen the nation state to facilitate control over national economies and further the adoption of state-led Keynesian policies. Their target is globalisation – sometimes as a component of capitalism but often as a separate phenomenon. The populist movement consists of a counter elite of people recruited from

---

[11] Ha-Joon Chang, The 2008 world financial crisis and the future of world development, in Calhoun and Derluguian, *The Deepening Crisis*, pp 39–64, quotation p 61.

[12] Streeck, *How Will Capitalism End?*, p 13. Italics in original.

[13] J.K. Gibson-Graham, *Postcapitalist Politics*. Minneapolis: University of Minnesota Press, 2006.

disaffected members of the dominant elites as well as disgruntled members of the public who have suffered as a consequence of post-industrialism and deindustrialisation. The objective is a move to a form of 'internationalisation' where states are interdependent but retain sovereignty and exercise control over boundaries. States can adopt macro-economic policies to protect their own industries and citizens through welfare state strategies.

Previous alternatives (state socialism as in the USSR, national capitalism as in inter-war Germany) are widely rejected as political and economic failures. The authors in the Calhoun and Derluguian three-volume collections cast doubt on the likelihood of any socialist outcome consequent on the 2007 financial and economic crisis. Daniel Chirot, for example, argues that Marxists are wrong to see crisis as the beginning of the end of capitalism. Taking the events of the 1930s as an example, he opines that depression and war are more likely outcomes, a view bolstered by the proxy-war between members of NATO and Russia in 2022.[14] Most criticisms of neoliberalism present challenges to aspects of capitalism rather than to capitalism as a whole. Forms of opposition to neoliberalism define the boundaries of left-wing politics rather than propositions for socialism. For example, leftist presidents, elected after Chavez in Latin America, define their policies as 'deepening democracy and limiting neoliberalism ... [T]he pursuit of a deeper democracy has been their common ground'.[15] Socialism is not envisaged as a viable counter-ideology and in these books, the idea of a communist alternative has no champions at all in the collections I have cited previously. For twenty-firstcentury critics the antinomy is between democracy and autocracy rather than socialism and capitalism. Socialist state regulation in my view has been prematurely dismissed by critics.[16]

Discussion of socialism and social democracy is a major component of this book. Early twentieth-century social democracy as well as Marxist–Leninist 'state socialism' have presented the only consistent and comprehensive theoretical and organisational challenge to capitalism. Investigating the reasons why they failed, help to understand why neoliberalism has been adopted on a world scale. The substitution of state planning in place of markets has traditionally been a major challenge to capitalism and is reconsidered in the context of digital communication technologies and computerisation.

Prominent specialists, such as David Harvey and Branco Milanovic, present China as moving to state capitalism, which poses a major alternative

---

[14] For a development of this point of view, see R. Desai, *Capitalism, Coronavirus and War.* London: Routledge, 2022. Chapter 7.

[15] F. Coronil, The future in question: History and Utopia in Latin America (1989–2010) in Calhoun and Derluguian, *Business as Usual*, pp 231–64, quotation pp 240–1.

[16] Such a possibility is dismissed by Georgi Derluguian, What communism was, in Wallerstein et al, *Does Capitalism Have a Future?*, pp 99–130.

to liberal capitalism (discussed in Chapter 15). China is a hybrid economic system with administrative forms of ownership and control and economic planning, coexisting with privately owned and capitalistically operating corporations trading on national and international markets. The Chinese economy, embodying both macro planning and market exchange, may hold the keys to future alternatives. In this book, I contend that forms of state-controlled capitalism appear to be the most likely alternatives to neoliberal globalisation. The conception of an administered form of state planning is viewed as a major challenge to a market society. The ideas underpinning socialist state planning are outlined in Chapter 4. Reasons for its failure, and the challenge of market socialism are presented in Chapter 5, where I consider some of the advantages and problems of market socialism.

Current views of the commentariat envisage only different forms of capitalism. Martin Vander Weyer[17] considers capitalism as the 'greatest engine of human progress ever invented', and Branco Milanovic, foresees a future only for global capitalism.[18] Such writers, nevertheless, concede that there are faults that need 'repair'. Even articles in the *Financial Times* point to its failings: 'neoliberal policy [since the 1970s] has fostered grotesque inequality, fuelled the rise of populist demagogues, exacerbated racial disparities and hamstrung our ability to deal with crises like climate change'.[19] This line of approach is also shared by many articulate critics on 'the left'. T.J. Clark, writing in the *New Left Review* in 2012 in an aptly titled article, 'For a Left with no future', contended that 'The important fact in the core territories of capitalism … is that no established political party or movement any longer even pretends to offer a programme of "reform". Reforming capitalism is tacitly assumed to be impossible; what politicians agree on instead is revival, resuscitation'.[20] Such an alternative in the wake of President Donald Trump is envisaged by Gary Gerstle[21] for the American Democratic Party under Joe Biden. There are alternative forms of capitalism, rather than alternatives to capitalism. Just what constitutes a reformed capitalism is a major concern of the book. But that is not all; I consider how earlier attempts have failed and contend that capitalism should, and can, be transformed.

---

[17] M.V. Weyer, *The Good, the Bad and the Greedy: Why We've Lost Faith in Capitalism.* London: Biteback, 2021; Paul Collier, *The Future of Capitalism.* London: Allen Lane, 2018.

[18] B. Milanovic, *Capitalism, Alone.* Cambridge, MA: Belknap Press, 2019.

[19] Larry Kramer, The market must not become an end in itself. *Financial Times* (London) 17 September 2022.

[20] T.J. Clarke, For a Left with no future, *New Left Review*, 74 (March–April 2012), pp 53–76, quotation p 74.

[21] Gary Gerstle, *The Rise and Fall of the Neoliberal Order.* Oxford: Oxford University Press, 2022.

Current discourses on building an 'alternative future' lack any discussion of the means of change: of how you transit from here to there. All have an intransitive approach: systems collapse with no consequent emergence of a new social formation. But social formations and modes of production do not 'collapse' spontaneously, they are changed and replaced by human action. And for human action to be successful requires an understanding of how societies function and fail to function. Without a sociology of an alternative there can be no vision of a realistic alternative. Margaret Thatcher famously contended that 'there is no alternative' to neoliberal capitalism. Current discourse, however, has moved on and puts Thatcher's point in rather a different form: in the twenty-first century, neoliberalism is recognised as a bad economic system, but the alternatives are worse. In this book, the alternatives are outlined and, despite their inadequacies, some of them are viewed to be better than neoliberalism.

The alternatives

Exceptionally, Randall Collins exemplifies the third approach mentioned previously. 'Schematically the only way to solve the crisis will be to replace capitalism with a non-capitalist system, which means socialist ownership and strong central regulation and planning'.[22] Erik Olin Wright[23] develops a strong case for emancipatory socialism and 'radical democratic egalitarianism'. This work, however, is somewhat speculative and explores theoretical proposals. Nick Srnicek and Alex Williams[24] critique leftist politics and call for a counter-hegemonic project, a transformation of capitalism. There are also other criticisms and proposals for reform, such as the call by Leo Panitch and Colin Leys for a new left type of socialism[25] and Chris Rogers for a 'bottom-up' alternative.[26] But these have not been articulated into an alternative set of political strategies linked to current political parties to bring these policies into being. The problem to be addressed is why, when its advocates put proposed 'alternatives' into effect in the twentieth century, they have failed not only to take root but have been replaced by economic and political formations strongly influenced by neoliberal ways of thinking and doing. I address these questions in Part II of this book.

Even reformist social democracy has been severely compromised by the rise of 'New Labour' parties, which have assimilated many neoliberal policies.

---

[22] Randall Collins, The end of middle-class work, pp 37–70, quotation, p 68.
[23] E.O. Wright, *Envisioning Real Utopias*. London: Verso 2010.
[24] Srnicek and Williams, *Inventing the Future*.
[25] Leo Panitch and Colin Leys, *Searching for Socialism: The Project of the Labour New Left from Benn to Corbyn*. London: Verso, 2020.
[26] Chris Rogers, *Capitalism and Its Alternatives*. London: Zed Books, 2014.

In the early twenty-first century, in the European Union (EU), social democratic parties have provided only a weak electoral challenge; in 2019, the most successful (Denmark and Spain) received only around a quarter of the electoral vote. The place of social democracy had been taken by ideologically diffuse populist protest parties that seek to re-establish political and economic control over their countries' borders. They are anti-globalisation rather than anti-capitalist. A notable development, nevertheless, has been the emergence of social democratic leaning politicians with significant social backing, such as Jeremy Corbyn in the UK and Bernie Sanders in the USA – but both lack support from the established political classes and neither has attained a position of political power. Corbyn's programme adopted some of Srnicek and Williams's proposals (such as a basic income), worker participation on boards of companies, greater public ownership and state banks. Labour under Corbyn, in 2017, received 12.9 million votes (some 40 per cent of those voting), which indicates considerable support for alternative policies. However, he suffered a significant set-back in the election of 2019 and has been marginalised and excluded by the subsequent leadership of the Parliamentary Labour Party under Keith Starmer.[27] A collection of essays, sympathetic to socialism, by Leo Panitch and Greg Albo,[28] casts doubt on the current possibility of a move to an alternative social democracy in the United Kingdom (UK), to which I return in the final chapter of this book.

Developments in China have moved to the forefront as a challenge and have engendered a focus on state guided capitalism,[29] which has divided commentators. Some regard China merely as moving to a corporate form of capitalism whereas others see a promise of an eventual transition to socialism. 'State capitalism' is an ambiguous term. I distinguish between an economy in which the state plays a major role in coordinating a privately owned economy (which may include state-owned assets), one in which the state owns and controls the means of production (state-capitalism, with a hyphen) and state-controlled capitalism in which political institutions are superior to economic ones (either privately and/or state owned). China fits into the latter category. Developments in China are detailed in Chapter 15.

Alternatives may be studied in terms of ideologies and programmes and/ or political movements and governments that put them into operation. Theoretical alternatives often appear as wishful thinking: they may have little support; there is widespread inertia; a lack of leadership; the political

---

[27] See M. Beveridge, *The Socialist Ideal in the Labour Party: From Attlee to Corbyn*. London: Merlin Press, 2021.

[28] Leo Panitch and Greg Albo (Eds), *Beyond Market Dystopia*. London: Merlin, 2019.

[29] Craig Calhoun, What threatens capitalism now?, in Wallerstein et al, *Does Capitalism Have a Future?*, pp 131–62, quotation p 151.

instruments are weak; opposing forces are ideologically and politically superior. It is to Milton Friedman, however, that we may turn for inspiration. In the introduction to his book *Capitalism and Freedom*, he noted the importance of:

> keeping options open until circumstances make change necessary. There is enormous inertia, a tyranny of the status quo in private and especially governmental arrangements. Only a crisis actual or perceived produces real change. When that crisis occurs, the actions that are taken depend on the ideas that are lying around. That, I believe, is our basic function; to develop alternatives to existing policies, to keep them alive and available until the politically impossible becomes politically inevitable.[30]

This book considers what policies should be available to 'achieve the politically impossible'.

Neoliberalism and the alternatives

Neoliberalism is the dominant ideology that shapes the form taken by contemporary globalised capitalism. To transcend it, any alternative must comprehend its ideology and organisational form. Neoliberalism has to be interrogated in both ideology, economic policy and political practice to discover if it provides something that organised capitalism and socialism have lacked. In the next chapter, I outline its diverse and ambiguous character, the ways its suppositions have affected capitalism and globalisation. I discuss the philosophical and economic principles that define the neoliberal project and shape domestic and international policies. In Chapter 3, I consider some of its shortcomings. The major focus of the book is to examine critically 'alternative' ideological and political movements – alternatives that have been tried and failed, as well as current proposals that have yet to be tried. These include alternative types of capitalism as well as alternative social formations to capitalism. I also distinguish between capitalism and globalisation and contend that globalisation can also take different forms. The objective is to provide an exposition, commentary and critical analysis of different approaches, and to suggest their strengths, weaknesses and likely political reactions.

The method I adopt is to describe the beneficial and adverse effects of global capitalism as they operate in modern societies and to suggest how

---

[30] Milton Friedman, *Capitalism and Freedom*. Chicago: Chicago University Press, 1982 (1962), p 7.

human progress may be achieved with something better. Not only is the experience of twentieth-century socialism revisited, but proposals are considered for its relevance today. These include the extension of public ownership, policies promoting full employment, the widening of the welfare state to a social state, environmental sustainability and peace, and reliance on planning rather than market forces. The development of high-tech communication and computerisation create new and more effective methods of economic coordination through planning.

The insight of Marx and Engels that capitalism was faulted as a mechanism to achieve human liberation because it was driven by economic exploitation is still valid. I distinguish between political domination and social oppression, on the one hand, and economic exploitation on the other. Claims for justice and an emphasis on diversity promotion to further equality of opportunity are worthy objectives to counter real forms of oppression. But my argument is that opposition to hierarchy and autocracy and claims for democracy and diversity have overwhelmed class interests. Social classes are the form taken by economic exploitation: dominant classes are drivers of modern societies, they shape law and control the mass media, as well as possessing disproportionate and unjustifiable levels of economic wealth and income. In this book, I reinstate classes at the centre of the analysis of capitalism.

In the final chapter, I present a revised form of market socialism, embedded in state planning, as an alternative to liberal market competition. Regulated market socialism is proposed as an economic system offering the advantages of a planned economy and the retention of consumer choice and individual entrepreneurship in the market sector. The objective is to combine the advantages of economic planning at the macro level with market relationships that satisfy individual needs and encourage entrepreneurship and innovative work. Planning is exercised at the macro level of states while markets and networks promote individual achievement and satisfy consumption at the micro level. Regulated market socialism delivers a minimalist answer to the problem of transition to socialism.

We might distinguish six main structural alternatives that will be developed later in this book. These are not mutually exclusive categories but classify more or less coherent ways of thinking about how economies should be organised.

- State socialism (state ownership and direction of the economy organised on a plan putting into effect socialist objectives).
- Social democratic corporatism (coordination based on a coalition of stakeholders – socialist parties, trade unions, business, government, civil society).
- State-capitalism (state ownership and control of economic assets realising profit for the benefit of a state bureaucracy).

- State-controlled capitalism (state institutions directing private and/or quasi-state corporations operating for profit).
- Market socialism (public ownership with market coordination).
- Autonomous self-sustaining economies composed of networks of self-sufficient, self-governing economic and social actors.

Organisation of the book

To examine these alternatives, the book consists of three introductory chapters followed by Part I dealing with twentieth-century socialist contenders and Part II, which considers contemporary critiques of global capitalism. In Chapter 1, I outline the significance of global neoliberal capitalism. In Chapter 2, I define *neoliberal capitalism* as a comprehensive model of how economy and society should be ordered in psychological, political, economic and social dimensions. In Chapter 3, I explain not only why it needs replacing but why, despite many crises and widespread public and academic criticism, it survives as a faulted but hegemonic ideology of the early twenty-first century.

In Part I, in Chapters 4 and 5, I turn to examine the historical legacy of challenges to capitalism of the twentieth century to build socialism in the Soviet Union, and social democracy in Western Europe. Here I follow Sidney Tarrow's approach when I compare two different types of society:[31] social democratic capitalism and state socialism exemplified by the cases of Great Britain and the Soviet Union. Comparing pairs of countries with inherent differences and similar outcomes, provides a perspective of the causal mechanisms of social change. In Chapter 4, I outline ideas that have driven the socialist movement – both social democratic and socialist. In Chapter 5, the early success of state socialism, the first comprehensive form of state-led industrialisation, ensured not only economic growth but a transformation of the social structure. As economic growth declined public demands were not fulfilled. State socialism was challenged ideologically by reformers who advocated market socialism and participatory democracy. A similar fate awaited the social democratic parties of Western Europe which, after the Second World War, promoted pluralist welfarist societies in Western Europe. In Chapters 6 and 7, I show how these political regimes, in different ways, failed to command public respect and support.

One explanatory theme of the book is that changes in the social structure of societies have had a major impact on the forms of social solidarity and political opposition and they provide drivers of neoliberal reforms. Neoliberalism from

---

[31] S. Tarrow, The strategy of paired comparison: Toward a theory of practice, *Comparative Political Studies*, 43:2 (2010), pp 230–59.

the 1980s became a potent international force because it provided feasible and tolerable answers to the inadequacies of post-war forms of economic and political coordination – in both the UK and the Soviet Union.

In Chapters 7 and 8, I discuss how the social democratic and the state socialist formations were inadequate and failed to counter the neoliberal alternative inspired by Prime Minister Margaret Thatcher. Epitomised by the rise of New Labour, a left-wing type of liberalism, defined in terms of individual rights, diversity promotion and equality of opportunity, provided a more attractive system of values compatible with neoliberalism. Relying on the experience of the USSR, I show how convergence to neoliberalism arose out of the failure of the coordinated statist economy to adapt to the technological advances that were under way in the transition from industrial to post-industrial society. Reform of state socialism led by President Gorbachev was also influenced by Thatcher's reforms and supported by the rising strata of professional educated people who formed the 'service class'. The geo-political dimension in favour of neoliberal reforms is shown to be crucial for the dismantling of state socialism. The methodology of the two area comparisons brings out how in both the Western social democratic and the East European socialist parties, the domestic social support for political reform was generated by the ascendant professional white collar social strata.

Neoliberalism in power, established universally in the late twentieth century, in turn has led to critical opposition and provides the content for Part II. In Chapters 9 and 10, I define globalisation and discuss the changing social and economic structure of the late twentieth and early twenty-first century: the movement from industrial to post-industrial structures, and the social, economic and political components of globalisation. I distinguish between globalisation as a spatial relationship of networks and transactions, and the form of neoliberal international capitalism in which, in different ways, it is embedded. Losers and winners are defined in terms of countries and social groups. In Chapter 10, I discuss the shift from national to international politics and the rise and composition of a transnational or global political class. I contend that the core capitalist states are no longer hegemonic but challenged by an ascendant semi-core led by China that threatens capitalist globalisation. Sanctions imposed on Russia and China lead to deglobalisation and the formation of regional blocs constituting competitive interdependence between core and semi-core.

In Chapters 11 to 13, I explain and criticise political and sociological critiques of global capitalism. In Chapter 11, I outline the views of those with a conviction that the development of global capitalism is leading to the formation of a new ascendant class predicated on information technology, economic abundance and collaborative production. It is claimed that contemporary capitalism is driven by ascendant forces, the 'creatariat', leading to a new form of production – post-capitalism (not necessarily socialism). Disillusion with previous forms of social democratic electoral politics and the 'vanguard party' leads to the rejection of organisational forms of leadership. The call is for autonomous action for spontaneous non-capitalist, cooperative social forms which, if multiplied, will replace global capitalism. This approach is considered to be over-optimistic as a means to overcome the dominant transnational corporations (TNCs) and hegemonic states.

In Chapter 12, I consider critics who wish to reverse globalisation to form areas of self-governing autonomous communities, which may run in parallel to industrial capitalism. The emphasis is on action, the 'here and now': the 'Occupy movements'. Many of these tendencies adopt an 'exit' strategy: the objectives are either to replace globalisation with autonomous economic democratic cooperative associations and/or to coexist with global capitalist forces. Informal networks, 'Twitter' revolutions enable mobilisation. These movements are considered expressions of social and political discontent that reveal and identify important forms of oppression, but many movements are limited to micro changes and present forms of coexistence with global capitalism. In Chapter 13, I turn to the environmentalists' critique of the exploitation of nature by Western industrial development, which they consider a threat to civilisation. The chapter contrasts Marxist and environmentalist approaches. The former considers that industrialisation is positive, the threat lies with the capitalistic nature of global capitalism, whereas environmentalists question the role of an urban–industrial civilisation and advocate degrowth policies. I discuss market and statist policies promoting sustainable development and who will bear the costs.

In Chapter 14, I outline the views of those who regard globalisation as a positive economic development but consider it necessary to democratise or regulate globalisation. All these proposals curb current globalisation policies, give states more powers and effectively move to internationalisation. The reformist social democratic approach includes making global organisations more democratic and responsive to societal interests of which one is corporate social responsibility (CSR). Socialists propose a different form of globalisation – here the institutions of capitalism are dismantled and globalisation pursues different objectives. Some, including the Chinese, advocate socialist policies to reshape globalisation. Major challenges to globalised capitalism are found in different varieties of 'state capitalism'. In Chapter 15, I distinguish between three types of political economy in which the state has a predominant role: state socialism, state-capitalism (with a hyphen) and state-controlled capitalism. All three present theoretical alternatives to liberal capitalism and the last two contemporary challenges. In the light of these definitions, I discuss the ways scholars use them to describe socialist societies, particularly in the ways that the Soviet Union was, and contemporary China is, 'state capitalist'. I present the discussion on whether countries can move from pre-capitalism to socialism missing out capitalism. In this framework, I consider the debate on state capitalism, and political capitalism presented by contemporary China.

In the concluding chapter, following a summary of the major alternatives discussed in the book, I examine how a form of regulated market socialism might provide a challenge to neoliberal theory and practice in the twenty-first century. I advocate a movement to a hybrid economy with public and private ownership. In this social formation, socialist planning is revisited in the context of computerised planning mechanisms. Economic surplus, made available from public ownership, is allocated through a state plan which allows for the production of use values in the public sector. In the retail sector, economic coordination continues to function through markets. A 'social state' is envisaged to provide a vision of a post-capitalist socialist political and moral order – without losing the satisfactions of a pluralist democratic consumer society. Self-motivating individualism is retained and economic democracy is introduced. Regulated market socialism is presented as a realistic alternative capable of transcending neoliberal capitalist globalisation.

2

Global Neoliberalism and What It Means

Capitalism can take many forms. Max Weber distinguished between political capitalism and modern industrial capitalism. I turn to political capitalism in the form of state capitalism in Chapter 15. Modern capitalism is distinguished from its earlier forms by virtue of its continuous quest for profit through capital investment, by the separation of business from the household, by monetary transactions through an impersonal market, and by the exploitation of wage labour. For Weber, the object of modern capitalism is the production of commodities and the provision of services for profit, backed up by rational accounting, rather than speculative money making. *Modern capitalism* might be defined as 'the pursuit of profit and forever renewed profit, by means of continuous, rational capitalistic enterprise'.[1]

Karl Marx produced a conception of capitalism as a historically determined mode of production. Social classes have a prominent place in the Marxist conception. The distinction of Marx, however, is that investment is derived from exploitation through the extraction of profit (surplus labour). The capitalist class is driven by the pursuit of continuous profit which accrues from investment through the market. This process creates classes and class conflict. Both thinkers agreed that capitalism is more than an economic system, it is a form of society[2] with a division of labour and interdependent institutions of the state, law, finance, markets, the family, education and research. How the different parts of the capitalist system fit together is the subject of 'varieties of capitalism'.

Neoliberalism is the dominant economic and social form that capitalism takes in the twenty-first century. In this chapter I consider how neoliberalism

---

[1] See H.H. Gerth and C. Wright Mills, *From Max Weber*. London: Routledge, 1961, pp 65–9.

[2] For a pertinent discussion of its societal form see Streeck, *How Will Capitalism End?*.

has outgrown classical liberalism and what its advocates consider its positive features and why it should be adopted. In the next chapter I consider its inadequacies. 'Neoliberalism' is an ambiguous concept. One commentator lists six uses of the term: an 'all-purpose denunciatory category', 'the way things are', an institutional framework to describe forms of national capitalism, a dominant ideology, a form of governmentality, and a theory and policy variant of liberalism.[3] Much of the literature refracts 'neoliberalism' through the prism of other theoretical positions (Marxist, Foucauldian, conservative, liberal), which rarely define the gist of 'neoliberalism'. A process of manufacturing types of neoliberalism to fit certain preconceptions is at work defining 'neoliberalism' to suit the observer's political constituencies.

Many critics regard neoliberalism to be the cause of any economic or political development of which they disapprove: inequality, migration, economic crises, 'populism', high rates of murder, excessive deaths from COVID-19, internal wars and foreign invasions are all portrayed as 'consequences of neoliberalism'. Neoliberalism is nothing more than 'a mask for practices that are all about the maintenance, reconstitution and restoration of elite class power'.[4] For its proponents, on the other hand, since its adoption in the last quarter of the twentieth century, neoliberal policies have secured vast increases of wealth and human well-being. Where it has been adopted, they contend, it has brought freedom, peace and prosperity. Consequently, these contrasting and contradictory approaches have led neoliberalism to be 'widely acknowledged ... as a controversial, incoherent and crisis-ridden term'.[5]

My approach is to identify a neoliberal economic paradigm that has antecedents in liberal economic and political theory. Elements of this core ideology have been adopted in the policies of international agencies, national governments, political parties and the practices of economic and political institutions. Neoliberalism, moreover, has to be considered as a part of a process of global liberalisation. It is not enough to analyse neoliberalism 'as a practice ... a "way of doing things" directed towards objectives and regulating itself by continuous reflection'.[6] A 'way of doing things' may be composed of both neoliberal and non-liberal components.

My objective is to uncover the components of what proponents of neoliberalism consider it to be. As Cahill and Konings have pointed out,

---

[3]   T. Flew, Six theories of neoliberalism, *Thesis Eleven*, 122:1 (2014), pp 49–71.

[4]   D. Harvey, *A Brief History of Neoliberalism*. Oxford: Oxford University Press, 2005, p 188.

[5]   Rajesh Venugopal, Neoliberalism as concept, *Economy and Society*, 44:2 (May 2015), pp 165–87, quotation p 165.

[6]   M. Foucault, *The Birth of Biopolitics*. New York and Basingstoke: Palgrave Macmillan, 2008, p 319.

to understand neoliberalism, one needs to identify the 'reconfigured institutional relationships brought about through processes such as privatisation, deregulation and new approaches to macroeconomic policy'.[7] I regard neoliberalism as a theory of society with interdependent components: namely, a form of economy, a set of psychological presuppositions, an institutional framework consisting of law, government and civil society; global neoliberalism presumes a world economy with a scope that erodes boundaries between states. There is a strong normative component in neoliberalism: advocacy of what is necessary to bring about a desirable capitalist society.

The economic basis of neoliberalism

At the core of neoliberalism is a theory of economic life. The major theorist of neoliberalism is Friedrich von Hayek,[8] who popularised and developed the ideas of Ludwig von Mises.[9] Its economics has been further elaborated in the USA by Milton Friedman.[10] They have provided the intellectual foundations of contemporary economic neoliberalism and are widely recognised as such. Hayek was awarded a Nobel Prize for economics in 1974, and he has directly and indirectly influenced the ways in which the reform of European welfare regimes and transformations of the state socialist societies have proceeded. His arguments have led to acceptance of the view that there is no better economic alternative to market capitalist competition. Hierarchical forms of planned coordination are not only deemed undesirable but also technically impossible to realise efficiently. He has formulated the ideological underpinning not only for neoliberal economies but also a fundamental critique of socialism. Neoliberalism is a normative theory and, as adopted in actual societies, it merges with the historical features of the host society.

The doctrine of neoliberalism evolved out of a nineteenth-century economic philosophy of liberalism that advocated the unhampered activity of individuals to further their own preferences through a market mechanism constrained by law. A focus on the activity of individuals gives a psychological foundation to neoliberalism. Classical liberalism's guiding principles entailed laws upholding private ownership, the absence of restraints on commerce,

---

[7]   D. Cahill and M. Konings, *Neoliberalism*. Cambridge: Polity, 2017, p 3.

[8]   Friedrich von Hayek's major books are *The Constitution of Liberty*, Chicago: Universty of Chicago Press, 1960; *The Individualism and Economic Order*, London: Routledge, 1948; and *The Road to Serfdom*, London: Routledge, 1944.

[9]   Ludwig von Mises, Liberalism. Indianapolis, IN: Liberty Fund, 2005.

[10] Milton Friedman, *Essays in Positive Economics*. Chicago: Chicago University Press, 1953. See also Friedman, *Capitalism and Freedom*.

firms acting to maximise their own profits and individuals their personal 'utility'; policy advocated free trade internationally. The state had an important role – to provide defence, to issue money, to enforce contracts, to maintain a framework for commerce and to supply public works; it also determined the terms of trade with foreign economies. Liberals conceded that social conditions could impede individual freedom and recognised that the state should act to reduce poverty, improve health, provide elementary education and reduce destitution by providing shelter. There was a benevolent component in classical liberalism.

Global neoliberalisation,[11] however, goes much further; it enlarges twentieth-century economic liberalism along four dimensions. First, the area of free interaction is extended from economic activities to many more aspects of human affairs; a social economy includes a 'multitude of different markets'.[12] Second, the scope of market relations is global. As a consequence of globalisation, the state loses its previous powers of control over its own borders and consequently over many aspects of national affairs; market relations increasingly replace statist regulation and coordination in a process of 'de-regulation'. Third, states not only enforce the rules of the socio-economic order but they promote the liberal order. As a provider of services, the state is weakened, but as an enforcer of rules it is strengthened. Government institutions themselves become the objects of economic rules defined by external organisations agreed by treaties and/or agreements. Fourth, to economic liberalism is added a dimension of financialisation, in the sense of the monetarisation of social exchange relationships, which extends the area of the economic

---

[11] For overviews see: Harvey, *A Brief History of Neoliberalism* and A. Saad-Filho and D. Johnston (Eds), *Neoliberalism: A Critical Reader*. London: Pluto Press, 2005. Important interpretations include: Foucault, *The Birth of Biopolitics*. A Marxist understanding: G. Dumenil and D. Levy, *The Crisis of Neoliberalism*. Harvard: Harvard University Press, 2011. Study of different state formations can be found in: *South Atlantic Quarterly*, 118:2 (2019), pp 343–61. Issue on Authoritarian Neoliberalism. Particularly, Bob Jessop, Authoritarian neoliberalism: Periodization and Critique, pp 343–61. These articles conflate neoliberal policies with other practices. Matthew Eagleton-Pierce, *Neoliberalism: The Key Concepts*. London: Routledge, 2016; Huw Macartney (Ed), *Variegated Neoliberalism*. London: Routledge, 2011; A. Burkin, *The Great Persuasion*, Cambridge, MA: Harvard University Press, 2012; P. Mirowski and D. Plehwe, *The Road from Mont Pelerin*. London and Cambridge, MA: Harvard University Press, 2009; Raymond Plant, *The Neoliberal State*. Oxford: Oxford University Press, 2010; D. Kotz, *The Rise and Fall of Neoliberal Capitalism*. Cambridge, MA: Harvard University Press, 2015; B. Van Apeldoorn and H. Overbeek (Eds), *Neoliberalism in Crisis*. Basingstoke: Palgrave Macmillan, 2012.

[12] Andrew Gamble, The free economy and the strong state: The rise of the social market economy, in R. Miliband and J. Saville (Eds) *The Socialist Register*. London: Merlin Press, 1979, pp 1–25, quotation, p 6.

mechanism of the market. These developments are bound by a set of philosophical and economic principles that enlarge the neoliberal project to make it a theory of society.

Liberal economics provides the taken for granted assumptions on which policy makers rely. Currently, it is the 'common sense' underpinning economic and social policy of the major governments in the modern world. As a doctrine, it prioritises the economic over the political and social. Economic liberalism, as advocated by Friedrich von Hayek, strongly influenced politicians and political institutions. Since the 1980s, it came to combines Hayek's academic analysis with a popular discourse. Margaret Thatcher, in 1975, after reading Hayek's, *The Constitution of Liberty*, is said to have declared: 'This is what we believe!'[13] Later, when in power she said:

> 'What's irritated me about the whole direction of politics in the last 30 years is that it's always been towards the collectivist society. People have forgotten about the personal society. And they say: do I count, do I matter? To which the short answer is, yes. And therefore, it isn't that I set out on economic policies; it's that I set out really to change the approach, and changing the economics is the means of changing that approach. If you change the approach, you really are after the heart and soul of the nation. Economics are the method; the object is to change the heart and soul.'[14]

Ronald Reagan, in the USA was converted to neoliberalism at roughly the same time and greatly contributed to its international implementation. To 'change the heart and soul', neoliberal economies take on psychological, social, and political dimensions.

Liberalism as a comprehensive ideology

I distinguish between neoliberalism as outlined in the works of Friedrich von Hayek and Milton Friedrich and later developments, introduced by Margaret Thatcher and Ronald Reagan and their economic and political advisers. While neoliberalism was, and remains, fundamentally an economic doctrine, for the economic mechanism to function properly, it requires matching political, legal and social institutions. Twentieth-century neoliberalism had

---

[13] She made him a Companion of Honour in 1984; later George Bush awarded him the Presidential Medal of Freedom in 2011.

[14] Margaret Thatcher in an interview with *The Sunday Times*, 1 May 1981. Available at: www.marharetthather.org/document/104475

different strands.[15] Michel Foucault, for example, emphasises governmentality, while others, following Hayek, stress that 'economic freedom' is founded on open markets. For all economic liberals, market capitalist economies are driven by entrepreneurs with privately owned assets, motivated to make profit from the sale of commodities and services, which satisfy consumers by fulfilling their wants.

An appropriate societal framework is necessary for a liberal economy to operate efficiently. Its nature may be illustrated by the indexes defining and measuring the extent of economic freedom; the criteria of the 'ways that things should be done'. Indexes constructed by Freedom House and the Fraser Institute are the best known and others include the influential measures compiled by the European Bank of Reconstruction and Development.[16] The Fraser Institute database was founded by Milton and Rose Friedman together with Michael Walker, a disciple of Hayek.[17] Its current Freedom Index is based on 42 data points, including the size of government, the legal system and property rights (including civil society), freedom to trade internationally and regulation (the right to exchange, gain credit, hire or work, operation of business). In 2018, the Cato and Fraser Institute published its Human Freedom Index, which includes 79 indicators of personal and economic freedom.[18] These indexes spell out the societal dimensions of current globalising liberalisation. These categories may be summarised into their main sociological components: the government, the social sphere (civil society), the forms of economic life and coordination. The scope of economic and political activities is complementary to form a neoliberal society.[19] The neoliberal model is adapted to the historically

---

[15] For an outline of the historical rise of neoliberalism see Gerstle, *The Rise and Fall of the Neoliberal Order*, Part 2.

[16] European Bank of Reconstruction and Development publishes the Transition report listing the extent to which the former state socialist societies have moved to a modern neoliberal society. Its measures indicate the importance of various components of the economy. See, for example, *Transition Report 1999*. London: EBRD, 1999 and other years.

[17] The following website carries numerous articles on economic freedom and related topics: https://www.atlasnetwork.org/news/article/economic-freedom-of-the-world-index

[18] These are: rule of law, security and safety, movement, religion, association, assembly, and civil society, expression and information, identity and relationships, size of government, legal system and property rights, access to sound money, freedom to trade internationally, and regulation of credit, labour, and business. See https://www.cato.org/human-freedom-index-new

[19] The Freedom House Index published in associate with the Cato Institute and Fraser Institute has 79 indicators of personal and economic freedom covering: Rule of Law, Security and Safety, Movement, Religion, Association, Assembly, Civil Society, Expression, Relationships, Size of Government, Legal System and Property Rights, Access to Sound Money, Freedom to Trade Internationally, and Regulation of Credit, Labour, and Business. See https://freedomhouse.org/

determined structures and processes of different societies. The resulting hybridity (measured by the range of scores in the Human Freedom Index and the Freedom House Index) is one of the reasons why commentators disagree over whether a society is neoliberal or not, or whether actions of governments constitute neoliberalism or not.

On the basis of these ideological and practical policy standpoints, *global neoliberalism* might be defined as a doctrine of market competition promoting, and promoted by, the unimpeded movement of capital, labour, goods, services, and the right of establishment[20] acting within the framework of law; the economy is predicated on private property secured by a minimalist regulatory state. To classical liberalism have been added the financialisation of 'non-economic' relationships, the subjection of the state to market regulation and the globalisation of national economies.

The components of neoliberalism are summarised in Box 2.1, and will be expanded later. Elements added to classical liberalism are shown in *italics*.

Maintaining stability and promoting progress

At the heart of the neoliberal project is the assumption that spontaneous exchanges and continuous adjustments motivated by the self-interest of economic actors maintain equilibrium, which is essential for the operation of a modern economy.[21] Such equilibrium is 'an optimum position', which secures the fulfilment of all social wants.[22] Underlying these assumptions are the subjective perceptions of individuals expressed in their choices. Individual propensities provide a psychological basis to neoliberalism and classical economics.[23] These ideas follow Alfred Marshall who emphasised that stable equilibrium occurs when prices oscillate around a central point[24]. Deviations from equilibrium lead to countervailing forces to restore it and concurrently to ensure that all material wants are optimally fulfilled. Liberal economists assume that there is a self-adjusting mechanism in the competitive market system, which constitutes a moving equilibrium in which adjustment is continuous.

The coordination of the economy is achieved through recurring spontaneous interactions between, and adjustments of, individual preferences. Of crucial

---

[20] That is the rights of corporations to set up and trade without restriction within the law.

[21] F. von Hayek, Economics and knowledge, republished in F. von Hayek, *Individualism and Economic Order*. Chicago and London: University of Chicago Press, 1948, pp 33–56, p 45.

[22] 'Wants' are what people express through their intentions to purchase and are not to be confused with 'needs', which are necessary to maintain a civilised life.

[23] F.A. Hayek, The use of knowledge in society. *American Economic Review*, 35:4 (1945), pp 519–30.

[24] A. Marshall, *Principles of Economics*. London: Macmillan, 1956, He uses the analogy that an egg cannot stand upright on one of its ends, pp 288–9.

Box 2.1: Societal components of neoliberalism

Psychological – motivations of personal self-interest act as drivers of economic development. Such psychological drives must be allowed to flourish in free associations, unfettered by the state;

Legal – supremacy of law: law defends liberty, defines rights to property, and enforces limits to state activity and the rules of the market;

Economic – unrestricted market coordination through competition at all levels of the economy; *marketisation is furthered by monetarisation and financialisation of 'non-economic' exchange to promote efficient allocation*;

Political – the state exercises law enforcement legitimated by electoral democracy; maintains property rights and actively promotes institutions of market exchange; *state activities are subject to market coordination, and open to audit of misuse (through state capture and corruption)*; the state is subject to law and *cannot override it*;

Social – rights to private property, autonomous civil society, *the promotion of anti-discrimination and diversity, the monetarisation of human relationships*;

Coordination – the market is the principal form of exchange; the process of catallaxy (mutual spontaneous adjustment) and exchange between actors promotes well-being. *International institutions set and enforce rules between national and global economic actors*;

Boundaries – the international system, mediated by agreements between states, promotes free geographical movement of capital, labour, goods and services. *Global institutions enforce rules to promote free capitalist intercourse on a world scale. Political intervention in 'unfree' states by liberal states is legitimate to secure freedom.*

Note: Italicised text indicates items added to classical liberalism by neoliberalism.

---

importance is the assumption that there are self-regulating economic mechanisms, which require political intervention. The market creates conditions for entrepreneurship, which identifies new wants, new products and new forms of association. The state enforces rules to make it work. Competition is essential for markets to function effectively and to promote efficiency. Stagnation is avoided because countervailing forces overcome inertia.[25] For example, areas of unemployment attract capital as the price of labour falls, individual entrepreneurs promote new products and hence the market brings about a new equilibrium. All these processes are spontaneous actions and reactions of individuals. If such processes are allowed to work, progress is secured.[26]

---

[25] See Andrew Gamble, Hayek and the left, *Political Quarterly*, 67:1 (1996), pp 46–53, discussion pp 49–50.

[26] For a current description, see Daron Acemoglu and James A. Robinson, *Why Nations Fail*. London: Profile Books, 2012.

Competitiveness between individuals coexists in separate spheres of politics and economics and is resolved through a process of catallaxy. For Adam Smith and the classical economists, coordination was ensured by the hidden or 'invisible hand'. His vision is of a society composed of individual self-motivated units. Hayek develops this insight with his concept of 'catallaxy'.[27] 'A catallaxy is thus the special kind of spontaneous order produced by the market through people acting within the rules of the law of property, tort and contract.'[28] It is through such mutual adjustments that economies are coordinated; it is claimed to be more effective and efficient than any form of state planning. Foucault's idea of a 'neoliberal governmentality'[29] sits most uneasily with this process, as the neoliberal idea is to minimise government control and to replace governmental activities with catallactic exchanges. Indeed, Foucault regards the process as originating in the Middle Ages, well before neoliberalism. Through the market, the autonomous business units, which compete one with another, are brought into harmony. For neoliberals, the market is considered a mechanism operating through conscious choices of actors not, as for Adam Smith, the result of an 'invisible' hand. The 'economic calculus' coordinating individual preferences operates through the price system embedded in the economic market.[30]

Promoting autonomous civil society ensures progress. Inequalities exist – but they are justifiable to the extent that they are deserved and have been earned. Discrimination based on race, sex and social origin is antithetical to neoliberalism:

> The great virtue of a free market system is that it does not care what color people are; it does not care what their religion is; it only cares whether they can produce something you want to buy. It is the most effective system we have discovered to enable people who hate one another to deal with one another and help one another.[31]

Governments are not laissez-faire. Policy objectives are to create an even playing field for all to compete equally: thus putting policies of diversity promotion on the government agenda. Such policies have been widely implemented across the political spectrum and include leaders ranging from

---

[27] F.A. Hayek, *Law, Legislation, and Liberty* (Vol 2). London: Routledge, 1976, pp 108–9. For an overview see Gamble, Hayek and the left.

[28] Hayek, *Law, Legislation, and Liberty*, p 109.

[29] See Foucault, *The Birth of Biopolitics*, p 246. Foucault completely ignores the idea of catallaxy, a crucial component of Hayek's paradigm.

[30] Hayek, The use of knowledge in society, quotation p 525.

[31] M. Friedman, *Why Government Is the Problem*, Essays in Public Policy, No 39. Stanford, CA: Hoover Institution Press, 1993, p 11.

George Bush to Barack Obama. They were strongly supported in the UK by Tony Blair's New Labour, as well as Margaret Thatcher. Diversity promotion and equality of opportunity are in keeping with neoliberal principles.

The individual and society

A fundamental belief of neoliberals is that the fulfilment of individual self-interests secures the 'increase of population and wealth'.[32] For Hayek: the objective of an economic system is to 'secure the best use of resources known to any of the members of society for ends whose relative importance only these individuals know'.[33] Social wholes, such as 'society' or 'collectivities',[34] are abstractions constructed in people's minds. Methodological individualism is a cornerstone of neoliberal thought. As Karl Popper has pointed out: behaviour cannot be reduced to collectivities. '[A]ll social phenomena ... should always be understood as resulting from the decisions, actions, attitudes ... of human individuals, and ... we should never be satisfied by an explanation in terms of so-called "collectivities" (states, nations, races, etc.).'[35] This approach is adopted by neoliberals in the economic sphere. 'There can be no collective consciousness superior to the aggregate of individuals' interests.'[36] Neoliberalism, moreover, extends the scope of classical liberalism: 'Everything ... becom[es] open to marketised forms of choice'[37].

In the neoliberal paradigm, market type exchanges should apply to many forms of 'non-economic behaviour'. Financialisation (the process of exchange through monetary transactions) of activities promotes effectiveness and increases personal choice. This is a major departure from classical economics in which the field for markets was limited to the economic sphere. Examples here are the introduction of prices for services in the public sector, such as healthcare, education, and the use of private companies to run prisons and probation services, fees for parking cars on public roads, for the use of public playing fields and toilets are other examples.

---

[32] F. Hayek, *The Fatal Conceit: The Errors of Socialism*. Edited by W.W. Bartley III. Volume 1 of the collected works of Friedrich A. Hayek. London: Routledge, 1988, p 6.

[33] F.A. Hayek, *Individualism and the Economic Order*. Chicago and London: University of Chicago Press, 1980, p 78.

[34] For an overview see Andrew Gamble, *Hayek: The Iron Cage of Liberty*. Cambridge: Polity, 1996, pp 53–6.

[35] K. Popper, *The Open Society and its Enemies, Vol 2*. London: Routledge, 1945. See Chapter 14, quotation p 91.

[36] See discussion of the ways that von Mises's thought has influenced the formation of a neoliberal sociological theory. N. Gane, Sociology and neoliberalism: A missing history, *Sociology*, 48:6 (December 2014), pp 1092–1106l, particularly pp 1094–5.

[37] Gane, Sociology and neoliberalism, p 1095.

Private property[38] is the heart of liberalism.[39] Economists such as Frank H. Knight, F.A. Hayek and Ludwig von Mises emphasise that the foundation of capitalism lies in the private ownership of productive resources, which provides the basis for the autonomy of the economic enterprise. 'The program of liberalism, therefore, if condensed into a single word, would have to read: property, that is, private ownership of the means of production ... All the other demands of liberalism result from this fundamental demand.'[40] Hayek considered that the development of trading in the formation of capitalism, which gave rise to a price system, was dependent on the security of private property and this requires state enforcement legitimated by law. Property and (to a lesser extent) inheritance ensure individual freedom. The logic of this position is that any alternative economic system to liberalism must replace private property.

Though Hayek concedes that private property reduces equality of opportunity, it is justifiable in that it promotes freedom and the alternative of state or collective ownership is bad. People 'get what they deserve' because rewards depend on their 'ability and enterprise' as well as fortuitous circumstance.[41] Milton Friedman put this clearly when he stated, 'The ethical principle that would directly justify the distribution of income in a free market society is, "To each according to what he and the instruments he owns produces"'.[42] Reducing inequality of opportunity, therefore, is desirable as it encourages 'free enterprise' and thus promotes progress. Equality of opportunity has seeped into social democratic politics and has effectively 'neoliberalised' the traditional socialist concern for social equality.

Spontaneity rather than conscious human design shapes individual behaviour. On the first page of Vol 1 of his collective works, Hayek contends that:

> To understand our civilisation, one must appreciate that the extended order resulted not from human design or intention but spontaneously: it arose from unintentionally conforming to certain traditional and largely *moral* [italics in original] practices, many of which men tend to dislike,

---

[38] A system of private property 'is the most important guarantee of freedom', Road to Serfdom. p 78.

[39] Remarkably, many commentators either marginalise or even ignore private property. For example, in Foucault's, *The Birth of Biopolitics*, there is not even a reference to property in the index.

[40] Ludwig von Mises, *Liberalism in The Classical Tradition*. San Francisco: Cobden Press, 1985, p 19.

[41] For further exposition see: A. Offer, The market turn: From social democracy to market liberalism. *Economic History Review*, 70: 4 (2017), pp 1051–71.

[42] Friedman, *Capitalism and Freedom*, pp 161–2.

whose significance they usually fail to understand, whose validity they cannot prove and which have nonetheless fairly rapidly spread by means of an evolutionary selection – the comparative increase of population and wealth – of those groups that happened to follow them.[43]

The paradigm denies any holistic understanding of society. Neoliberals contend that 'society' does not exist and is a creation in the minds of sociologists (and socialists).

Sociologists, such as Emile Durkheim, would contend, on the contrary, that individuals cannot flourish alone and society is created by people and gives sustenance to human life. Socialism sought to change society and to do this one had to understand its laws of development. Socialism is based on the contention that human development is predicated on 'a conscious, rational regulation of human social life'.[44] All this is denied by neoliberals who, nevertheless, have views on how human behaviour should be conducted. They 'impose [their] vision' of how society should be organised and, in this sense, sustain Francis Fukuyama's views of the ultimate validity of their own theories.'[45] Only market mechanisms operating through competition can achieve optimum results – satisfying the wants of individuals.[46] One important conclusion follows from such reasoning: planning by governments cannot satisfy individual human wants because the information required cannot be known to any aggregating unit (which in practice is the state).[47]

A liberal market society is a pluralistic one: there is no one single centre of control. No collectivity can know the wants of individuals: governments cannot truthfully promote the 'interests of society'.[48] The state promotes its own interests, which does not coincide with individual interests. Freedom is achieved through the 'spontaneous processes of ordering that emerge from the actions of individuals and which find concrete expression through acts of exchange and competition in markets.'[49] In an institutional sense, political and economic authorities must be separate autonomous components of civil society. Coordination of the multiple sectors occurs through a process of mutual exchange (catallaxy). Continuous state intrusion cannot be reconciled

---

[43] Hayek, *The Fatal Conceit*, p 6.
[44] Tom Bottomore, *Sociology and Socialism*. Brighton: Wheatsheaf books, 1984, p 1.
[45] See discussion in P. Mirowski and D. Plehwe, *The Road from Mont Pelerin*, London and Cambridge, MA: Harvard University Press, 2009, p 445.
[46] Hayek, *Individualism and the Economic Order*, p 79.
[47] See particularly, Hayek, Economics and knowledge.
[48] F. von Hayek, *Individualism: True and False*, 1945. Available at: http://econdse.org/wp-content/uploads/2014/09/hayek.pdf. See p 19.
[49] Gane, Sociology and neoliberalism, p 1102.

with a liberal market theory as the state cannot 'know better' than a freely functioning market.

The growth of state regulation and interference with market processes is deplored by neoliberals who seek to dismantle government agencies.[50] As Friedman points out: '[O]n the whole, market competition when it is permitted to work, protects the consumer better than do the alternative government mechanisms that have been increasingly superimposed on the market'.[51] Milton and Rose Friedman condemn bureaucratic government, which 'increasingly interposes itself between the citizenry and the representatives they choose'.[52] As to monopolies, the neoliberal argument is that under conditions of free international trade very few would exist. For those that do, Friedman makes it clear that he considers a private monopoly to be more desirable than public regulation or public monopoly.[53] These views assume that any form of collectivism is 'essentially authoritarian'. The criticism that markets require 'constant intervention' by the state for them to function neoliberals consider to be quite wrong. Laws must be strongly enforced to secure free market operations, but states should not meddle in market processes.

The rule of law

The boundaries of a market system and the enforcement of legitimate market relationships are secured through the legal system. A neoliberal economy is not only a form of economic exchange but a social system predicated on a wide variety of psychological norms, of pluralistic political institutions, of values and competition, of personal satisfaction derived from consumption and entrepreneurial innovation and, fundamentally, on the enforcements by an independent legal system.

Political and legal institutions provide the framework in which neoliberalism can operate. Neoliberals promote civil society in the formation of 'intermediate formations and associations' which are 'essential factors in preserving the orderly working of human society'.[54] In participating in the social processes, an individual 'must be ready and

---

[50] See discussion in Simon Choat, The iron cage of enterprise or the restoration of class power? Approaches to understanding neoliberalism. *Political Studies Review*, 17:4 (2019), pp 416–27, p 420.

[51] See particularly, M. Friedman and R. Friedman, *Free to Choose*. London and New York: Harcourt Brace, 1990, p 222.

[52] Friedman and Friedman, *Free to Choose*, p 295.

[53] Friedman, *Capitalism and Freedom*, p 28; on role of free international trade, see Friedman and Friedman, *Free to Choose*, p 53.

[54] Hayek, *Individualism: True and False*, p 22.

willing to adjust himself to changes and to submit to conventions' to further human freedom.[55]

Liberty cannot be undermined by democracy (in the sense of majority rule or Parliamentary decision). All states, including democratic ones, are bound by law that promotes 'democratic choice'. Friedrich von Hayek maintains that majority rule must be consistent with the community's common beliefs or principles and cannot override them: 'it is necessary that the majority submit to these common principles even when it may be in its immediate interest to violate them.' 'The power of the majority is limited by those commonly held principles and there is no legitimate power beyond them.'[56] Democracy is 'a rule of procedure whose aim is to promote freedom'.[57] Hence there are important legally constituted limitations on the ways that states, including democratic ones, should act.

All forms of government activity must be defined by law; an important consequence here is that law limits democracy. The liberal state, it should be emphasised, must be strong in its definition and enforcement of the rules that maintain liberal market society. The rule of law, enforced by the state, maintains the fundamental features of capitalism, which cannot be subject to alteration even by majoritarian democratic decision. Hence the sphere of government is limited: the state bureaucracy is subject to law, which even elected governments cannot abrogate. In politics, competitive elections are the parallel to the free economic market. They provide a rational political mechanism to secure individual self-interest – through competition involving free entry of candidates and rational choice on the part of electors. Hence, electoral democracy must be promoted.

Progress is promoted by institutions that ensure both stability and development; competition and self-interest safeguard the success of free enterprise; laws enforced by the state secure rewards for innovation and industry. For Hayek:

> the spontaneous actions of individuals will, under conditions which we can define, bring about a distribution of resources which can be understood as if it were made according to a single plan, although nobody has planned it. [This] seems to me indeed an answer to the problem which has sometimes been metaphorically described as that of the 'social mind'.[58]

---

[55] Hayek, *Individualism: True and False*, p 22.
[56] Hayek, *The Constitution of Liberty*, pp 106–7.
[57] Quotation attributed to Hayek, cited by P. Mirowski, Postface: Defining Neoliberalism, in Mirowski and Plehwe, *The Road from Mont Pelerin*, pp 417–56, quotation p 446.
[58] Hayek, Economics and knowledge, p 54.

There is neither state planning nor anarchy: free autonomous social institutions interact through a process of catallaxy to promote human well-being. Law and social institutions provide an essential framework in which freedom may be realised. Thus, in my view, there is a tension in neoliberalism between the state which maintains the institutions of capitalism and the freedom of individuals acting through the market. Freedom is attained through market competition, which ideally should form the basis of interaction between people.

The neoliberal social system

An idealised version of the neoliberal social system is illustrated in Figure 2.1. The social system operates as a self-regulating whole promoting human well-being. The diagram illustrates the interconnectedness of the psychological, legal, economic and political processes. Neoliberal governments promote a neoliberal type of society, a kind of 'sociological liberalism'. Moreover, proponents of global liberalisation adopt a missionary zeal – the paradigm can and should be applied globally.

Globalisation is endorsed as it widens the market and strengthens economies. The values embodied in twenty-first-century liberalism transcend the boundaries of nation states; neoliberal institutions and processes should be replicable on a global basis unhindered by states maintaining economic, personal and financial borders. In the autumn of 2007, Alan Greenspan, the former chairman of the US Federal Reserve, when asked which candidate he would support in the presidential election, replied, '[We] are fortunate that, thanks to globalisation, policy decisions in the US have been largely replaced by global market forces. National security aside, it hardly makes any difference who will be the next president. The world is governed by market forces.'[59] There may be some wishful thinking here as later the presidency of Donald Trump illustrated that US state policies can curb and limit the influence of globalisation. But the point is that political power is mediated through the global market. In the neoliberal paradigm, the free combination of the factors of production promotes human wealth and well-being on a world scale – global liberalisation. Here neoliberals follow earlier liberal thinkers who lauded the civilising effects of international trade. Organisations such as the European Bank for Reconstruction and Development (EBRD), the WTO and the IMF promote these neoliberal economic objectives.

---

[59]   Cited by Adam Tooze, *Crashed*. London: Allen Lane, 2018, p 574.

Figure 2.1: Neoliberal pluralist sectors of society

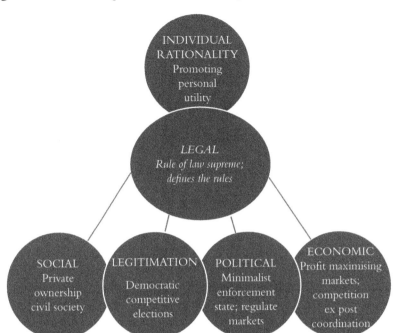

Hence the open processes of globalisation, which have grown in the twenty-first century, find support among neoliberal writers and policy makers who contend that the benefits of the good society should not be confined to the privileged West. 'Democracy promotion' is endorsed if it brings freedom. Globalisation, however, should not be conflated solely into a component of neoliberalism; globalisation is a phenomenon that can take different, even socialist, forms (see Chapter 14).

Financialisation and speculation

The financial system plays a crucial role in the allocation of assets, the coordination of the economy and everyday life. In some forms, it is consistent with, and a development of, the neoliberal narrative of Hayek. Financial motives and criteria, financial actors and institutions mediate between the person and social life. Financialisation of relationships promotes a regime of accumulation – financial criteria determine the allocation of investment; economic and non-economic organisations and associations are subject to financial scrutiny; and everyday life becomes financialised though the monetarisation of relationships.[60] These processes promote individual choice concurrently with the creation of profit. Speculation on various forms of currency evaluation (derivatives, futures) comes to replace the sale of goods and services. Hence critical writers such as Gerard Dumenil and Dominique Levy recognise neoliberalism as a 'new social order' consequent on the reassertion of the interests of the 'financial fraction of the ruling classes'.[61] They consider the rise and dominance of financial institutions in the twentieth century to be a new stage of capitalism.

Financialisation facilitates transactions and enables banks to increase levels of debt, thus enabling 'debt instruments [to] far outweigh equity instruments' as sources of revenue in relation to gross domestic product.[62] The state (or central) bank should be independent of government, and thus be free to act as an economic, or a political, player. Financialisation, however, is a process that has been grafted onto neoliberal economies and in some respects is not compatible with its original forms. Financialisation has facilitated the rise of the 'debt economy' and it, rather than economic liberalism, is believed to be responsible for the financial crisis of 2007. Many neoliberals would emphasise the need for firm regulation by governments of the financial sector. Consequently, neoliberal politicians, in the USA, objected to government 'bail-outs' of financial companies that had acted speculatively and had insufficient capital reserves. The fault here, it is contended, lies with faulty and inadequate regulation, not with the neoliberal market mechanism.

However, these 'faults' indicate more serious problems with the liberal mechanisms. Markets under modern capitalism operate through money, and transactions on the stock exchange do not necessarily lead to economic development and wealth creation, though they may increase profit. Financialisation raises transaction costs without adding any real value to the national product. Liberal economics does not sufficiently distinguish between speculation and enterprise. Financial markets lead to the 'risk of the predominance of speculation'.[63] This tendency was recognised by Maynard Keynes, well before neoliberalism, when he pointed out that investors were not motivated by the prospective yield of an investment (which may be low)

[60] N. van der Zwan, State of the art: Making sense of financialisation. *Socio-Economic Review*, 12 (2014), pp 99–129; O. Orhangazi, Financialisation and capital accumulation in the non-financial corporate sector: A theoretical and empirical investigation on the US economy: 1973–2003. *Cambridge Journal of Economics*, 32 (2008), pp 863–86.

[61] Gérard Duménil and Dominique Lévi, Costs and benefits of neoliberalism: A class analysis. *Review of International Political Economy*, 8:4 (Winter, 2001), pp 578–607, quotations pp 596, 578.

[62] See T. Di Muzio and R.H. Robbins, *Debt as Power*. Manchester: Manchester University Press, 2016.

[63] J. M. Keynes, *General Theory of Employment, Interest and Money*, London: Palgrave Macmillan, 1936, p 158.

but looked for 'a favourable change in the conventional basis of valuation' – in plain English, a speculative gain.[64]

Financial markets involve spontaneous exchanges but not always the virtuous kinds envisaged by writers like Milton Friedman. They promote computer-based trading in which speculators' profit is derived from rises and falls of stock market prices. Investment has been directed to financial instruments that, through speculation, have given very high returns. Securitisation (a process promoting the purchase of cash flow from debt such as mortgages) has also greatly furthered speculation in the financial sector leading to global financial instability. The cumulative pursuit of financial profit consequently has led to financial and economic crises. This is not an aberration of financial capitalism but a tendency built into the ways in which unregulated financial markets have operated. It is a consequence of the unregulated movement of capital on a global scale – private gain and public loss.

Neoliberal economists, however, would lay the blame on the lack of rules to order the market which, they insist, is a maxim of neoliberalism. The absence of any mutual economic correction became obvious in 2007 following the financial collapse of the British bank Northern Rock and later of the American Lehman Brothers, which entailed the serious malfunctioning of the financial system. In September and October 2008, according to Ben Bernanke, economies faced 'the worst financial crisis in global history, including the Great Depression'.[65] The Great Depression, however, had very strong rules governing the issue of credit and was caused by inadequate levels of demand. The antidote to booms and slumps as well as financial crisis is not self-adjusting economic mechanism but policies enacted by the state, which intervenes to overcome market failure.

The regulatory role of the state

In the neoliberal paradigm, the state is required to provide a strong legal framework for the enforcement of a system of private property and market exchange and to ensure the enduring value of money. Its role is to enforce a body of rules, not to promote political objectives such as justice or welfare.[66] Milton Friedman acknowledges that a major distinction between what he called

---

[64] 'When the capital development of a country becomes a by-product of the activities of a casino, the job is likely to be ill-done. The measure of success attained by Wall St, regarded as an institution of which the proper social purpose is to direct new investment into the most profitable channels in terms of future yield, cannot be claimed as one of the outstanding triumphs of *laissez-faire* capitalism.' Keynes, *General Theory*, p 159.

[65] Cited by Tooze, *Crashed*, p 163.

[66] For a discussion of neoliberalism and the state, see Plant, *The Neoliberal State*, especially Chapter 1.

'nineteenth century liberalism' (classical liberalism) and the 'new liberalism' (neoliberalism) is the more positive role for the state in the latter.[67] As he has put it: '[Neoliberalism] must give high place to a severe limitation on the power of the state to interfere in the detailed activities of individuals; at the same time, it must explicitly recognise that there are important positive functions that must be performed by the state'.[68] It provides a framework for the enforcements of laws for a market society. The state has a role to promote a market economy and to secure conditions for effective competition. The doctrine does not exclude objectives of ensuring justice and welfare, but these are not its major concerns.

Friedman is clear that economic coordination should be based on 'voluntary co-operation, ... the technique of the market place, and of arrangements involving voluntary exchange'.[69] An understanding of neoliberalism as promoting some sort of 'neoliberal bureaucratised state', suggested by some of its critics, cannot be found in the works of any of neoliberalism's major economic theorists. Milton Friedman explicitly rejects this kind of interference: 'Government can never duplicate the variety and diversity of individual action ... [B]y imposing uniform standards ... in the process, government would replace progress by stagnation, it would substitute uniform mediocrity for the variety essential for that experimentation which can bring tomorrow's laggards above today's mean'.[70]

Under the new liberalism, 'the spread of market relations is inevitably spearheaded by state actors'.[71] In the practice of current neoliberal policies, states have taken functions not anticipated or theorised by economists such as Hayek. The transactions required in maintaining an equal and competitive market call for state regulation. The internal organisation of state institutions should also follow neoliberal principles – there should be internal markets and, wherever possible, competition. Processes of catallaxy are subject to such laws. The objective of promoting 'fair competition' then comes to override the freedom of individual actors. In all these activities, market exchange is increasingly replaced by state regulation constituting a tension within neoliberalism.

Foucault highlights the extent of penetration of government into social life in what he calls 'a grid of governmentality',[72] which applies to a vast range of conduct – market rules for example are applied to the processes within government or government run institutions (such as universities or

---

[67] Friedman, *Capitalism and Freedom*.
[68] Milton Friedman, *Neoliberalism and its prospects*, Oslo: Farmand. (1951), pp 89–93. Collected works can be found at: https://miltonfriedman.hoover.org/friedman_images/Collections/2016c21/Farmand.
[69] Friedman, *Neoliberalism and its prospects*, p 4.
[70] Friedman, *Capitalism and Freedom*, p 4.
[71] Mirowski, *The Road from Mont Peleri*, p 437.
[72] See discussion in Foucault, *The Birth of Biopolitics*, pp 186–7.

national health service hospitals). This form of 'neoliberal governability',[73] I contend, is not compatible with the views of leading neoliberals, such as Hayek and Milton Friedman who condemn reliance on bureaucratic rules and favour catallactic exchanges between units that are direct and mutually sustaining. The intrusion of 'governmental personnel and advisors' in the USA,[74] are not a consequence of neoliberalism but occur despite it. Foucault's ideas about 'sociological government' which promotes a 'society that has now become the object of governmental intervention and practice'[75] are opposed by neoliberals. As the Friedmans complain: 'The bureaucracy that is needed to administer government grows and increasingly imposes itself between the citizenry and the representatives they choose. It becomes both a vehicle whereby special interests can achieve their objectives and an important special interest in its own right – a major part of a new class.'[76]

Paradoxically, however, the neoliberal policy of the extension of the market to non-economic associations and government bodies has led to bureaucratic regulation to audit and police market exchanges. As one commentator has put it: to ensure the unimpeded 'marketisation of the state', 'processes, institutions and actors must be monitored, audited, evaluated and certified, to ensure that they are efficient, cost-effective, transparent and accountable'.[77] Such developments can become bureaucratic distortions (like authoritarian structures) and are not part of the neoliberal way of thinking – bureaucracy is a perversion of neoliberalism because it curbs the market. Neoliberals have condemned the 'bureaucratic inflation' of regulatory bodies and endorse Adam Smith's 'propensity to truck, barter and exchange'[78] without the imposition of excessive bureaucratic procedures and rules. The irony here is that bringing markets into state administration and making procedures subject to rules (to counter patronage and corruption) raise levels of bureaucracy. Regulatory bodies set up to promote competition have the same bureaucratic effects.

Self-regulating markets

Milton Friedman in 'Neoliberalism and its Prospects' makes it clear that 'the goal of the competitive order ... supersedes the nineteenth century goal of laissez-faire'. Coordination for Friedman is furthered not by 'administrative

---

[73] See discussion in Foucault, *The Birth of Biopolitics*, p 192.

[74] Foucault, *The Birth of Biopolitics*, p 193.

[75] See discussion in Foucault, *The Birth of Biopolitics*, pp 145–7, quotation, p 146.

[76] M. Freidman and R. Friedman, *Free to Choose*, p 295.

[77] See discussion in Simon Choat, The iron cage of enterprise. Quotation p 419. Choat analyses this development from a Foucault perspective.

[78] Noted by Choat, The iron cage of enterprise, p 418.

order' but by 'the exercise of individual initiative by millions of independent economic units'; it is the 'impersonal price system [which coordinates] the detailed economic activities of these units'.[79] What is missing here is any consideration of the very high transaction costs that are involved in 'making markets' work.

Friedman makes it abundantly clear that statist forms of coordination involve 'people telling other people what to do' whereas under neoliberalism it takes place through 'voluntary co-operation'.[80] In *Why Government Is the Problem*,[81] he explicitly declares that the activity of government has led to it 'becom[ing] a self-generating monstrosity ... What we now have is a government of the people, by the bureaucrats, including the legislators who have become bureaucrats, for the bureaucrats'. Rather than promoting neoliberalism, political and economic elites operate to secure their own sectional interest by making rules which benefit themselves.[82] I would agree with Friedman that commentators who consider the invasive and growing role of state regulation as a form of neoliberalism are quite mistaken. As the Friedmans object: 'High level bureaucrats ... [issue] rules and regulations as "interpretations" of laws that in fact subtly, or sometimes crudely, alter their thrust; of dragging their feet in administering those parts of laws of which they disapprove, while pressing on with those they favor'.[83]

The bureaucratisation of governmental and of daily-life cannot be attributed to the suppositions of neoliberalism. Here followers of Foucault lapse into reductionism – to seek the cause of everything in 'neoliberalism'. The functions of 'auditing', 'monitoring' and control performed by the interventionist state,[84] and 'active governmentality' in Foucault's terms, are not part of neoliberal philosophy at all but represent elite interests that have captured state apparatuses. Friedman makes this clear when, in criticising 'the growth in government at all levels', he concludes that 'In the government sphere, as in the market, there seems to be an invisible hand, but it operates in precisely the opposite direction from Adam Smith's'.[85] State bureaucracies provide spaces for the exercise of bureaucratic self-interest and

---

[79] Friedman, Neoliberalism and its prospects, quotations pp 3–4.

[80] Friedman, *Capitalism and Freedom*, p 6.

[81] Friedman, *Why Government Is the Problem*, p 7.

[82] See the examples with respect to 'protectionism as an elite strategy' in Vo Phuong Mai Le, Patrick Minford and Eric Nowell, European economic policy: Protectionism as an elite strategy, in A. Gamble and D. Lane (Eds), *The European Union and World Politics*. Palgrave: London, 2009, pp 217–34.

[83] Friedman and Friedman, *Free to Choose*, p 296.

[84] See Choat, The iron cage of enterprise, p 420.

[85] Friedman and Friedman, *Free to Choose*, p 5.

opportunities for corruption. The neoliberal solution is not to introduce bureaucratic monitoring of the executives but their replacement by private competing bodies.

Neoliberalism, even in theory, recognises other human values: 'All of us are willing to sacrifice some efficiency for other goals', markets have some undesirable consequences (such as pollution) which require state regulation'.[86] Though individuals should insure themselves against risk (such as ill-health and unemployment) Hayek concedes that a 'safety net' should be provided for the needy. While the state (as well as charity) should take on a function of 'relieving misery and distress' it should not interfere with the operation of the market. Welfare provision should not be a monopoly for governments, which should face competition for providing services from the private sector.[87] In the neoliberal approach, there is a separate moral place for charity to provide for the needy. However, the provision of social welfare (unlike in socialism) is not part of any conception of social justice. People should make provision for their own welfare (through, for example, insurance).

Conclusion

Neoliberal capitalism proposes that assets are privately owned and transactions are conducted in a market, driven by competing units to secure profit. Politically, the state provides a legal framework of enforcements promoting market processes and political freedom. Socially, civil society in the form of free autonomous associations separates the individual from the control of the state thus securing liberation. Institutions and processes are secured by law which is autonomous and is superior to politics, including democratic politics. Private business rather than collective state provision is considered the most effective way to provide services. The scope of neoliberalism is universal and not confined within the boundaries of nation states, and its institutions are replicable on a world scale. Neoliberals contend that its mechanisms provide the best economic system to promote growth and human well-being, thus they justify promotion and adoption by other non-liberal societies.

No 'real existing' polity fits completely into the model I have described. There are contradictions and inconsistencies in the processes of neoliberal

---

[86] M. Friedman, *Market or Plan?*. London: Centre for Research into Communist Societies, 1984, quotation p 20.
[87] Hayek, *The Constitution of Liberty*, p 150.

regimes.[88] However, discrepancies between theory and practice are to be expected as liberal economic philosophy is normative and states,embedded in their own history and culture, depart in many ways from the principles listed earlier. Milton Friedman concedes that every economic system is a combination of voluntary cooperation and command elements: 'The problem is one of proportion' of keeping a balance between market processes and securing other human objectives outside markets.[89] States selectively adopt policies of neoliberalisation. 'Neoliberal' regimes in Latin America, for example, have been shown to be authoritarian in character;[90] China has adopted many tenets of liberal competition, but the state retains monopoly powers over the operation of significant branches of the economy. Self-defined neoliberal governments may also preside over bureaucracies, sometimes controlled by political and/or economic elites who institute market type processes within the state to counter state capture by economic interests and corruption on the part of government executives. These are part of the traditional state's role of defining and enforcing the rules of the market.

Writers often wrongly identify historically determined elements of regimes as neoliberal practices. The neoliberal prescriptions described here have to be contextualised in the institutional structures and values in which they have developed – conservative, liberal, patriarchal, social democratic, populist and state capitalist. Regimes embody their own footprint. There is a process of liberalisation, furthered by political and economic elites, which is mediated by existing structures and processes. Global neoliberalism includes contradictory economic formations and leads to a variety of outcomes. The notion that a 'new political order' of neoliberalism initiated by President Donald Trump has been reversed under Joe Biden is premature.[91] While neoliberals reveal the positive features of the doctrine, in the next chapter we turn to consider the inadequacies of the neoliberal approach and why alternatives are necessary.

---

[88] Ha-Joon Chang, Breaking the mould: An institutionalist political economy alternative to the neoliberal theory of the market and the states. *Cambridge Journal of Economics*, 26 (2002), pp 539–59.

[89] Friedman, *Market or Plan?*, quotation p 16.

[90] Dieter Plehwe, Introduction, in Mirowski and Plehwe, *The Road from Mont Pelerin*. Plehwe cites the example of 'authoritarian' neoliberal regimes in Latin America, p 3.

[91] See Gerstle, *The Rise and Fall of the Neoliberal Order*, Chapter 8.

3

Neoliberalism: A Critique

In evaluating neoliberalism as a social and economic theory, one should avoid
the trap of attributing all the virtues and/or faults of contemporary capitalist
society to neoliberalism. Often critics link the practices of governments
which they dislike to political and economic outcomes having no, or only
an indirect, affinity to any neoliberal ideology or policy. Many denounce or
praise 'the way things are' as consequences of neoliberalism. Consider Alan
Greenspan's list of the achievements of global neoliberalism:

> During the past century, economic growth created resources far in
> excess of those required to maintain subsistence. That surplus in
> democratic capitalist societies has, in large measure, been employed
> to improve the quality of life along many dimensions. To cite a short
> list: (1) greater longevity, owing first to the widespread development of
> clean, potable water, and later to rapid advances in medical technology,
> (2) a universal system of education that enabled greatly increased social
> mobility, (3) vastly improved conditions of work, and (4) the ability
> to enhance our environment by setting aside natural resources rather
> than employing them to sustain a minimum level of subsistence. At
> a fundamental level, we have used the substantial increases in wealth
> generated by our market-driven economy to purchase what many
> would view as greater civility.[1]

However valid such endorsements of economic and civilisational
advancements may be, these achievements may not be consequences
solely of neoliberal policies. Advances in scientific technologies, provision
of universal education and improvement in working conditions would

---

[1]   Alan Greenspan, 'On globalisation', Lecture delivered at the Institute for International
Economics' First Annual Stavros Niarchos Foundation Lecture 24 October 2001. Available
at: https://www.piie.com/events/greenspan-globalization

have happened anyway as they occurred in statist societies such as Nazi Germany, social democratic Britain, the socialist USSR, and contemporary China – all countries operating under different economic and political systems to neoliberalism. Capitalist countries have adopted neoliberal policies on a piecemeal basis and their introduction has been mediated by the history and institutions of the societies in which they are embedded. Advanced capitalist economies with neoliberal governments, for example, often manipulate interest rates, subsidise failing industries and support welfare subsidies.

As a contribution to economic theory, neoliberalism has made some advances. The network idea of catallaxy is superior to Adam Smith's concept of the 'invisible hand'. The elimination of entry barriers to labour markets has led governments to further policies of inclusion and diversity and to enhance the upward mobility of labour. Liberal market policies, adopted in societies such as China, have opened up the economy by rewarding entrepreneurship and enterprise; policies of the World Trade Organization have facilitated free trade and the movement of capital and labour and consequently the industrial development of Asia and, to a more moderate degree, in Latin America. Adding markets to planning has had positive effects – notably, in China. The neoliberal criticism that promoting the interest of 'society' furthers the personal interests of politicians and elites is sometimes true; politicians can be self-serving and corrupt – but not always. Individual freedom and the notion that people receive 'what they deserve' have a widespread appeal under conditions of possessive individualism. Neoliberalism commands wide support and, as a normative theory, has been adopted by a very diverse set of political parties to shape public policy. But not all countries have benefitted and many liberalising economies have faced de-industrialisation, unemployment, poverty and economic crises. State-led industrialisation has also had successes. Neoliberal economics are predicated on maximising the satisfaction of individuals whereas the economies are often driven by the interests of corporations and firms, which have different operational principles.

Here we consider not the application of neoliberal policies but the underlying theoretical assumptions of global neoliberalism. Neoliberalism contextualises and affects the ways that politics, economics and globalisation operate. I turn to discuss seven dimensions where capitalism rooted in neoliberalism may be faulted. These are listed briefly, then elaborated in the text that follows:

- that the aggregate of individuals' market behaviour is an inadequate basis for economic policy;
- that individualistic catallaxic exchanges do not cumulatively meet the needs of collectivities;

- that countervailing economic power does not operate to overcome inertia or to stabilise economic cycles;
- that financialisation of economic relations is often perverse and may lead to speculation;
- that private ownership of productive assets can distort economic incentives, stifle entrepreneurship, and lead to idleness;
- that neoliberal policies ignore conflicts caused by class relations;
- that the continual and cumulative pursuit of consumption does not fulfil human needs, and the operation of markets does not always give people 'what they deserve'.

Psychological subjectivism

Neoliberal methodology is predicated on the subjective propensities of individuals to make their own choices. Such economic thinking is a form of subjectivism: suppositions and motivations in people's minds guide behaviour. This has the merit of putting the individual at the centre of economics but concurrently ignores recurring human associations, such as companies, and social classes. Corporations are collectivities with multiple aims. Ownership and the division of labour give rise to social classes whose leaders and associations promote collective interests. By putting individuals at the centre of its analysis, neoliberalism does not take adequate account of the unequal division of economic and political power. It is a psychological rather than a sociological approach. To explain economic conduct, institutional structures as well as dominant and subordinate social classes should be taken into account.

To promote collective well-being and optimum welfare, one must consider the social distribution of physical and financial assets. Demand fulfilled through the market mechanism satisfies individual wants. However, those with the most financial assets exert a disproportional influence on the market while concurrently short-changing those with the least. Fulfilling individual wants, created by advertising, is not the same as meeting human needs. Hence the emphasis on choice given by the market does not necessarily promote a just distribution of human welfare. The institutional framework and unequal distribution of wealth limit the choices of the poor. The London property market fulfils the wants of the rich, while the needs of the poor and even the moderately well off cannot be met. The latter lack the assets to enter the market; their 'choice' is determined by their means, by the distribution of income and wealth, which shape their market preferences. While market exchanges enable properties to be sold to the highest bidder, they do not ensure an equitable distribution of properties. Consequently, demand for expensive property stimulates the building of more of the same kind.

This is not a fault of the market but of unequal income and wealth distribution. The market is a neutral mechanism, what is ignored in neoliberal theory and practice is that market players in capitalist societies are grossly unequal. We experience no countervailing economic forces to meet the needs of the poor for housing as they are not expressed in terms of economic 'wants'. The articulation of 'wants' as expressed in personal demands is not the same as social needs. The rich can buy healthcare at any price thus utilising scarce medical resources for trivial wants, such as cosmetic surgery, while the needs of the sick, who may be poor, remain unattended. This is even more unjust if the wealth has been achieved without merit.

Equilibrium analysis is concerned with satisfying existing individual wants efficiently. In neoliberal thinking there is an absence of holistic knowledge (considering the economy as a whole), only the sum of the perceptions of free individuals, fulfilling their 'choices' in the selection of goods and services, is considered. 'Wants' may also be created artificially through advertising thus leading to spiralling demand for commodities, consequently depleting nature's resources and contributing to environmental costs. The market might be a mechanism promoting public welfare if the distribution of assets was made equal, but this would undermine a cardinal component of neoliberal capitalism: the freedom to own unlimited assets. Reducing the barriers to equality of opportunity for the poor to become richer, or promoting diversity in the labour market does not address the levels of institutionally determined inequality. The constitution of inequality is inherited wealth. A concept of 'society', however, implies that human beings can calculate how to meet human needs on a collective basis. Democracies can justifiably limit liberty by promoting equality based on consideration of needs or desert, rather than, as in a liberal framework, promoting equality of opportunity. Democracies bring values, other than economic ones, to consider the constitution of human needs.

Catallaxy and the fulfilment of wants

The process of catallaxy does not achieve the optimum fulfilment of people's wants. Hayek and other neoliberal writers do not sufficiently take into account the fact that knowledge is imperfect. As equilibrium depends on the compatibility of the subjective plans of all people who interact, we cannot assume that all people will adjust their own plans to make them mutually compatible. Individuals cannot know the intentions of others; they must guess and in so doing will make mistakes. Hence, without compatibility, the market cannot operate in an optimum way. Catallaxies take the form of continual adjustments and readjustments, which do not always lead to moving equilibriums. Such incompatibilities have led to serious market failures, enduring slumps and damaging crises. Neoliberals assume that with time compatibility will develop and lead to a single equilibrium which will satisfy the wants of all actors. However, economies can sustain different market structures with their own equilibriums. There can be 'multiple equilibriums' caused by information asymmetries and institutional rigidities. Capitalist countries have severe regional divisions and imbalances. 'The market' does not create one equilibrium through complementary flows of investment and labour. Regions maintain their own equilibriums through inertia. For example, the regions of Arkansas (US), Tyneside (UK) and Ivanova (Russia) have not attained the levels of other prosperous national regions but remain in a static state of poverty well below their economic potential. Taking account of such imbalances, governments can introduce policies to remedy them.

Social institutions (such as corporations and economic organisations) form the major economic units in globalised capitalism. Hegemonic economic power in the form of corporate global companies can shape outcomes, rather than autonomous and anonymous processes involved in the operation of catallaxies.[2] Economic activities in households are largely separate from the operation of the national economy[3] and do not figure in market exchange. Institutions (such as schools, universities), economic enterprises (corporations), and political entities (states, parties) contain diverse and often conflicting interests, which makes catallactic exchanges problematic.

In a global market economy, as countries have different living standards, outsourcing of production leads to poor countries with low wage costs providing labour at a fraction of the cost of developed countries. Hence capital flows to the former concurrently lead to unemployment in the latter. A free labour market encourages cross-national migration, which causes disruption to families, depopulation in declining areas (and poverty for those who remain, despite the receipt of remittances) and strain on resources in immigrant areas. The ideology of neoliberalism legitimates migration as a social good in promoting social welfare and wealth creation, the other side of the coin is social stress, not only in the host areas but also in the parent ones. The 'problem' of migration is not to be resolved by adjustments in regulation but by developmental policies in the areas of origin. Catallaxy operates at the level of individual exchange and ignores the collateral cost on third parties and on society. There is no calculation of social cost. As social costs may even be higher than individual costs (when, for example,

---

[2] See Andrew Gamble, The new political economy, *Political Studies*, XLIII (1995), pp 516–30, especially pp 526–7.

[3] See J.K. Gibson-Graham, *The End of Capitalism (As We Knew It)*. Minneapolis: University of Minnesota Press, 2006.

noise, water and air pollution are involved) then satisfaction of individually perceived wants is not an optimum solution.

The market can operate to the disadvantage of employees as they have considerably less bargaining power than employers and, in poor countries, employees have even less power and weaker labour laws.[4] The fault in neoliberalism is that it considers individuals who are assumed to be equal in relation to the market, not organisations, which are unequal. Neoliberal policies have led over time to rising levels of income – which is positive – as well as concurrently to vast increases in differentials within countries. However, between countries, as I show in Chapter 9, the differential between the leading Western countries, on the one side, and China and some East Asian and Pacific countries, on the other, has narrowed. Since the mid-1970s, outsourcing due to globalisation has had positive effects in the host countries but not in the parent countries.

Economic outcomes are not optimal

A state of equilibrium may not be optimum from the point of view of the utilisation of resources on a societal level. While Hayek emphasises that there is movement towards equilibrium, to reach it may take a long time. The economic history of capitalism is punctuated by cyclical movements, by periods of slumps as well as economic crises. In Hayek's terms, a catallactic movement to a sub-optimal equilibrium is achieved through marginal adaptations. Self-correcting or countervailing forces of the market may be weak or non-existent resulting in underemployment settling at a sub-optimal use of capital and labour. This is a fault of market capitalism. As Keynes put it: the economic system 'seems capable of remaining in a chronic condition of subnormal activity for a considerable period without any marked tendency either towards recovery or towards complete collapse'.[5] Equilibrium can settle at a below optimum level and is not corrected through the economic mechanism.[6] Even a rise in the prospective yield of capital may not be followed by investment (as greater profit may result from speculation on the stock exchange) and hence does not result in a rise in employment.[7] Structural unemployment of labour and capital can continue, ensuring a condition well below a Pareto optimum. There is no *economic* countervailing

---

[4] See discussion in D. Rodrik, *The Globalisation Paradox: Why Global Markets, States and Democracy Can't Coexist*. New York: Norton, 2011, particularly Chapter 9.

[5] Keynes, *General Theory*, p 249.

[6] See discussion in Keynes, *General Theory*, pp 249–54. Joan Robinson showed how imperfect competition led to firms producing below the optimal level. J. Robinson, *The Economics of Imperfect Competition*. London: Macmillan (2nd edn), 1969.

[7] Keynes, *General Theory*, p 250.

power. Such countervailing power as exists is that of governments, which are not a form of market adaptation.

A convincing case can be made for state-led investment. As William Janeway writes: 'neoclassical economics is irrelevant to understanding how the Innovation Economy evolves through historical time, for its core purpose is to identify the conditions under which a competitive market economy will reach an efficient, timeless equilibrium in the allocation of resources'.[8] Developmental economics in contrast is predicated on securing economic growth, which requires long-term capital investment which is quite rationally denied if short-term financial gain is the economic objective.

In neoliberal thinking, there is an excessive emphasis on meeting consumer wants. As Hayek put it: '[T]here is no known way, other than by the distribution of products in a competitive market, to inform individuals in what direction their several efforts must aim so as to contribute as much as possible to the total product'.[9] The emphasis here ignores the economic benefits of state welfare provision which is instituted when markets fail. Shifting provision away from collectively provided health services often leads not only to higher costs but to deterioration in overall provision.[10] Transaction costs of marketisation should be set against potential benefits. It is often claimed that state managed health provision provides not only a comprehensive but also a more efficient service for the population as a whole than those run on a profit-maximising basis. The latter certainly provide better services for those with the ability to pay – the market rewards the rich.

Ownership and control

What is lacking in the neoliberal approach is any consideration of the perverse ways in which economic and political power are unevenly distributed. Security of rights to private property is justified by von Mises and Hayek as a necessary condition for the development of capitalism. For its initial rise, they have been correct. But the literature, even of the 1930s, on the modern corporation and the separation of ownership from control, is ignored.[11] Such division in the structure of corporations puts in question whether private corporate ownership is any longer a necessary, let alone a positive, feature of a modern market society. The point here is that the state representing the

---

[8] W.H. Janeway, *Doing Capitalism in the Innovation Economy: Markets, Speculation and the State.* Cambridge: Cambridge University Press, 2018, p 8.

[9] Hayek, *The Fatal Conceit*, p 7.

[10] P. Watson (Ed), *Health Care Reform and Globalisation*. London: Routledge, 2013.

[11] Of note is the work of A. Berle and G. Means, *The Modern Corporation and Private Property.* New York: Commerce Clearing House, 1932; and later work such as R.K. Marris, *The Economic Theory of Managerial Capitalism*. New York: Free Press, 1964.

public interest (as with nationalised companies) can act equally as well as, or even better than, thousands of individual shareholders who are powerless. In such cases, under free enterprise, managerial control remains unchecked and leads to enormous unjustifiable financial rewards to company executives.

Neoliberals conceive of ownership as promoting freedom, but they ignore the 'unfreedom' that is experienced by those who do not own corporate property. The alternative posed by Hayek is between substituting state ownership for private ownership. State ownership, he explains, would put the state 'in a position whereby its actions must in effect decide all other incomes'. He contends that 'a world in which the wealthy are powerful is still a better world than one in which only the already powerful can acquire wealth'.[12]

The reality of modern capitalism is that the 'already powerful' are those who possess wealth and they determine who are the ones best placed to acquire more wealth. It is quite remarkable that Hayek relies on Trotskyite literature of the late 1930s to conclude that, as a consequence of political power, income differentials in the USSR were greater than in the USA.[13] Studies show that differentials, even if we include payments in kind, were absolutely and relatively lower in the USSR and later in the European socialist states. Even the most extreme estimates of income differentials for the USSR in the 1960s gave the maximum salary at 300 times higher than the minimum wage. Whereas Gerhard Lenski, writing at that time, found a ratio of 11,000 to one for the USA between the highest and the lowest earnings.[14] (We consider recent data on income differentials in Chapter 5 of this book.)

Differentials have risen greatly in post-socialist European states (exponentially in some states of the former Soviet Union). In capitalist states the unequal inherited ownership of wealth is the greatest source of unjustifiable income inequality. Hayek concedes that state planning can secure 'a more just and equitable distribution of wealth ... It is indisputable that if we want to secure a distribution of wealth which conforms to some predetermined standard ... We must plan the whole economic system'.[15] However, he continues that it is not worth the 'price to pay' for the oppression it will create, and he gives preference to increases in productivity to increase national wealth rather than redistribution.[16] These are debateable propositions. He does concede that one should not

---

[12] Hayek, *The Road to Serfdom*, discussion and quotations from pp 77 and 78 respectively.
[13] Hayek, *The Road to Serfdom*, fn 1, p 77.
[14] David Lane, *The End of Inequality?* London: Penguin, 1971, p 74.
[15] Hayek, *The Road to Serfdom*, p 74.
[16] Hayek, *The Road to Serfdom*, p 155.

'depress large classes as to turn them into determined enemies of the existing order'. In such cases, presumably, redistribution is justifiable.[17] Providing equal opportunity for individuals to become unequal (freedom of opportunity) does not address the unequal personal distribution of private capital. Modern governments are (or should be) subject to public accountability, whereas private corporations are responsible only to their share-holders, who expect profits, and they are controlled by directors who regulate the proceeds. Neoliberals endorse financial incentives as a stimulus for efficient work performance and promote the model of the individualistic innovative wealth-making entrepreneur. But they ignore the idle rich who live on the proceeds of inheritance or unearned profits. The logic of the neoliberal position to further individual striving, and innovation should be to curb inheritance as it deters its beneficiaries from taking work.

The emphasis on the need for the economic system to provide profits as an incentive for hard work and entrepreneurship sometimes has positive effects, but not always. Often, the rewards of top banking executives and financial market managers are a consequence of greed for personal income, rather than a reward for innovative work. To take one example: hedge funds returned an average earning of 3 per cent in 2014 (compared with 9 per cent in 2013) and underperformed the US S&P index. Despite this mediocre performance, the 25 best paid fund managers earned $11.62 billion in 2014 – Ken Griffin of Citadel $1.3 billion and James Simons $1.2 billion. While this is less than in 2013, it is quite disproportionate to other earnings.[18] It beggars belief to suggest that these incomes are legitimate rewards for efficient management or to act to stimulate innovation and reward effort. The question must also be raised as to whether the services of fund and asset managers could be replaced with some other method of financial management.

Global economic crisis

Capitalism has always experienced economic crises, and it has fallen to states, rather than 'the market', to restore financial equilibrium. The extent of economic dislocation that occurred during the economic crisis of 2007–08 cannot be underestimated: capital equity loss of US banks was $3.6 trillion;[19]

---

[17] Hayek, *The Road to Serfdom*, p 155.

[18] Data cited in *Financial Times* (London), 8 May 2015.

[19] M. Richardson and N. Roubini, *Washington Post*, 15 February 2009. Cited by J. Crotty, Structural causes of the global financial crisis: A critical assessment of the 'new financial architecture'. *Cambridge Journal of Economics*, 33 (2009), pp 563–80, reference p 569.

unemployment has been estimated to have risen world wide by 50 million people and more than 200 million people were pushed into poverty.[20] As Adam Tooze has cogently put it:

> The 'great trade collapse' of 2008 was the most severe synchronised contraction in international trade ever recorded. Within nine months of their pre-crisis peak, in April 2008, global exports were down by 22 per cent ... In the United States between late 2008 and early 2009, 800,000 people were losing their jobs every month. By 2015, over nine million American families would lose their home to foreclosure - the largest forced population movement in the United States since the Dust Bowl. In Europe, meanwhile, failing banks and fragile public finances created a crisis that nearly split the eurozone.[21]

The question to be addressed is what components of the world economic system were responsible for the crisis. In its Global Financial Stability Report for April 2007, the IMF pointed to weaknesses in the structure of the world's financial system: there had been a significant rise in private sector debt and the globalisation of business had led to a weakening of individual banks.[22] By October 2008, the Fund pointed out that 'the global financial system has entered a new phase of the crisis where solvency concerns have increased to the point where further public resources have had to be committed to contain systemic risks and the economic fallout'.[23] There were many underlying causes that cannot be considered in detail here; major factors were that companies in the financial sector had issued credit to high risk clients with insufficient liquidity to honour claims by depositors. Consequently, major banks defaulted when they had insufficient cash reserves to meet withdrawals; financial companies (Lehman Bros, Northern Rock and others) became bankrupt; insurance companies, such as AIG, also faced financial instability (AIG was saved by the US government buying its stock). The geographical interdependence of financial corporations, especially the crucial role of American corporations had global effects.[24] The weakness of international coordination of the financial corporations led the public sector, at great public expense, to finance rescue operations which, in turn, turned private debt

---

[20] Data cited in S. Blankenburg and J.G. Palma, Introduction: The global financial crisis. *Cambridge Journal of Economics*, 33 (2009), pp 531–38, p 532.

[21] Adam Tooze, The forgotten history of the financial crisis, *Foreign Affairs*, 97:5 (September 2018), pp 199–210, quotation p 199. For a detailed account of the crisis see: Tooze, *Crashed*.

[22] IMF, *Global Financial Stability Report*. Washington DC: IMF, April 2007, p ix.

[23] IMF, *Global Financial Stability Report*, pp 4–5.

[24] See Tooze, The forgotten history of the financial crisis.

into public debt. Public debt was financed through government financial stringency, particularly 'austerity programmes'.

The crisis, however, cannot be attributed to 'neoliberal' economics in a strict sense. While it is true that lax financial conditions promoted choice through easy credit, neoliberal economists have emphasised the importance of a regulatory framework for the market. It was a 'crisis of financial capitalism';[25] of striving for profit by the under- or un-regulated banks in an unsustainable system. Many neoliberals opposed government support for the ailing banks on the grounds that they had acted negligently. Senator Richard C. Shelby, the senior Republican to the Senate banking committee, opposed the US Treasury's proposal to use $700 billion to support the banking industry. He contended that 'bank capital standards' were not designed to 'ensure safety and soundness'; 'financial firms were leveraged heavily to maximise profits'.[26] Opposition was also voiced by Bernie Sanders who opposed the provision because it did not stipulate limits to housing repossessions and did not limit executive income. The US government would bail out the rich at the expense of the poor who would lose their homes. In Hayekian terms, the market mechanism did not have any economic countervailing power; the financial system lacked financial rules, which are a systemic requirement for neoliberal economics. While American Republicans opposed state bail-outs, the banking system nevertheless was saved by state regulation to prevent a complete economic collapse. State intervention showed that market mechanisms were unable to solve the economic crisis without unacceptable economic costs. The state rescue of the financial system effectively maintained the (badly managed) financial institutions at public cost.

Political power and possessive individualism

Underlying the theoretical framework of economic liberalism are the psychological motivations of individuals. Possessive individualism is the bedrock of neoliberalism.[27] Its model of capitalism lacks a dimension of political power. The role of social classes, as well as ruling economic and political elites, are either excluded from or are marginal to the paradigm.

It is incorrect to claim, as does Hayek, that competition does not lead to oligopoly and monopoly.[28] The free market, free trade and free mobility of

---

[25] Tooze, The forgotten history of the financial crisis, p 2.

[26] Speech quoted in D.M. Herszenhorn, A curious coalition opposed bailout bill, *New York Times*, 2 October 2008, available online.

[27] See C.B. Macpherson, *The Political Theory of Possessive Individualism: Hobbes to Locke*. Oxford: Oxford University Press, 1963; Gamble, *Hayek: The Iron Cage of Liberty*, Chapter 3.

[28] See discussion in Hayek, *The Road to Serfdom*, pp 32–3.

capital have led to the growth of global oligopolies. Neoliberal globalisation has had the effect of making it easier for transnational corporations to acquire subsidiaries irrespective of their geographical location. Side effects have been de-industrialisation and the shift of industrial production to cheaper geographical sites, often leading to economic hardship for the displaced workforce and its dependent population. As we note in Chapter 9 on globalisation, the dominant class becomes global. In the neoliberal approach, all parties are supposed to gain through competition but in practice some gain at the expense of others.

Neoliberalism is predicated on a simplistic economic theory of human behaviour. Many claims are based on assumptions about individual free choice. 'Choice' is limited by an individual's stock of economic, social and political assets. Individual choice is only one and not the most important criterion of human progress and welfare. Security, health, family, a regular income and a worthwhile occupation, social solidarity and fraternity all contribute to human happiness.[29] Such objectives should also find a place in political and social policy. In denying the existence of 'society', neoliberals ignore the fact that human civilisation is a social construct. Without society, human existence would remain at a pre-civilisational level. Human beings consciously create institutions, such as universities, trade unions, codes of law, corporations and governments. Hayek dismisses the capacity of human collaboration to further development; 'socialist aims and programmes are factually impossible to achieve or execute ... [O]rder generated without design can far outstrip plans men consciously contrive'.[30] Planning is held to be not only impossible but harmful. 'Economic liberalism ... regards competition as superior not only because it is in most circumstances the most efficient method known, but even more because it is the only method by which our activities can be adjusted to each other without coercive or arbitrary intervention of authority.'[31] This conclusion can be challenged on theoretical and empirical grounds. The planning mechanisms already used by major capitalist corporations can be utilised in state decision-making.[32] As conscious control of the economy, of which planning is a part, constitutes a cornerstone of collectivist policy, I postpone until Chapter 4 a discussion of the advantages of planning.

---

[29] For further development see: Robert E. Lane, *The Market Experience*. Cambridge: Cambridge University Press, 1991.

[30] Hayek, *The Fatal Conceit*, pp 7–8.

[31] Hayek, *The Road to Serfdom*, p 27.

[32] L. Phillips and M. Rozworski, *People's Republic of Walmart: How the World's Biggest Corporations are Laying the Foundation for Socialism*. London: Verso, 2018.

Conclusion

'Neoliberalism' is an ambiguous and overused term. It should not be conflated with the effects of globalisation, bureaucratisation, faulty financial processes (excessive lending) and the geo-political interests of states. All these forces may influence the nature of policies and become intertwined with neoliberal policies, but they should be distinguished from them. Neoliberalism has psychological, economic, political and social dimensions. The psychological basis at the heart of neoliberalism is that the pursuit of self-interest (enabled by the institutions and processes of neoliberalism) gives people what they deserve as well as what they want. The institutional complex best suited to fulfil this objective is given by competitive capitalist market relations.

In repudiating the role of the state to achieve self-realisation and social protection, neoliberalism has undermined collective agency and replaced it with individualistic competitive activity. It has had more appeal and success at a micro level, as its frame of reference is individuals. It has validated a belief in diversity, in the fulfilment of consumer wants and market choice; it has appealed to those who seek individualist solutions to public problems. The process of marketising the operations of the state also has involved enormous transaction costs and hyper bureaucratic controls. Ironically perhaps, the criticism of excessive bureaucratic control made by the Friedmans[33] is often a consequence of neoliberal practices to promote internal competition and legal procedures to counter corruption within government and international organisations.

As a theory of how economies should be coordinated, neoliberalism has faults. Economic forces have historically been crucial as a driver of development, but economic preferences and interests must be considered in relation to the political and the social. The fulfilment of individual wants does not address inequitable social outcomes that are a consequence of the unequal allocation of wealth, power and income. 'Choice' is always socially conditioned. The ownership of property historically has played a positive role in the development of trade and the rise of capitalism, it has also been a cause of wars. Since the second quarter of the twentieth century, the separation of ownership from control in the modern corporation has led to a strengthening of executives and a weakening of the mass of shareholders (though corporate owners remain significant). Consequently, neoliberal capitalism serves some people's interests better than others. It seeks to fulfil consumer wants rather than addressing social needs which can only be calculated when non-economic values are considered. A catallaxy may lead to equilibrium which in many cases is optimal but in other cases may be

---

[33] Friedman and Friedman, *Free to Choose*. See discussion in Chapter 2 of this book.

sub-optimal and continue to be so for long periods of time. A market driven by possessive individualism does not calculate social and environmental costs.

During economic crises or depressions, countervailing economic forces have not stimulated a new equilibrium and this function has been assumed by the state. Rather than 'countervailing forces', the existing tendencies reinforce each other. Essentially, initial inequalities are amplified in a pattern of circular and cumulative causation.[34] In equilibrium economics, a negative change in the economic system will lead to a countervailing tendency to reverse the induced change. Hence, if a factory closes workers are made redundant, the conventional economist's response is that they will seek other work; if none is available, they will either start their own businesses or accept lower wages and hence attract investment, which will provide new employment. In this way a new equilibrium is attained. This does not always happen: countervailing forces do not equalise conditions. On the contrary, the system moves in the same direction. Social processes are cumulative: rich areas become more prosperous and poor ones become more impoverished. Foreign investment is not automatically attracted to areas of high unemployment. There is no stimulus for investment as the unemployed have low spending power, and the lack of economic demand leads to decline in retail trade. There are important social consequences: the mental and physical health of the unemployed suffers, they incur debts, and their family life disintegrates. If there is free movement of labour, workers move elsewhere hence changing the age and sex structure of the areas of origin, making the remaining labour force less viable.

The process of cumulative causation explains the persistence of 'depressed areas' within countries as well as the decline of many national economies. When liberal economic policies fail, the state intervenes to correct the imbalances created by the market. Neoliberal policies have led to the withdrawal of the state as supplier of comprehensive welfare without replacing it, consequently, social solidarity has weakened. The free movement of labour and capital has led to localised long-term levels of unemployment and underemployment of labour and the underutilisation of capital; migration of labour has caused social dislocations and severely disrupted communities. Catallaxies do not solve these imbalances. Competing and self-serving units often lead to social and political polarisation. The free and unregulated operation of markets may be challenged as not providing effective forms of coordination.

---

[34] Here I follow the reasoning of Gunnar Myrdal, *Economic Theory and Underdeveloped Regions*. London: Duckworth, 1957. The self-sustaining and cumulative process of inflation, which was particularly applicable to the post-socialist economies in the early years of transformation, has a similar effect.

The socialist alternative is of a social-welfare state based on the idea that all persons have social rights: to employment, to an occupation and to receive a comprehensive range of social services – to meet collectively their needs. What is not assured in the neoliberal paradigm is what state-regulated economies can provide – societies with comprehensive development plans, full employment, regular income and public provision of education and health services, free at the point of delivery.

Despite the destabilisation of the world economic system following the 2007 crisis, the thinking of the dominant elites is that modifications of financialisation, establishing effective regulation in the financial sector as well as retrenchment in state spending, can rectify the faults. Even critical economists have accepted much of the neoliberal competitive economic framework within which Keynesianism or post Keynesian policies could operate to manage capitalism.[35] A more effectively managed capitalism seems to be the answer favoured by radical Western economists[36] and major electoral political parties. Other criticism has come from islands of resistance (the anti-capitalism of 'Occupy Wall St' and later the Extinction Rebellion) far removed politically and institutionally from the centres of power.[37] (These are considered in Chapter 12).

As Colin Crouch put it, 'The ... task today is ... *not* to explain why neoliberalism will die following its crisis, but the very opposite: how it comes about that neoliberalism is emerging from the financial collapse more politically powerful than ever' [italics in original].[38] The answer, I think, is that an elite consensus accepts neoliberal suppositions. The mass media, major political parties, economic and social science academia are strongly influenced by the basic concepts of neoliberalism in its applications in the economic, political and social spheres. Adopted by regional organisations (such as the EU) and international institutions (such as the WTO and IMF) neoliberalism has become an unchallenged ideology with a global spread. Andrew Gamble concludes: 'the main dispute in political economy in the modern era has been settled, and settled substantially in favour of neoliberalism ... [W]hile there certainly remain important choices between alternatives within this neoliberal

---

[35] See the editorial by Blankenburg and Palma, Introduction: The global financial crisis.

[36] J.G. Palma, The revenge of the market on the rentiers: Why neoliberal reports of the end of history turned out to be premature. *Cambridge Journal of Economics*, 33 (2009), pp 829–69, quotation p 867.

[37] John Holloway, *Crack Capitalism*. London: Pluto, 2010; Rogers, *Capitalism and Its Alternatives*.

[38] Colin Crouch, *The Strange Non-Death of Neoliberalism*. Cambridge UK and Malden, MA: Polity, 2011, p viii. Crouch has no solution to transcend neoliberalism, though he believes that civil society can modify and obtain better outcomes from a corporation dominated capitalism (see p x).

framework, few any longer make the argument that there are realistic choices between alternative frameworks'.[39] The neoliberal consensus sustains the view that competitive individualism gives people 'what they deserve'. It endorses a limited role for the state, it recommends the introduction of sounder financial procedures, a coherent competition policy, technology transfer, sustainable development, transparency, it proposes social diversity programmes, the promotion of equality of opportunity and a competitive democracy governed by law.[40] These conclusions are found to be somewhat overdetermined and invite a challenge.

In later chapters, we consider other options: alternatives to capitalism or alternative forms of capitalism. Alternatives need to consider the social and the political, and reassert the interests of society. One approach is a reversion to self-sustaining development, an increase in barter and networking, a revival of spontaneous democratic forms of association. The major alternatives share an assumption that the state should further a political and economic agenda in the public interest. To a greater or lesser extent these statist forms advocate the substitution of the spontaneity of market competitive catallaxies by collective forms of direction or planning, combined in different proportions with market forces. Statist alternatives may lead to different types of intervention, which is not, and has not always been, successful. A major objective of this book is to show where state intervention went wrong, and why it has been rejected in favour of neoliberal forms of capitalism. Before we turn to current alternatives, I consider in the next chapters how and why, in the twentieth century, state-managed economies failed. I discuss social democracy and socialism as the major twentieth-century challenges to capitalism: state socialism as it developed and then fell in central and Eastern Europe and social democracy, as it attained and then lost power, in Western Europe.

---

[39] Andrew Gamble, The Western ideology, *Government and Opposition*, 14:1 (2009), pp 1–19, quotation p 5.

[40] J.E. Stiglitz, More instruments and broader goals: Moving toward the post-Washington consensus. Annual lecture to WIDER (Helsinki), 1998. Available at: http://citeseerx.ist. psu.edu/viewdoc/download?doi=10.1.1.471.9764&rep=rep1&type=pdf

PART I

Socialist Contenders and Their Demise

4

Socialist Visions

The French Revolution heralded capitalism with declarations of human rights: Liberty of the individual, Equality before the law, Fraternity between people and Property for the bourgeoisie.[1] All people had the right to freedom of association for common purposes and to own property. Neoliberalism is the current expression of these ideals which apply not only to individual countries but on a global scale. While socialists have accepted the values of the Enlightenment in the sense that life based on reason would free human beings from oppression, they have been critical of liberal-democracy, which they consider to be an expression of bourgeois ways of thinking and doing. Socialism is a social and political system that is predicated on the universal fulfilment of human needs, which can only be met by the attainment of another three objectives: public property, social equality and a classless society. Whereas liberalism in its various forms was grounded on the rights of individuals, socialism promotes collective rights, which in turn liberate individuals. Socialism, as an ideology and, in the former socialist states, as a form of government, provided the major challenge to capitalism in the twentieth century.

We might distinguish between socialism as an ideology (a set of assumptions about how society should be arranged), as a political movement or movements (an instrument of political change), and as an existing society – a political system that has transcended capitalism. In this chapter, I outline the normative basis of socialism. In Chapter 5, I consider how these principles were translated into practice in the Soviet model of socialism, and in Chapter 6 under Western social democracy. In Chapters 7 and 8 I consider how they gave way to neoliberalism.

---

[1] Property, I have added from the Declaration of the Rights of Man and of Citizens, National Assembly of France 1804. Reprinted in William Doyle, *The French Revolution*. Oxford: University Press, 2001, pp 12–15.

Socialism as a normative order

While there are significant differences in the origins, theoretical justifications and political movements subscribing to 'socialism', all are critical of capitalism. Capitalism is unjust because it generates unwarranted inequalities, it is inefficient because it wastes human and material resources and it is evil because it leads to war. Its advocates contend that socialism is morally, economically and politically superior to capitalism.[2] *Socialism* in a generic sense might be defined as 'a system of communal (or social) ownership of the means of production, established for the purpose of making (or keeping) the distribution of income, wealth, opportunity and economic power as nearly equal as possible.'[3] By the beginning of the twentieth century two distinct approaches to socialism may be delineated, based on the theorising of John Stuart Mill,[4] and they have remained the two foremost adversaries of capitalism.

The first is a piecemeal gradualist policy of cumulative reforms, distinguished as a social democratic approach. It is a political movement with decentralised and pluralist forms, seeking to achieve its aims through electoral processes. It is a hybrid pluralist political formation that includes ideas held by people with a Christian outlook, as well as by those influenced by Marxism. Its ideology contains a tension between an economy containing significant elements of private property and market relationships, and a state-led economy with a significant level of public ownership. The second calls for revolutionary change and is referred to as 'socialist' or 'communist'. It is more critical of the institution of private property and electoral democracy (though not of 'real democracy').

Both movements operated through political parties that articulate ideologies, secure activist and mass support, and either challenge the state through revolution and/or use it to further particular reformist objectives. In practice, social democratic and socialist (or communist) parties vary in their ideological cohesion; they have ambiguous, often contradictory, policies promoted by different factions advocating different kinds of reform or different strategies of revolution.

The two approaches also share an appeal to democracy as a legitimating process but are divided about what democracy means. Despite these differences, socialism as an ideology and as a political movement is closely linked to three major objectives: public ownership of the means of

---

[2] David Schweickart summarises the superiority in terms of its economic efficiency, its propensity for economic growth, its promotion of liberty, equality, democracy and autonomy. David Schweickart, *Against Capitalism*. Boulder: Westview Press, 1996.

[3] Carl A. Landauer, *European Socialism*. Berkeley: University of California Press, 1959, vol 1, p 5.

[4] John Stuart Mill, *On Socialism*. New York: Amherst, 1976, pp 115–6.

production, distribution and exchange; social equality of all citizens; and the promotion of the interests of all people who work. Socialists differ on the importance of these different components as well as the ways to achieve them resulting in divisions in the socialist movement.[5] Here I define the major normative approaches which give rise to 'socialist alternatives'.

Socialism defined

John Stuart Mill in 1869 defined socialism as:

> The joint ownership by all members of the community of the instruments and means of production; which carries with it the consequence that the division of the produce among the body of owners must be a public act, performed according to rules laid down by the community. Socialism by no means excludes private ownership of articles of consumption; the exclusive right to each of his or her share of the produce when received, either to enjoy, to give or to exchange it … The distinctive feature of socialism is … that the instruments of production are held as common property.[6]

At the heart of the socialist idea is public ownership for the public good.

These views are shared by traditional social democrats as well as Marxists. The objectives of the British social democratic Fabians were 'the emancipation of land and industrial capital from individual and class ownership and the vesting of them in the community for the general benefit'. They called for the 'transfer' of assets from owners without compensation, though 'expropriated individuals' would be given 'relief'.[7] Public ownership is the economic means to achieve equality which enriches the citizens' range of positive freedoms.

The concept of equality conjoined with that of socialism has a long history and is particularly prominent in reformist social democratic thought. William Morris thought that socialism was 'a condition of equality'.[8]

---

[5] For an historical overview see: Alexander Gray, *The Socialist Tradition: Moses to Lenin*. London: Longmans, 1946; Landauer, *European Socialism*; Donald Sassoon, *One Hundred Years of Socialism*. London and New York: Tauris, 2014; S. Padgett and W.E. Paterson, *A History of Social Democracy in Post-war Europe*. London and New York: Longman, 1991.

[6] Mill, *On Socialism*, pp 117–18. The essay was published after Mill's death in 1879.

[7] Socialists they considered would work to achieve this goal though various political organisations such as the British Fabian Society, in M. Beer (ed), *A History of British Socialism* (Vol 2). London: Routledge, 1920.

[8] William Morris, *Letters on Socialism*, London (privately printed), 1894, p 5. Cited by Steven Lukes, Equality, in L. Kolakowski and S. Hampshire, *The Socialist Idea*. New York: Basic Books, 1975, p 79.

By the late twentieth century, social democracy became almost synonymous with the pursuit of equality, and this difference marks the division between socialists and social democrats. As Roy Jenkins has put it, 'The desire for greater equality has been part of the inspiration of all socialist thinkers and of all socialist movements'.[9] It is contrasted with the competitiveness of capitalism, which is legitimated not by equality but by the organising principle of freedom which, when linked to competition, promotes inequality.

But equality has ambiguous connotations.[10] One may distinguish between relational equality, which has to do with reciprocity in human relationships, and distributive equality, which entails parity in the availability of resources of wealth, income, education and status. The ethical basis of socialism is that distribution should be on the principle of human need and that relational power should be based on equal rights. The claims of equality as a social ideal, however, are not solely the prerogative of socialists. Conservative political leaders and international organisations such as the World Bank and International Monetary Fund deplore excessive inequality. Equality was advocated by the rising bourgeoisie against the inherited privileges of the aristocracy who had illegitimately taken the property which belonged to all people in the state of nature. These views were cloaked in nineteenth-century philosophical discourse and lacked a sociological dimension. It is Durkheim and Marx who have analysed in sociological terms the relationship between inequality and socialism.

Marx and Lenin regarded inequality as being a consequence of class relationships. Unlike traditional social democrats, they did not regard social equality per se to be a major objective. And this is a major difference between social democracy and the communist movement. 'Vulgar socialism [social democracy] ... has taken over from the bourgeois economists the consideration and treatment of distribution as independent of the mode of production and hence the presentation of socialism as turning principally on distribution.'[11] Lenin pointed out that:

---

[9]   Roy Jenkins, Equality, in *New Fabian Essays*. London: Turnstile Press, 1952, p 69.

[10] '[Equality] may either purport to state a fact, or convey the expression of an ethical judgement ... It may affirm that men are, on the whole, very similar in their natural endowments of character and intelligence ... (or) it may assert that while they differ profoundly as individuals in capacity and character, they are equally entitled as human beings to consideration and respect, and that the well-being of a society is likely to be increased, if it so plans its organisation that, whether their powers are great or small, all its members may be equally enabled to make the best of such powers as they possess.' R.H. Tawney, *Equality*. New York: Harcourt, Brace, 1929, p 34.

[11] K. Marx, *Critique of the Gotha Program I, Selected Works* (Vol 2). London: Lawrence and Wishart, 1951, pp 23–4.

General talk about freedom, equality and democracy is in fact but a blind repetition of concepts shaped by the relations of commodity production ... Engels in his Anti-Duhring explained that the concept of 'equality' is moulded (by) the relations of commodity production; equality becomes a prejudice if it is not understood to mean the abolition of classes.[12]

Emile Durkheim not only provided a sociological explanation for inequality but also linked it to a notion of socialism. For Durkheim, the division of labour was a fundamental feature of industrial society. The development of the process of the division of labour, he believed, led to the 'progressive decline' of hereditary caste-like inequalities and to the rise of the principle of merit. Inheritance of property gave rise to incompetent ownership classes.[13] For Durkheim, socialism involved the conscious control of the arrangements of society. Socialism, 'is above all an aspiration for a rearrangement of the social structure, by relocating the industrial set-up in the totality of the social organism, drawing it out of the shadows where it was functioning automatically, summoning it to the light and the control of the conscience'.[14] Socialism is the object of science[15] and sociology as a science of society was a means to achieve socialism. It is perhaps this notion of society that Margaret Thatcher opposed so forcibly. In Durkheim's way of thinking, sociology threatens capitalist market relations.

Marxism and socialism

The Marxist approach is important, not only for its normative value, but also because the successful twentieth-century socialist revolutions were legitimated by their supporters as expressions of Marxist theory. Karl Marx and Friedrich Engels endorsed a modern society (scientifically based, secular, economically developed, wealthy and politically democratic). But they identified a fault, a contradiction, in modern capitalism: it promoted human liberation while practising economic exploitation.[16] The labour theory of value is a cornerstone in Marx's approach: it reveals the illegitimate extraction of surplus value (through a process of exploitation) promoting a class contradiction under capitalism. The socialist future

---

[12] V.I. Lenin, *Economics and Politics, Collected Works* (Vol 30), pp 116–7. See also A. Zdravomyslov, Socialism, welfare and equality, *Social Sciences*, 2 (1982), p 58.
[13] E. Durkheim, *Professional Ethics and Civic Morals*. Glencoe: Free Press, 1958, p 213.
[14] E. Durkheim, *Socialism*. New York: Collier Books, 1958, p 39.
[15] E. Durkheim, *Socialism*, p 42.
[16] Goran Therborn, *From Marxism to Post-Marxism*. London: Verso, 2008, p 68.

visualised by Marx's followers would transcend capitalism by destroying the exploitative elements (the domination of capital and market relations), which had been historically necessary for progress but which had become a fetter on development.

The normative operating principles under socialism were as follows: psychologically, human beings would be able to fulfil their potential; economically, the economy would operate for public good not private gain; and politically, it would promote a real participatory (rather than electoral) form of democracy. Socialism proposes to bring about the emancipatory elements of modernisation, concurrently promoting the development of the productive forces, without the bourgeoisie and private property. It promises the birth of a civilisation without economic exploitation predicated on principles of mutuality and human cooperation. The approach here might be contrasted with neoliberalism which is predicated on fulfilling individual interests through competition (see Chapter 2, this volume).

Followers of Marx adopted a world view that had three interrelated components: the method of historical materialism, a socio-economic analysis of capitalism and a politics of class revolution to move to socialism. The first two components identify law-like tendencies: capitalism is revealed as having inherent structural contradictions that inevitably lead to revolution and a new synthesis, socialism. The unfolding of these contradictions provides the basis for an interpretation of Marxism as scientific socialism.[17] However, in the third component mentioned previously, the process of revolutionary change, there is a recognition of the need for human action, for a political praxis. In the politics of revolution, twentieth-century followers of Marx, in countries with governing Communist Parties (notably, the USSR and China), controversially, added a fourth component to Marxism: the legitimation of Communist Parties as ruling parties and their programme to build communism.

For Marxists, relational and distributive inequality may be attributed to two fundamental causes: property relationships that, through the extraction of surplus labour, give rise to antagonistic classes, and the division of labour, creating stratification in authority, income, culture and life chances. Like Durkheim, Marxists argued that the division of labour, and its attendant inequalities, are an inevitable consequence of the capitalist mode of production. But, unlike Durkheim, they do not see it as a necessary feature of a socialist organisation of industrial society. In their earlier writings, Marx

---

[17] The linkage is best known from Friedrich Engels speech of 1883 where he explicitly compares Marx's discovery of the law of human history to Darwin's law of the development of nature. Speech at the Graveside of Karl Marx, *Selected Works*, Moscow: Foreign Languages Publishing House, 1951, p 153.

and Engels envisaged the abolition of the division of labour. In *The German Ideology*, it was contended that in communist society nobody would have

> one exclusive sphere of activity but each can become accomplished in any branch [a person] wishes, society regulates the general production and thus makes it possible for [people] to do one thing today and another tomorrow, to hunt in the morning, fish in the afternoon, rear cattle in the evening, and criticise after dinner, just as [they] have a mind, without ever becoming hunter, fisherman, shepherd or critic.[18]

These activities, of course, must be interpreted in a symbolic sense, not literally. There is an alternative here in the form that life would take under socialism.

This is a vision of a way of life based on a notion of freedom quite different from that of liberalism. The abolition of economic exploitation creates a different context in which the division of labour takes place. Marxist writers anchor their notion of freedom in the mode of production.[19] Communism is only possible in a highly developed economy, a post-scarcity economy, to which we return in Chapter 9. These views have provided the intellectual background for contemporary discussions of inequality and social structure. Social democrats and liberals seek to reduce the initial advantage enjoyed by certain social groups so that achieved inequalities may be rewarded justly. Hence increasing equality of opportunity, favoured by both social democrats[20] and liberals, does not reduce the inequality of wealth, income or power. Policies promoting 'diversity' also fall into this trap. We will return to these ideas in Chapter 7. During the twentieth century, social democrats shifted the object of socialism from changes in property relations to the attainment of equality of opportunity – a proposal quite compatible with an alternative form of capitalism.

The state socialist alternative

The state socialist alternative to liberalism entails the formation of a society distinguished by system rationality, a planned economy and a hegemonic state.[21] Substantive rationality supplants the instrumental rationality of the

---

[18] K. Marx and F. Engels, *The German Ideology*. London: Lawrence & Wishart, 1965, p 45.

[19] See discussion in A. Rattansi, *Marx and the Division of Labour*. London: Macmillan, 1982, especially Part V, and T. Bottomore, Socialism and the division on labour, in B. Parekh, *The Concept of Socialism*. London: Routledge, 1975.

[20] C.A.R. Crosland, *The Future of Socialism*. London: Cape, 1956, pp 150–1.

[21] For further discussion see: Ivan Szelenyi et al, The socialist economic system, in N.J. Smelser and Richard Swedberg (Eds), *The Handbook of Economic Sociology*. Princeton University Press, 1994, pp 234–254.

market with a plan for the whole society; public property takes the place of private property; cooperation and planning replace competition; politics, in the form of the state led by the Communist Party, provides a single centre of control and replaces the multiple reciprocity of exchange relationships. This 'totality' of the planning system has led to criticisms from the Left and the Right, with both sides objecting (though for different reasons) to the powers taken by the state over the individual.[22]

In the theory of a socialist system, rationality is a major value and is achieved through conscious political guidance and control administered collectively in the interests of all the people. Such socialists believe, quite contrary to neoliberals, that it is possible to decide collectively and rationally the kind of society in which people wish to live and bring it about through a plan. In Marxist terms, socialist planning promotes the satisfaction of use values (consumption satisfying needs) whereas the market prioritises exchange values (sales by merchants). In the first volume of *Capital*, Marx described the difference between the worst architect and the best of bees in that the architect raises his structure in his imagination before he erects it in reality.[23] When the socialist movement developed in the late nineteenth and early twentieth century, socialists contended that people's needs could be fulfilled most effectively through a national plan. Such a plan, devised and coordinated by the political leadership and executed by the state, would promote the Benthamite proposition of achieving the greatest happiness for the greatest number of citizens.

The planned economy: the theory

The intellectual justification for planning, which later shaped the outlook of Soviet policy makers, was provided by Friedrich Engels. Engels envisaged 'an entirely new organization of society in which production is no longer directed by mutually competing individual industrialists but rather by the whole society operating according to a definite plan and taking account of the needs of all ... and with the participation of all members of society'.[24]

Engels is not just concerned with the economic inefficiencies of the market, but with the impossibility of a capitalist competitive market system to satisfy human needs. He also links planning to universal public participation

---

[22] See Christoph Sorg, Failing to plan is planning to fail: Toward an expanded notion of democratically planned postcapitalism. *Critical Sociology*, 17 March 2022. Available at: https://doi-org.ezp.lib.cam.ac.uk/10.1177%2F08969205221081058

[23] K. Marx, *Economic Manuscripts: Capital, Vol I*, Chapter 7. Available at: https://www.marxists.org/archive/marx/works/1867-c1/ch07.htm

[24] F. Engels, The principles of communism, in *Collected Works of Marx and Engels, Vol 25*. Available at: http://www.marxists.org/archive/marx/works/1847/11/prin-com.htm

(though he leaves open the form it would take). In *Anti-Duhring*, he reiterated that under a socialist system, 'Anarchy in social production is replaced by plan-conforming, conscious organisation.' Thus 'the whole sphere of the conditions of life ... which have hitherto ruled mankind, now comes under the domination and control of mankind [which], for the first time, becomes ... the master of his own social organisation'.[25] The principles of hierarchical economic coordination could not be clearer; it should also be added that he anticipated some form of collective participation 'by all members of society'.

With the abolition of private property and its transfer to the state, the duality of power (between government and economy) would be eliminated and the state would become the dominant institution. 'National property stands above private property, and the state is the true owner. This latter principle is the one generally accepted ... and public property [is administered] for the public good.'[26] Concepts of hierarchical coordination have strongly influenced economists who have socialist inclinations. Thus, Maurice Dobb contended that a socialist economy must 'necessarily be a planned economy, in the sense that major economic decisions (such as ... entrepreneurial decisions in a capitalist economy) are taken by some central governmental body, and embodied in a general complex of decisions, or conspectus, coordinated *ex-ante* for a defined planning period'.[27]

Socialist planning – the antithesis of a competitive neoliberal capitalist market economy – puts into effect the political, economic and social components of the socialist vision.[28] Planning of a modern economy is a mammoth task. The objectives must reconcile and prioritise the relative merits of investment and consumption, economic growth, the satisfaction of individual needs in terms of material, spiritual and welfare (health, education) needs, defence and security, levels of income distribution and income differentials, the balance of current and future needs and environmental security. The neoliberal objection is first, that such a plan gives far too much power to the planners to determine 'what people should have' and second,

---

[25] F. Engels, *Anti-Duhring*. Moscow: Foreign Languages Publishing House, 1954, p 392.

[26] F. Engels, Speech at Elberfeld, on February 8 and 15, 1845. *Marx–Engels Collected Works, Vol 4*. Available at: http://www.marxists.org/archive/marx/works/1847/11/prin-com.htm

[27] Maurice Dobb, *Welfare Economics and the Economics of Socialism*. Cambridge: Cambridge University Press, 1969, p 126.

[28] A late twentieth-century listing of socialist planning's objectives is offered by W.P. Cockshott and A. Cottrell: the improvement of the cultural and living standards of the people, the provision of social provision and consumer goods, the reduction of working time and improvement of the work environment; a long-term development path recognising environmental constraints; an economic structure which promotes economic equality between all categories of employees both within national economies and between them on a world scale. See W. Paul Cockshott and Allin Cottrell, *Towards a New Socialism*. Nottingham: Spokesman Books, 1993, p 62.

that it is practically impossible accurately to make the calculations required by the plan. The market mechanism will always trump the planning process.

Justification of a planned economy

The traditional socialist theoretical justification is that only state management of publicly owned enterprises can promote economic rationality. Planners contend that a plurality of independent competing economic units coordinated by a market, even if they were publicly owned, would not result in rational outputs at a societal level, as the sum of the individual interests would not be the same as the interest of the whole. The neoliberal alternative of market catallaxy (discussed in Chapter 2), socialist writers contend, cannot satisfy people's needs in an optimum way. Directive planning takes a hierarchical form with targets detailed in a central plan. Here the amounts and prices of goods and services are calculated to match up the production and supply of components for products and services. Led by Hayek, neoliberals contend that economic calculations are too numerous and complex to be done effectively by planners and that the experience of the Soviet Union proved it. Planners, they declare, decide what they want, not what the public needs. We return to this issue in Chapter 16.

As listed by socialist economists, one can identify five major social and economic advantages of a planned economy over market coordination. The following are postulated qualities, not necessarily what happens under existing planning arrangements – which I discuss in Chapter 5. The first argument in favour of directive planning is that it directs the amount, timing and composition of investment and employment. The irrationality of the market, giving a cyclical character to economic developments (booms and persistent slumps), is abolished. It eliminates the waste of time and resources created by competition[29] – the duplication of resources, advertising and transaction costs.

Second, state planning promotes long-term security and eliminates uncertainty, unlike under market conditions in which uncertainty leads to investment for short-term gain – to ensure profits before market conditions change. Better to take profits when you can, than risk the uncertainty of the long term. Even under market capitalism, the state plays a major role in long-term investment projects where private business is averse to the risk and uncertainty involving possible financial loss.

---

[29] As Engels put it in *Anti-Duhring*, 'The socialised appropriation of the means of production does away with ... the positive waste and devastation of productive forces and products that are at the present time the inevitable concomitants of production.' Engels, *Anti-Duhring*, p 391.

Third, planning considers and coordinates a wide range of social, individual and political values and interests. Social costs can be considered by the plan. For example, the endemic unemployment of capitalism gives rise to gross regional disproportions, to the underutilisation of resources, to environmental damage which is excluded in market calculations (unless there is state interference with market calculations).

Fourth, planning can ensure economic equality by stipulating wage rates and social transfers; profits accrue to the state (community) not to individuals or private companies. Economic rents in the form of excessive salaries or bonuses are precluded. (This includes celebrities, such as film or sports stars as well as company directors). Poverty can be avoided through an employment policy providing all citizens with paid labour or a social wage. New inventions (such as life-enhancing drugs) can be immediately available and are not subject to copyright.

Finally, planning is politically more just and democratic than the market. Whereas market societies promote the autonomy of economic entities in civil society, a planned economy is inclusive and the units of the economy are in principle subject to democratic control. What has been achieved in the political sphere through electoral procedures can be extended to democratic control of the economy.

Under an ex-post market system, on the other hand, the totality of outcomes at a national level is unintended and consequent on a multitude of decisions made by the autonomous units of civil society (included here are business firms). Whereas ex-ante planning brings about a national pattern of investment, consumption, income distribution and employment. The objective of socialist planning is to maximise the welfare of the population. Policy should be made not only on the basis of unity and consistency, but also with 'maximum vision' of the welfare criteria that form the basis of the economic plan.[30] Backward regions, which would fail under a market system, could be supported on social grounds. Ecological costs can be included in the plans. The criteria to be used in evaluating the planning system are not levels of economic growth or productivity, but a judgment of how the effects of planning contribute to the overall economic, political and social goals of the people's well-being. Thus, employing and paying people with disabilities might not be economically rational in a market economic sense, but it would be justified in promoting social solidarity and human well-being. The socialist claim is that under capitalism rationality is limited: the market promotes only a formal or instrumental rationality – a rationality of means rather than, as under a planned system, a substantive rationality of ends.

---

[30] See Dobb, *Welfare Economics and the Economics of Socialism*, p 133.

A word of caution is necessary here. The previous claims are the principles underlying planning; in practice, actual procedures may be imperfect and other conditions (including human failings) may undermine these assumptions. I turn to the criticisms and failures of planning in Chapter 5.

Modern capitalism also depends on types of employment and production which in the view of socialists are superfluous and even injurious – advertising, over-consumption and speculation in the financial sector. The consumer society is a product of the artificial creation of wants through the mass media. In a market society, this is economically rational as it is necessary to maintain demand for products. The socialist response is that under planning the harmful effects of over-development can be avoided. So too, the social costs of pollution and environmental damage are considered in the estimation of costs and built into the plan in a way that is impossible in a competitive profit maximising economy.

Even in conventional economics, some recognise that hierarchical control (rather than market coordination) has advantages. Oliver Williamson, for example, considers that it may enhance rationality as decisions may be made sequentially and adapted as events unfold. Though he considers corporations, the arguments can equally be applied to governments. Hierarchy may better control opportunistic behaviour by reducing potential gains and it has the advantage of strong social control over behaviour.[31] In practice, capitalism has adopted various forms of regulation, usually by the state or state sponsored bodies, to promote public well-being. These measures are partial, as indicated previously, generally ex-post, and often at variance with neoliberal principles. Large commercial corporations[32] as well as governments successfully employ planning strategies.

A system of directive planning, to be successful, entails the introduction of corresponding economic and social institutions. Economic coordination is not achieved through competitive transactions and a self-regulating price mechanism. Success is not measured in terms of income, wealth and profit; there is no institutionalised competition or individual calculation of self-interest by players. There is one ultimate centre of control which coordinates action (though disaggregation can take place on a functional and spatial basis); state, economy and society are not separate autonomous interacting entities. This fusion and the powers that accrue to the state form the basis of the liberal critique of 'totalitarian' planning. From a socialist point of view, central planning is based on people working together, for each other, on principles of mutual trust. In practice, these principles are often undermined by other values and norms (the instrumental rationality of bureaucracies), which we consider in Chapter 5.

---

[31]   Oliver E. Williamson, *Markets and Hierarchies*. New York: Free Press, 1975, p 26.
[32]   Phillips and Rozworski, *People's Republic of Walmart*.

Figure 4.1: Scheme of socialist planning and control

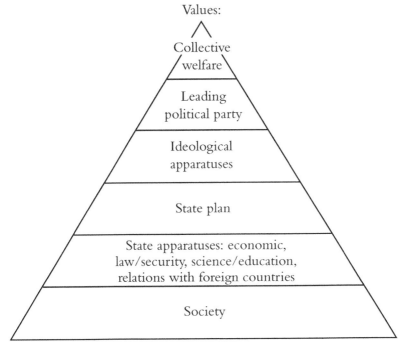

Embedding planning in society

As we noted in the discussion of neoliberalism, an economic market must be embedded in appropriate institutions. To complement the operating principles of state economic coordination, a system of socialist planning has corresponding social, economic and political sectors. These principles are quite different from those of liberal-democratic societies. I illustrate the structure of the system in Figure 4.1. At the top of the scheme is the objective of collective welfare – unlike in the liberal model, where individual satisfaction is the objective. The ideological institutions formulate the plan – under the control of the hegemonic political Party. The state plan is binding on the economy and on the state apparatuses. All these institutions then engage with members of society, as shown at the bottom of Figure 4.1.

Study of Figure 4.1 illustrates not only the hierarchical nature of a proposed planning system but also significant differences from market capitalism. In the theory of state socialism, collectivist (socialist) values are articulated by the Communist Party, aggregated by the state plan and executed through the state bureaucracy. Of note is the fact that values of possessive individualism are replaced by those of the collective. Society has priority over the individual. However, not everything is planned. Areas of individual choice remain – notably in the selection of occupations and in the purchase of consumer goods. Socialist economies may contain, and even sponsor, areas of autonomous activity within the planning system (creative arts and research can be autonomous) though these have been relatively minor. Individual initiative and entrepreneurship, however, must be expressed within the parameters secured by the plan. This way of thinking influenced the form of coordination that was instituted in the USSR and later the other socialist states. The political market (democratic competitive elections) and competitive economy (market price reconciling demand and supply) were replaced by a state organised planned economy under a hegemonic Communist Party.

In the state socialist paradigm, a fundamental change occurs in the organisation of the economy. Whereas under capitalism, the state exercises ex-post economic coordination, under central planning, the state acts ex-ante. Not only does it have the enforcement rights of the capitalist state but it determines the nature and levels of investment and employment as well as the distribution of goods and services to members of society. The rationality of firms under capitalism – to maximise profits, is replaced by a rationality of plan fulfilment. It is claimed that factors of production can be utilised more effectively to produce the kinds of products and services that are most socially useful, rather than, as under capitalism, fulfilling 'wants' for things that are desirable. Supporters of the planning system contend that a culturally induced social consensus is generated in which motivation to work and to cooperate is a distinctive part of a socialist system. Critics, however, point to the coercion, administrative wastefulness and corruption which occurs in practice (rather than the theory) of state planning which I return to in Chapter 5.

The previously discussed outline of the socialist planning system is normative and presents only one component of the actual changes that took place in the Soviet Union. Unlike in capitalist societies, where governments have regulated markets for hundreds of years, the ambitious Bolshevik planners had no experience to guide them in setting up a planned socialist economy. Their policies have to be interpreted in the context of a statist form of economy inherited from economic development under the Tsars, of a peasant-based society emerging from feudalism, of foreign invasion and bitter civil war. These factors influenced the policies adopted by the political leadership. The Soviet form of planning, which we consider in Chapter 5, took shape under the most inauspicious circumstances and perpetuated autocratic state power.

Conclusion

As they developed in the twentieth century, despite many differences, social democracy and socialism as ideologies and as political movements were closely linked to three major objectives: public ownership of the means of production, distribution and exchange; social equality, and the promotion of the interests of the working class. When in power they have presented robust challenges to liberal capitalism. While in the late nineteenth century there was only one socialism in the form of a generic social democracy in opposition to capitalism, later the political movement split into two major parts. The first, the social democratic, based on political pluralism, presented a piecemeal gradualist policy of cumulative reforms; the second, the socialist or communist, based on one-party leadership, called for revolutionary change. Social democracy has become a welfarist alternative form of capitalism; state socialism evolved as a statist alternative to market capitalism. Both movements use the state to further particular aims. A collectivist or communal, rather than an individualistic, framework of action has also been a socialist principle shared to varying degrees by supporters of the social democratic movement. 'Society' rather than the 'individual' is foremost. And this assumption leads many to regard the socialist-controlled state as the promoter of the general interest − rather than it being a consequence of the sum of individuals pursuing their own interests, with some having more power than others.

Movements for socialist planning at the state level have been eclipsed by globalised capitalism. In the following chapters we consider how this change has come about and whether the fortunes of these movements can be revived. Before we turn to discover how the British social democratic model of capitalism developed, I outline the policies pursued in Soviet Russia and discuss what were considered at the time to be successes of state socialism. Also, of crucial contemporary relevance, I consider how, when confronted with neoliberalism, both social democracy and state socialism were replaced.

5

The State Socialist Challenge and Its Market Socialist Critics

After the Second World War, state socialism provided a model of socialist development for Europe and Asia. The socialist states presented a theory of how society should be organised, and the countries of the Soviet bloc offered an example of how socialism could be put into practice. These developments, economically and politically, posed a strong challenge to liberal capitalism. Socialism, as it developed in the USSR, represented an economic alternative based on the principles of hierarchy and central control. It provided a template for other societies to copy: a social system coordinated by a plan rather than a competitive market, by public property rather than private property. The major contention of its supporters is that it promoted the Marxist objective of human emancipation through the abolition of economic exploitation. In contrast, its detractors, from the social democratic and liberal traditions, have emphasised the subjugation of the individual to a state that they consider to be equally exploitative and oppressive. Others suggest that the alternative to capitalism is to be found in a form of market socialism in which economic relations are set in a market shell, and democratic participation replaces hierarchy as the organising principle.

Building the basis of socialist society

The theoretical considerations outlined in Chapter 4 guided the Soviet leaders. The Soviet system, state socialism, was a process of state-led comprehensive modernisation. It had six major components: rapid industrialisation and urbanisation; land reform (transfer of land to peasants) followed by collectivisation of agriculture (state control of peasant farms); cultural revolution, a drive for mass literacy and numeracy; centralised forms of state ownership and control and political mobilisation; state ownership and control of the productive forces financed from surpluses derived from labour; autonomous economic development coupled to relative isolation from the world economy.

In the early years following the October Revolution and the First World War, the economic and political leadership procured full state control of the economy and nationalised productive assets and land; private production for the market and for profit was forbidden. Central direction and control of the forces of production were established under the hegemony of the Communist Party. Planning determined what should and could be produced. Investment was prioritised for defence, industrial development (with priority to heavy industry) and social provision (education, public health, housing); consumer goods had a low priority. Money lost its role as a means of accumulation; it could not be invested (there was no stock exchange) nor could it be created independently (by the issue of credit) by financial institutions.

Hierarchical state administration replaced markets. State ministries were given control over production assets. The coordination of finance, production, labour, prices and product mix was performed on an administrative basis. One partial exception to the state system was to be found in agriculture where assets (animals, seeds, products but not land) were owned collectively by farmers. They were organised into collective farms that supplied their produce to the state, in return for revenue. Not all agriculture was organised in this way as many 'state farms' were in state ownership and had the same economic status as non-agricultural industries. All farmers were also able to own small plots of land and animals (these were considered possessions, rather than private property), and their products could be traded freely on a collective farm market.

A state planning commission (Gosplan) was set up and established economic plans over five-year periods. The government had a monopoly of foreign trade, it controlled the money supply and coordinated production and investment. It allocated plans to each economic ministry detailing production targets, a wage fund for distribution to employees, and the prices of commodities and labour rates were fixed by state committees. Economic enterprises were subject to vertical commands from ministries which in turn were controlled by state planners in Gosplan (as well as other state bodies). Of considerable importance is that the system was a federation of republics (Ukraine, Armenia, the Russian Federation and so on, a total of 15 at the end of the Soviet Union): some Republican ministries operated at the level of the constituent republics of the USSR, which had their own plans coordinated by Gosplan USSR.

In a Marxist perspective, as adopted by Soviet leaders, the 'superstructure' of society had to conform to the basis. Consequently, a cultural revolution was instigated by the government. This involved the formation of a state-financed free and comprehensive system of education (private schools had been abolished), which accompanied mass literacy campaigns. Attempts were made to create a different system of socialist values: honours and symbols were instituted to reflect the virtues of the socialist revolution (for example, the medal of Hero of the Soviet Union, streets and buildings were renamed after socialist heroes). Income differentials remained but were significantly equalised, with non-manual professional and executive salaries moving towards those of manual workers.[1] A remarkable long-term equalisation of income was achieved.[2] As shown in Figure 5.1, the top 1 per cent of the population possessed 18 per cent of the national income in 1905; from 1927 onwards, it fell to between 4 and 6 per cent. During the period between 1916 and 1935, the comparable share in the USA was around 22 per cent. The rising levels of equality can largely be explained by the abolition of income from the ownership of property, the low level of unemployment, state levelling of differentials (the plans determined income levels) and a large increase in the employed work force, including a massive increase in the number of women employees.

After the Second World War, these developments also occurred in all the European state socialist societies where pre-war differentials between salaries and wages, male and female, skilled and unskilled, industrial and agricultural earnings all fell considerably.[3] J.-C. Asselain illustrates the enormous change by revealing that between 1931–32 and 1969, meat consumption fell from 47.5 kg (per capita per annum) to 44.9 kg for managerial and white-collar households, and rose from 33.8 kg to 49.5 kg for working-class households.[4] These figures illustrate the decline in social conditions for the middle classes to the advantage of the manual working class.

Differentials of income and power, however, were considered necessary for the effective and efficient building of socialist society. Policy makers sought to arrange differentials to reward merit and effort; wage scales were constructed that rewarded skill, the arduousness and complexity of labour.[5] In practice, compared to capitalist market societies, wage differentials were

---

[1] For details see D. Lane, *The Rise and Fall of State Socialism*. Cambridge: Polity, 1996, pp 40–7.

[2] This is the case even when payments in kind are taken into account. A major difference as far as distributive income was concerned was limited scope of the leisure and consumption industries for people to spend their money on. State control over production made it very difficult to practice conspicuous consumption.

[3] Data cited in Jean-Charles Asselain, The distribution of incomes in East-Central Europe, in Pierre Kende and Zdenek Strmiska (Eds), *Equality and Inequality in Eastern Europe*. Leamington Spa and New York: Berg, 1987, pp 21–62. Citations pp 26, 27. See particularly note 2 (p 26) for comparisons between 1937–39 and 1948 in Czechoslovakia. See also David Lane, *The End of Social Inequality?*. London: George Allen & Unwin, 1982, pp 58–9.

[4] Asselain, The distribution of incomes in East-Central Europe, p 30, fn 12.

[5] See Zdravomyslov, Socialism, welfare and equality.

Figure 5.1: Russia: share of top 1 per cent of families of national income (pre-tax), 1905–1985

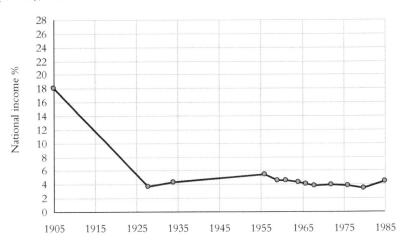

Source: F. Novokmet, T. Piketty, G. Zucman, *From Soviets to Oligarchs: Inequality and Property in Russia 1905–2016*. NBER, Working Papers Series. No 23712. 2017.

relatively small and manual labour was better off compared to non-manual employees. Though the family and the educational system still reproduced social inequality, the immense industrialisation which took place led to very high levels of social mobility. Western European social democratic achievements in welfare state provision (which we consider in the next chapter) were on a considerably lower scale and in many respects less significant than the attainments in the socialist countries, where there was no private education or medical practices.

The rise of state socialism

Whatever weaknesses were latent in the Soviet form of economic and social organisation, they were not widely recognised in the years following the end of the Second World War. The inter-war turmoil of collectivisation (including famine and deportations) was overshadowed by the successes of industrial developments. Furthermore, the Allied victory over the Axis powers, in which the USSR, at great cost, played a major role, enhanced its credibility as an economic and political model. The Soviet Union had demonstrated that a state-owned and centrally organised economy was viable and effective. The Soviet leadership had successfully industrialised and modernised what was one of the most economically backward societies in Europe. The urban population increased from 28.1 million in 1929 to 63.1 million in 1940. Alexander Gerschenkron has shown that output of Soviet large-scale industry increased at an annual rate of between 15 and 17 per cent between 1928 and 1938. Soviet industrial output as a ratio of American rose from 6.9 per cent in 1913, to 27.3 per cent in 1932 and 45.1 per cent in 1938.[6] By the 1950s, educational standards had risen exponentially: universal literacy had been achieved and most of the population had a full secondary education; the Soviet 'intelligentsia' had increased with important political implications (discussed later).

The USSR became the first comprehensively planned developmental state. By the end of the 1960s, the experience of the USSR was widely acclaimed; planning appeared to have triumphed over the market. Soviet science, high-tech space technology, nuclear weapons, successful military industries (and even sports science) were all held in high esteem, even awe, in the West. The social and political context also appeared to be positive: the socialist societies secured high levels of employment, universal educational and health services that were provided free at the point of delivery, and there were low levels of crime.

But there had been considerable costs, which considerably clouded the Soviet modernisation drive and led to many critics to condemn the Soviet experience. There had been severe repression and coercion, particularly in the countryside.[7] As we noted in Chapter 2, liberal economists such as Hayek had long criticised the faults inherent in the planning process and many of the issues were taken up by critics in the socialist countries. The most general objection was that 'planning' hid from view the political power of those who controlled the state. Critics here point to the collectivisation campaigns and to the oppression of groups opposing the political system. In more general and unmeasurable terms, hierarchical control places officials in a position where they can exercise uncontrollable power, and to the subordination of people to the administrative system. Such hierarchical power may be acceptable in capitalist profit-making organisations, but they are inimical to socialism. The censoring of media, restrictions on individual research and bans on foreign travel were forms of subjugation consequent on central control. These criticisms were outweighed by the other more positive achievements of the Soviet system. Academic discourse, such as E.H. Carr's *The New Society* (London: Macmillan, 1941, a series of lectures first broadcast by the BBC) and Peter Nettle's, *The Soviet Achievement* (London: Thames and Hudson, 1967) commanded wide public respect and sustained beliefs in the Soviet socialist alternative.

---

[6] A. Gerschenkron, The rise of growth in Russia, *Journal of Economic History*, 7 (1947), Supplement, p 166. Other scholars gave similar figures.

[7] To give just one example. Agricultural policy led to 1.8 million kulaks being deported in 1930–31 and 340,000 in 1932–3. Terry Martin, The Affirmative Action Empire: Nations and Nationalism in the Soviet Union, 1923–1939. Ithaca, NY: Cornell University Press, 2001, p 326.

The Soviet system was greatly enlarged after the Second World War. The 'Soviet system' was either imposed on, or consciously copied by, countries that came to form the world communist movement.[8] By 1980, there were 16 communist states that formed the core of the 'world socialist system'. These included China and the states of Eastern Europe. The bloc was also influential in many countries in Africa and Asia, who considered themselves societies of 'socialist orientation'. At that time, the Soviet bloc claimed one third of the world's population and 40 per cent of its industrial production. Though the state socialist societies remained economically relatively poor and lacked the consumer artefacts available in the West, by the 1950s, they had achieved rates of economic growth higher than comparable capitalist states and, when account is taken of the initial level of development, were comparable in levels of public social welfare, such as health and education. However, there was a concealed weakness. The Soviet bloc was led by the industrial power of the Soviet Union but otherwise composed of relatively poor, Third World countries, with large peasant populations (exceptional were the small central European states of the German Democratic Republic and Czechoslovakia). The level of productive forces was very much below that of the Western capitalist countries. China, for example, in 1979, only had a gross annual domestic product (GDP) per capita of $260[9] (the USSR's per capita income was $4110).

Whatever their faults and deficiencies, a modern industrial society had been constructed without an economy based on private property and market relations driven by profit and legitimated by competitive electoral democracy. What all supporters and critics of the state socialist system agreed upon was that there was a fusion of politics and economics. The political determined the economic and social, whereas under capitalism, politics was dependent on, and an outgrowth of, civil society, which included a powerful bourgeoisie. Under state socialism, the Communist Party was the dominant power: it articulated a hegemonic ideology; aggregated political and economic interests; and it had a monopoly of formal political power. The state was unitary in character, though some had a federalist political form. There was no pluralistic division of powers into executive, legislative and judiciary. It was assumed by the leaders of Soviet-type states that in a unitary class society there would be no major contradictions. Notions of the division of powers were regarded as ineffective under capitalism and irrelevant under socialism as the dominant Party represented and exercised the will of

---

[8] For further discussion see: Ivan Szelenyi et al, The socialist economic system, pp 234–54; Lane, *The Rise and Fall of State Socialism*, Part I.

[9] World Bank, *World Development Report*. New York: World Bank, 1981.

the working class. This doctrine effectively strengthened the executive of the party-state formation as a bureaucratic power.

In terms of analysis of the social structure, the class structure departed considerably from capitalism and we deal in more detail with its composition in Chapter 8. Here we may note that the extraction of surplus value did not occur through a market mechanism and accrue to a capitalist class but was utilised by the state for economic and social development. Soviet Marxists were motivated to abolish economic exploitation derived from class relations rather than by social democratic concerns for social equality and justice. (I consider the designation of state-capitalism in Chapter 15). Wlodek Wesolowski, a leading Polish sociologist, writing in the1970s, reflected the views of many socialists at the time when he claimed that the domination of the bourgeois class is assured in the capitalist system

> chiefly through the law of property, and control of the utilisation of the means of production and appropriate of the surplus value created in production by the workers'labour. [T]he socialist revolution eliminates this type of relationship and, through nationalisation, introduces common ownership of the means of production ... [T]his is the basis of the claim that 'economic domination' of a class has been eliminated, since the control over the means of production is broadly societal and the benefits from production go into the societal fund.[10]

By the middle of the 1960s, state socialism appeared to be an effective form of industrial society, which could operate without a capitalist class and an economic free market; it provided a full employment economy, widespread welfare services free at the point of delivery and had, despite hostile relations created by the Cold War, preserved peace.

However, the hopes and confidence that state socialism would provide an effective alternative to capitalism was short-lived. State socialism was not copied in the advanced capitalist countries and did not institute, even in the USSR, a mode of production economically superior to capitalism. As the societies matured, they experienced a period of disenchantment and were finally dismantled in the late 1980s. Doubts about the efficiency of planning, concerns about the absence of democracy and apprehension about human rights were to appear in a new context. How and why the reversal to capitalism occurred is crucial to socialism's credibility as an alternative. The main reasons for this reversal were the backward conditions inherited by the socialist governments, mistakes by the political leadership, the consequences

---

[10] W. Wesolowski, *Classes, Strata and Power*. London: Routledge, 1979, p 120.

of the modernisation process and the hostile world environment. I turn to discuss these features in Chapter 8.

Economic and social consequences of modernisation

By the 1970s, as a consequence of the post-war policies of industrialisation and urbanisation, a transformation had taken place in the social structure. Such developments put considerable strains on the socialist economies and traditional forms of party and state control. State socialism had been introduced into relatively undeveloped agrarian economies, and the modernisation processes led to urbanisation and a shift in employment away from agriculture to industry and then to services.

By the mid-1980s there was a demographic mass of urbanised non-manual workers and a significant number with higher education. The working population shifted from manufacturing to the service sector and employees' educational levels rose. By 1983, in Bulgaria 32 per cent of employees were in the services sector, 36.5 per cent in Hungary, and 40.7 per cent in the USSR.[11] Educational standards rose considerably and led to significant changes in the social structure. In the USSR in 1939, there were only 1.2 million people with a full higher education, by 1959 the figure had risen to 3.8 million, and another massive rise to 20.1 million occurred in 1986.[12] People with higher and specialist secondary education rose in the USSR from 16.841 million in 1968–70 to 28.612 million in 1980. Comparable changes took place in the other East European socialist societies. Figure 5.2 shows the ratios in each country of those people with tertiary education employed in the economy between 1970 and 1987. In 1987, there were 35.7 million people with higher education. Moreover, they were grouped in the younger age cohorts. In 1985 alone, 859,000 young people in the USSR graduated with higher education and joined the work force.[13] This involved the rise of a social stratum known in these countries as the 'socialist intelligentsia' – people with higher educational qualifications. This group, in my opinion, was to constitute the ballast of support for the elite led reforms that would dismantle state socialism.

The growth of a large middle class with higher levels of expectations had significant political implications. As expectations rose, there appeared commensurate aspirations for improvements in living conditions as found

[11] *Statisticheski ezhegodnik stran-chlenov SEV 1984*. Moscow: Finansy i statistika, 1984, pp 363– 7.

[12] *Narodnoe khozyastvo SSSR V 1985g*. Moscow, 1986, p 27.

[13] *Statisticheski ezhegodnik stran-chlenov soveta ekonomicheskoy vzaimopomoshchi 1988*. Moscow, Finansy i statistika, 1988. pp 439–40.

Figure 5.2: Employees with tertiary education: Bulgaria, Poland, USSR, Czechoslovakia, 1970, 1987 (000s) (or latest date)

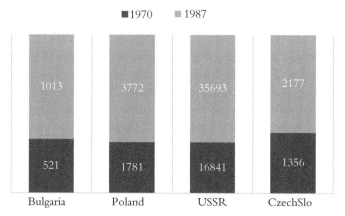

Source: *Statisticheski ezhegodnik stran-chlenov SEV 1988.* Moscow: Finansy I statistika, 1988, p 422.

in the market economies of the West. While living conditions had risen considerably in the early period of socialist development, from the mid-1970s, the countries of Eastern Europe and the USSR all suffered falls in their rates of growth. The decline in the growth of real income can be gauged from the official figures for Bulgaria, Hungary, the USSR and Czechoslovakia as shown in Figure 5.3. Concurrently, the communist leaders were confronted with increasing demands for consumer goods and better-quality services.

These figures in themselves, however, do not condemn the system of state planning. If one takes a more realistic view of economic growth than the overstated claims of communist party leaders, such as Khrushchev who in 1961 had boasted that the Soviet Union in ten years would overtake the GDP of the USA,[14] one would expect that rates of growth would fall as the economy increases in size.

During the 1980s, the world economy was in depression and all the advanced societies had declining growth rates, including successful economies such as West Germany. The USA also experienced similar declines in rates of growth. In the period 1980 to 1987, Western Germany had a growth rate of 1 per cent, the UK 1.3 per cent and France 0.5 per cent. The European socialist countries had not suffered any economic 'collapse' and Western

---

[14] Nikita Khrushchev, The tasks of the Communist Party in building a communist society. Speech to the 22nd Congress of the CPSU. Moscow, 31 October 1961. Reprinted in G. Hodnett (Ed) *Resolutions and Decisions of the CPSU* (Vol iv). Toronto: University of Toronto Press, 1974, quotation, p 211.

Figure 5.3: Increase in real income per capita of population (%): Bulgaria, Hungary, USSR, Czechoslovakia, 1956–57, 1971–75, 1981–85

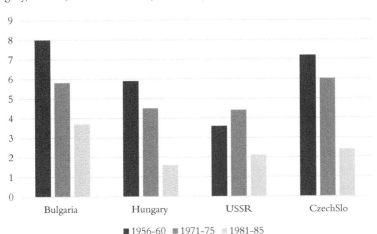

Source: *Statisticheski ezhegodnik stran-chlenov SEV 1988.* Moscow: Finansy i statistika, 1988, p 25.

European countries with similar declines in growth did not seek any form of systemic change. While the European socialist states were no longer closing the gap with the capitalist West, the planned economies were not doing too badly. When compared to the advanced societies of the West, which were increasingly used as a reference point, the decline in growth rates, however, coupled to the rising expectations of the rapidly growing middle-class populations, led to an expectations gap. For comparison, later, China, having embarked on economic reform, had achieved growth rates of 8.69 per annum in the 1980s, which have been maintained. The East European countries were not fulfilling the expectations of the population. In some states, notably Poland and Hungary, there were falls in real income between 1981 and 1986, as illustrated from the official statistics in Figure 5.4.

The centralised political system became a target for political opposition. Here there is a major difference compared to liberal capitalism where the separation of institutions gives rise to the autonomy of the units of a market society with many different foci of economic and political power. Not so under state socialism: its political centre is the state-party bureaucracy. When things go well, it enhances its own legitimacy. When things go badly, however, it increasingly becomes the focus of popular discontent. In other words, a defining feature of an administrative system is that responsibility for the management of the economy is clear. Under capitalism, there is an 'invisible' human hand guiding the market whereas in the latter there is human 'design' visibly formulated by the political and economic leadership. While bringing down governments in capitalist societies does not change

Figure 5.4: Real income of manual and non-manual workers, 1981 to 1986: Bulgaria, Hungary, Poland and Czechoslovakia

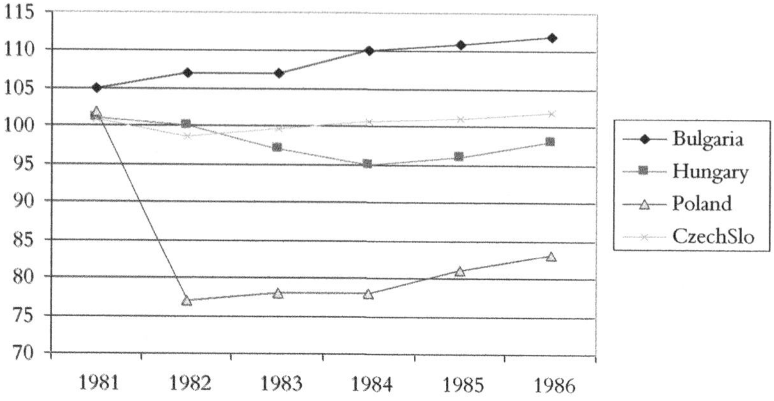

Index: 1980=100

Source: *Statisticheski ezhegodnik stran-chlenov Soveta Ekonomicheskoy Vzaimopomoshchi 1988.* Moscow, 1988, p 81. Other countries not shown in source.

the substance of the social order, under state socialism, a challenge to the communist regime – demands for greater 'pluralism' or the institution of markets – would change the design.

Criticism of the planning system

The planning system also had shortcomings in the delivery of goods and services, and the questionable quality of consumer goods led to calls for reforms, including market reforms. By the early 1970s, the decline in economic growth levels and other indicators led to concern that the planning system was not working or, at least, not working as well as expected. One must disentangle here different causal mechanisms. One should not attribute all the malfunctions of socialist regimes to the system of planning. The footprint of revolution, civil war, Tsarist autocracy and foreign intervention had left their marks on the political system of the Soviet Union. All these factors, in different ways, had deleterious effects on the evolution of Soviet regimes. The centralising of decision making and bureaucratic power inherent in hierarchical control do have harmful consequences. Here the lack of democratic participation presents a problem to which I return later in this chapter.

Other objections focussed on faults in the administered mechanism. Corruption was one such problem.[15] If prices are set too low and lead

---

[15] Corruption as a factor in collapse is detailed by Leslie Holmes, *The End of Communist Power.* Cambridge: Polity, 1993.

to shortages, profit could be made by (illegally) reselling commodities. Administrative allocation in appointments, in the distribution of resources (such as access to quality healthcare and education) and even recreation (holiday hotels, foreign travel) gave immense power to people with administrative responsibility. There was no labour market for professional and executive jobs which were subject to administrative procedures of promotion/demotion. Consequently, corruption became recognised as a negative component of administrative control. In response, various agencies of people's control and Party control were set up to prevent abuse of administrative power and to create administrative transparency. But anecdotal evidence would suggest that these mechanisms were only partially effective.

Other difficulties arose from the absence of a freely functioning price system and competition. In a market, coordination of transactions takes place through the price mechanism. In theory, at least, this should ensure the efficient combination of factors of production. Critics began to express concern about the 'distortions' that they saw arising in the economy.[16] One of the underlying structural features of the planned economy was that the authorities in the state apparatus and the economic enterprise had conflicting interests. The tension arises because the planning institutions control access to resources used by the enterprises. The production enterprise must bargain with the planning bodies for inputs (the amount of capital and labour that can be used in production) rather than to procure them on a market. The economic enterprise then bargains for more resources than it needs. A general criticism was that the plan did not fulfil individual needs – it did not heed consumer demands. Shortages of consumer goods were endemic and the assortment and quality of goods produced in the socialist states compared poorly with those produced abroad, which became a measure of the legitimacy of the system.

Underlying these inefficiencies, was the fact that the state socialist economies had become much bigger and more complex by the end of the 1960s – and consequently, more difficult to plan. Eugene Zaleski has revealed that in the USSR in 1953, there were 9,490 indexes and 20 million industrial products.[17] State planning appeared unable to cope with the more complex advanced industrial economy. The planning system was set up in the context of extensive development: that is, adding cheap factors of production (labour which was abundant) to capital (which was scarce). As the economy developed, labour supply began to dry up as reserves were depleted. Labour

---

[16] Probably the best known is Janos Kornai, *The Economics of Shortage*. Amsterdam: North-Holland, 1980.

[17] E. Zaleski, *Stalinist Planning for Economic Growth, 1933–1952*. London: Macmillan, 1980, p 486.

productivity also was in decline. Reformers clamoured to set up a system in which labour input would have a market value and would distinguish between returns to different outlays of capital. Such a policy would lead to increases in wage differentials – to the benefit of qualified and professional non-manual labour.

It was recognised that the planning system was imperfect as the authorities lacked up-to-date knowledge necessary for efficient coordination. Enterprises also retained significant areas of autonomy. Three areas may be distinguished in which the central control of the economy was circumscribed.[18] First, there were spaces between enterprise management and higher-level administration that led to enterprises having control of the proceeds of sales – for example, from production in excess of the plan. In practice, 'profit-sharing' was 'as old as the first five year plan'[19] (enterprises kept some of the income they generated). Second, enterprises developed their own interests as a form of protection from excessive production targets; they also sheltered themselves by accumulating emergency reserves of stocks and manufacturing their own spare parts. Third, enterprises ignored directives. They inflated costs and overspent the wage funds. According to Asselain, enterprises 'viol[ated] the fundamental principle of the centralised economy: the absolute primacy of centralised directives'.[20] The conclusion to be drawn here is that, without modern computing power, the planners had insufficient information and imperfect tools to analyse what data they had.

These imperfections in the system led enterprises to 'hoard' resources, which gives rise to what Jarnos Kornai defines as a 'shortage economy'. Capital and land had no price, and rent was not charged for the use of land. Land use in cities then led to inefficiencies, scarce house space was under-utilised because there was no incentive for occupants to find smaller and (cheaper) accommodation. As there was no housing market, geographical mobility was restricted. Problems arose when demand outstripped supply; as prices were fixed, there were shortages and queues appeared. Waiting in queues also has economic costs.

The absence of a market led to the inefficient combination of factors of production. For example, gas was sold based on its production cost as there was no need to make a profit. An unintended consequence was that people did not economise on heating, which led to waste of energy. Factories did not economise on the use of resources. Soviet products contained more metal and were much heavier than comparable Western counterparts.

---

[18] See Jean-Charles Asselain, *Planning and Profits in Socialist Economies*. London and Boston: Routledge, 1981.

[19] Asselain, *Planning and Profits in Socialist Economies*, p 32.

[20] See Asselain, *Planning and Profits in Socialist Economies*, pp 32–5, citation p 35.

Labour also was extravagantly used: the labour market did not respond to shortages by raising wages and, as there was no profit motive, there was no need to economise on labour. The state had the responsibility to provide a full employment economy, unlike in market economies where labour costs are reduced to maximise profits. Hence state socialist enterprises had many more workers than comparable capitalist ones, and the rhythm of work was slow as labour had no wage incentive to increase the intensity of labour. Even the introduction of new Western labour-saving technology did not, in many cases, lead to the shedding of labour.

These strictures all had some substance but must be understood within the system of socialist economic planning. The planners' answer to these criticisms was that, as the plan determined industrial location, there was no need for interest or rent. Planners could respond to shortages of commodities as well as 'the market' by organising the production of more goods or services. In practice, shortages of labour led to (often unregistered) mobility of labour from areas of low wages. Deficiencies of services could be met by the informal market which continued within the context of planning. Defenders of state planning considered that the objective of full employment is itself a social good. What was criticised in the West as 'underutilisation' of labour was a form of social security. Provision of jobs to ensure that all citizens have an occupation has positive social advantages. Rather than funding unemployment benefits through taxes, the socialist system accepted higher levels of employment even if this meant using an 'excessive' amount of labour.

Underlying these criticisms, however, is the problem raised by Western market economists. For Friedrich von Hayek, Ludwig von Mises and Max Weber, rational economic calculation is considered impossible in a modern economy in the absence of freely negotiated prices.[21] The infeasibility of calculating the thousands of equations necessary to simulate a market has been the major reason put forward to deny the possibility of a rational price system under a planned socialist system.[22] Without an efficient price system, bottlenecks and shortages occurred as supplies of products and services fell short of demand.

By the mid-1970s, economists and politicians in the state socialist societies conceded that the state planning system needed reform. The economic outputs of the socialist states were compared unfavourably to the economies of rising

---

[21] See discussion in F. von Hayek, *Individualism and Individual Order*. Chicago University Press, 1980, pp 145–6.

[22] L. von Mises, *Economic Calculation in the Socialist Commonwealth*. Auburn: Ludwig von Mises Institute, 1990; F. von Hayek, *Collectivist Economic Planning*. London: Routledge, 1935; O. Lange, On the economic theory of socialism: Part one. *Review of Economic Studies*, 4:1 (Oct 1936), pp 53–71. See discussion pp 55–57.

capitalist states such as South Korea, Taiwan and Singapore. Even the incumbent Communist leaders recognised that significant changes were required. Just what these changes would entail, however, was a contentious issue. Economic reformers, prompted by the successful model of the Asian 'tigers', turned to the market price mechanism to remove queues, to act as indicators for investment, to stimulate innovation, to act as a spur to productivity and to improve the quality of goods and services. We return in Chapter 8 to consider the reforms that were adopted under President Gorbachev in the latter half of the twentieth century. Here I summarise the achievements and failings of state socialism as they appeared in the late 1970s and outline the theoretical alternatives, posed by socialist critics, to the Soviet planning system.

State socialism: an appraisal

The Soviet system provided an effective form of modernisation for a country emerging out of feudalism. The USSR was the first state-led developmental economy. The state effectively utilised economic surplus for economic and social development. Its contours were as much dependent on the outcome of war, both civil and international and the economic and political heritage of the feudal Tsarist Russian Empire, as on the economic models constructed by socialist intellectuals and planners. The socialist states were successful developmental models designed to catch up to the levels of the forces of production of the capitalist core. This 'catch-up' was achieved without market competition and private property, though it had its own costs during the civil war in Soviet Russia and the periods of collectivisation and severe repression under Stalin. The Soviet experience was transferred, with some important modifications, to Eastern Europe and later to China. Planning was carried out under conditions of backwardness and post-war reconstruction, which caused considerable distortions in the ways in which activity was organised.[23] On the positive side, in terms of economic development, international comparative advantage did not determine the location of investment. Rather, policy was to foster the all-round economic development of each country – ensuring energy-power and diversified industrial development, as well as comprehensive social provision of education and welfare. Money and markets led by profits had no influence on the allocative operation of the economic system though they remained important in the process of distribution.[24]

---

[23] Eugene Zaleski describes in some detail the distortions in planning that took place. See his *Stalinist Planning for Economic Growth*.

[24] *Kurs politicheskoy ekonomii, Vol II (Sotsializm)*. Moscow: Izdatel'stvo ekonomika, 1974, quotation pp 125–6.

State socialism accomplished an effective, but imperfect, alternative to liberal market capitalism. But the history of twentieth-century revolutions, carried out in the name of Marx, shows that abolishing private property and market relations does not abolish all forms of political and economic inequality and oppression. Critics of state socialism have argued that the societies were not 'truly socialist' but state-capitalist.[25] From this point of view, they provide not an alternative to capitalism but an alternative type of capitalism based on economic exploitation. Even after the Second World War, the relative economic backwardness compounded by military confrontation with the West, made the fulfilment of consumer expectations impossible. In the last quarter of the twentieth century, practical problems of economic coordination in the advanced industrial state socialist economies became acute and economic growth was on the decline. Popular aspirations to outstrip the Western countries in terms of consumer welfare were not fulfilled. Without the knowledge available through advanced computing systems, the apparatus of planning was inadequate and led to faulty coordination.

Two major theoretical positions arose to reform the state planning system. The first, which originated from critics within the socialist countries, was to graft markets onto the system of central socialist planning. The second, which was articulated by Leftist Western critics, was for a participatory and democratic system of planning quite different from the Soviet style of state planning. Discussion has revolved around different types of collective ownership, the form and powers of the state, and how the proposed market economy would fit into a democratic framework. Many complained that state-owned industries were undemocratic and their management acted in similar ways (with respect to labour relations for example) as privately owned corporations. I consider the 'state capitalist' critique in Chapter 15. The 'socialist market' alternative to central planning was articulated to resolve the difficulties of the planned European socialist economies and it was also proposed for the social democratic forms of state planning which had occurred under the nationalised industries in Western Europe, particularly the UK.

---

[25] See, for example, A. Callinicos, *The Revenge of History*. Cambridge: Polity, 1991, and Chris Harman, The storm breaks. *International Socialism*, 46 (Spring 1990). State capitalism, Harman argues, was a phase of development of capitalism, which has now ended. '[T]he transition from state capitalism to multinational capitalism is neither a step forward not a step backwards, but a step sideways' (p 82).

Market socialism in theory

The theoretical assumptions of market socialism[26] were developed in the twentieth century between the two world wars.[27] Oskar Lange, in a seminal article written in 1935, pointed out that the principles of economic theory are applicable to all developed economies.[28] Markets, he argued, have the same economic effects in all economic formations. The technical aspects of markets (as a means to reconcile demand and supply through prices) make them appropriate instruments under socialism. Socialism, it was contended, was secured through the state ownership of property and the domination of the working class through the hegemony of the Communist Party. An economic market mechanism could be put in place to regulate prices and determine the production of goods and services without changing the socialist mode of production.

But market socialism was something more than an economic mechanism, it too required a political and social framework. Reformers in the socialist states following the lead of Lange claimed that in terms of class relationships the relations to the means of production would remain socialist under a system of market socialism. The legal and social system under the leadership of the Communist Party could remain intact. The bourgeoisie had been dispossessed and the working class remained the dominant class. Market mechanisms could be grafted onto the planning system.

Other writers, especially market socialists in the West, however, brought out other important factors. Many claimed that socialist markets should be embedded in a democratic pluralist framework, which at that time the Soviet system lacked. As David Miller put it:

> The market is recognised as the centre piece of economic life, both for its efficiency as a means of providing goods and services and for its more general liberating qualities. But the market economy cannot function in an acceptable way unless complemented by a democratic state that sets appropriate ground rules, monitors the evolution of

---

[26] Yugoslavia was the path-breaking example of market socialism embracing workers' control. Due to limitations on space, in this chapter discussion is limited to the states that were reforming the Soviet planning process.

[27] For a summary of the early literature see K. Landauer, *European Socialism*. David Schweickart has a cogent summary of the market socialist case against capitalism (see *Against Capitalism*). J. Kornai, *The Road to Freedom: Shifting from the Socialist System*. New York: W.W. Norton, 1990, p 58. See also Joseph E. Stiglitz, *Whither Socialism?*. Cambridge, MA, and London: MIT Press, 1998, p 9.

[28] Oskar Lange, Marxian economics and modern economic theory, *Review of Economic Studies*, (June 1935), pp 68–87, see p 81.

particular markets over time, rectifies the distribution of income, and directly supplies a range of public goods.[29]

Here economies are not embedded only in market structures but require their own forms of rule making and enforcements. Market and state are counterbalancing institutions and are mediated by participant democratic structures and procedures.

From the late 1970s, in the state socialist societies, reformers relied on Lange's arguments: the introduction of markets, in the context of publicly owned property controlled by a hegemonic socialist or communist party, could make the socialist economy work more effectively. The principal reasons put forward for reform of Soviet type planning accepted many of the arguments made by liberal economists: notably, that markets would provide a more efficient form of price formation, would fulfil consumers' needs through a better distribution of goods and services and a more effective allocation of resources. It is important to note here that the party-state would remain hegemonic to preserve the socialist basis of property ownership. Remember the quotation from Wesolowski, cited previously. Public property relations secured by the party-state apparatuses would be necessary and sufficient, to sustain the socialist social system. The major problem here was how in practice the market mechanism would be integrated into the state system and how socialist political objectives would be secured in a competitive market system.

What has confounded the market socialist reformers is how to resolve the contradiction between the objectives of socialism (a classless society, moral commitments to work, equalitarian outcomes, full and meaningful employment, direct provision of use values) and the social and political consequences of the economic market, usually measured by the criteria of economic efficiency, profitability and satisfying consumers. Whether there is an irreconcilable contradiction here is debatable. Some supporters of market socialism believe that a socialist market and socialist planning can and should be effectively combined. We return to these issues in Chapter 8 when we consider the reform and dismantling of European state socialism.

Participatory socialist planning

A second set of reform proposals were articulated, which considered that the very conception of central state planning as it had developed in the USSR should be transformed. In response to the Soviet experience, proposals for a

---

[29] David Miller, *Market, State and Community: Theoretical Foundations of Market Socialism*. Oxford: Clarendon Press, 1989, pp 18–19.

different kind of socialist planning have been made by Ernest Mandel, Fikrit Adaman and Pat Devine. Their remedy lies in a form of participatory planning and greater democratic control. Ernest Mandel has been a stalwart defender of the principles of socialist planning; he has argued that the isolation and backwardness of the USSR conditioned its bureaucratic mismanagement.[30] Its distortions could have been avoided under 'a democratically centralised system of workers' management in mature industrialised countries, on an international scale'.[31] Leaving aside the profound difficulties involved with the international scale of globalised capitalism, Mandel envisages the setting up of national self-management bodies (with regional and local branches), which would take over the formation of detailed plans. His proposals would involve 'the great masses of citizens' in decision-making thus reducing 'bureaucracy'.[32]

Fikrit Adaman and Pat Devine also claim that bureaucratic control leads to inefficiency and that a bureaucratic system lacks entrepreneurial drive. They contend that participatory planning is necessary to ensure not only efficiency but also a democratic transformative dynamic for socialism. Participatory planning is not just a version of planning but a form of socialism in its own right. For Adaman and Devine it is a system 'in which the values of individuals and collectives interact and shape one another through a process of cooperation and negotiation'.[33]

Soviet-type planning, they argue, entailed coercion. A participatory system 'dispenses with coercion, whether by the state or by market forces'.[34] 'Negotiated coordination' takes place between 'representatives of those affected by the decisions involved, informed by participatory discussion among the multiplicity of affected interests'.[35] Their general proposition is that 'at each level of decision making, those who are affected by the decisions participate in making them'.[36] The process does not involve

---

[30] E. Mandel, The myth of market socialism. *New Left Review*, I/169 (May/June 1988), p 109.

[31] Mandel, The myth of market socialism, p 109.

[32] See the discussion in Ernest Mandel, In defence of socialist planning. *New Left Review*, I/159 (September–October 1986), Section 7, Articulated Workers' Self-Management.

[33] F. Adaman and P. Devine, On the economic theory of socialism, *New Left Review*, (1997), p 75.

[34] Adaman and Devine, On the economic theory of socialism, p 75.

[35] Adaman and Devine, On the economic theory of socialism, p 76. Here Adaman and Devine summarise the argument made in *Devine, Democracy and Economic Planning*. Cambridge: Polity, 1988.

[36] F. Adaman and P. Devine, Participatory planning as a deliberative democratic process: A response to Hodgson's critique. *Economy and Society*, 30:2 (2001), pp 229–39, quotation p 234. See also G.M. Hodgson, Socialism against Markets? A critique of two recent proposals. *Economy and Society*, 27:4 (1998), pp 407–33.

coordination with pre-existing plans but is 'a discursive process of deliberative democracy'.[37] In the course of the deliberative process, Adaman and Devine are confident that:

> a consensus will occur ... based on mutual recognition of the legitimacy of the interests involved and the application of reason informed by the prevailing value system(s). The social interest is not arrived at through aggregation [as it might be in a market system], nor is it imposed from above [as in central planning], it is negotiated.[38]

They propose a form of stakeholder participation and control. Their scheme would encompass competition between enterprises and production for profit. In this sense it is a form of market socialism. Enterprises would meet changes in supply and demand through the process of negotiated coordination. Adaman and Devine incline away from an ex-ante planning process to the Hayek-like catallaxy of spontaneous exchange (discussed in Chapter 2). The result, they contend, would be a system shorn of the distorting effects of capitalist ownership relationships. Negotiated coordination takes place at many levels and involves actors appropriate to the level. Decisions with global scope, 'such as those concerned with international redistribution, the global pattern of economic activity or activities with global ecological consequences, would be negotiated at the global level'.[39] The general idea is that 'self-governing associations in civil society exercise control through their representatives over the economic activities of society'.[40]

Such a system could not work unless there was a general consensus on values and ways of doing things. The problem is that priorities differ between people and institutions. Outcomes depend on how differences between interests are resolved, and it is not always possible to attain a consensus. When a consensus cannot be reached, compulsion might be necessary to execute plans[41] – examples abound in capitalist countries when governments plan new airports or expressways or when they introduce measures to reduce global warming. In all societies, the ends to be pursued entail conflicts of opinions and interests over levels of economic growth, on the balance between individual and national needs, between the interests of present and future generations and on the use and preservation of the environment.

---

[37] Adaman and Devine, Participatory planning as a deliberative democratic process, p 234.

[38] Adaman and Devine, Participatory planning as a deliberative democratic process, p 237.

[39] Adaman and Devine, On the economic theory of socialism, pp 77–8.

[40] Firkit Adaman and P. Devine, The promise of participatory planning: A rejoinder to Hodgson. *Economy and Society*, 35:1 (2006), pp 141–7, quotation, p 146.

[41] This is the thrust of Hodgson's critique. G.M. Hodgson, Socialism against markets?, see p 408.

One cannot deny that consensus may be reached through democratic discussion. The point that different interests have to be consulted and coordinated is well taken. However, there are limits. The need for a body with authority (that is, legitimate use of power) entails compulsion when different interests cannot be reconciled. The consequences of democratic decision making often involve winners and losers – the latter (in the final analysis) will have to accept the 'democratic decision' in the same way that they would also have to accept a bureaucratic decision of which they strongly disapprove. Truly, democratic decisions might make the coercion more just and acceptable. But it does not alter the fact that when interests are irreconcilable, in a democracy the majority can legitimately coerce the minority to accept the majority decision. The units in which the democratic process occurs also lead to conflicting results. In federal states, for example, constituent republics often seek, quite democratically, outcomes that differ from the federal power, sometimes even leading to secession. (The decisions of the European Union are often not shared by the majority of citizens in many of the member states. Another example, is that the UK's decision to leave the EU was not shared by a majority of people in Scotland.)

Compulsion cannot be avoided either by a centralised plan or by a market mechanism: putting planning into a participatory democratic framework legitimises compulsion. Moreover, the outcomes of such participatory deliberations may be incompatible with a national socialist economic plan. For example, plans made at a higher level promoting environmental benefits or to advance equal opportunities might be incompatible with the views and interests of those negatively affected by such policies who might, if they constituted a majority, quite logically claim a 'democratic' mandate to reject them. The socialist state, like any state, has to maintain and enforce its rules. 'Planning' involves ex-ante decision-making. Hence planners, like architects, have an image of the type of society they wish to construct. The alternative perspective is that a planning body (constituted on a participatory basis) would fulfil social needs determined on an interactive piece-meal basis.

I accept that the pluralist nature of the economic formation could lead to positive results, especially at lower levels. Adaman and Devine's ideas about participation have virtues in challenging bureaucratised central control. Participation in the 'running of ... society's economy in one way or another'[42] is to be commended. But if negotiated participation is possible under social pluralism, by the same logic, why is it not possible within the parameters of state planning? To pose a 'dilemma' between 'authoritarian' planning

---

[42]   Adaman and Devine, The promise of participatory planning, p 146.

and 'democratic' markets is to pose the wrong question, as planning can be democratic and markets do not claim to be democratic.[43] There should be no barrier against citizen participation in the formulation and monitoring of a central plan. State planning does not have to be tyrannical – it should and can be grounded on the views and interests of subjects, of stake holders.

The limits to reform under state socialism

The arguments considered earlier are ideological and theoretical in character. In practical politics in the state socialist societies there were major obstacles to reform of the planning processes. Before the mid-1980s, the prospects for any significant departures from the established state planning were remote. The institutional structure of state socialism, the constraining role of the party-state apparatus and its ideology of risk-free, equalitarian welfarism, prevented any significant move to a market type economy within the constraints of state planning. In the West, critics considered that the 'totalitarian' nature of Soviet type societies made them 'revolution proof' as Zygmund Bauman[44] put it. By this he meant that any significant internal transformation of the Soviet system was impossible due to the oppressive controls. He was wrong. In both the socialist European states and in China the introduction of markets led to the incursion of neoliberal components into the economy and, notably, considerable privatisation.

Before we consider, in Chapter 8, how the state socialist economies were dismantled, we turn to the social democratic governments in Western Europe. Concurrently with the building of the planned economies in central and Eastern Europe, crucial developments were taking place in Western Europe where a milder form of social democratic statism had been installed after the Second World War. A second real alternative to competitive capitalism had presented itself: a social democratic welfare state. In the next chapter, I shall show how the social democratic parties had similar initial successes but faced comparable problems before they were electorally defeated by the forces of neoliberalism. The history of state socialism and social democracy followed a similar trajectory. Ronald Reagan and Margaret Thatcher became an inspiration to the nascent proponents of political and economic reform in the state socialist societies as well as in social democratic capitalist societies. We turn then in the next chapter, to review how social democracy (illustrated by the British Labour Party) was captured by neoliberalism.

---

[43] Johanna Bockman, *Markets in the Name of Socialism: The Left-Wing Origins of Neoliberalism.* Stanford: Stanford University, 2011, p 200.

[44] Z. Bauman, Social dissent in the East European political system. *European Journal of Sociology*, 12 (1971), pp 25–51, see p 26.

6

The Decay of Social Democracy

Following the Second World War, the victorious Western capitalist countries were confronted with problems of reconstruction. Three major paradigms of economic and political organisation presented themselves: competitive market capitalism, hierarchically organised state socialism and welfare social democracy. Competitive market capitalism continued in the USA, but in the rest of the world it had suffered serious set-backs. The inter-war depression and the resounding defeat of right-wing forces during the war had weakened the legitimacy of capitalism and the Western European countries were also confronted by indigenous liberation movements in their colonies. The Soviet planned economy had emerged as a challenge to capitalism. The Western states had to 'win the peace'. and to do this coordinated welfarist societies were devised. In this chapter, I outline the initial successes of West European social democracy which introduced coordinated welfarist economies. The focus here is on the British Labour Party, which is used as a reference point for European social democracy.[1]

In 1945, only 28 years after the Bolshevik Revolution in Russia, social democratic-led governments (sometimes in coalitions or with the support of communist or liberal parties) came to power through the electoral process in the major Western European countries. Governments took office that offered an alternative social democratic form of capitalism to the liberal capitalism of the inter-war period. These governments adopted a piece-meal gradualist policy of reforms, which was predicated on the promotion of equality, and social justice. In practical politics, 'social democratic' policies – promoting equality of opportunity and a wider democracy, which often included

---

[1]   It is beyond the scope of this book to consider other social democratic countries. See Sassoon, *One Hundred Years of Socialism*.

the extension of public ownership – were also supported by liberal and conservative parties.

In the UK in the 1945 general election, the Labour Party gained 47.7 per cent of votes – giving Labour a majority of 146 Parliamentary seats. Similar political developments occurred in Western Europe: socialists and communists secured sufficient electoral support to form or to participate in governments.[2] In the Scandinavian countries social democracy was particularly strong. Thought the Left was clearly in the vanguard, conservative political groups had a significant following. In the UK, for example, the Conservatives received 39.7 per cent of the vote, giving them 210 seats. Even in what has been called a landslide victory, Labour received only just over a third of the votes of the electorate (the total number registered to vote).[3] In Germany in 1949 the conservative Christian Democrats constituted the largest single party with 35 per cent of the votes and 207 seats. If this was a 'red tide', it certainly carried with it many large right-wing boats.

In the advanced capitalist states, major movements counter to capitalism also took the form of well-supported communist parties in Italy, France, Finland and Greece. The socialist movements in all these countries were influenced in varying ways by the ideas of Marxists as well as the experience and practice of the Soviet Union. They were anti-capitalist in the sense that unregulated markets and uncontrolled private ownership were rejected as means to further human development. The communists, however, were not strong enough in any of the West European countries to gain state power. Nevertheless, they had an influence over politics as well as an important role in local government and in trade unions. The British Labour Party, after the Second World War, was reformist, democratic and Parliamentary. The Party contained members and supporters who sought the transformation of capitalism, and those who believed that, through cumulative reforms, capitalism could be reformed in favour of a superior type of socialist society.

---

[2]   In Western Germany in 1949, the Social Democratic Party of Germany (SPD) gained 29 per cent of the vote and 140 seats, and the communist parties (15 seats) 5.7 per cent; in France, in the 1945 elections, the Communist Party received the highest proportion of votes (26.2 per cent and 161 seats) and the Socialist Party (23.4 per cent with 150 seats); in Italy, the Italian Socialist Party in 1946 received 20.7 per cent with 115 seats and the Communists 19 per cent with 104 seats. For Germany see: Parties and Elections in Europe, http://www.parties-and-elections.eu/germany2.html. For details of election in Western Europe 1941–1950, see Sassoon, *One Hundred Years of Socialism*, Chapter 5, especially p 118.

[3]   See http://www.parties-and-elections.eu. See data under UK.

The social democratic post-Second World War alternative

Parliamentary socialism was the template of the Labour Party. It was set as a moderate, gradualist, electorally acceptable movement, national in orientation. Similarly, across Western Europe, major reforms were instigated by the newly incumbent left-wing and liberal parties. It is important to note that many of these welfare reforms were accepted by non-socialists. Indeed, in the UK, plans for reconstruction in the post-war period had been devised during the Second World War. The Beverage Report (1942), chaired by William Beverage, a liberal economist, under the war-time coalition government of Conservative and Labour parties, sought to abolish 'five evils': squalor, ignorance, want, idleness and disease, which became the basis for the British welfare state after 1945.

Unlike the world-wide significance of the Bolshevik victory as pronounced by Lenin and his followers in Russia, the social democratic parties presented their programmes as reactions to the insufficiencies of capitalism.[4] The British Labour Party is an iconic example of progressive social democracy in government. In 1945, its policy document, *Let Us Face the Future*, declared:

> [W]hen [the people] had won [the First World War] they lacked a lively interest in the social and economic problems of peace, and accepted the election promises of the leaders of the anti-Labour parties at their face value ... The people lost that peace. And when we say 'peace' we mean ... the social and economic policy which followed the fighting ... Similar forces are at work today. [But vested] interests have not been able to make the same profits out of this war as they did out of the last. The 100% Excess Profits Tax, the controls over industry and transport, the fair rationing of food and control of prices ... all helped to win the war. With these measures the country has come nearer to making 'fair shares' the national rule than ever before in its history.[5]

British social democracy is a protest against injustice, inequality and poverty generated by capitalism. The Labour Party accepted the parameters of

---

[4] For overviews of Labour Party post-war history see: Henry Pelling and Alastair J. Reid, *A Short History of the Labour Party*. Basingstoke: Palgrave Macmillan, 2005 edn; Raymond Plant, Matt Beech and Kevin Hickson, *The Struggle for Labour's Soul: Understanding Labour's Political Thought since 1945*. London: Routledge, 2004; Ralph Miliband, *Parliamentary Socialism*. London: Merlin, 1972. For an overview of socialism in Western Europe see Sassoon, *One Hundred Years of Socialism*.

[5] Quotations from 1945 Labour Election Manifesto, *Let Us Face the Future*. Available at: www.labour-party.org.uk/manifestos/1945

capitalist society – parliamentary democracy, private ownership and a pluralist society. Its 1945 programme was based on statist, welfarist, anti-free-market assumptions. It was accepted that full employment would be a responsibility of government – to be achieved through government management of the economy using Keynesian methods. There was general agreement on the part of reformers that the state should and would take a leading role in the economic and social welfare of the population which would include public ownership of failing industries. An important conditioning factor here was that the West European states had all emerged from the war when market processes had been suppressed. The forms of enterprise introduced by the social democratic governments were state-managed and included state-owned corporations operating within a market economy.

The statist credentials of the British Labour Party

Though many commentators are often dismissive of social democratic parties on the grounds that they work within the confines of capitalism, it should be acknowledged that the British Labour Party significantly modified British the liberal capitalism of the pre-Second World War period. In the aftermath of the Second World War, the UK nationalised the iron and steel industry, aircraft and ship construction, road, rail, canal and air transport, electricity, gas, water. The Bank of England was nationalised and some banks ('Municipal banks') were under local council ownership. The government had significant holdings in large private corporations, such as British Petroleum. It also exercised control over the exchange rate of sterling and the export of capital and, until the 1950s, it exercised price controls over a large number of commodities. It had a monopoly, exercised by the British Broadcasting Corporation (BBC), of radio and the nascent television services.

High rates of taxation had been instituted to finance the Second World War and continued into the post-war period. In the UK, the highest rate of tax remained at 90 per cent of income between 1953 and 1970[6] (which included the period of Conservative government between 1951 and 1964). Consequently, post-war governments had a strong tax base on which the welfare state could be financed. During the post-war period up to 1979, income distribution became much more equal. The changes are captured in Figure 6.1, which shows the national income share for the UK of the top 0.5 per cent of the population.

---

[6] Thomas Piketty, *Capital in the Twenty-First Century*. New York: Harvard University Press, 2014, p 499.

Figure 6.1: UK: top 0.5 per cent of incomes, 1913–2012

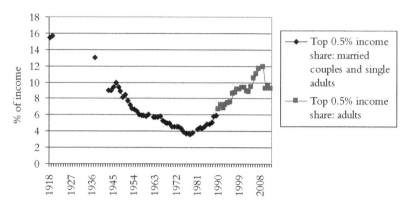

Source: The World Top Incomes Database. Available at: http://topincomes.g-mond.parisschool ofeconomics.eu/

The share of the top income group was declining even before the Second World War and more so during the post-war periods of the Labour governments (1945–51, 1964–70, 1974–79) and continued under Conservative governments (1951–1964 and 1970–1974). Anticipating discussion in later chapters, we note from the graph that the trend reversed from 1979 under Margaret Thatcher and continued to spiral upwards under Tony Blair. The early post-war period witnessed a political culture in the Labour Party with a strong belief in promoting equality and an aversion to many aspects of capitalism. The welfare regimes were encased in mixed economies with considerable state ownership and control operating through a market. While the reforms heralding the introduction of the welfare state had cross party-political support, the Labour Party gained the credit for putting them into effect.

The legitimacy of public ownership was substantiated in terms of its greater economic efficiency rather than the Marxist notion of abolishing exploitation. 'Public ownership of gas and electricity undertakings will lower charges, prevent competitive waste, open the way for co-ordinated research and development and lead to the reforming of uneconomic areas of distribution.'[7] Other major industries such as motor production, textiles, chemicals, building, publishing as well as smaller businesses continued under private ownership. The model for the nationalised industries was strongly influenced by Herbert Morrison's experience with the organisation of the (pre-war) London Passenger Transport Board – rather than being based on

---

[7] Quotations from 1945 Labour Election Manifesto, *Let Us Face the Future.*

any socialist principles of co-determination.[8] Public ownership was extended to public utilities. Later British governments intervened to nationalise companies that were facing collapse, Ferranti and British Leyland – one of Britain's largest motor companies – were taken over. The state also supplanted the market as provider of social welfare services. Public health was promoted by a National Health Service. Public housing under local government was supported and enhanced through the centralisation and pooling of building materials and was accompanied by price control. While in these ways market capitalism was curbed, demands by Labour Party Conferences for the public ownership of land, heavy industry and the banks, as well as claims for a 'shopping list' of the top 200 companies, were disregarded by Labour governments. Later, such proposals were completely repudiated by the leadership of the Labour Party under Tony Blair. The objective of Labour in power was less ideological than practical politics, and the legitimation for public ownership has been on pragmatic political grounds of efficiency and effectiveness. Nevertheless, social democracy in power represented a form of state coordinated welfare capitalism, distinctive from liberal capitalism and certainly very different from what was to follow – neoliberalism.

Labour governments also pursued progressive, tolerant measures in domestic politics. They ended the death penalty and passed other social legislation: reforms legalising homosexuality and abortion. Later, in foreign policy, armed forces were not committed to the Vietnam War. However, the Labour government did not show sympathy towards the evolving communist bloc. The Party was a signatory to the Treaty of Brussels, signed on 17 March 1948, which was the precursor of the North Atlantic Treaty Organization (NATO) directed against the Soviet Union. In 1947, it also reintroduced conscription into the armed forces for all 18-year-olds who were to serve in Labour's foreign wars – in Malaya and Korea. The Labour Party endorsed the dominant political world order, and later,under Tony Blair, Britain's regular army was heavily involved in Iraq and Afghanistan.

Social democracy adopted a political ideology and practices to reduce the uncertain outcomes of a market economy, to address social injustice and to alleviate distributive inequality of capitalism by gradual piecemeal democratic reforms. Social democratic parties do not operate as counter-cultures to capitalism but as sub-cultures working within it – promoting an alternative form of welfare capitalism.

The post-war period in Britain, at least at the level of political elites, was one of social consensus. Conservative governments up to the time of Margaret Thatcher accepted the reforms, notably public ownership. Neither denationalisation of state-owned industries nor reversal of welfare institutions,

---

[8] B. Donoughue and G.W. Jones, *Herbert Morrison*. London: Weidenfeld and Nicolson, 1973.

such as the National Health Service set up by the Labour government, occurred. As a result of this reforming spirit, the UK had a significant publicly owned industrial sector, considerable powers of control over the economy; and the social sector – education, social services (including comprehensive health provision and state pensions) – was financed by the government through taxation. State ownership was not solely a Labour Party policy but part of managed European capitalism in the 1970s. In most of Western Europe, electricity, gas, coal, airlines and steel were largely state owned, and in Austria, France, Britain, Italy and West Germany the state had considerable stakes in the motor industry; railways, the post and telecommunications, and nuclear power were in public ownership.[9] Later, neoliberal governments would target and privatise the state-owned industries.

There were four main developments that predisposed British governments towards statist welfare policies. First, the failure of capitalism in the inter-war period to maintain high levels of employment consequent on economic depression, followed by the loss of markets in the Empire after the Second World War. Second, the defeat of right-wing movements (in Germany, Italy and Romania) in the Second World War. Third, the social advances achieved by state socialism. Fourth, wars played a crucial part in the process of political change – either directly or indirectly. Governments had organised the war effort, private companies had been brought under state control, market competition had been superseded by war-time planning and a highly progressive tax regime was in place.

In Western Europe, the aftermath of war created conditions for incumbent governments to effect civil changes – to 'win the peace'. They secured a form of capitalism significantly different from liberal capitalism through partial public ownership, economic control over the market and policies of social equality.[10] The strategy of social democratic and reformist parties was to win control of the state; the principal means were Keynesian policies of economic management. The form of social democratic capitalism differed not only from the liberal market variety but also from the socialist countries in Eastern Europe and, later, China. While there were considerable differences between social democratic regimes, there were enough similarities to demarcate social democratic societies in terms of their political formation, dominant values, types of property and role of the state.[11] They provided an iconic model of a socially managed type of welfare capitalism. The major differences between

---

[9] See details in J. Foreman-Peck and G. Federico, *European Industrial Policy*. Oxford: Oxford University Press, 1999, pp 441–2.

[10] For an outline of developments in Europe see Padgett and Paterson, *A History of Social Democracy in Post-war Europe*.

[11] Bruno Amable classifies Denmark, Finland and Sweden as 'social democratic capitalism'. Here I include the UK in the post-war period under the social democratic heading. The

Table 6.1: Capitalist, social democratic and communist organising principles

Social factors	Market–capitalist	Social democratic	State socialist
Social goals	Freedom of the individual	Equality of opportunity	Communist society
Type of freedom	Freedom 'from'	Freedom 'to'	Freedom 'to'
Form of coordination	Market	Market/state	State/market
Integration/values	Individualistic	Individualistic/ collectivist	Collectivist planning
Property	Private	Public/private	Public
Class structure	Multiple	Multiple	Unitary
Economic efficiency	Profit maximisation	State regulation/ private profit	State regulation/ planning
Political legitimacy	Electoral competitive	Electoral competitive	Collectivist/statist
Extent of markets	National/regional/ global	National/regional/ global	National/regional
Social base of parties	Class + nation	Class/division of labour	Class/ownership relations

liberal market capitalism, welfare social democracy and state socialism are summarised in Table 6.1.

As indicated in Table 6.1, social democratic organising principles are embedded in a capitalist framework. While the state socialist form of economic coordination was hierarchical (albeit with some market components), the social democratic formation was pluralistic and hybrid. The market and profit maximisation still operated in a large private sector. Political parties, usually with strong class allegiances, competed for parliamentary office. Despite the inroads of public ownership, corporate property was still mainly privately owned. Political objectives were to secure an equalisation in levels (principally) of income as well as promoting positive values of freedom: this involved restricting the market and enhancing the freedom of citizens to access social goods such as housing, education and healthcare. However, social democratic parties failed to achieve their wider objectives. By the late 1970s, social democracy in government was confronted by a revival of market capitalism that would take the form of neoliberalism.

UK was later to move towards the US as a market-based model. B. Amable, *The Diversity of Modern Capitalism*. Oxford: Oxford University Press, 2003, pp 171–80.

Both Western social democracy and Soviet socialism would lose power and legitimacy in the 1980s.

Undermining social democracy's power and appeal, and underpinning the rise of neoliberalism, were fundamental changes in the organisation of capitalism, which transformed national capitalism into transnational capitalism, which we discuss in Chapter 8. But first we consider the electoral politics of the UK and the failure of social democracy to consolidate its position into the last quarter of the twentieth century. This failure, concurrent with the rise of neoliberalism, also had significant effects on the state socialist societies in Eastern Europe and China.

The transformation of Western social democracy

In the immediate post-war years, the British economy under the Labour government did relatively well.[12] Welfare social democracy was popular. The UK made a successful recovery from the war and exported to ravaged European as well as to Commonwealth markets. As European countries recovered, the British economy faced considerable difficulties. From the late 1960s, inflation gripped the country, a trade deficit led to devaluation, and in June 1969, the government required a standby loan from the IMF. Trade deficits continued in the 1970s. In the initial post-war period, full-employment had effectively been achieved, with registered unemployment falling to 2.5 per cent. From the mid-1970s, unemployment rose to over 5 per cent, which at the time was regarded as excessive. What was novel about the unemployment figures of the late seventies was that they coincided with high levels of inflation – a phenomenon known as stagflation.

A root cause of the economic problems was the inability of British industry after the post-war economic boom to compete successfully. Gross national product (GNP) per capita did not rise between 1970 and 1978. Inflation was far greater than in other Organisation for Economic Co-operation and Development (OECD) countries – even though interest rates were 12.5 per cent in 1978, compared with 3 per cent in Germany. Unemployment was also high, reaching 6.1 per cent in 1978 compared with 3.9 in Germany. It was widely believed that the policies of the Labour government under Harold Wilson (elected in 1964 and 1966) were responsible, though the Conservatives had been in power between 1951 and 1964. Critics of the

---

[12] Many works deal in more detail with the Thatcher epoch, see particularly: Edgar Wilson, *A Very British Miracle: The Failure of Thatcherism*. London: Pluto, 1992; Geoffrey Wheatcroft, *The Strange Death of Tory England*. London: Allan Lane, 2005; Martin Pugh, *Speak for Britain! A New History of the Labour Party*. London: Bodley Head, 2010; Ralph Miliband, *Socialism for a Sceptical Age*. Cambridge: Polity, 1994; Desmond S. King, *The New Right: Politics, Markets and Citizenship*. London: Macmillan, 1987.

Labour administration, following the line of liberal economists, argued that a regulated form of social democratic capitalism can only function with considerable economic and social costs.

Three main arguments were put forward for the failure of the British economy at this time, which applied to all political administrations, including that of the One Nation conservatives under Harold Macmillan. First: structural and managerial: these included inadequate skill levels of the work force, a lack of entrepreneurial spirit and management, low levels of investment and insufficient renewal of capital. The outcome was low productivity, inability to compete in world competitive markets and falling profits and wages. Many contended that the exchange value of the pound was too high and that devaluation should have taken place to make exports more competitive.

Second: trade union practices. The UK had a decentralised trade union structure with localised negotiation between employees and employers. From the 1950s, industrial disputes became widespread and, in some companies, shop stewards took the initiative in organising 'wild cat strikes'. Successive governments tried to legislate to control union activity. 'In Place of Strife', which would have limited the powers of unions, was tabled under the Wilson government in 1969 but was withdrawn after opposition by the trade unions. The Conservative government under Edward Heath introduced further legislation, the Industrial Relations Act 1970. This in turn led to a dramatic rise in strike activity. From an average of around 3 million lost days in 1950, it rose to 23.9 million in 1972. The Labour government elected in 1974 was also dogged by strikes; notably in 1979 there were 29.5 million days lost.[13] The unions were widely regarded as the villains who had made Britain an ungovernable country. Certainly, labour-management relations were confrontational. While the unions were publicly blamed, their actions were precipitated by underlying structural conditions.

Third: Keynesian economic theory. Keynesian policies, as interpreted in the 1970s, were not working. Demand management (increased government spending) did not reduce unemployment; neither did it increase economic growth. And rises in the rate of interest did not curb inflation. Many concluded that Keynesian theories of economic management were no longer applicable to post-war conditions. A major turning point was the speech of James Callaghan who, when Labour Party leader, contended at the Labour Party Conference in 1976 that:

> We used to think that you could spend your way out of a recession and increase employment by cutting taxes and boosting government

---

[13] For details see Wilson, *A Very British Miracle*, p 11.

spending. I tell you in all candour that that option no longer exists, and in so far as it ever did exist, it only worked on each occasion since the war by injecting a bigger dose of inflation into the economy, followed by a higher level of unemployment as the next step.[14]

Underlying the Labour government's problems was a financial crisis: to maintain the value of the pound, the government agreed a massive IMF loan ($3.9 billion), which required an austerity programme involving public expenditure cuts. Keynesian policies of government spending to end recession and unemployment were rejected. As we shall discover, Thatcherism was to take their place. Other social changes also had significant effects in weakening the traditional Labour Party policies to which I return later.

Reasserting Labour's traditional values

The leadership of the British Labour Party pursued its traditional policy. It proposed further nationalisation of industry and significant moves in foreign policy away from the hegemony of the USA. Up to and including the leadership of Michael Foot, the Party leadership resisted calls for internal 'modernisation', and, though there were important divisions within the leadership, it provided an overtly socialist platform. In 1973, under the influence of Tony Benn, the Party's programme included proposals for the nationalisation of 25 major companies[15]. Benn strongly advocated that future proposals for public ownership would include policies of industrial democracy. The Labour Party's *Parliamentary* leadership, notably Harold Wilson, elected by and responsible to Members of Parliament, disavowed such strategies.

The Party pursued a policy that, if executed, would have considerably weakened liberal capitalism to achieve its goal towards a statist form of socialism. The 1983 Labour Manifesto – New Hope for Britain[16] – adopted a radical social democratic perspective. Keynesianism was endorsed as a policy capable of achieving full employment. The Manifesto proposed the nationalisation of key industries, it reiterated support for public services and the preservation and development of the National Health Service; it advocated more equality at work and the abolition of the House of Lords. There were to be major changes in foreign policy, effectively breaking

---

[14] Labour Party, Annual Conference Report 1976, p 188. Cited in Wikipedia in entry under James Callaghan.
[15] See discussion in Panitch and Leys, *Searching for Socialism*, pp 58–63.
[16] Quotations from 1983 Labour Manifesto, The New Hope for Britain. Available at: http://www.labour.org.uk/manifestos/1983

away from the US military alliance and NATO and leaving the European Economic Community (later to become the European Union).

The Manifesto envisaged 'a major increase in public investment, including transport, housing and energy conservation'. There would be major changes in foreign affairs, including the banning of nuclear weapons and leaving NATO. The Manifesto details the transformative proposals of the Labour Party, which provided a template for a radical social democratic alternative to liberal capitalism. The first objective was to increase public investment, especially in new technology. A second goal was 'to rebuild British industry, working within a new framework for planning and industrial democracy'. Third, Labour would 'create a fairer Britain, with decent social services for all'. Fourth, Labour would 'Introduce positive action programmes to promote women's rights and opportunities, and appoint a cabinet minister to promote equality between the sexes'. Finally, in international affairs, the Party would 'take new initiatives to promote peace and development'. Policies included cancelling the Trident nuclear submarine programme and a refusal to employ American cruise missiles. Britain would also prepare to leave the European Economic Community. Other policies included support for the nationalised coal industry, the protection of pensions, sustaining council house dwellers as well as support for owner–occupiers, the improvement of legal aid, the introduction of a freedom of information bill and devolution to Scotland.

Thus, under Michael Foot, a radical policy, in advance of the achievements of the post-war Labour Party, was advocated. The vision was of a socialist Britain: an enhanced welfare state, independence from the European Economic Community (which was considered to be controlled by corporate business) and an independent foreign policy anchored around nuclear disarmament. A further advance from market capitalism would be achieved by extending state ownership, management and regulation. If implemented, this would have been a significant alternative economic formation moving from competitive capitalism in the direction of socialism. But it was not to be realised. Critics, such as Gerald Kaufman, dubbed Labour's 1983 Manifesto as the 'longest suicide note in history'.

A major blow for the social democratic alternative was defeat at the polls. Labour lost the 1983 election. It constituted a reversal from which the Labour Party has never completely recovered and effectively killed off the social democratic alternative.[17] The Conservatives were returned and Margaret Thatcher consolidated her Parliamentary majority, which rose from 43 to 144. Labour received only 27.6 per cent of the vote – only half a million votes more than the Social Democratic Party and Liberal Alliance

---

[17] In a wider context see also G. Moschonas, *In the Name of Social Democracy, The Great Transformation: 1945 to the Present.* London: Verso, 2002.

Table 6.2: Electoral support of major parties, UK Parliament 1979–1992

Prime Minister	UK elections							
	Election				Election			
	Year	Vote (%)			Seats Won			Turn out (%)
		Con	Lab	Lib	Con	Lab	Lib	
Thatcher	1979	44	37	14	339	268	11	76
Thatcher	1983	42	28	25	397	209	23	72.7
Thatcher/Major	1987	42	31	23	375	229	22	75.3
Major	1992	42	34	18	336	271	20	77.7

Source: Parties and Elections in Europe. Available at: http://www.parties-and-elections.eu. See data under UK.

(SDP–Liberal Alliance). The SDP had been formed by the defection of some leading moderate Labour politicians (Roy Jenkins, Bill Rogers, David Owen and Shirley Williams) in 1981. Margaret Thatcher came to power on a wave of public criticism of the Labour government. Prior to Thatcher's Parliamentary victory in May 1979, Britain had experienced a period of economic and political disorder leading up to the Winter of Discontent in 1978/79. Unemployment reached some 3 million people in 1982. Whereas the government sought to limit wage increases to 5 per cent, unions (to meet inflation) were claiming up to 25 per cent rises. To support their claims, massive and widespread strikes and demonstrations took place and included public sector workers such as grave diggers, refuse collectors and hospital staff.

The general malaise led to Labour suffering consecutive electoral defeats in 1987 and 1992 as illustrated in Table 6.2. While the Conservatives in all the elections had the highest number of votes, they lacked an absolute majority: their share of the total electorate in the elections of 1979, 1983, 1987 and 1992 was 33.1 per cent, 30.8 per cent, 31.8 per cent and 32.6 per cent respectively (not shown in Table 6.2). These results fortified critics both within the social democratic movement and those outside it who agitated for a move away from ideas of statist socialism to more moderate social democratic policies.

The rise of a neoliberal conservatism

The stagnation of the economy and the disorder caused by British labour relations provided the underlying basis for an alternative economic and social policy. This came from the pro free-enterprise wing of the Conservative Party led by Margaret Thatcher. The Conservatives as well as Labour's internal critics explained Britain's malaise and decline in terms of the statist policies to which both Labour and One Nation Conservatism had subscribed. The underlying principles of Keynesian economic ideology were not working. Trade union power, unemployment, inflation and economic decline were all true and unpalatable facts. The period leading up to the 1979 election was one of economic crisis amplified by the print media, especially the Murdoch press, which propagated a hostile and negative account of Labour governments.

The conclusion drawn by opponents of the Labour Party was that there was too much socialism, too much nationalisation, too much power to the unions and too much state interference with the market. Some of these criticisms also could be levelled at previous Conservative governments, which had administered the country and maintained statist provisions. But the previously described criticisms are somewhat one sided and ignored the structural problems facing Britain as well as constraints on the government exercised by the International Monetary Fund (IMF). There had been a lack of post-war investment compared to continental Europe, especially Germany. Labour's opponents were blind to the failures of British private companies. British shipbuilding, automobiles, cycles, small tools, as well as textiles and general manufacturing lacked investment and innovation. The nationalised industries – particularly coal and railways – had been run down in the war and were not sufficiently renewed thereafter. Government policy favoured low prices in the nationalised industries; they were required to break even and not make profits. This policy effectively subsidised private business users of energy and socialised losses, which were borne by the government.

The international interests of British banks maintained an over-valued exchange rate to protect sterling. Had the exchange value of the pound fallen, it would have stimulated exports and reduced imports. The role of the USA and the IMF in securing the value of the pound sterling illustrates the external constraints faced by governments with any significant level of international trade. British capitalism had failed to adapt to the competitive post-Second World War international economy. Strikes were not just due to the weakness of the Labour government but a consequence of real wage erosion over many years. (Miners were not particularly privileged and earned around the average for all manual workers.[18]) Many on strike were low-paid public service workers who suffered wage restraint as well as the effects of inflation. Margaret Thatcher adopted a confrontational

---

[18] See details and discussion in Wilson, *A Very British Miracle*, p 52.

policy towards the unions and defeated the miners. Thereafter organised labour was broken.

Neoliberalism as a political project

Margaret Thatcher and the New Right were successful not only in discrediting Labour policies but also in transforming traditional Conservative ones. After her election as leader of the Conservative Party in 1974, she moved Conservative Party policy away from its 'One Nation' philosophy. Policy shifted from the post-war consensus of social democratisation and state regulation to the free operation of the economic market. Whatever their faults, her policies were electorally successful. Margaret Thatcher was re-elected for three consecutive terms, with very large majorities in 1983 and 1987 (see Table 6.2). Thatcher's governments systematically carried out policies resting on neoliberal policies.

What accounts for her success? Her policies worked. She managed to control inflation; she secured political stability by ending strikes and undermining the trade union movement. This was at the cost of breaking the traditional Conservative value of a one-nation social consensus. Britain entered a period of economic growth, albeit based on the financial and services sector, and she was also aided by fortuitous tax revenues from North Sea oil. Her policies had resonance with ascendant groups of the population, which had no affinity with the Labour Party's socialist proposals. It was attractive to people who wanted to be rewarded as they thought they deserved. The Labour Party, in which some prominent members also shared Margaret Thatcher's views, was deeply divided. Reformers in the Labour Party blamed left-wing policy articulated by the leadership as being unworkable and unwanted. It was an electoral handicap, they contended, which had to be changed.

The demise of the social democratic alternative

The previous analysis is in terms of current events and faults of political leadership. There were, moreover, three underlying developments which contributed to the decline of social democracy in the late twentieth century, and which predisposed many to accept neoliberal policies and reject socialist ones.[19] First, the changing nature of the class structure of the advanced societies; second, the political strategy of reformist social democracy, and

---

[19] A. Lavelle, *The Death of Social Democracy: Political Consequences in the 21st Century*. Aldershot: Ashgate, 2008.

Figure 6.2: Voting by occupational background: British elections, 1983, 1987

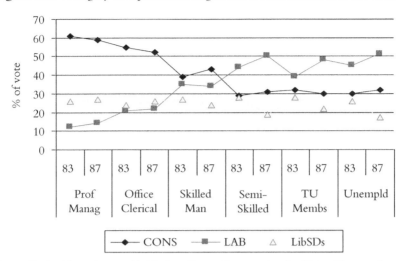

Source: Derived from data provided by Ivor Crewe, How to win a landslide without really trying. Based on BBC/Gallup polls. *The Guardian*, 15 June 1987.

third, the global character of capitalism. These features were shared by other capitalist countries but the move to neoliberalism happened first in the UK due to the more severe problems caused by the loss of Empire, lack of domestic commercial enterprise, competition from European countries and the political leadership of Margaret Thatcher and her advisers.

Fundamental changes in British society directly influenced political preferences. Labour's electoral decline, it was widely argued, was a result of the depletion of Labour's electoral base. Figure 6.2 records Labour's votes by occupational categories in 1983 and 1987. Labour received over 40 per cent of the votes of semi-skilled, trade union members and unemployed in both years; but the vote of only a third of the skilled manual working class, around a fifth of the lower non-manuals and fewer than 15 per cent of the professional and managerial voters. The shape of the lines illustrates the fact that British politics was still class based – as one moves from the upper classes, Labour's votes rise and the Conservatives' declines; the SDP/Liberal Alliance is fairly evenly spread throughout the class structure. Labour still commanded significant support among the semi-skilled manual workers, trade union members and the unemployed. However, the non-manual occupational groups were growing and here Labour was losing support particularly to the new and more moderate SDP/Liberal Alliance.

Table 6.3 details the social background of selected groups of voters in more detail at the 1987 election. It shows the significant shortfall in the Labour vote in the middle classes where in each category Labour came

Table 6.3: Voting by social class in 1987 General Election

	Middle class			New WkCl		Trad WkCl	
	Univ ed	Pub sec	Pvt sec	Owner occ	NonTU	Coun HsOc	Sct+NI
Con	34	44	65	44	40	25	29
Lab	29	24	13	32	38	57	57
Lib/SD	36	32	22	24	22	18	15

Key: WkCl = Working Class. Univ ed = University education. Pub sec = Public sector. Pvt sec = Private sector. Owner occ = Owner occupier (owned own house). NonTU = Not a member of a trade union. Coun HsOc = Council house occupant. Sct+NI = Scotland and Northern Ireland.

Source: Ivor Crewe, How to win a landslide without really trying. Based on BBC/Gallup polls. *The Guardian*, 15 June 1987.

bottom of the poll – even after the SDP/Liberal Alliance. The largest group of voters from the 'new working class' – those owning their own houses and not members of trade unions – voted for the Conservatives. In 1987, the only social constituency to return a majority of those voting Labour were trade union members living in council houses or in Scotland and Northern Ireland. Only in the latter did Labour retain a clear majority of its traditional support.

The obvious inference from these facts is that Labour had failed to attract the growing middle-class sections of the population. The Conservatives received the most votes from the professional, clerical and skilled manual workers as well as gaining significant support from Labour's traditional working-class constituencies. The occupational structure was changing and it was widely asserted that the 'decomposition' of class underpinned not only the electoral decline of social democratic parties but also the demise of socialism as a political movement. Socialism's working class base was simply withering away. A 'post-industrial' political culture, it appears, no longer supports a collectivist statist approach. This was not just a British phenomenon: neoliberal marketisation replaced the social market in the EU and, as we shall discover in later chapters, was copied by the radical reformers in Eastern Europe. Its major theoretical assumptions were worked into the New Labour Policy espoused by Tony Blair, to which we turn in the next chapter.

The shift in voting to the conservatives discussed previously was correlated with the appearance of new generations with different values. A long-term decline has occurred in the salience of social democratic and socialist ideology. The technological base of capitalism has changed and is taking a global form. Writers on post-industrial society have drawn attention to new features of capitalism. Notably, the forces of production are 'post-industrial' or 'informational', and the interface between politics and economy is global. We consider these changes in Chapter 9. Here we may note that it coincided with the flight of industrial production to Asia and the South.

There developed a New Spirit of Capitalism,[20] a revival of capitalism as a consumer-focussed as well as a profit maximising economic system with global dimensions. At the heart of this 'New Spirit' was the ideology of neoliberalism: the emphasis on freedom, private personal property, mass consumption and individualism. Neoliberal policies had a global appeal. They were welcomed and adopted in the socialist societies of Eastern Europe with devastating effects, which we turn to in Chapter 8. A major realignment in the class structure of the Western industrial societies was taking place which undermined the class basis of socialism, to which we return in Chapter 9.

The second set of issues underlying Labour's decline was a complementary shift in the development of capitalism, which became increasingly global in character. Even in the 1970s, as noted previously, conditionalities imposed by the International Monetary Fund (IMF), constrained expenditures by the Labour government. Globalisation amplified the powers of transnational corporations and international economic institutions. To maintain international financial credibility, governments must follow international rules which, mediated through international organisations such as the IMF and the World Trade Organization (WTO), limit state policies and champion private enterprise. Very few states captured by social democratic governments are able successfully to withstand their pressures. As I show in later chapters, globalisation has reduced the powers of the nation state.

Third, social democracy was politically challenged as a means to achieve an alternative to capitalism. The British Labour Party had demonstrated that there could be an alternative to competitive liberalism in the form of a welfare-state industrial society. The electorate has had a choice. The parliamentary road depends on popular electoral support. In the case of the British Labour Party, which is typical of social democratic parties, less than half of the electorate, even at the height of its success, voted for the Party. Thus, to maintain electoral support in the context of hostile mass media, the Party can only adopt policies which have wide political endorsement – or it will lose power through the ballot box. The dilemma is that political strategy becomes predicated on 'winning elections'. The Party leadership is constrained by reforms of 'what the public will accept' (which often reflects what the corporate mass media will accept) rather than the promotion of socialism. A consequence is that such reforms become assimilated into the existing system and, unintentionally perhaps, the Party morphs into a

---

[20] This idea is developed in L. Boltanski and E. Chiapello, *The New Spirit of Capitalism*. London: Verso, 2007.

democratic Party of reform. Such a strategy gives rise to the dilemma that public support is divided; there is strong opposition to socialist parties from private financial, industrial and agricultural interests. And any malfunction of socialist measures is amplified by the hostile media. Consequently, there follows a loss of parliamentary power. The Party is labelled as 'unelectable'.

These scenarios pose questions of whether a 'socialist alternative' to capitalism is any longer realistic, of whether socialism can overcome the challenges presented by contemporary industrial civilisation, and of whether a socialist alternative can be achieved through electoral reforms. I intend to answer these questions in the final chapter. In the next two chapters I discuss how and why Western European social democracy and Eastern European socialist parties rejected the socialist alternative that had been offered and, in the guise of renewing socialism, moved towards a neoliberal economic and moral order.

7

The Conversion of Social Democracy to the 'Third Way'

In Chapters 5 and 6, I showed that in the final quarter of the twentieth century, the decline in support for social democracy in Western Europe, as well as scepticism about the performance of socialism in Eastern Europe, led many commentators to question whether the statist, collectivist, classed-based alternative to capitalism proposed by left-wing parties was any longer practical or desirable. While the conditions in the state socialist societies were very different from those in Western Europe, the outcomes had many similarities. I contend that comparable underlying processes were at work which undermined the socialist perspective. Social democracy, which promised a welfare-related form of capitalism, and state socialism, which succeeded in forming a coherent economic alternative, were renounced by many of their former supporters and both social formations disintegrated and were replaced, to different degrees, by neoliberal regimes. While the underlying social determinants were analogous, the rise of neoliberalism in Western and Eastern Europe occurred in ways that could not have been more different. In this chapter, I consider theorising on the left, which sought a 'third way' between capitalism and socialism, placed in a democratic shell. In the next chapter, I turn to parallel developments that occurred under state socialism, in this case the changes were more substantive and involved regime change.

Against the background of electoral defeat and occupational realignment, Labour leaders and supporters considered that significant changes were required to make the Party successful. Such critics called for a profound shift in traditional social democratic ideology as described in Chapter 4. Discussion took place in two domains: in academia and the media where the fundamental causes and remedies were identified, and in the Party which focused on the policies and images which would further victory at the ballot box. In the former I outline a turn to a left neoliberalism, which became the foundation for a significant change in the kind of alternative that social democracy would present in Britain. These discussions framed the policies that would be adopted by reformers in the Labour Party, which was relaunched under Tony Blair under the banner of 'New Labour'. Unlike its Conservative advocates, neoliberalism was never proposed as a legitimating ideology – quite the contrary. A discourse in terms of welfare and individual rights continued and appealed to leftist (rather than socialist) democratic progressive movements. 'Left-wing' politics had the character of a 'progressive' movement predicated on promoting diversity, democracy and human rights. Indeed, the popular left-wing media referred positively to its readers as 'progressives' rather than socialists. In place of the dualism between capitalism and socialism, the political antithesis was now defined as being between 'democracy' and 'authoritarianism'. Left neoliberal thinking appeared in New Labour disguised as the 'third way'.

Identity, diversity and class

Shifts in social democratic policy were part of the changing ideological framework of leftist and critical ideology. It is pertinent here to make a distinction between 'left wing' and 'socialism'. The 'left' is a general term that can be applied to theories or discourses in opposition to the status quo and is usually associated with demands for justice, more equality, more democracy and less hierarchy. It is applied as an identifier not only to socialists but also to the peace and anti-globalisation movements and includes identification with feminism, sexual politics, anti-colonialism and anti-racism. Some types of populism also share the 'leftist' values mentioned previously, but most are labelled as 'right wing' due to their association with traditional often nationalist values and support for hierarchical processes. As we noted in Chapter 4, socialism is a component of 'the left' specifically linked to the working class (in the sense of all people who work) and public ownership to achieve an equal and classless society. Socialists do not necessarily share the other views associated with 'leftist thinking' which, in the twenty-first century, has moved away from traditional socialist ideals and mostly ignores economic exploitation.

One of the earliest attempts to bring social democratic political thinking into line with the changes in social and economic structure (see Chapter 9) was provided by C.A.R. Crosland in his book *The Future of Socialism*.[1] As early as the 1950s, he considered that capitalism had changed and social democracy had already achieved many of its primary goals. He argued that economic growth and development had led to the all-round improvement of the condition of the working class which had been transformed from a mass of unskilled manual workers in manufacturing to a socially differentiated

---

[1]   Crosland, *The Future of Socialism*.

non-manual service sector. In the economy, the enterprise was no longer dependent on the capitalist entrepreneur who, consequent on the separation of ownership from control, had been superseded by financial, executive and managerial employees. These features of modern capitalism, while preserving the market and private ownership, secured stability and, crucially, rising incomes for working people. For Crosland, the first stage of socialism had already arrived. Social action had to address new problems: 'the freedom of personal and leisure life, and social responsibility for cultural values'.[2] He set the scene by moving the political agenda away from class and economic issues to the social: to divorce laws, the licensing of alcohol, abortion, sexual orientation, censorship and gender rights.[3] He emphasised the need to promote equality of opportunity.[4] It was incumbent on the Labour Party to adapt, to refocus and to complete the good society.

The conclusion reached by this kind of reasoning was that a new post-capitalist, post-socialist society is qualitatively different from traditional capitalism[5] and socialism was no longer its antithesis. These views were expanded and developed by a new cohort of leftist rather than socialist writers in the 1980s who set the ideological agenda for New Labour, for what they considered to be a 'Third Way'. They contended that the high level of technological division of labour and new forms of production required greater levels of cooperation and interdependence between management, technical and manual staff. The traditional forms of confrontation between management and unions were now self-defeating. Deindustrialisation and a geographical shift of manufacturing and extractive industries to rising Third World powers were also taking place.

Much of this thinking was led by sociologists who turned from an analysis of class to culture. In so doing, an ideological shift relegated class to a concept similar in standing to gender, caste, race and nationality, and usually of less social relevance than these divisions. This approach moves substantially away from a Marxist paradigm. Writers reconstitute class with an emphasis on its relational and symbolic aspects.[6] Mike Savage, for example,[7] identifies

---

[2] Crosland, *The Future of Socialism*, p 354.

[3] Crosland, *The Future of Socialism*, p 355.

[4] Crosland, *The Future of Socialism*. See Chapter VIII, Is equal opportunity enough? Here he emulates the 'egalitarian ideology of contemporary America', p 151.

[5] Scott Lasch and John Urry, *The End of Organized Capitalism*. Madison: University of Wisconsin Press, 1988.

[6] See, for example, F. Devine, M. Savage, J. Scott and R. Crompton (Eds), *Rethinking Class: Culture, Identity and Lifestyle*. Basingstoke: Palgrave, 2005. For Russia a similar position is taken by authors in *Rethinking Class in Russia*. Edited by Suvi Salmenniemi. Farnham, Surrey: Ashgate, 2012.

[7] M. Savage, *Class Analysis and Social Transformation*. Oxford: Oxford University Press, 2000.

class in terms of people's self-worth and social distinctions. Consequently, attention has shifted to consider 'non-economic capitals' (cultural, social, symbolic) and dwell on how people behave – how they dress, how they live and form identities, and how they cope with life in general.[8] This approach diminishes the economic relevance of class. Tony Giddens opined that 'class … is no longer experienced as class … and becomes individualised and expressed through the individual's "biography"'. 'Lifestyle and taste' are markers of social differentiation. The 'generational transmission belt' of class, he contended, has been broken.[9]

Responsibility for well-being moves from state welfare to the individual. The welfare state was designed 'to cope more with external than with manufactured risk':

> Welfare state bureaucracies, like bureaucracies everywhere, have tended to become inflexible and impersonal; and welfare dependency is probably in some part a real phenomenon, not just an invention of neoliberalism. Finally, the welfare state was consolidated in the post-war period at a point where chronically high levels of unemployment seemed unlikely to return.[10]

> Positive welfare, by contrast, places much greater emphasis on the mobilising of life-political measures, aimed once more at connecting autonomy with personal and collective responsibilities.[11]

Here we have the neoliberal orientation: only taking individual responsibility will 'give people what they deserve'. The focus in this liberal form of society shifted to changing lifestyles and life values, environmental protection, and 'reducing toxicities'. Ecological issues and movements also arrived at the centre of politics[12] (see Chapter 13). This approach effectively removed the welfare state component of Labour Party policy.

This intellectual tendency spawned a leftist neoliberalism. In an influential book published in 1989, *New Times*, Stuart Hall remarked that 'Another major requirement for trying to think through the complexities and ambiguities of new times is simply to open our minds to the deeply *cultural* character of the revolution of our times … The material world of

---

[8]　See Beverley Skeggs, *Class, Self, Culture*. London: Routledge, 2004.

[9]　Anthony Giddens, *Beyond Left and Right: The Future of Politics*. Cambridge: Polity, 1994, pp 143–4.

[10]　Giddens, *Beyond Left and Right*, p 10.

[11]　Giddens, *Beyond Left and Right*, p 18.

[12]　Giddens, *Beyond Left and Right*, pp 196–7.

commodities and technologies is profoundly cultural'.[13] The Left, he argued, had to be committed to 'diversity and difference'; it had to confront a 'politics of the family, of health, of food, of sexuality, of the body'.[14] Sociology was captured by cultural studies.

These ideological developments rode on the tide moving towards a Leftist social orientation and away from socialist politics – to consider forms of subordination, subservience and inequality, epitomised by the movements of feminism, sexual politics, and issues of racial, national and ethnic identification, as well as environmental concerns. The stress was on the promotion of social diversity, social mobility and individual rights. In addition to structural and global changes there also occurred a revision in sociological interpretation and understanding. Sociology became cultural in orientation predicated on how people perceive their social identity and relationships.

The criticism levelled against existing claims to socialism (Soviet type socialism and Labourist social democracy) was that they were hierarchical and lacked consideration of diversity and choice. Socialist politics, it was contended, was bureaucratised, rigid and regimented: the state provided uniform council houses and a uniform school system – citizens had to take what they were given. State socialism for such thinkers was symbolised by Chinese citizens all dressed in grey tunics – Sun Yat Sen's uniform, though there were other colours (black, blue – often worn by students, green – worn by the military) giving a little disciplined diversity.

State control was inimical to individual rights. What was advocated instead was a leftist 'democratic individualism' that echoed neoliberal 'consumer individualism' – though consumers as citizens were part of the left neoliberal rhetoric. For Charles Leadbeater, the Left's stress should be on 'individuality, diversity and plurality in lifestyles.'[15] 'Reflexivity' became the catchword of liberal sociologists – the self shapes its own values and norms, rather than taking them from society. The sociology of social wholes found in Comte and Durkheim was discarded. In its place reliance was put on various forms of autonomous association as well as a revival of markets. 'The market [and] competition can be useful economic tools to deliver consumer choice' and the Left will only 'succeed if it starts asserting an alternative individualism'.[16] As a critical reader in a socialist paper complained: 'you call abortion

[13] Stuart Hall and Martin Jacques, *New Times*. London: Lawrence and Wishart, 1989; Stuart Hall, The Meaning of the New Times, in *New Times*, pp 116–36, citation p 128. Italics in original.

[14] Hall, *The Meaning of the New Times*, p 130.

[15] C. Leadbeater, Power to the Person, in *New Times*, eds S. Hall and M. Jacques. London: Lawrence and Wishart, 1989, pp 191–204. Quotation, p 145.

[16] Leadbeater, Power to the Person, p 149.

pro-choice, while failing to look at what lies behind that choice ... It is as if disabled people are unsatisfactory and so it is all right to snuff out a life. It's just a choice, just like that of buying a box of cornflakes.'[17]

This shift defined a left neoliberalism. Social class is ignored as an organising principle (it is not mentioned to a significant degree in any chapter in the collection by Hall and Jacques and does not even occur in the index of *New Times*). In their discussion of citizenship, for example, Stuart Hall's and David Held's discourse is in terms of the 'diversity of arenas in which citizenship is claimed and contested'.[18] Such ideological developments contributed to the formation of social and political identities. Ironically perhaps, whereas the neoliberalism of Margaret Thatcher tightened the links between capital, the market and politics, the 'new left' had a class identity crisis. Though concurrently claiming to be opposed to neoliberalism and particularly to its Thatcherite variant, the new left developed its own forms of liberalism. Class was decoupled from socialist politics and was replaced with a leftist individualism and identity politics.

Identity politics

'Identity' politics is a form of 'essentialism'. It means that members of a group with certain characteristics (age, ethnicity, gender, nationality) possess an 'essence' that gives them a common distinctiveness worthy of recognition. It is a politics of identification rather than a movement for social change.[19] Such groups may be constituted by those who dominate (white Anglo-Saxon men) or are subjugated (people who are gay, persons of colour, females). Left-wing thinkers appeal to subaltern groups to assert a positive image of their identity. Issues and interests are expressed through concerns about race, ethnicity, gender, diversity, animal rights, and green issues. The idea of 'intersectionality' defines groups that experience multiple forms of discrimination that combine ('intersect') to form a subject, or social cluster. These social clusters share some of the characteristics of classes (a self-consciousness and oppression by other dominant clusters). Gender and ethnic groups, for example, reproduce themselves demographically; they have an awareness of their often unequal life chances compared to other groups and this social identity provides a basis for political action.

---

[17] *Morning Star* (London), 14 September 2021.

[18] Stuart Hall and D. Held, Citizens and citizenship, in Hall and Jacques, *New Times*, pp 173–88, citation p 176. I exclude here the two chapters by Mike Rustin and Paul Hurst written as critical responses to the *New Times* and *Marxism Today* outlook.

[19] See N. Fraser, From redistribution to recognition? Dilemmas of justice in a post-socialist age. *New Left Review*, 212 (1995), pp 68–93.

But there are important differences in the objectives of the groups committed to identity politics, compared to class interests. They seek a more positive evaluation – recognition of their specific identity coupled to removal of actual and perceived discrimination and subjugation. Identity politics mobilises around the configuration and recognition of the identity of a group, rather than to what the group shares with others belonging to a wider community. Hence support for 'unemployed women' is not a form of identity politics if it is directed at the unemployment liabilities of the group, but it is identity politics if it politicises only the sex of the unemployed. Feminism is an identity in the sense that it includes 'any ideology, activity or policy whose goal is to remove discrimination against women and to break down the male domination of society'.[20]

Such movements call for the affirmation of identity and respect for the dignity of the identity: public carnivals celebrate gay identity; public buildings and professional football matches sponsor gay pride by displaying the rainbow flag, or 'taking the knee'. Intersectionality (white middle-class males, black unemployed lesbians) are defined by what they have in common as a social in-group; there is no linkage with a wider class consciousness (white working class males exclude black working class males from their in-group). 'Black lives matter' creates cohesion among black people but divides by class – white and brown lives appear excluded and 'don't matter' – hence creating divisions between people with different skin colour and sometimes a hostile environment between them. All these actions can be accommodated within a framework of liberal capitalism and are endorsed by political, economic and cultural elites. The argument here is not intended to disparage these movements but to place them as movements within a democratic civil society framework.

What these social groups and movements do not have, and which is essential for a socialist identity, is a shared and common economic position that determines life chances and social consciousness. Social class is an objective feature that defines the economic constitution of capitalist society. The elimination of social 'discrimination' of identity groups does not eradicate exploitation – the extraction of profit (surplus value, defined further in Chapter 15). The socialist objective is not only to do away with conditions of discrimination (which can be cultural in form) but to abolish exploitation that is economic in character. While I recognise that there are many forms of discrimination and oppression (ethnic, gender, colonial and bureaucratic), to advocate a 'divorce' of Marxism from historical materialism,[21] is to discard the role of economic exploitation – the driving force of capitalism. I am not dismissing the pursuit of identity struggles as meaningless, they identify

---

[20]   J. Lovenduski and V. Randall, *Contemporary Feminist Politics*. Oxford: OUP. 1993, p 134.
[21]   Gibson-Graham, *The End of Capitalism*, p 264.

important inequalities, but I contend that they diminish, even occlude, issues of class which are more comprehensive in character and have much greater political relevance.

From ruling classes to pluralistic elites

'Progressive' left-wing ideology, formulated in academia and articulated by mainstream print and television journalists, has abandoned a ruling class approach and considered political elites (rather than ruling classes) to be arbiters of politics. Elites come to agreements on 'fundamentals' – on how social and political change should take place. They define the issues and the beneficiaries in terms of identity politics. Political management by elites ensures the absence of a critical class ideology, to ensure the construction of a consensus politics. Consequently, the convergence of left- and right-wing neoliberalism entailed that competing electoral political parties shared the same values. The well-known statement of Margaret Thatcher – 'there is no alternative' – accurately describes what these developments promised. Elections revolved around personalities, 'celebrity politics', rather than competing policies. It is not surprising that protest movements take a 'populist' form – such as the French Front National and later UKIP – and have attracted significant numbers of working class supporters. In common with progressive left-wing ideology, right-wing parties, such as the British Conservative Party, claim credit for legalising homosexuality, gay marriage and abortion. The socialist idea of a movement based on the working class leading to a different mode of production and human emancipation from capital – the abolition of class itself – is superseded by a Leftist conception of justice, democracy, equality and individual rights promoted by informal groups and non-governmental organisations.

The effects of neoliberal economic policies, which lead to greater competition on the labour market – the out-sourcing of jobs and an increase in the number of low-paid insecure jobs – remain. Employees in such jobs include poor men and poor women whether or not are they are gay, black, white or feminist. The identity argument is that some core characteristic (ethnicity, nationality, gender) binds its holders together socially and politically. But this is erroneous as these groups exhibit a wide range of social, economic and political attributes. They are separated by occupational and educational inequalities – particularly inequalities caused by class position. [22]

---

[22] In the summer of 2019, only four clubs in the Premier League paid the living wage as their minimum wage to their non-playing employees (£8.21 per hour in April 2019). A black cleaning worker at Manchester United would earn around £390 per week and one black player (Paul Pogba) earned £170,000 per week. His net worth is estimated at £106 million.

The fallacy in much left thinking lies in muddling different forms of identity and diversity involving discrimination with the more fundamental relational process of economic exploitation and political power derived from corporate ownership and control. It does not really matter for the operation of a capitalist system whether it is managed by men or by women, by white Americans or African Americans. What matters is that management is motivated to ensure the constant accumulation of capital and maximum profits. Capitalist systems therefore adapt to cultural practices – sometimes (as in colonial regimes) excluding subordinate groups (racial or gender) from elite positions, but in other more enlightened times, by promoting an open recruitment policy. Oppression of homosexuals, for example, is a form of cultural discrimination and oppression that requires a change of beliefs – a respect for social difference. Diversity policies call for the abolition of discrimination against certain minorities, ('it doesn't matter if you are gay or a woman').

The point I am making here is that identity politics is not a challenge either to capitalism or to its neoliberal form. Governing elites and ruling classes are no less elites and classes if they have a diversified social composition. The greater equality of opportunity given to people to escape from their underprivileged group does not concurrently decrease inequality between privileged and underprivileged groups. Minority groups are not socially homogeneous, and many of the advances secured by diversity promotion give advantages to the middle class members of these groups who have a stronger social identity with middle class people (white middle-class men with black middle-class women) than they do with working-class people within the group (black middle-class men with black working class men). Take another example, more middle-class black women getting middle-class jobs is good in itself but it does not help women in working-class jobs who remain confined to low-paid insecure work. Measures prioritising women may diminish the chances of working class men from securing middle-class jobs that are secured by middle-class women. Another example, the effects of austerity policies may negatively affect a higher proportion of black men from working-class backgrounds, but the total number of white men, even if they are a lower proportion from working-class backgrounds, may be considerably larger. Hence prioritising black identity divides the working class.

Under capitalism, class is a mobilising principle and provides a structure of identification at a higher level than that given by the essentialism of identity politics. Social class shapes the economic and social character of race and gender. This is not to deny the significance of other forms of oppression, domination and subordination. And I recognise that some forms of oppression and inequality (patriarchy, for example) are independent of class and capitalism. There is a strong case for supporting movements opposing various forms of discrimination. Successful socialist policies may undermine capitalism but should not be expected to put right all forms of inequality, political oppression and social domination.[23] The most one can hope of socialism is that in abolishing class exploitation it can facilitate conditions in which other forms of unjustified domination can also be remedied.

Social democracy moves towards neoliberalism

Following Labour's electoral defeat in 1992, the move to the Right in the Labour Party gathered momentum and cumulated in 1994 in the election of Tony Blair. It was claimed that traditional left-wing policies had made Labour 'unelectable'. (An assertion later to be made against Jeremy Corbyn.) Blair, assisted by Gordon Brown, adopted a platform of reform known as New Labour. The discourse surrounding the introduction of New Labour was one created in response to conservative neoliberalism and the failure of the traditional Labour Party to attain power. New Labour initially defined its policy as a 'third way' or, as many of its advocates labelled it, the 'radical centre'.

Tony Blair, a charismatic and assertive leader, transformed the Labour Party into what became a new political party – New Labour. However, the leadership, while replacing traditional ideology. utilised the Labour Party machinery and respected its traditions. Blair also accepted many of the assumptions and policies of the Thatcher government: 'Some things the Conservatives got right',[24] he recalls in his memoirs. When in government he retained key aspects of Thatcher's policy: privatisation, deregulation and a prominent role for the City of London (Britain's financial centre), which Labour recognised as a major source of wealth creation. Like the Conservatives, Blair sought to 'safeguard the basic principles of the National Health Service'. However, he introduced the market into public health and social services and allowed many state activities to be franchised to private businesses.

The cornerstone of Old Labour's socialist principles was commitment to public ownership. Before New Labour, Clause IV of the Party's constitution proclaimed the goal of 'the common ownership of the means of production, distribution and exchange, and the best obtainable system of popular administration and control of each industry and service'. Tony Blair recalls: 'After the 1992 defeat, and without discussion with anyone ... I formed a clear view that if ever I was leader, the constitution should be rewritten and the old commitments to nationalisation and state control would

---

[23] H.I. Hartmann, and B. Reskin, *Women's Work, Men's Work, Sex Segregation on the Job.* Washington, DC: National Academy Press, 1986.

[24] Tony Blair, *A Journey.* London: Hutchinson, 2010, pp 86–7.

be dumped.'[25] For Blair, the idea of public ownership was an anachronism – something that had prevailed in early twentieth century political thought but which 'had become hopelessly unreal, even surreal, in the late-twentieth-century world.'[26] Clause IV was replaced by a 'commitment to enterprise alongside the commitment to justice'. The role of the trade unions in the Party was also weakened. Changes in Labour Party procedures gave the leader of the Parliamentary Party effective control of policy making.[27]

In 1994, the Labour Party was re-launched. As Tony Blair has described it: 'We kept at the beginning the phrase "democratic socialism"'. What followed was a statement that ignored any reference to the state as the principal economic actor:

'The Labour Party is a democratic socialist party. It believes that by the strength of our common endeavour, we achieve more than we achieve alone so as to create for each of us the means to realize our true potential and for all of us a community in which power, wealth and opportunity are in the hands of the many not the few, where the rights we enjoy reflect the duties we owe and where we live together, freely, in a spirit of solidarity, tolerance and respect.'[28]

Labour adopted the image of, and was increasingly marketed as, an American-type of Democratic Party conjoined with a presidential type of political leadership (in the person of Tony Blair). It adopted the ideological framework of identity politics described previously. New Labour converged to the neoliberal programme of Margaret Thatcher in five major ways: marketisation, privatisation, financialisation, deregulation and an interventionalist foreign policy.

The significant departure of New Labour from traditional Labour Party politics can be gauged from the Party's 1997 Manifesto, the introduction to which was signed by the Party leader, Tony Blair. Rather like the traditional Conservatism of Harold Macmillan, it envisaged 'a Britain that is one nation [with] shared values and purpose, where merit comes before privilege, [which is] run for the many not the few, [and is] strong and sure of itself at home and abroad'.[29] 'We are a national Party, supported today by people from all

---

[25] Blair, *A Journey*, p 75.
[26] Blair, *A Journey*, p 76.
[27] For a detailed account see Panitch and Leys, *Searching for Socialism*, Chapter 6.
[28] Labour Party statement cited by Tony Blair, *A Journey*, pp 86–7.
[29] Labour Party 1997 Election Manifesto, New Labour Because Britain Deserves Better. Available at http://www.labour.org.uk/. The slogan 'for the many not the few' was originally made by Iain Macleod at the Conservative Party Conference on 9 October 1969.

walks of life, from the successful businessman or woman to the pensioner on a council estate.'

Blair sums up New Labour's policy as:

> no return to the old union laws; no renationalisation of the privatised utilities; no raising of the top rate of tax; no unilateralism [nuclear disarmament]; no abolition of grammar schools ... [but] investment and reform in public services; pro-Europe and pro-US; opportunity and responsibility together in welfare ... even-handedness between business and labour (employees might have additional individual rights, but not collective ones).[30]

This self-declared 'Third Way' formed a liberal, rather than socialist, mould for the Labour Party. Its values were economic growth and wealth creation, entrepreneurship and social justice. These were universal values, which could and should be applied on a world scale. As Giddens puts it:

> One could say that the two old political philosophies – the old left and Thatcherism – were 'half theories'. Old Labour was strong on social justice but never successful in fostering a dynamic economy. Thatcherism was strong on competitiveness but took no account of social justice. The Third Way seeks to reconcile these two, recognizing the difficult trade-offs that have to be confronted ... The new social democracy seeks to preserve the basic values of the left – a belief in an inclusive society, a commitment to combating inequality and protecting the vulnerable – but it holds that many traditional perspectives have become counter-productive.[31]

Tony Giddens here combines social democratic ideas about social justice with an explicit acceptance of many of Margaret Thatcher's views on competitive markets. New Labour conceived an alternative neoliberalism. It became the acceptable face of Thatcherism. For example, when asked by Allyson Pollock what the rationale was behind the use of private finance for public investment, given that the costs were higher and the risks were borne by the public sector, Gordon Brown is reported to have said that: 'the public sector is bad at management and only the private sector is efficient and can manage services well'.[32] As Pollock concludes, 'by 2003 the business paradigm was

---

[30] Blair, *A Journey*, 2010, p 94.

[31] Tony Giddens, There is no alternative: The Third Way is the only way forward. *Independent* (Newspaper, London), 8 January 2002.

[32] Allyson Pollock, *NHS Plc: The Privatisation of Our Health Care*. London: Verso 2004, p 3.

the only model that the Treasury and senior Department of Health officials could relate to'. The EU and the USA made the case with the World Trade Organization to open up public services to private provision by companies based anywhere in the world.[33]

Foreign affairs: the global perspective

Foreign policy under New Labour became interventionist. Opposition to nuclear weapons was dropped and membership of European associations (such as the EU) was reaffirmed. Underlying these changes was a view that globalisation leads to the 'overlap' (in Giddens's terms) of domestic and foreign policy. 'Interventionalism becomes a necessary doctrine when national sovereignty has lost much of its meaning and where there are universal humanitarian concerns that override local interests. Transnational terrorism, itself a creature of globalisation, is a threat far greater than the more localised forms of terrorism prevalent in the past.'[34] Intervention abroad was legitimated as serving two objectives: national interest and humanitarian concern. It also widened the market and operated under neoliberal economic conditions and laws that were shaped by the hegemonic Western powers, under the leadership of the USA.

Politically, New Labour strengthened the American alliance. Blair stood 'shoulder to shoulder' with America in its war on terrorism. After the September 11 bombing of New York, he was 'determined' to fulfil his obligations to the USA.[35] In his speech to the US Congress in 2003 he endorsed values held in common with the US: 'Members of Congress, ours are not Western values, they are the universal values of the human spirit. And anywhere, anytime ordinary people are given the chance to choose, the choice is the same: freedom ...; democracy ...; the rule of law.'[36] The Labour leadership forged an American alliance with a commitment to foreign wars not only to protect but also to promote freedom as endorsed in the neoliberal perspective. Policy enhanced Blair's own status:

> I [Tony Blair] counted, ... [I] was a world and not just a national leader ... [O]ur alliance with the US gave Britain a huge position. Those who thought our closeness to America was a problem in the rest of the world could not have been further from the mark. On the contrary, it gave us immediate purchase.[37]

---

[33] Pollock, *NHS Plc*, p 60.
[34] A. Giddens, *New Statesman*, 17 May 2010.
[35] Blair, *A Journey*, p 412.
[36] Tony Blair's speech to the US Congress. Available at: theguardian.com, Friday 18 July 2003.
[37] Blair, *A Journey*, p 410.

The Blair administration sought a positive political role in the new world order. Its policies were interventionist. It is debatable whether the military interventions in Bosnia, Kosovo and Sierra Leone were successful or not. Certainly, involvements in Iraq and Afghanistan were serious miscalculations and liabilities. It quickly became evident that the invaded states have not moved, as Blair predicted, to 'prosperity, democracy and calm'. Though not faced with any direct threat, between 1991 and 2012 the British government spent over £100 billion on military and associated capabilities.[38] No political gain followed from Blair's interventions. According to Wars in Peace (the organ of a British military think tank) the war in Iraq helped the rise of al-Qaeda and led to 100,000 Iraqi deaths and at least 2 million refugees. Policies of 'democracy promotion' and foreign intervention were not a consequence of democratic decisions by the UK electorate and did not secure 'beacons of calm'. Quite the opposite. The Blair leadership manipulated the Labour government cabinet and coerced Labour Members of Parliament to support what are widely regarded, even by members of the political classes, as illegal wars.

An appraisal of New Labour

While New Labour projected itself as an alternative to the Thatcher government, the policies of the Blair/Brown governments followed, even strengthened, the major trends of Margaret Thatcher's policy. As Blair put it:

> I even decided to own up to supporting changes Margaret Thatcher had made. I knew the credibility of the whole New Labour project rested on accepting much of what she wanted to do in the 1980s was inevitable, a consequence not of ideology but of *social and economic change* ... [T]he basic fact: Britain needed the industrial and economic reforms of the Thatcher period.[39]

Evaluation of Labour's record in government depends on one's criteria and standpoint. Before we appraise New Labour's government from a critical position, I summarise the major attainments. On the positive side, aided by North Sea oil revenues, New Labour presided over ten years of economic growth. A national minimum wage was introduced. People were able to borrow more and were able to do so more easily. Public resources available to the educational system and National Health Service were increased. The levels of registered crime fell. Child poverty was reduced.

---

[38] *Wars in Peace: British Military Operations since 1991.* London: RUSI, 2014, p 11.
[39] Italics added, Blair, *A Journey*, p 99.

A freedom of information act was introduced. The UK signed the EU Social Chapter (which ensured certain minimum standards) and the European Convention on Human Rights. Civil partnership for same-sex marriages was legalised. Winter fuel payments and tax credits were introduced as was free museum entry. Foreign aid was increased. In 1999, the automatic right of hereditary peers to a seat in the House of Lords was abolished, though the participation of the peers continues (when elected by members of the upper House). Devolution of government to Scotland and Wales was achieved. The civil war in Northern Ireland was successfully ended. These were significant achievements.

Rather more controversially, the economy continued its movement away from manufacturing to services, and financial services became a major British sector of the economy. Economic policy was set in Margaret Thatcher's footprint and the shift from manufacturing to services continued. Gordon Brown, Blair's Chancellor of the Exchequer, pursued a policy of deregulation of financial services to the advantage of the City of London. At the London Guildhall in June 2005, he declared:

What I said when I made the Bank of England independent remains even more true today, I said that our new monetary and fiscal regime was founded on stability first, foremost and always, stability yesterday, today and tomorrow. And I mean not just stability by securing low inflation but stability in our industrial relations, stability through a stable and competitive tax regime, and stability through a predictable and *light touch regulatory environment* – a stability founded on our strength to make the right long term decisions, the same strength of national purpose we will demonstrate in protecting our security in this Parliament and the long-term – strong in defence in fighting terrorism, upholding NATO, supporting our armed forces at home and abroad, and retaining our independent nuclear deterrent [italics added].[40]

'Globalisation' and deregulation were key building blocks in the New Labour strategy. Foreign policy strengthened the American alliance and pursued an interventionist foreign policy.

Gordon Brown extolled the global financial system, which he considered to be beneficial.[41] The 'light touch' allowed the deregulated financial system

---

[40] Gordon Brown's Mansion House speech, 22 June 2006. Available at: http://www.theg uardian.com/business/2006/jun/22/politics.economicpolicy

[41] Gordon Brown, Speech to Mansion House, 20 June 2007. Available at: National Archive: http://webarchive.nationalarchives.gov.uk/+/http:/www.hm-treasury.gov.uk/2014.htm

to pursue unsustainable profits based on a deluge of unproductive financial operations. Not long after Brown's congratulatory speech, major British financial companies collapsed and subsequent financial rescue packages had to be paid for by British governments, which funded private losses at substantial public cost. The City contributed to the global economic crisis, which had roots in the British deregulated financial system. A new world order indeed was created. But not the one described by the Labour leadership. A world financial crisis, fuelled by the deregulated banking system, emerged and led to a significant decline in the world economy. Gordon Brown would be called on to use the financial resources of the state to maintain financial stability. To pay for this state financial subsidy, policies of financial austerity would be introduced in all major economies.

Deepening economic inequalities

Neoliberal policies had led not only to growth but also to unjustifiable inequalities. The de-regulation of commerce and trade brought in a massive increase in differentials. Freedom of movement of labour in the EU led to an inflow of cheap labour, which had a dampening effect on British wage levels. A decline in wages as a share of gross national product (GNP) affected all the neoliberalising countries of the industrial West (see Figure 7.1). In the UK, the share fell from 65 per cent to 58 per cent between 1960 and 2014, though under the Harold Wilson administration in 1975, it had risen to 70 per cent. The member states of the EU followed a similar trend with a large drop after the accession of the former communist countries. Even if GDP was growing, labour's share of it was falling.

It comes as no surprise that New Labour's policies increased levels of wage inequality. In Figure 7.2, data for the ratio of profits to wages are shown for various dates, coinciding with a new government, between 1950 and 2009. The annual growth of wages for each year is shown by the line joined by a shaded box (right-hand index). The vertical blocks show the ratio of profits to wages; by the end of the Wilson government the ratio of profits to wages had declined very considerably and was even lower than after the Second World War – this ratio also coincided with very high wage settlements, which made considerable inroads into profits. The upward sloping trend line shows the rising ratio of profits to wages (left-hand index). The Wilson period was one of low investment and productivity, though concurrently (as a consequence of trade union activity) workers were able to maintain wage rates and 'squeeze' profits. The decline in profits was also caused by other rising costs for business – particularly the severe rise in oil prices. The reversal coincided with the Thatcher administrations from 1979.

The Conservative administration first under Margaret Thatcher then John Major restored the ratio to favour profits. The gap actually increased

Figure 7.1: Wages as percentage share of GDP: UK, US, EU 15, EU 28, 1960–2014

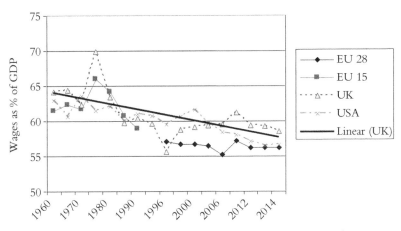

Note: Adjusted wage share: total economy, as percentage of GDP at current market prices (compensation per employee as percentage of GDP at market prices per person employed).

Source: AMECO database (ALCD0).

Figure 7.2: UK: trends of profits and wages, 1950–2009

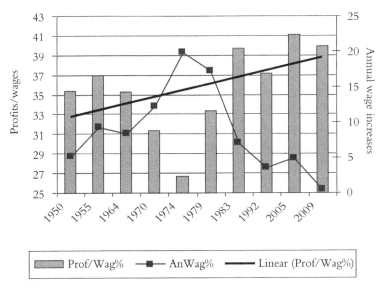

Note: Profits are surpluses for corporations.

Source: UK Office of National Statistics. Available at: http://www.ons.gov.uk/ons/datas ets-and-tables/data-selector.html?cdid=KH4M&dataset=pn2&table-id=D. Tables CGBZ and DTWM, annual growth of wages Table KH4M.

under New Labour with profits rising to over 40 per cent of wages in 2005. The Blair administration achieved the highest ratio of profits to wages in the post-Second World War period (41.1 per cent). From this perspective, Labour was far from being the Party of working people. The slight fall in profit to wage ratio and the very slight growth in wages in 2009 are clearly consequences of the global recession.

It should also be borne in mind that these data reflect prices, the state of the market and also refer only to corporations in the private sector. Nevertheless, they are a fairly robust index of the changes taking place – a significant shift of redistribution away from wage labour. Quite simply: Old Labour diminished profits whereas the Conservatives and New Labour boosted and preserved them. Differences between types of salary earnings have to be taken into account. Executive salaries increased at an exponential rate and the share of income received by the top 1 per cent of employees took a very high proportion of the increase in the wage fund, which we discuss later. Concurrently, lower paid employees had no or little increase in wage income. Brown had boasted to the City in his Mansion House speech of 2006 that the public sector pay settlement would be 'founded on our 2 per cent inflation target'. This was one part of his recipe for keeping down inflation, the other unstated consequence was to enhance profits. For New Labour, the market realised the rewards that many well paid people thought deserved – regardless of their real contribution to society and irrespective of how such rewards meet people's needs.

New Labour's income policy

Despite there being no rise in the disposable incomes of most employees, living standards increased during the Blair administration. Consumer spending rose due to a significant increase in credit (and consequently debt). Credit liberalisation had been introduced as a neoliberal policy under the Margaret Thatcher administration: between 1980 and 2008, UK banking sector assets (loans of domestic and foreign banks) had increased tenfold; and domestic credit increased fourfold.[42] The increase in debt has been documented by Stewart Lansley.[43] He points out that between 2000 and 2007, a period coinciding with the Blair/Brown administration, consumer spending rose by £55 billion more than income, and retail sales rose by 35 per cent. Between 1997 (the advent of the first Blair government) and 2003, the total annual of lending rose steadily from £14 billion to £36 billion,[44] then

---

[42] Data cited by A. Offer, The market turn, p 1060.
[43] Stewart Lansley, *Life in the Middle.* Touchstone Pamphlet no 6 London Trade Union Congress. Nd. Available at: www.touchstoneblog.org.uk
[44] Landsley, *Life in the Middle*, p 17.

fell back to around £27 billion in 2007. Deregulation allowed householders to secure loans against property to finance all kinds of consumer spending. The ratio of debt to disposable income rose from 98 per cent in 2000 to 154 per cent in 2007.[45] Small businesses were able to borrow more easily. However, they also suffered: personal bankruptcies rose from an annual average of 22,000 in the 1990s to 106,700 in 2007.[46]

Even if earned income was falling, as described previously, the reader might ask: does it matter if people were better off? It matters because the rise in living standards was based on increased lending. People were able to procure credit to facilitate the maintenance of living standards. Financialisation encouraged household debt.[47] Households borrowed on average 45 per cent of their income in 1945 which rose to 157 per cent in 2007.[48] These high levels of debt – on mortgage loans, credit cards and overdrafts – fuelled the economic crisis that occurred in 2007. They were facilitated by the 'light touch' of the financial services sector.

The fruits of economic growth were disproportionately distributed. During the Labour governments between 1964 and 1979, the Gini coefficient fell from 27 in 1964 to 23 in 1978 (the higher the number, the greater the inequality). From 1979, with the advent of the Thatcher administration, measurement of inequality followed an upward curve, which continued right through the administration of New Labour. For the UK, the Gini index of gross income distribution was 35 (average 2001–2005) and one of the highest in Europe (Austria was 27, France 31, Germany 33, but Italy 38 and Portugal 41). When taxation is considered, Britain's ranking did not change – it fell to 30, whereas for Austria it was 23, France 26, Germany 27, Italy 35 and Portugal 36.[49] By 2007/08, the Gini coefficient had reached an all-time high of 36. As the authors of the National Equality Panel conclude, 'the increasing inequality after 2004–05 meant that by 2007–08 it had reached its highest levels in the years covered since 1961. Moreover … comparison with measures based on tax records suggests that this is the highest level of income inequality since soon after the Second World War'.[50]

---

[45] Landsley, *Life in the Middle*, p 18.

[46] Landsley, *Life in the Middle*, p 19.

[47] On the significance of debt and credit see: Di Muzio and Robbins, *Debt as Power*.

[48] Figures cited by Stewart Lansley, *Unfair to Middling*. Touchstone pamphlets, 12 November 2009. Available at: http://touchstoneblog.org.uk/2009/11/unfair-to-middling-how-middle-income-britains-shrinking-wages-fuelled-the-crash-and-threaten-recovery/

[49] Data cited in *An Anatomy of Economic Inequality in the UK: Report of the National Equality Panel*. London: Centre for Analysis of Social Exclusion, London School of Economics, 2010., p 56.

[50] *An Anatomy of Economic Inequality in the UK*, p 39.

In 1990, the top 1 per cent of the population received 8 per cent of total income rising to 10 per cent in 2000.[51] The increasing polarisation of incomes during the Blair/Brown administration is illustrated by the fact that the income of people in the 99th percentile (the 1 per cent below the very richest) rose by over 70 per cent between 1996/7 and 2005/6, whereas the fifth percentile (the fifth from the bottom) rose 29 per cent.[52] Measuring the distribution of wealth over time is difficult as value is influenced by fluctuations of stock exchange prices. Evidence from HMRC (the British tax collector) shows that the Gini coefficient of wealth ownership increased considerably during the New Labour administrations: in 1995 it was 65, rising to 71 in 2000, though it fell back to 67 in 2003.[53]

Not all these changes were due to the Labour government. The transformation of the occupational structure also had important consequences for the income distribution of the population. An increase took place in the number of jobs in lower non-manual occupations (social care, security, hotel and catering) which are not unionised and often recruited from immigrant labour; these jobs are at the bottom of the income hierarchy. Managerial positions and professionals in finance and law as well as in the public sector have not only grown but have been subject to a (spurious) market evaluation of 'what they deserve' – very high incomes. The number of employees in middle income employment decreased by around 20 per cent during this period.[54] Many of these middle-income working class jobs were lost due to the outsourcing abroad of production and services and led to unemployment for many skilled employees. (We return to income and globalisation in Chapter 9.)

New Labour maintained some progressive taxation policies (minimum wage legislation, for example), which, to some extent, offset the inequality in income distribution noted previously. However, despite these measures, the tax system was still regressive. As Lansley points out, whereas income tax is progressive, other taxes (council tax and VAT) are regressive. The lowest income group, 10 per cent of tax payers, contributed 44 per cent of income to tax in 1996/7 and 46 per cent in 2006/7; whereas the top per centile paid 37 per cent in tax and 37.5 per cent respectively in the two dates. Taxation policy did not reverse the increasing overall levels of income inequality. The New Labour administration continued the free market policy of Thatcherism and had no significant impact on the distribution of income and wealth. Rather than a 'third way' between old Labour and Conservatism,

---

[51] *An Anatomy of Economic Inequality in the UK*, p 387.
[52] HMRC data cited by Lansley, *Life in the middle*, p 22.
[53] Data cited in *An Anatomy of Economic Inequality in the UK*, p 60.
[54] Lansley, *Life in the middle*, p 24.

the Blair/Brown administration delivered another form of neoliberalism, though disguised as a modernised version of social democracy. The defeat of the Blair–Brown Labour government was not a defeat of socialism but of neoliberalism.

At the root of these developments was a significant shift by Labour towards the philosophy of New Labour. Policies of collective ownership had been swept into the dustbin of history. Now the objective was the enlargement of consumer choice, and opening up the market to facilitate that choice. As the political elites in the three major parties were in agreement on all major aspects of policy, parliamentary democracy became increasingly distant from the electorate. Only the speed and timing remained the topics of debate. The traditional social democratic goal of reducing the inequality of outcomes (or situations) moved to creating conditions of equality of opportunity, to making the conditions more equal to become more unequal, and thus fulfilling a leftist neoliberal agenda.

New Labour had a positive 'diversity' agenda. At the centre of its social policy were concerns about civil liberties. It sought to equalise opportunities for women, for ethnic minorities, for the underprivileged and campaigned for the recognition of sexual diversity. It promoted 'health and safety' issues. These are views shared by the major political parties in their goal of building a 'one nation' Britain, David Cameron's 'big society'. What was ignored by New Labour were the effects of industrial restructuring: the weakening of the security which had been provided by full employment, the decline in well-paying jobs for the manual working class, the significant growth in long-term unemployment in the old industrial areas and the rise of a new class of non-manual lowly paid workers with insecure and often part-time jobs. The acceptance, by all the major political parties, of freedom of movement (within Europe) given by membership of the EU, led to high levels of immigration and to further depression of the labour market which affected many in traditional Labour voting areas. The traditional working class base of the Party gradually realised that Labour no longer defended their interests, and abstained from voting. Rather than constituting an alternative to neoliberal capitalism, New Labour created an alternative form of neoliberalism, which failed.

The fall of New Labour

New Labour's domestic and foreign policies disillusioned its supporters. Electoral defeat followed. Tony Blair resigned as prime minister on 27 June 2007, making way for Gordon Brown, and he consequently also resigned his Parliamentary seat. Blair's fall was principally caused by his role in the invasion of Iraq. However, other factors contributed to the unpopularity of the government and to the decline of the Labour Party. The involvement of Gordon Brown and Ed Balls in the de-regulation of the City – and the consequent bankruptcy of leading financial companies – also cast doubt on their economic policies. New Labour undermined the idea of public enterprise and outsourced public services to the private sector. The Private Finance Initiative, which involved contracting out building and maintenance of public works to private firms, which are then leased back to the government, proved to be costly. Such schemes led to enormous capital and interest payments by the government with no risks to the companies, leading to claims that they involved the privatisation of profits and the socialisation of risks. Such policies, which followed Margaret Thatcher's neoliberal agenda, have led many critics to declare that New Labour settled for 'global capitalism, inequality, authoritarianism and deception'.[55] A harsh but justified summary.

Against this background, Labour's electoral support (as well as Party membership) had been falling and are recorded in Table 7.1. Votes cast for New Labour severely declined: in 1997 they were 43.2 per cent; in 2001, 40.7 per cent; in 2005, 35.3 per cent; and in 2010 they fell to 29 per cent. Seats won fell from 356 in 2005 to 258 in 2010 when Labour received votes equal to only 18.9 per cent of the electorate (not shown in Table 7.1) and suffered a resounding electoral defeat.

An achievement of Margaret Thatcher, she boasted, had been to persuade the leaders of the Labour Party that there could be 'no alternative' to free market economics and politics. Under Tony Blair, the British Labour Party had turned full circle. Its leadership became modelled on the American presidency. Its conference an endorsement of its leader. It had become for many an acceptable form of Thatcherism. The Labour Party's popular base had eroded, its membership decimated, and its internal processes emasculated by the Party leader. The election of 2010 ended New Labour. Social democracy as a New Labour project presented neither an alternative to capitalism nor an alternative form of capitalism. Even one of its ideological architects (*The New Statesman*) conceded that 'New Labour as such is dead and it is time to abandon the term'.[56]

The revival of socialism in a democratic framework?

As we note on Table 7.1, following the collapse of the Blair–Brown government, under Jeremy Corbyn's leadership, the 2017 election reversed the decline in Labour's electoral fortunes. His share of the vote rose to 40 per cent, even with the loss of Scottish Labour votes, which had switched

---

[55] Anthony Barnett, *New Statesman* (London), 22 March 2010.

[56] Leader, *New Statesman*, 17 May 2010.

Table 7.1: UK Parliamentary elections, 1997–2019

	Prime minister	Blair	Blair	Blair	Cameron Clegg	Cameron	May	Johnson
	Year of election	1997	2001	2005	2010	2015	2017	2019
Conservatives	%	30.6	31.7	32.3	36.1	36.9	42.4	43.6
	Seats	165	166	197	307	331	318	365
Labour	%	43.2	40.7	35.2	29.0	30.4	40.0	32.1
	Seats	419	413	356	258	232	262	203
Liberal Democrats	%	16.7	18.3	22.0	23.0	7.9	7.4	11.5
	Seats	46	52	62	57	8	12	11
SNP	%	2.0	1.8	1.5	1.7	4.7	3.0	3.9
	Seats	6	5	6	6	56	35	48
UKIP	%	0.3	1.5	2.2	3.1	12.6	1.8	
	Seats	–	–	–	–	1	–	
Total	Seats	659	659	645	650	650	650	650
Turnout	%	71.4	59.4	61.4	65.1	66.1	68.7	67.3

Key: % = percentage of votes cast. SNP = Scottish National Party. UKIP = United Kingdom Independence Party.

Source: http://www.parties-and-elections.eu. See data under UK. Derived from http://www.bbc.com.

from the Labour Party to the Scottish Nationalist Party after 2005. Corbyn had successfully fought an election based on traditional Labour's policies. Corbyn's views were much more radical than the Party's official policy. His statements and political actions over a long parliamentary period define him as a traditional 'old Labour' socialist, as outlined in Chapter 4.[57] Corbynista policy promised a qualitative shift away from the economic and political consensus of the Tony Blair and Teresa May administrations. He promised a significant move away from 'austerity politics', a more progressive tax policy, the Bank of England would print money ('people's quantitative easing') to invest in a high-tech economy; nationalisation of key utilities, including railways and energy companies, were promised; collective bargaining would be strengthened; the welfare state would be enhanced with further investment and the abolition of the private finance initiative; in education, higher

---

[57] Alex Nunns, *The Candidate: Jeremy Corbyn's Improbable Path to Power*. London: OR Books, 2018; Robin Blackburn, The Corbyn project: Public capital and Labour's new deal. *New Left Review*, May–June 2018.

education tuition fees would be abolished. Corbyn is a long-time critic of the monarchy, but, apart from reforming some of its rituals (the opening of Parliament by the monarch, for example), it would continue; in foreign affairs, he had consistently campaigned against NATO and its enlargement and Britain's nuclear deterrent, policy here would be more cautious in supporting British intervention abroad, though the UK would remain in NATO; he had tenaciously opposed Britain's membership of the EU but, when leader, proposed remaining in the single market after the UK voted to leave; he has strongly supported environmentalist policies.

Overall, Corbynism was a moderate policy of state involvement and high taxation, predicated on democratic ownership and accountability. There was no likelihood of large-scale nationalisation or of exit from NATO. Nevertheless, policy provided a challenge to liberal capitalism and electoral success indicated that a more socialist orientation was not an electoral 'suicide pact'. Corbyn's success gave hope for an 'alternative' social democratic party. He represented a popular socialist platform but the incompatibility of his leadership with the Blairite composition of the Parliamentary Labour Party led to confused and contradictory policies, particularly the demand for a second referendum on exit from the EU. Corbyn, moreover, was confronted with a massive hostile press campaign as well as immense criticism from within the Parliamentary Labour Party (composed of Labour's MPs).[58] Corbyn was vilified by his own Members of Parliament. All this weakened Corbyn's electoral chances and defeat followed in the election of 2019; Labour attracted only 32.1 per cent of the votes, Corbyn resigned as leader of the Parliamentary Labour Party. Subsequently, under the leadership of Keir Starmer, he was excluded from the Parliamentary Labour Party, and completely marginalised by the Labour leadership, which turned to revise the policy position of New Labour to regain the middle ground.

Electoral defeats, and the exclusion of the Corbinista faction from the Labour's parliamentary leadership, raise the question of whether capitalism has changed to such an extent that social democratic and socialist goals are undesirable. The short answer is that, from the ascendancy of Tony Blair, the Parliamentary Labour Party has presented another unacceptable form of neoliberalism. Socialist policies have not been tried. It is therefore premature to rule them out as an effective alternative. The question remains as to what reforms are possible and desirable in current conditions and how could they be implemented. Before we turn to these issues, I consider the way in which the turn from statist social democracy in Western Europe was paralleled in the Soviet bloc, with spectacular results.

---

[58] For an insider account see: Andrew Murray, *Is Socialism Possible in Britain? Reflections on the Corbyn Years*. London: Verso, 2022.

8

State Socialism Moves to a Market Economy

In Chapter 5, I described how state socialism developed in the Soviet Union and later in East European societies. But it was not copied in the advanced capitalist countries. In the 1980's the slowing of economic growth and the unfulfilled expectations of the populations led to movements for economic reform. A successful reform was considered essential to meet the conditions and expectations of a more advanced modern society, though by the beginning of the 1980s economic reforms in the European state socialist societies had had little success. Proposals from the reformist economic and political intelligentsia (outlined in Chapter 5) shifted to calls for a deeper form of restructuring.[1]

A major division arose between reformers. Some proposed a move to a market economy consequent on severe reductions in the role of economic planning but, crucially, they endorsed the continuing hegemony of the Communist party-state system. Other campaigners sought a move to a market system that would disband (or effectively curtail) not only central planning but also the hegemonic role of the Communist Party. Implicitly, their ideas moved to an acceptance of markets which, if they were to work as in the West, could only operate in the context of autonomous economic institutions (independent banks, corporations, stock exchanges). Market forces could not be introduced, they claimed, if politicians (and political institutions) prevented the market from operating. They contended that a market system was much more than a market economy, it was dependent on a corresponding socio-political infrastructure and institutions to make it work – just what neoliberal theory required (as described in Chapter 2).

---

[1] For a more detailed account see D. Lane, *The Capitalist Transformation of State Socialism*. London: Routledge, 2014, Chapter 11.

Their critics considered, correctly as it was to transpire, that such a course would lead to the restoration of capitalism.

Within system market-type reform was limited by the high levels of state ownership and extensive economic and political controls exercised by a hegemonic Communist Party that appeared immovable. A major impetus for transformation was to come from outside – from the example of neoliberal governments in the West, as well as external conditions for reform. Socialist reformers found political inspiration in the success of neoliberalisation in Western Europe, particularly from the policies pursued by Margaret Thatcher in Britain. She had privatised state-owned assets, severely weakened state management, defeated the militant trade unions, strengthened the market and diluted the welfare state. And she had enjoyed public support. As we noted in Chapter 7, one of her boasts was that she had converted Tony Blair's New Labour to Thatcherism. She was to capitalise on the weaknesses of state socialism to capture Mikhail Gorbachev as another convert.

Perestroika: from reform to transformation

In the 1980s, the Sovietised states not only experienced falling growth rates and economic stagnation but also were confronted by hostile Western policies led by President Bush and Prime Minister Margaret Thatcher. The Western-supported war in Afghanistan drained the USSR's resources, and the American Star Wars programme increased the need for defence expenditure. There were strong movements for economic reform in the socialist countries and Eurocommunism provided a critique of the hierarchical Party-led one-party system.

Following the death of Konstantin Chernenko, Mikhail Gorbachev was elected General Secretary of the Communist Party of the Soviet Union in March 1985, and reform of the political and economic processes was anticipated. His proposals, moreover, exceeded the expectations not only of Western leaders but also of the reform movements in the communist states. On 25 February 1986 Gorbachev introduced a new version of the Programme of the Communist Party of the Soviet Union. In his speech, he outlined what he and other reformers considered to be fundamental problems of the Soviet state and his proposals for the ways solve them. This was the policy of perestroika. As we noted in Chapter 5, the institutional structure of state socialism appeared to preclude any significant reforms involving a transition from Communist Party rule to a market pluralist system. Such a transformation, however, was proposed by Gorbachev.

The political objectives of Gorbachev were to put in place the legitimacy of markets and democratic competition, the conditions for a move to private property and, most important of all, a political settlement with the West. Gorbachev had a vision of the future. The Programme of the Communist

Party of the Soviet Union was to provide a new beacon for progressive forces predicated on human rights, a pluralist society, a market led economy and a return to European civilisational values. It was Gorbachev's hope that the West would accept the USSR as a friendly world power. It was a humanistic version of Western social-democracy. Acceptance by the West, however, entailed meeting the conditions demanded by the Western powers, led by the USA. Both domestic developments and foreign pressures on Gorbachev would lead to the dismantling of the Soviet party-state, and a move to free market capitalism.

The mobilising strategies were those of glasnost (a more open form of the media); democratisation, which meant a more pluralist system in which the Communist Party would lose its monopoly of political power in the context of more open elections; the introduction of market relations and private ownership of productive assets; in international relations a more devolved policy towards the European countries of the Soviet bloc and, most important of all, a move towards détente with the USA and NATO. In combination these proposals undermined the state structures of the USSR. The transformation of state socialism was predicated on neoliberal reforms. In my view, similar underlying social factors to those in Western Europe conditioned these developments.

The social bases of radical economic reform and counter-revolution

In Chapter 5, we noted that following the processes of industrialisation, the state socialist societies had become urbanised, the workforce highly educated, occupationally skilled and socially differentiated. The socialist countries had a growing educated middle class whose expectations were much higher than the manual working class that had arisen in the years of rapid industrialisation.

Social classes, in my view, underpinned Gorbachev's reforms and class actors were at the heart of the transformation from state socialism to capitalism. The class structure in the socialist societies differed from that in the capitalist countries. The state, not individuals or private institutions, owned the means of production. Apart from the collective farm peasants, all employees engaged in wage labour constituted, in Soviet terms, the working class, and all were employed by state institutions. By the 1970s, the socialist regimes were becoming much more socially differentiated. One might distinguish a group of executive and higher management officials responsible for policy making and having control of various sectors of the economy which I define as an administrative stratum. This group formed part of, but was separate from, the rising 'service' class composed of non-manual employees with higher education and professional qualifications. These two groups (the administrative stratum and the upper non-manual strata) formed the basis of a latent ascendant class predisposed to a market type of society.[2]

Members of the administrative stratum were in a contradictory position. They occupied influential, secure and privileged positions and formed a base from which the ruling elites were recruited. (By ruling elites, I mean the people who occupied positions that exercised political and economic power within the USSR and/or the Republics.) The administrative stratum included personnel with positions of authority in the Party, leading executive positions in government institutions (including the economic and 'power' ministries, educational and health institutions, the media). Potentially, they could turn their administrative control into ownership of property if they were able to valorise their administrative and executive capital through a market.

The difference with market capitalism was that positions of authority did not allow their holders to inherit or to dispose of the state owned assets under their control. They did not 'own' state property (they could not sell the factories under their command) and neither could they use their knowledge and authority to form their own businesses. Control of surplus yielded from production was managed by the executives of the party-state, which severely limited the expropriation of surplus by officials. (Whether this led to state capitalism is considered in Chapter 15.) A move to markets and private ownership would transform membership of a privileged salaried administrative stratum into a capitalist class with legal rights over the expropriation of surplus value derived from private property. The strata that could benefit from this kind of transformation constituted a counter elite – in the Soviet context, a counter-revolutionary class.

The second impetus for change came from the rising professional and executive strata. This occupational group is often defined as a 'service class' by Western sociologists, such as Karl Renner and John Goldthorpe, and includes non-manual senior managers and executives with professional qualifications employed in government administration, the economy, law, the media and social services (health, education) – in the state socialist societies, these were all state run institutions. Such personnel had considerable influence and the political elites were dependent on their loyalty and support. With the maturation of the social system, the political elites began to absorb, and to reflect the interests of the new younger university educated professionals which differed from the older generation.

The 'service class' differed from that in the capitalist market economies. In the planned economy, all personnel were paid for their labour by a state

---

[2]   I detail these changes in David Lane, *Elites and Classes in the Transformation of State Socialism*. Transaction Publishers: New Brunswick, 2011, especially Chapters 4, 9 and 10.

enterprise or institution: the state had a monopoly over employment and fixed wage rates and conditions. The exchange of labour power for money remained a feature of state socialism and income derived from employment was important in the determination of living standards. Whereas under capitalism, the market mediates between owners and employees (who enjoy profits and salaries respectively), under state socialism, the economic rewards were not determined by market conditions, but administratively. Based on the socialist assumption of a common purpose and community of interests in a workers' state, there were relatively low real income differentials as we noted in Chapter 5 (see Figure 5.1). Executives were paid bonuses but they did not receive 'surplus value' comparable to profits. They could receive benefits in the form of consumption goods and services but could not buy productive assets. Relative to manual industrial workers, real income of skilled non-manual employees had declined in the socialist system (see Figure 5.4). This relative *equality* created a sense of alienation for many in the professional strata (the 'socialist intelligentsia'), what I defined as the 'service class'. Unlike neoliberal policy in the Western capitalist states, which promoted equality of opportunity by 'levelling up', in state socialist society, there had been a considerable levelling down.

The literary and artistic intelligentsia also resented the administrative control over cultural expression which weakened their professional standing. The difference between the actual level of incomes and what their recipients thought they deserved (prompted by knowledge of Western societies) led them to believe that the market would give higher material benefits and/ or enhanced cultural status.

These conditions led many policy makers to argue that the relativities were insufficient to reward innovation and the acquisition of skills. The cultural and academic intelligentsia resented the restricted cultural and political restraints that limited their freedom and compounded the material injustices. There emerged a new 'middle class' that valued individualism (often expressed in demands for cultural and political freedom). A move to markets, they believed, would ensure that they received what they deserved, which would justly reward their higher qualifications and skills.

Already in the late 1960s, scholars were aware of the discord between members of the new middle class and an older generation of activists. Frank Parkin, generalising about developments in Poland, Hungary, Czechoslovakia and Yugoslavia in 1969, noted

> the quite sharp antagonisms ... between the younger generation of graduates and technocrats on the one hand and the older party veterans and partisans on the other ... In Czechoslovakia ... opposition to the economic reforms came from factory managers whose appointment

owed more to their politics and proletarian origin than to their technical abilities.[3]

By the 1980s, the constitution of the 'service class' had been transformed. As we noted in Chapter 5, a new middle class had emerged constituted of people with higher educational qualifications.

The social recruitment of the political elites had been transformed. Table 8.1 shows the ways in which the educational background of the Communist Party of the Soviet Union's leading cadres had changed between 1971 and 1986. Whereas in 1971, only 20 per cent of the leading cadres had higher education (this included part-time and 'incomplete' higher education) by 1986 this figure had risen to 31.8 per cent in a group that had doubled in size. More importantly, however, people with higher education dominated in the executive and representative echelons of the party. The Party's central committee included representatives from the major institutions and groups in Soviet society. In 1986, some 70 per cent of its members had higher education and 7 per cent higher university degrees; whereas, of the rank-and-file Party membership, 68 per cent had secondary education or less.

My contention is that the Party elites had become socially decoupled from the mass membership, which earlier could be relied upon to support the centralised administrative system. Here then we detect the embryo of the changes in class structure that underpinned the transformation of state socialism. The traditional planning and administrative system was supported by the older Party members from manual worker or peasant backgrounds who had worked their way up the system. A move to markets was supported by an ascendant stratum formed by occupational groups with professional skills. I define these groups as latent classes because they were developing an identity with a common interest opposed to the incumbent ruling class.

We may define class boundaries operating on the basis of these two criteria of stratification (control of assets and marketability of knowledge/skills). Driving the reform process were the interests of these two groups: a faction of the state/Party bureaucracy with the latent support of middle-class occupational groups (the 'service' class) who believed that they would personally benefit if their life chances became dependent on the free market. Both groups could turn their occupational positions into class rights by securing an economic market, and some could benefit by acquiring rights to property.

---

[3] Frank Parkin, Class stratification in socialist societies. *British Journal of Sociology*, 20:4 (1969), pp 365–7. He does not, however, provide any hard evidence for the validity of this assertion.

Table 8.1: Higher education of Party cadres, Communist Party of the Soviet Union, 1971, 1986

	1971		1986	
	N	**%**	**N**	**%**
All Party members:	2.81 mill	19.6	6.8 mill	31.8

Leading cadres:

Members and candidates of city, district (raykom) and area (okrug) committees and auditing commissions, elected prior to the 27th Congress (1986)

	N	**%**
Higher education	230,926	56.7
Higher academic degrees	6,408	1.6

Members and candidates of central committees and auditing committees, and central committees of Union Republican parties and provinces (obkom) and territories (krai) committees (1985–86)

	N	**%**
Higher education	22,118	69.4
Higher academic degrees	2,295	7.2

Source: *Partiynaya zhizn'* (Moscow), No 4 (1986): 20, 23.

It is important to emphasise, however, that these were not homogeneous coherent political groups. Many in the service class found themselves in contradictory positions as state socialism provided secure and privileged positions as well as a platform to achieve socialist goals. Both these strata contained loyal supporters of state socialism who sought its continuation through 'within system' reform and a limited market, rather than its transcendence. Others, however, formed a counter administrative elite, which constituted the political forces supporting Gorbachev when General Secretary of the Party, not just in the introduction of market reforms but of opening up to the West and later moving to private property.

Support for radical reforms

A faction of the political elite under Gorbachev played an important role in leading the movement for radical reform and in doing so responded to, and cultivated, the new middle classes. Initially, Gorbachev sought a move to the market within the context of a Communist Party-led political order, rather than a move to capitalism with private property. To secure support for change, the Gorbachev leadership shifted the political balance within the political elites from those favouring the traditional forms of administrative political control to a counter administrative elite drawn from the new service class. Here he could rely on significant political support from the growing number of middle class people in elected positions in the Communist Party as well as in the more heterogeneous representative bodies.

Gorbachev opened up the discussion of reform, which enabled opposing views to be articulated. In the early reforms put into effect in Czechoslovakia, Hungary, Poland and the German Democratic Republic (GDR), the state planning system and state ownership were not infringed – the reformers were aware of the direct Soviet intervention in Hungary in 1956 and political intrusion by the Warsaw Pact countries in Czechoslovakia in 1968. Before Gorbachev, the political leadership of the USSR severely restricted the mobilisation of counter-political forces and used physical force against opposition. Gorbachev, however, allowed public criticism under the policy of 'glasnost' (openness).

Reformers were emboldened to call openly for a move to a competitive market system and private property. In the Supreme Soviet of the RSFSR, in July 1990, voting on the 'Silaev reforms', which proposed to introduce market reforms in the Soviet Union, illustrates which social strata were driving the reform process. In support of market reforms were over 70 per cent of the government and Party elites, as well as over 80 per cent of deputies who had a professional or executive background.[4] However, when one examines backing for privatisation, government and Party elites were divided. In December 1990, the vote on the introduction of private property was defeated, with nearly 70 per cent of the political elites voting against it. On the other hand, of the professional strata, under 40 per cent voted against.[5] Clearly some would have welcomed a move to capitalism, which they saw as opening up a land of opportunity, giving them 'what they really deserved'. Others feared the uncertainty that a market society would bring, and a considerable number opposed such reforms on ideological socialist grounds. They were in contradictory class positions.

Such domestic developments, however, provided insufficient political ballast, even if led by Gorbachev, to move to a market system. The domestic political elites were too divided, and lacked the motivation and political consensus to abolish their own established political base under state socialism to move to the uncertainties of capitalism. The tipping point was the crucial

---

[4] See voting details in D. Lane and C. Ross, *The Transition from Communism to Capitalism*. New York: St Martin's Press, 1999, pp 129–33.

[5] Lane and Ross, *The Transition from Communism to Capitalism*, pp 129–33.

role of external class forces. To precipitate change, Gorbachev had to cultivate and then rely on external support.

Here one must take into account the development of a world network. Changes in communication media influenced the expectations of populations, which became global in scale. Margaret Thatcher's brand of neoliberalism was well-known not only through reform-oriented circles but also through her appearances on domestic television in the socialist countries. Her message applied to welfare states such as the UK and to the statist communist societies, where people thought that a market system would give them what they deserved and most thought that they deserved more than they then received. We must also bear in mind that previous leaders, such as Nikita Khrushchev, had claimed that they could not only catch up with, but would surpass, the countries of the capitalist world. In the socialist countries, despite their communistic façade, regime self-legitimacy was measured in terms of economic progress and the people's levels of consumption.

Transformation and the role of transnational interests

The policy of perestroika proved a futile attempt at economic reform of state socialism. Gorbachev's drive to the market was initially stalled by his political opponents in the Party and state apparatuses. As a consequence of domestic elite opposition, the Gorbachev leadership was pushed into dependence on outsiders to sustain the move to a market economy. A decisive role was played by what Leslie Sklair has called the global capitalist class, which widens the definition of class to include 'globalizing politicians, bureaucrats and professionals' (discussed in Chapter 10).[6]

Whereas in the capitalist economies, the international capitalist class had a direct presence through the ownership of companies, Western transnational corporations (TNCs) could not be hosted in the socialist countries and national enterprises were not available for purchase or sale. The interests of foreign TNCs, however, were furthered through Western global political elites which promoted their business interests. The external foreign dimension was a crucial driving force to privatise and 'open up' the state-owned corporations. Transnational political forces, through government leaders such as Margaret Thatcher, George Bush and later Tony Blair, as well as international organisations, such as the IMF and the WTO, influenced the domestic economic and political elites in the socialist countries. Indeed, they were crucial to sustain Gorbachev's internal policy. As a former adviser to Gorbachev has cogently put it:

---

[6]   L. Sklair, *The Transnational Capitalist Class*. London: Blackwell, 2001.

[T]he task of [Gorbachev's foreign policy] was not to protect the USSR from the outside threat and to assure the internal stability but almost the opposite: to use relations with the outside world as an additional instrument of internal change. He wished to transform the West into his ally in the political struggle against the conservative opposition he was facing at home because his real political front was there.[7]

While this statement rather understates the domestic support for Gorbachev, it does focus attention on the crucial role of the West. The politics of the radical reform leadership, first under Gorbachev and then under Yeltsin, sought an agreement with foreign world actors. Gorbachev's objective became what he called a 'perekhod' (to move from one place to another) from state socialism to a 'social market economy'[8].

The West had its own agenda. As Michael MccGwire, in a Brookings Paper has pointed out, Western policy in respect to the Soviet Union entailed 'a sustained attempt to achieve military superiority ... a general militarization of the international arena ... [and] a massive "psychological" attack against the socialist community'.[9] This involved the development of space-based weapons, 'special forces' (that is, undercover agents) in Eastern Europe, the exercise of economic sanctions through trade policy and embargoes on the export from the West of advanced technology. Aid was promised to Eastern European states (such as Hungary and Rumania) as a reward and compensation for movement away from Soviet influence.[10] In 1989, during the critical turn of events that led to calls for independence in the Baltic states, the US National Endowment for Democracy gave financial assistance to pro-Western groups in the Baltic republics, the Ukraine and the Caucasus.[11] To this one could note the parallels and successes of US policy of

---

[7] Andrei Grachev, Russia in the world. Paper delivered at BNAAS Annual Conference, Cambridge, 1995, p 3.

[8] Despite claiming that perestroika was promoting 'more socialism and more democracy' (Mikhail Gorbachev, *Perestroika*. London: Collins 1987, see pp 36–7) Gorbachev, as correctly quoted here by Archie Brown was intent on dismantling planning and moving on to a social market system. See A. Brown, *Seven Years that Changed the World*. Oxford: Oxford University Press, 2007. See pp 211–2.

[9] Michael MccGwire, *Perestroika and Soviet National Security*. Washington, DC: Brookings, 1991, pp 117–8.

[10] See MccGwire, *Perestroika and Soviet National Security*, pp 110–13.

[11] Evidence is contained in a letter of Yazov, the Soviet Defence Minister, see Raymond L. Garthoff, *The Great Transition: American-Soviet Relations and the End of the Cold War*. Washington, DC: Brookings, 1994, p 395, fn 39. A secret Politburo document, referring to contacts between Soviet citizens and foreign UK emigre Balts, Radio Free Europe and others, expressed concern at activities of an anti-Soviet and anti-communist character. Ibid, p 396.

'covert operations in Chile and Nicaragua'.[12] These confrontational policies undermined the state socialist system through Western political identification with, and sometimes financial support for, the movements for radical reform.

The conditions offered to Gorbachev in support of his reform initiatives required a move to a Western liberal form of competitive capitalism. It is here that the ideas of economic liberalism made their mark. A social democratic type of regime, coupled to a gradual move to markets under a mixed economy retaining the state-owned financial and manufacturing companies, was not supported by Western advisers and transnational coordinating bodies. Neoliberalism's objective is to make institutions appropriate for free market capitalism. Western leaders insisted on a policy of competitive markets in the polity (parties and competitive elections) as well as an open international economy (privatised production for exchange, and money which would be negotiable in international markets). A neoliberal system would be assured by establishing the rule of law to guarantee rights to property and its proceeds. A marketised form of exchange paved the way for the introduction of Western products and capital (to purchase domestic assets), and access to a low wage labour force. International relations would require the socialist East European states to move from the Soviet sphere of influence and for the USSR to repudiate any military or political confrontation with the West. The Warsaw Pact (the military alliance of the socialist bloc) would have to be dismantled.

The linkage with foreign powers provided the impetus in the process of capitalist transition. In combination, the mutual support of these elements (the administrative counter elite, the new 'service' class and the capitalist West) enabled the leadership under Gorbachev to carry out the systemic reforms that ended state socialism. The weakening of the power of the Communist Party of the Soviet Union and the installation of liberal-oriented political and economic elites enabled a transition to a neoliberal form of capitalism to take place. The West, led by policy makers in, and the leaders of, the USA, laid down the ground rules for such integration into the world liberal order. Later, international bodies, such as the International Monetary Fund, World Trade Organisation and World Bank would oversee these developments. The drivers in the transformation to global capitalism were the international components of the transnational capitalist class (which we turn to in Chapter 10).

It is in this context that Gorbachev and the economic reformers presented a 'democratisation' of the political institutions to break up the control of the

---

[12] Military aid was sent to anti-communist guerrilla movements in Cambodia and Angola as well. The communist states, of course, also engaged in ideological, economic and political subversion, with manifestly little success in the stable Western democratic countries.

administrative elites intent on maintaining the centralised system of controls.[13] He advocated a more democratic political system, a major provision of which, however, was that it would not be a multi-party competitive political system. His leadership proposed a form of political pluralism – a choice of candidates (people could be nominated as individuals - rather than Communist party nominees), and freedom for various types of informal groups (but not formal political parties), which could contend for political power. The Communist Party would remain hegemonic, though it would have to rule by popular consent. Gorbachev claimed that socialism would be strengthened. He shared the vision of the democratic market socialists, the planned economy would function in a democratic context but unlike them, defined by a hegemonic Communist Party. With the process of perestroika, reforms went much further than Gorbachev initially had proposed, and led to major systemic changes.

What was to transpire, as the most important measure of all, was a shift in authority from the Party to the Soviets (the elected Parliaments). In March 1990, the exclusion of the Party's 'leading role' from the Soviet constitution broke the Party's constitutional and symbolic monopoly of power. The ideological and institutional framework which, from its founding under Vladimir Lenin, held together state socialism was consciously dismantled. Political reforms effectively destroyed the party-state apparatus that controlled the planned economy. To enable the market reforms to work, the planning organs were disbanded. Enterprises were allowed to trade one with another as in market societies. The unintended consequence of these economic and political reforms was that the leadership under Gorbachev was unable (and some did not want) to contain the more radical forces which sought a transition to a liberal form of capitalism.

Gorbachev's policies dismantled the coordinating economic institutions and led to the disintegration of the economic system, to spiralling inflation, a significant decline in production and a general crisis of state socialism – as a state and as a form of socialism. The complex catallaxies (described in Chapter 2) that coordinated the liberal market system were not in place. It was utopian to assume that the processes and institutions of Western market economies, which had been formed over centuries, could be established spontaneously. The economic system of the Soviet Union 'collapsed', not as a consequence of the many faults of the planning mechanism but under the weight of the Gorbachev reforms.

Three major stabilising institutions of the Soviet order were dismantled: the centralised system of state planning, the apparat of the communist Party

---

[13] These developments are detailed in Lane, *Elites and Classes in the Transformation of State Socialism*.

of the Soviet Union, and the nomenklatura system of appointments. The sum of these developments constituted the precondition for the breakup of the USSR. Secession from the Union by the Republics was declared first on 11 March 1990 by the Lithuanian Soviet Socialist Republic and completed on 12 December 1991 when the Russian Federation left the Union. Republican leaders were set on the path to break the USSR. On 8 December 1991, the Belovezh Accord was signed by the heads of state of Russia (Yeltsin), Ukraine (Kravchuk) and Belarus (Shushkevich). The Accord recognised each other's independence and declared the formation of the Commonwealth of Independent States (CIS). The USSR no longer existed and on 25 December, Gorbachev resigned as president. On 26 December the Supreme Soviet of the USSR dissolved the USSR. On 31 December 1991 the USSR ceased to exist. The assets of the USSR were taken over by the 15 Republics that previously had formed the USSR.

The was not only the end of the USSR as a state formation but the termination of an era of state socialism. State socialism no longer presented a viable alternative to capitalism.

Reform movements in the socialist countries of Eastern Europe followed the lead of Gorbachev. Here, anti-communist political forces were stronger: in the electoral process, legislatures lacking a communist majority were elected in Poland and Hungary. As in the Soviet Union, the political hegemony of the Communist Party was broken, the planning ministries were dissolved and economic transformation led in the direction of privatisation and marketisation. It was a matter of time before the whole structure disintegrated. The Communist Party command system was transformed into a political polyarchy and planning was hastily replaced by a market economy predicated on privatised property. Under President Yeltsin, and concurrently in the European socialist states, privatisation occurred on a large scale between 1989 and 1995.[14] Communist ideology was renounced. State socialism was ended and its institutions disbanded. State socialism did not collapse due to its internal contradictions. It was dismantled by its own leadership. Subsequently, the West under the leadership of the USA, legitimated by the universalistic goals of neoliberalism, defined the conditions on which the post-socialist European states joined the world international order.

When we compare the underlying factors leading to the decline of socialism (in the form of social democracy) in the UK (Chapter 7) and in the USSR, we distinguish common processes at work. Both economies experienced internal decline in the final quarter of the twentieth century and

---

[14] See Hilary Appel, *A New Capitalist Order: Privatisation and Ideology in Russia and Eastern Europe*. Pittsburgh: University of Pittsburgh Press, 2004; Richard Pomfret, *Constructing a Market Economy*. Cheltenham: Edward Elgar, 2002.

both, in different ways, had contested political regimes. Both had experienced similar trends in the social structure in the rise of non-manual executive and professional occupations consequent on the decline of the manual working class. The growing professional non-manual strata provided the social and political base in support of a more competitive market and less state-managed system. Both countries were subject to foreign influences that had impacts on internal politics. In the socialist bloc, reformers sought to join the world economic order, in the West, countries were becoming part of a liberal global system. In both countries, there occurred a significant destatisation entailing privatisation and marketisation. The developments in all the state socialist countries were at a qualitatively more advanced level and involved a regime change and the establishment of a capitalist class. In the Western European states, in contrast, the outcome resulted in the weakening of nation states and the assimilation of parts of the dominant classes into global networks. In both areas the traditional socialist appeal of collective provision significantly declined and was replaced by possessive individualism.

State socialism, as a form of industrial development and modernisation, provided an effective practical alternative to capitalism but was faulted politically and economically. The socialist societies had developed their own forms of irrationality. To explain such developments, one cannot rely on the writing of Marx to seek explanations of faults in the state socialist societies or remedies to their inadequacies.

Explanations have to be found not only in the approach of historical materialism, but also may be derived from other theories and approaches, and legacies of history – notably from the continuation of processes inherited from previous social and political formations. Bureaucracy, patriarchy, militarism and credentialism (the exercise of 'expert' knowledge) also constitute forms of political and economic power and have their own origins and laws of development. It is mistaken to attribute all the malformations, inadequacies, and injustices to features inherent in the class structures of capitalist or socialist regimes. Following writers such as E.O. Wright[15] we might widen the notion of domination and control to include not only ownership of capital assets but organisational power that may be utilised by people in authority – officials, bureaucrats, lawyers. Other lower levels of control include those based on credentials that include a range of professionals from school teachers to doctors and accountants.

Developments not anticipated by Soviet Marxists, such as those concerned with environmental exploitation as well as the consequences of nuclear war, have assumed greater political importance in the twenty-first century. The oppression of marginalised groups (gender and caste) has cultural and

---

[15] E.O. Wright, *Classes*. London: Verso, 1985.

historical roots. These dimensions of power might be shaped by, but are not constituent parts of, economic exploitation and must be analysed separately. However, they cannot be equated with economic exploitation. Marx has been vindicated in giving to the ownership of private property and the extraction of economic surplus, obtained through market relationships, a qualitatively different level of power than other forms of domination and discrimination. Modes of production, with distinctive levels of productive forces, form and limit human relationships. The formation of classes is an explanation not only of how the social structure generates major conflicts based on property but also one of how, historically, societies change and in whose interests changes take place.

The transition to capitalism

Following the dissolution of the Soviet Union in December 1991, the state socialist societies began the journey of transition to capitalism. Transition implies an intentional movement from an existing state to a specified type of society; in this case the target is a market type of capitalism, legitimately encased in an electoral competitive democracy. The policy of transition initially contained five components: domestically, the creation of national sovereign state units, a market system based on privately owned property, democratic competitive electoral politics and a pluralist civil society. The fifth component was in the international sphere which called for exposure to the world economy and normalisation of political relations with the dominant political powers. These features took as their model a liberal framework.

In the transformation process, the European post-socialist states took two different roads: first, inclusion as New Member States (NMS) in the EU; second, the formation of a Commonwealth of Independent States (CIS) composed of the remaining republics of the former Soviet Union. Both regional groups of countries, at least initially, subscribed to liberal economic and political policies. A pluralist political system predicated on electoral democracy and a competitive market economy anchored in private property were adopted. Later, many lapsed into forms of oligarchic state-led capitalism. The promised transition to democratic freedom, wealth and prosperity did not arrive in the form expected – though some benefitted immensely from the transformation. An alternative could have been a hybrid, social democratic welfare-state form of economic formation, which would have moved to market economic relations and a more pluralistic political system while retaining public property and state-led markets. This course was the intended consequence for some of the reformers who sought a form of market socialism, but this was not recommended by foreign economic advisers and not supported by coordinating institutions, such as the International Monetary Fund. One other important transformation occurred in China. Here the Communist leadership moved to the market and introduced significant privatisation including large corporations. These changes, however, were conducted in the context of a state plan, foreign investment was circumscribed and, perhaps most important of all, the Communist Party maintained its hegemony over society and the state, which retained ownership and control of crucial financial and non-financial enterprises (discussed further in Chapter 15). One conclusion is quite clear: the dissolution of the Soviet Union marked the end of one alternative to capitalism: state socialism.

PART II

Capitalist Globalisation and Its Adversaries

9

From Industrial
to Global Capitalism

In previous chapters I showed how political movements and governments met the challenges of national and world politics after the Second World War. Policies were influenced by two major interconnected and cumulative developments. First, occurred a transformation of manual worker based developed industrial economies to a predominantly nonmanual service sector. Economies of the advanced nations experienced the rise of transport, trade, electronic communications, insurance, education, banking, health, recreation and research. Industrial production continued, often in an attenuated form, but with a smaller more skilled work force, which was able to harness machines and robots to perform not only industrial tasks but commercial and personal ones. The armies of factory workers were gradually replaced by a much smaller number of scientific, technical and professional employees. Second, a qualitative shift took place in the spatial relationships between countries and regions consequent on the globalisation of economic and social relations. These developments together may be described as a movement from national industrial capitalism to globalised post-industrial capitalism. Such structural developments have conditioned the framework of politics.

The groundwork for theories of 'post-industrial', 'informational' or 'knowledge' based societies may be traced back to the 1960s. The works of Clark Kerr,[1] J.K. Galbraith[2] and Daniel Bell[3] all contributed to the concept of post-industrial society. A consequence of the changes they identified is that knowledge and intellectual property became major economic resources.

[1] Kerr, C. et al., *Industrialism and Industrial Man*. Cambridge, MA: Harvard University Press, 1960.
[2] Galbraith, J.K., *The New Industrial State*. London; Hamish Hamilton, 1976.
[3] Bell, D., *The Coming of Post-Industrial Society*. London: Heinemann, 1974.

In post-industrial society, the use and 'codification of theoretical knowledge' became a fundamental component of the economy. Knowledge is 'a set of organised statement of facts or ideas, presenting a reasoned judgement or an experimental result, which is transmitted to others through some communication medium in some systematic form'.[4] Post-industrial society was composed of three domains: the tertiary sector (transportation), the quaternary sector (trade, finance, insurance, real estate) and the quinary sector (health, education, research, government and recreation). These sectors provided a social base for a 'post-industrial' type of politics. What also emerged after the third quarter of the twentieth century were multi-national corporations, which strongly influenced states, and financial companies, rather than productive enterprise, which drove investment.

From national to global capitalism

One might distinguish between three spatial types of capitalist economies having different forms of coordination, types of economic systems and related class structures: national, international and global. In practice, states contain parts of all three but in different proportions.

A national economy is defined by the main economic forms of coordination being situated within the borders of a given country. During the rise of capitalism in the late eighteenth and early nineteenth century, companies were national in ownership, largely producing for, and receiving inputs from, the home country. National economies were enclosed politically by states. The Treaty of Westphalia signed in 1648 defined citizenship, and declared that states were sovereign within their boundaries. The state provided a major form of economic coordination and shaped laws for the conduct of business and property. National economies were linked to a nation's culture – language, religion, and 'ways of doing things'. National economies were part of the first phase of industrial capitalism and states exerted direct territorial control over their overseas possessions or colonies, and they made treaties on a bi-lateral or multinational basis. States regulated the movements of capital and labour, and national laws governed the ownership and rights of companies. States also controlled the massive nineteenth-century migration from Europe (generally with little restriction) and defined citizenship. The home country ruled directly over colonies, and armies enforced imperial laws often through intermediaries in the host countries – a territorial form of power. Treaties and agreements were initiated and sanctioned by nation states.

---

[4]   Bell, *The Coming of Post-Industrial Society*, pp 117, 175. Like Bell, J.K. Galbraith defines the 'technostructure' in terms of 'specialised scientific and technical knowledge'. Galbraith, *The New Industrial State*, pp 61–3.

National economies expanded greatly in the nineteenth century and the international economy was formed by intercourse between states. Capitalism was a major driver of economic change. Marx and Engels noted its spread in the Communist Manifesto:

> The bourgeoisie has through its exploitation of the world market given a cosmopolitan character to production and consumption in every country ... In place of the old local and national seclusion and self-sufficiency, we have intercourse in every direction, universal inter-dependence of nations. And as in material, so also in intellectual production. The intellectual creations of individual nations become common property.[5]

Internationalisation implies interactions between predominantly national economies. The nation state continues to have coordinating roles and determines laws that regulate international political exchange. National companies trading on a world scale remain embedded in their countries of origin. Under conditions of 'internationalisation', national state intervention is decisive – states make and abrogate treaties, and control national economic corporations. National sovereignty predominates and national businesses with foreign interests seek government intervention to secure their assets abroad.

In the final quarter of the twentieth century, capitalism moved from its international form to a more fluid economic order, global capitalism. States began losing some of their powers of economic coordination and also their political sovereignty. Internationalisation turned into globalisation.[6] National boundaries between states were broken down to facilitate the unimpeded movement of the factors of production – particularly capital – given by the 'right of establishment' of companies in host countries. World trade in merchandise increased in volume from $3,500,000 million in 1990, to

---

5   Communist Manifesto, p 16. Available at: https://www.marxists.org/archive/marx/works/download/pdf/Manifesto.pdf
6   There is a vast literature on 'globalisation'. Colin Crouch, *The Globalisation Backlash*. Cambridge: Polity, 2018; Frank J. Lechner and John Boli, *The Globalization Reader* (2nd edn). Oxford and Malden: Blackwell, 2004; P. Dicken, *Global Shift* (7th edn). New York: Guildford Press, 2015; Rodrik, *The Globalization Paradox*; Leslie Sklair, *Sociology of the Global System*. London: Prentice Hall/Harvester, 1991; D. Held and A. McGrew A., *The Global Transformations Reader* (2nd edn). Cambridge: Polity, 2002; J.-A. Scholte, *Globalization: A Critical Introduction*. Basingstoke: Palgrave, 2000 (2nd edn). 2005; J. Bhagwati, *In Defence of Globalization*. Oxford: Oxford University Press, 2004; H.-J. Chang, *The Bad Samaritans: Rich Nations, Poor Policies & the Threat to the Developing World*. New York: Random House, 2007; Sklair, *The Transnational Capitalist Class*; Immanuel Wallerstein, *World-Systems Analysis*. Duke University Press, 2004; J.E. Stiglitz, *Globalization and Its Discontents*. London: Penguin, 2002.

$6,450,000 million in 2000 and $19,000,000 million in 2019.[7] Migration of labour increased, especially within regional blocs such as the EU, but remained subject to state controls. Production took the form of outsourcing and off-shoring, creating global value chains: by 2013, 453 million jobs, approximately 20 per cent of world employment, were involved in global value chains and accounted for approximately half of world trade.[8]

The globalisation phenomenon

Globalisation in its most general sense has been defined as 'a process that erodes national boundaries, integrates national economies, cultures, technologies and governance, and produces complex relations of mutual interdependence'.[9] Globalisation involves the compression of time; interaction between actors is rapid, often instantaneous. It differs from internationalisation, which is a process in which flows across states and relationships between them are mediated by the states themselves – through bi-lateral or multi-lateral treaties and/or agreements. Globalisation has a seamless character: knowledge, communications, goods, people, capital and services flow quickly without restriction across national borders. Local and national cultures are transcended by global media and transnational culture. Globalisation from this technical point of view is an interterritorial logic concerned with spatial flows of goods, people, services and capital.

The significance of *capitalist* globalisation, however, is a disputed issue.[10] The most popular approach is to uncouple capitalism from globalisation and to treat the latter as a consequence of technological change – particularly the development of advanced forms of communication and information technology. David Held and Antony McGrew, in a widely accepted definition, refer to globalisation as 'the historical process which transforms the spatial organisation of social relations and transactions, generating transcontinental or interregional networks of interaction and the exercise

---

7   See Unctadstat (United nations Conference on Trade and Development) database available at: https://unctadstat.unctad.org/wds/TableViewer/tableView.aspx. Table on total merchandise in world trade.

8   *World Development Report 2020*. Washington, DC: World Bank, 2020. For data on employment see International Labour Organisation, *World Employment Social Outlook*. Geneva: ILO, 2015.

9   S. Gygli, F. Haelg and J-E. Sturm, *The KOF Globalisation Index – Revisited*. Zurich: Swiss Economic Institute, 2018. Available at: https://www.ethz.ch/content/dam/ethz/spec ial-interest/dual/kof-dam/documents/Globalization/2018/KOF_Globalisation_Index_ Revisited.pdf

10   For a sceptical treatment of 'globalisation' ideas, see: P. Hirst and G. Thompson, *Globalization in Question*. Cambridge: Polity, 1996 and 1999.

of power'.[11] Like industrial society theories, the approach is predicated on technological developments. For these writers, globalisation has four major components.[12]

- Action at a distance (social agents in one locale have significant consequences for 'distant others').
- Time-space compression (instantaneous electronic communication erodes distance and time on social organisation and interaction).
- Accelerating interdependence (enmeshment among national economies and societies – events in one impact on others).
- Spatial integration (intensification of interregional interconnectedness).

Globalisation has to be understood as consequences of technological invention – the electronic revolution in which communication transcends time and space. The greater complexity and interdependence of actors has led to the rise of global regulatory frameworks, including the arrival of institutions such as the International Monetary Fund, the World Bank and the World Trade Organization, which have provided financial and economic backing to these developments. The coordination of world politics and economics has moved from agreements between states, to regulation by global organisations.[13]

Western social science academia, as well as political and economic commentators, generally regard globalisation as positive. It enhances investment, communication, the spread of knowledge, the interaction of people, trade and production from which all gain economically and socially. The core post-industrial states benefit from low-cost imports, and the rest of world profits from Western outsourcing of manufacturing operations, high-technology and, more contentiously, Western political processes and cultural artefacts. Globalisation economically, it is contended, has led to higher living standards both in the core capitalist countries as well as in the rest of the world. Martin Wolf is representative of Western economists and opinion makers when he writes that 'Today's liberal democracies are the most successful societies in human history in terms of prosperity, freedom and the welfare of peoples'.[14] Though he concedes that they experience crises which create problems.

---

[11]   David Held and Anthony McGrew, The end of the old world order? Globalization and the prospects for world order. *Review of International Studies*, 24 (December 1998), p 220. See also Anthony Giddens, *Beyond Left and Right*, p 80.

[12]   The great globalization debate: An introduction, in D. Held and A. McGrew (Eds), *The Global Transformation Reader*, p 3.

[13]   See discussion in Scholte, *Globalization*, Chapter 4.

[14]   M. Wolf, 'In defence of democratic capitalism', *Financial Times*, 21 January 2023. See also *The Crisis of Democratic Capitalism*. London, Penguin Books, 2023.

Globalisation as a form of capitalism

Globalisation is set in a capitalist framework which, as J.A. Scholte has pointed out, spurred globalisation in four principal ways.[15] First, through the expansion of trade. As home markets have become saturated, firms, pushed by a capitalist logic, have pursued global markets as a means to maintain or increase their sales volume through export. The larger market facilitates economies of scale and hence raises profit margins. Second, foreign direct investment (FDI) and the global mobility of companies between countries expand markets and thereby promote profits through new locations for the subsidiaries of multinational corporations (MNCs). Third, global sourcing and the building of internationally dispersed production networks have reduced costs; capital is mobile and compensates for the rigidities of labour markets, notably, where workers have been unionised. Host countries welcome inward investment as it brings employment, foreign technology and knowledge; on the other side, host countries can provide tax havens for foreign businesses. Fourth, financialisation has enabled portfolio investment in foreign companies and increased currency trading.

Economic globalisation is underpinned by capitalist interests and corporations working through governments or, in some countries, by governments themselves. International economic corporations are driven by their desire for expansion and the quest for cheaper factors of production as well as markets to ensure profits. Globalisation from this point of view is a form of capitalism: a transnational form of ownership and market production; globalisation has a capitalist logic. Marx pointed out that capitalism involved the 'annihilation of space through time'.[16] The economic drivers are transnational corporations (TNCs) which are embedded in global networks of suppliers and purchasers. Their strategic management rests in the home country where decisions are taken about investment and the location and sources of production. Governments bodies may influence their policies, but they have no command over them. The allocation of investment on a global scale gives transnational companies significant economic powers and the search for profits leads to the incessant production of commodities. 'Wants' can be manufactured making the desires for goods and services of consumers unlimited. Consequently, they consume the products of nature and concurrently production leads to pollution and contributes to global warming. We return to environmental concerns in Chapter 13.

---

[15] Scholte, *Globalisation*.

[16] Cited by David Harvey, *The New Imperialism*. Oxford: Oxford University Press 2003, p 98. See also David Harvey, *Limits to Capital: The Condition of Postmodernity*. Oxford: Blackwell, 1989, Part III.

By recognising these cultural, political and economic conditions, one moves from a paradigm of globalisation as a particular set of transnational networks and forms of exchange, to globalisation as an expression of capitalism as a set of norms adopted in the latest phase in capitalist development. Digital technology is analogous to machines of the nineteenth-century industrial revolution: then mechanical engineering provided the tools, the driving forces were capitalist entrepreneurs supported by banks and governments, the facilitators were armies of industrial workers. Under globalisation, electronics and the internet are the tools utilised by TNCs, which are facilitated by transnational economic, financial and political organisations.

We might then define *globalised capitalism* as a system of production of goods and services taking place through unhindered international market exchange; productive assets are collectively or individually owned; profit leading to accumulation is a major motive of economic life; the state, embedded in a pluralistic society, secures private property and rights over the proceeds of production. States operate in a global market in which transnational institutions not only limit their powers but, in many (but not all) ways, supersede them.

The economic underpinning of globalisation

All these developments are promoted through liberalisation processes that remove political restrictions on movements of capital, goods, workers and services in order to create an open, borderless world. Trade agreements specifying the freedom of establishment strengthen the ability of companies to form foreign affiliates. Corporations formed foreign affiliates in the late nineteenth and early twentieth centuries, but major developments occurred during the last quarter of the twentieth century. On a world scale, in 1982, the total world foreign direct investment (FDI) outflow was $28 billion, which rose to $1,216 billion in 2006; between 1986 and 1990, the annual growth of FDI inflows was 21.7 per cent, and between 1996 and 2000 it rose to 40 per cent.[17] Such flows had an enormous impact on national economies and led to deindustrialisation in the core economies of the world system. FDI was not channelled only to developing countries. Figure 9.1 illustrates the inflows of FDI to the major regional economies from 1990 to 2018. By far the major recipients of FDI are developed economies. We note the steep rise of world FDI between 1990 and 2000, a significant fall after 2000, the recovery to 2007, followed by a fall after the recession of 2007. There has been a shift towards developing economies since around 2010,

---

[17] United Nations Conference on Trade and Development, *World Investment Report (WIR) 2007*. New York, Geneva: United Nations, 2007, p 9.

Figure 9.1: FDI inflows, by region and economy, 1990–2018

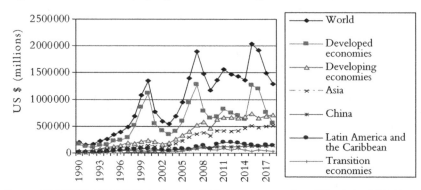

Source: UNCTAD, FDI/MNE database Available at: www.unctad.org/fdistatistics. WIR19-tab01.xlsx.

and the graph shows the rising gap between the world total and developed economies since 2008.

Despite the widely held belief that China's growth was a consequence of FDI, the table shows that, between 1990 and 2017, it was just below Latin America and the Caribbean. 'China' here excludes Hong Kong, but even if added, it would not change the general picture. Outsourcing was a significant factor in Chinese economic growth. The transition economies of the post-socialist states also accounted for a very small proportion of world FDI; much of which was channelled into energy extraction in Russia, Kazakhstan and Azerbaidzhan. As to borders and acquisitions, between 1990 and 2018, developed countries accounted for 80 per cent of the volume, and China had a negligible share.[18] This figure indicates the way in which China was outside the core of the world capitalist economy.

The global economy

International corporations/TNCs earn a considerable proportion of their profits from sales in host countries. The major countries contributing to outward direct investment are the USA and the UK followed by Germany (well behind with only 8 per cent).[19] These data provide an empirical base to show that the corporate capitalist class has a global dimension with its epicentre in the USA. They also shed considerable light on the nature of 'post-industrial society'. FDI has significantly changed its direction. Before

---

[18] UNCTAD cross-border M&A database. Available at: www.unctad.org/fdistatistics.
[19] UNCTAD, data cited by Peter Dicken, *Global Shift*. London: Sage, 2007, p 81.

the Second World War, FDI was channelled away from the centre to the developing world which absorbed four-fifths of FDI. From the 1960s to the 1980s, the largest FDI flows took place between the core regions.[20] Three-fifths of FDI in 1997 took the form of mergers and acquisitions – it was not investment at all. Citing data collected by UNCTAD, Jerry Harris points out that in 1995, some 40,000 companies had (multiple) headquarters in more than three countries.[21]

The global economy is constituted of transnational companies that replace both the autonomous units of the national and dependent economies. Mergers and acquisitions favour dominant corporations located in hegemonic states, which can utilise their economic power to buy and control less powerful companies, often (but not always) located in weaker economies. Their objective (for example, the take-over of UK's Cadbury Schweppes) is to increase market share rather than to achieve any improvement in economic efficiency (though increased market share can create conditions for greater productivity). Corporations become 'global'. While they have affiliates in one or more of the hegemonic core countries, they are not responsible for the host countries' state apparatuses – though they may be influenced by them. They act as multiple units on a global basis (for example, Toyota, Google, Vodafone, BP, Royal Dutch Shell, J.P. Morgan, CitiBank, HSBC, Rio-Tinto, Microsoft, China National Petroleum). The rise of global companies has led to a qualitative shift in their political power. Such companies have a registered home base (or bases) but are not dependent on any one national government.

The US and Western Europe have a dominant presence among the world's top 100 non-financial transnational companies. In 2019, of the world's top 100 non-financial companies (ranked by foreign assets), the USA had 19 companies, followed by France with 15, the UK with 13, Germany with 10 and Japan with 9; China had 9 companies (plus 1 in Hong Kong) (the Russian Federation had none).[22] China, however, is growing rapidly: in 2016, China had only two companies in the list. Most of the Western companies had more than half their assets, sales and employment located abroad. Though the host countries gain from taxes, net profits are repatriated to the owners in the home countries.

Clearly, these facts have significant implications for geo-politics and help to explain 'the West's' hegemony over other states. It adds a global dimension to

---

[20] Jerry Harris, *The Dialectics of Globalisation: Economic and Political Conflict in a Transnational World*. Newcastle: Cambridge Scholar Press, 2006, p 60.

[21] Harris, *The Dialectics of Globalisation*, p 60.

[22] Top 100 Non-financial corporations ranked by foreign assets, 2019. Annex WebTable 24. Available at: http://unctad.org. Annex-Web Tables. 24.

the transformation of the post-socialist societies, considered in Chapter 8. What shapes the structure of any given country's economy is the relative weighting and importance of national companies, dependence on foreign companies and the location of affiliates. The combination of these factors makes the economies of nation states more or less global in character. Linkages to other states in turn influence government policy in maintaining a presence, and the nature of that presence, in international affairs. States operate in a global space that is subject to weak or no state regulation (let alone democratic control). Subsidiaries, of course, are subject to state and regional bloc regulations in the host country. Such companies appeal to, and expect, their own governments to support their trading interests – as they usually do.

Transnational corporations possess significant geo-political economic power. Their geographical mobility enables them to switch (or threaten to switch) location if faced with government-imposed tax rises or adverse environmental conditions. Earnings derived from foreign subsidiaries lead to a concern with political and economic stability of regimes in countries where the assets of global companies are located. They support friendly governments sharing liberal values. Profits from sales in the home country are often smaller than repatriated profits from affiliates abroad. Hence it is obvious that the 'rule of law', 'peace keeping' missions and 'democracy promotion' are not simply altruistic in intention but have implications for the security and profitability of global companies – and the states in which they have their boardrooms.

National political elites in host countries backing global economic interests however come into conflict with domestically based economic elites. The former emphasise the advantages brought by foreign companies – the provision of employment and technical knowledge. Domestic elites often emphasise economic dependency, the drain of profits, the dangers to domestic production and the consequences for employment should domestic firms fail. Here is a base for economic nationalism. The point must be emphasised that globalisation is furthered by and, in turn, promotes the liberalisation of economies. Critics of capitalist globalisation contend that nation states have lost sovereignty to international corporations and organisations. They are faced, to varying degrees, by the economic power wielded by conglomerations of internationally structured business firms. Home-based political elites mediate not only between domestic interests, but they also have to take into account those that operate regionally and globally. Hence domestic political elites, and media outlets, are often divided between those leaning towards home or foreign interests.

To maximise profits, transnational companies are able to locate enterprises in areas of political stability, low pay and minimal taxation, but they also invest in developed countries where employees have higher levels of education and technological knowledge. Foreign investment has some positive effects in the host countries: TNCs are usually able to pay higher wages than local companies and usually bring with them better commercial practices and working conditions. Within national labour markets, freedom of movement enables the unemployed or under-employed workers to move to more prosperous areas with the consequences of enlarging the labour supply and depressing local wage rates. The extent to which governments lose power is dependent on their economic constitution: on the mix of national companies, home based transnationals and foreign affiliates. The level and significance of 'globalisation' varies considerably between countries.

Variations of globalisation between states

Figure 9.2 shows the growth from 1970 to 2019 along three dimensions of globalisation as measured by the KOF index: political, social and economic. 'Economic globalisation characterises long distance flows of goods, capital and services as well as information and perceptions that accompany market exchanges.' The economic index comprises cross-border trade, investment, income flows and capital movements. Social globalisation measures personal cross-border contacts (telephone calls and letters), tourism, information flows, such as TV and internet, and cultural global spread (including book exports and imports) and the availability of McDonald's and IKEA shops. 'Social globalisation expresses the spread of ideas, information, images and people. Political globalisation characterises the diffusion of government policies'.[23] Political globalisation, as defined by KOF, is measured by the number of foreign embassies, international organisations joined, United Nations (UN) peace missions in which a country is involved, and bilateral and multilateral agreements. It should be noted that this index includes measures of transactions and interdependencies negotiated between countries (internationalism) in addition to multi-national flows. The index shows the continuous rise of multiple economic, social and political links between countries over time.[24]

Globalisation after 1990 increased considerably in scope and intensity on all three indicators. In the mid-1990s, a sharp upturn in globalisation,

---

[23] Savina Gygli, Florian Haelg and Jan-Egbert Sturm, The KOF Globalisation Index – Revisited, February, 2018. Zurich: Swiss Economic Institute, KOF Working Papers, No 439. February, 2018KKOF Working Papers, No. 439, February 2018OF Working Papers, No. 439, February 2018KOF Working Papers, No. 439, February 2018.

[24] For the full details of the 41 variables used to construct the indexes see: Indexes and variables, 2018 KOF Globalisation Index: KOF Globalisation Index 2015 (Published 2018). https://www.kof.ethz.ch/en/forecasts-and-indicators/indicators/kof-globalisat ion-index.html. The index covers 209 countries.

Figure 9.2: World globalisation index: economic, social, political

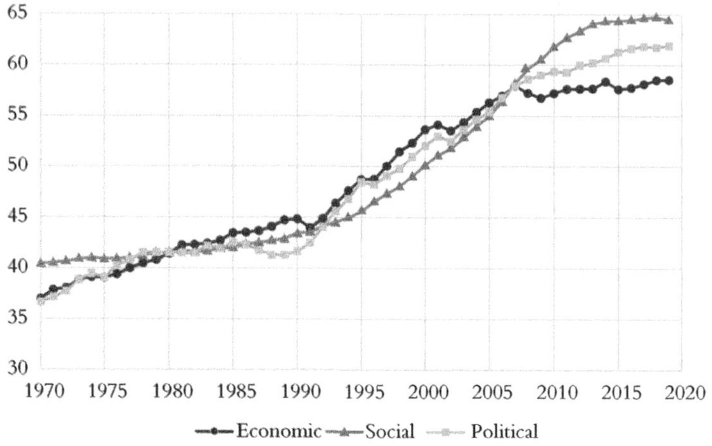

Note: Total number of countries: 209.

Source: KOF Globalisation Index. Available at: https://www.kof.ethz.ch/en/forecasts-and-ind icators/indicators/kof-globalisation-index.html.

Figure 9.3: Economic globalisation, 1970–2019: China, Russia, UK and US

Note: Principle components: trade as per cent, FDI stock, Portfolio investment, income payable to foreign nationals.

Source: KOF database

driven by economic globalisation, occurred, which continued in parallel for all three indexes up to 2007 when the global economic crisis led to a significant fall in economic globalisation. Political and social globalisation was uninterrupted, indicating that these dimensions were self-sustaining. After 2015, economic globalisation continued with a slight increase (at least up to 2019). As shown in Figure 9.3, the UK and the USA maintained their levels after 2008, despite a considerable decline in 2006; after 2012, China has maintained a steady rise. Russia, however, experienced a substantial and continuous fall after 2006.

This relative stability of economic globalisation (except for Russia) is perhaps surprising as many economic pundits have remarked on the declining interdependence of national economies and a tendency for states to become more economically autonomous. One reason for this is that economists measure 'globalisation' in terms of international trade and ignore other important features of globalisation. Figure 9.4 plots just world trade: indeed, in 2008, there was a significant fall, but from 2010 world trade has remained fairly constant with another small fall in 2018. Overall, the level of globalisation, even measured by international trade, has remained high and well over the 1990 levels. Following the COVID-19 pandemic and the Ukraine/NATO–Russia war, global interaction has fallen considerably mainly as a result of economic and political sanctions enacted on Russia and to a lesser extent on China. International value chains and multinational

Figure 9.4: World international trade, 1970–2019

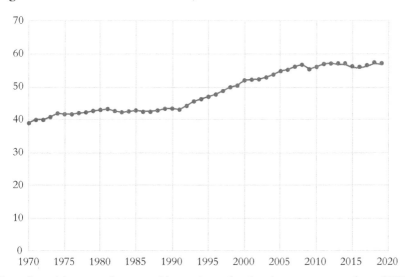

Data refers mainly to sum of exports and imports in goods and services as a percentage share of GDP.

Source: Derived from KOR database.

corporation (MNCs) are firmly set and take time to respond to external changes, regionalisation between 'friendly' ('outfriending') blocs is the most likely outcome.

The nation state may have been weakened by the power of international forces, though some states are more globalised or internationalised than others. The KOF index for 2019 for selected countries is shown in Figure 9.5. The core industrialised states are the most globalised. Size of countries as well as type and complexity of the economy are important in determining the extent of globalisation. Small developed countries are likely to be highly globalised economically and culturally as they are more dependent on both imports and exports of commodities and cultural goods. On the other hand, China has enormous exports but has a relatively low overall globalisation index: it is less dependent on imports and has a lower exposure to foreign cultural goods and services.

Cultural and informational globalisation

While economic globalisation attracts the attention of most politicians, cultural and informational globalisation has a noteworthy impact. Cultural globalisation is concerned with the ways in which a common international system of values and ways of doing things impact on local cultures. The local and national are replaced or modified by globally accepted values; there is instant communication of 'world news', entertainment and beliefs.

Figure 9.5: Total Globalisation Index (KOF), 2019: Netherlands, UK, US, Japan, Russia, China and Brazil

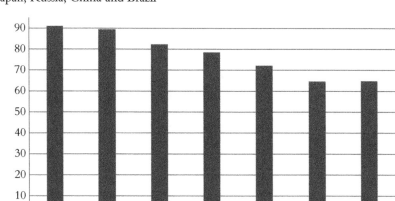

Source: KoF Globalisation Index. Available at: https://www.kof.ethz.ch/en/forecasts-and-ind icators/indicators/kof-globalisation-index.html.

The widespread access to digital media facilitated by the internet and mobile phones giving access on a global basis to 'social media', has had an immense impact. Data for changes between 1970 and 2019 on 'cultural globalisation' for four countries (China, Russia, US and Brazil) are shown in Figure 9.6. This index considers the number of McDonald's restaurants (per capita) and IKEA shops (per capita), trade in cultural goods (sum of exports and imports), trademark applications (non-residents as a proportion of all applications) and trade in personal services (sum of exports and imports). The major increases took place from the end of the 1980s. China shows a convergence: a big jump in 1995, and a constant rise after 2001, the latter being a consequence of joining the WTO in 2001. It is notable that even before the dismantling of the USSR, Russia's cultural globalisation was greater than China's or Brazil's. Brazil has had a smoother rise of cultural convergence with the USA. Russia also had a significant increase after the end of communism, though from 2015, following the beginning of hostilities with Ukraine, it has fallen considerably and shows a significant decline and divergence from the USA.

While these data are not perfect, they show that globalisation has amplified interdependence by opening up economies and social life. The scale of globalisation and increased internationalisation have brought about a reconfiguration of economic, political and social space. Consequently, the interaction of technical globalisation and liberal capitalism has had significant cultural effects, particularly since the mid-1990s. It is widely considered that these developments lead to cultural as well as economic hegemony which is exerted by Western powers, particularly the USA.

Interpersonal globalisation

Interpersonal globalisation is more than migration. It also includes the volume of international telephone calls, personal transfers of goods, financial transfers or remittances, arrivals and departures of international tourists and the number of foreign-born residents as a percentage of the total population. Interpersonal globalisation has risen significantly since 1970. Great Britain has the highest interpersonal movement.[25] Interchange with Russia has risen sharply after its economic transformation to exceed the world average in 2012, only to fall to the world average in 2015. China's index is very much below the world average; international population mobility and interpersonal forms of communication remained relatively low and stable between 2012 and 2019.

---

[25] See data in KOF database. KOFIpGldf (Col P).

Figure 9.6: Cultural globalisation, 1970–2019: China, Russia, US and Brazil

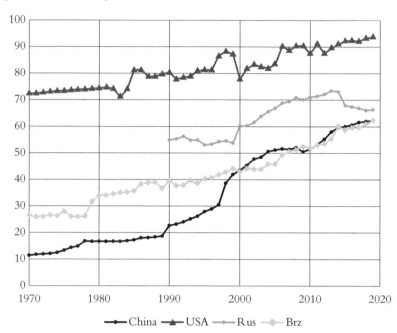

Note: This is an index calculated by KOR which indicates changes over time.

Source: KOR database

Unrestricted migration is a parallel social movement to economic free trade: trade involves the movement of goods, migration that of people. The increase in trade and uneven economic development have been accompanied by a large rise in migration. Unemployed or underemployed people move to developing areas to find work. Neoliberal economics legitimates these developments in terms of enhanced efficiency and increased economic growth. States, however, are subject to public pressure. People oppose immigration for both cultural and economic reasons. Nevertheless, despite states restricting immigration, the scale of worker migration is immense: in the countries of the EU, there were over 40 million foreign born people (9 per cent of its population).[26]

The consequences of migration on a massive scale have led to significant changes in the perception of people with different origins and cultures. In the earlier period of colonialisation, overt racism was practised by policies of hegemonic capitalist states, which frequently maligned the indigenous

---

[26] See Dicken, *Global Shift*, p 345; on Europe, H. Fassmann, M. Haller and D. Lane, *Migration and Mobility in Europe*. Cheltenham: Edward Elgar, 2009, p 1.

peoples in their colonies and other dependent countries. Under conditions of globalisation and large-scale migration, economic liberalism calls for the elimination of discrimination on the basis of social characteristics. Policies of diversity are widely favoured and adopted by transnational organisations. While prejudice on the basis of skin colour and sex continue in more attenuated forms, the rise of greater interpersonal mobility leads to political, economic and cultural elites condemning overt forms of discrimination. Economic elites are generally in favour of free geographical mobility, whereas the publics in host societies are opposed.

Glocalisation

Do these developments lead to the cultural domination of the Western states? John Gray has contended that while globalisation makes economic activity 'more interconnected', it 'has not produced any convergence in economic systems or regimes'.[27] Gray, however, refers only in general terms to different varieties of capitalism, and he ignores the homogenising effects of social, cultural and interpersonal globalisation. Roland Robertson[28] is a fervent denier of the rise of a unitary and dominant 'globalised' culture emanating from the USA through media of mass communication. Robertson emphasises the 'interpenetration' of the local and the global,[29] which creates a pattern of 'glocalisation'. For him, 'the local is essentially *included* [italics in original] within the flexible conception of the global' (p 200). Global media, he contends, are 'absorbed' locally in different ways and globalisation incorporates culture from the locality.[30]

However, there is no empirical content to his assertions, merely the opinion of others offered in support of 'glocalisation'. Food selling outlets, such as McDonald's, in different countries, include local variations of food content, but these are relatively minor. McDonald's franchises strive to provide the service expected 'from McDonald's' and the supply of materials is carefully monitored by the company. Consumers go to McDonald's to sample the real thing – not only the famous Big Mac but also the informal ambiance of the setting. Another example, cited by Robertson, CNN news, indeed differs between regions of the world, but the differences are minor compared to the style, content and messages of the news, which reflect Western liberal concerns. Both examples illustrate that globalisation brings something new

---

27 J. Gray, *False Dawn*. London: Granta Publications, 2002, p xxii.
28 R. Robertson, Globalisation or glocalisation?. *Journal of International Communication*, 18:2 (2002), pp 191–208. Published online 2012, originally published 2002.
29 See Robertson, Globalisation or glocalisation?, p 197.
30 See also R. Robertson (Ed), *European Glocalization in Global Context*. London: Palgrave, 2014.

to the host countries. In the culinary sphere, the flow is not only from the developed countries to the periphery. Internationalisation takes place through the movement of Indian, Chinese and other Asian restaurants and eateries to developed countries; Germany now boasts a ubiquitous glocalised curry wurst (sausage).

In state-guided societies, such as Russia under President Putin and Xi Jinping in China, globalisation is more controlled and 'glocalisation' takes a different form. Writers like Ning Wang, for example, contend that China has adapted to globalisation: 'glocalisation with Chinese characteristics' has been successful.[31] The Chinese government restricts access in line with its law and custom, and adopts a form of internationalisation: it erects borders. Cultural globalisation in China has been subjected to political control, which has precluded some of its effects. However, consumer society has arrived in China and strongly influences people's life styles. Moves to greater national independence, and the greater reliance on self-sufficiency, following the world economic slowdown after 2007 and the COVID-19 pandemic in 2020, have slowed economic globalisation.[32] The effects of global interdependencies are also illustrated by the sanction regimes instituted during the Ukrainian/NATO–Russian war. Russia's political, economic and social interactions with the Western core countries have been significantly reduced. Consequently, the dominant players in international trade are shifting policy towards regionalisation which excludes Russia and China from Western markets and networks. Economic and social intercourse moves on a regional scale, Russian products are still exported, but more go to markets outside NATO.

Does globalisation lead to inequality?

A widely held criticism of the process of globalisation is that it perpetuates the hegemony of the Western states and in doing so amplifies inequality. There are three major issues involved in attempting to study these assertions empirically. First, are inequalities increasing *between* states? Second, are there growing inequalities *within* states? And third is the question of whether there is growing polarisation between different groups of states (hegemonic and dependent).

I address the question of income inequalities by showing the distribution of world income between geographical areas from the middle of the twentieth century to 2017. Figure 9.7 plots the growth in GDP measured in income

---

[31] Ning Wang, Globalisation as glocalisation in China: A new perspective. *Third World Quarterly*, 36:11 (November 2015), pp 2059–74, quotation, p 2066.
[32] See Jeremy Green, *Is Globalisation Over?* Cambridge: Polity, 2019.

Figure 9.7: Economic growth, 1960–2017: selected countries and areas

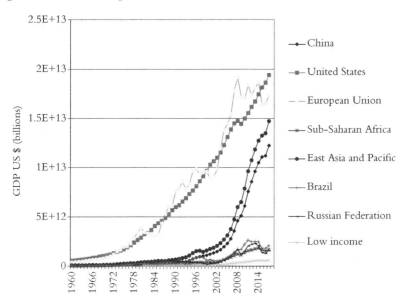

Data are in current US dollars (billions). Dollar figures for GDP are converted from domestic currencies using single year official exchange rates. The notation in the graph deals with large numbers: i.e. 2E+13 represents 20 000 000 000 000 dollars.

Note: GDP at purchaser's prices is the sum of gross value added by all resident producers in the economy plus any product taxes and minus any subsidies not included in the value of the products.

Source: World Bank GDP Indicators, NY.GDP.MKTP.CD. Available at World Bank database.

between 1960 and 2017 for selected countries and groups of countries. Study of the figure will show if there has been an increase in differentials between different groups of countries.

As one would expect, Figure 9.7 shows the continuous rise of income in the European Union and the USA. At the bottom of the scale come all 'low-income' countries, Brazil, Sub-Sahara Africa, and the Russian Federation. It is clear that the gap between these countries and the core states has increased. In the middle of the chart are China and a grouping of East Asian and Pacific countries. Until around 2008, the gap in absolute terms between them and the Western countries increased, thereafter it has significantly declined. As far as *countries* are concerned, we can fairly confidently conclude that the industrialised ones had a healthy growth rate in this time period – despite some downward movements since the financial crisis beginning in 2007. We can also safely say that poor countries, including a significant number of countries in Africa and Latin America, have experienced some growth but have not reduced the gap between themselves and the northern states.

M. Rosner and E. Ortiz-Espena[33] have shown that since around 1975, the greatest change has come in China, East Asia and the Pacific where there has been not only rapid economic growth but also a narrowing of the gap in national GDP between them and the core industrial powers.

As to longer term trends, Figure 9.8 shows the distribution of world income on three dates: 1800, 1975 and 2015. The world income cake is divided into four areas: Europe, Asia-Pacific, Africa, and North and South America. The world poverty line ($1.75 per day) is shown in each graph. In the three periods most of the world's income was in the Asia-Pacific region. However, by 1975 there was a bi-polar distribution with the populations of Asia-Pacific being grouped at the very lowest part of the distribution – most of the populations here were below the poverty line (shown by the vertical line). The European and American areas were skewed towards the richer incomes. The economic and political core, the USA and Europe, received a disproportionate per capita share of the increase in the world's wealth. In 1975, the Asia and the Pacific areas retained most of the world's poor population – roughly 80 per cent of their populations were below the international poverty line.

By 2015, however, a major transformation had taken place. Whereas the European and American populations remained in roughly the same place (with a slight increase overall in the total incomes received), there had been a massive upward shift in the world's wealth. Most residents in the Asia-Pacific area had moved above the international poverty line and there was also a significant increase in the number of people with higher incomes. The gap between America and Europe, on the one side, and Asia-Pacific, on the other, had significantly decreased. If one considers the affluent people, defined here as receiving over $30 per day, the numbers in the two continents were roughly equal. An Asian middle class, predominantly in China, had arrived. For the Asian-Pacific countries, increases in globalisation were correlated with an increase in national wealth. Africa is a loser. While the graphs show that there are more people in Africa in the middle income groups, in 2015, by far the highest proportion of people in the world in poverty are to be found in Africa.

While these data consider shifts in income *between* countries over time, they do not define the differentials between those groups of people *within* countries.[34] If we consider the entire increment in global income between 1988 and 2008, 44 per cent of the gain went to the richest 5 per cent of

---

[33] M. Rosner and E. Ortiz-Espena, Income Inequality, 2016. Available at: https://ourworl dindata.org/income-inequality#global-income-inequality. Graphs constructed by Ola Rosling. Available at: https://www.gapminder.org/tag/ola-rosling/

[34] Branco Milanovic, *Global Inequality*. Cambridge, MA: Belknap Press, 2016, pp 24–6.

Figure 9.8: Division of world national income by continents and per person: 1800, 1975 and 2015

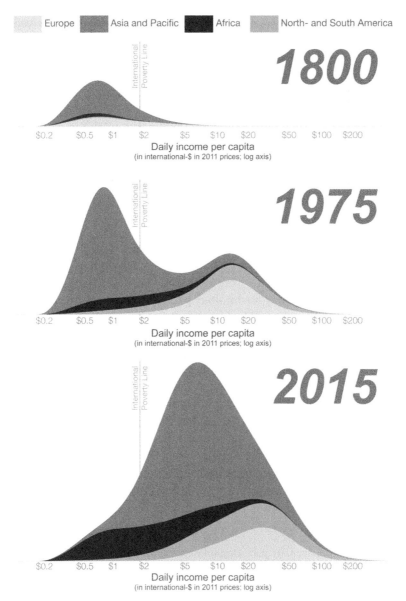

Source: M. Rosner and E. Ortiz-Espena (2016), Income Inequality. Available at: https://our worldindata.org/income-inequality#global-income-inequality. Graphs originally constructed by Ola Rosling available at https://www.gapminder.org/tag/ola-rosling/

people, with almost one-fifth of the total increment being received by the top 1 per cent. As Christopher Lakner and Branco Milanovic[35] point out: the 'emerging global middle class' received only between 2 and 4 per cent of the increase. Whereas in real income terms the top 1 per cent received on average (and after tax) $71,000 compared to the median income of $1,400, the poorest earned $450 (all figures are in 2005 international dollars). Even their statistics, however, indicate that the poor were better off than previously. Christopher Lakner and Branco Milanovic conclude:

> The 'winners' were people in country-deciles that in 1988 were around the median of the global income distribution, 90 percent of whom in terms of population are from Asia. The 'losers' were the country-deciles that in 1988 were around the 85th percentile of the global income distribution, almost 90 percent of whom in terms of population are from mature economies.[36]

The 'losers' were manual and non-manual workers whose work had been outsourced to Asia or been made redundant through technological innovation.

These changes in income were related to economic development for which improved advanced technology played an important part. The role of globalisation was to enable a significant shift to take place from the industrial Western core to the semi-periphery of the world economic system. Here then we have one of the major causes of the changing fortunes of the working classes in the European countries, which we discussed in Chapter 7.

The claims made about the success of globalisation, by authorities such as the World Bank,[37] apply to the countries of South and East Asia, particularly China. 'Tracking the evolution of individual country-deciles shows the underlying elements that drive the changes in the global distribution: China has graduated from the bottom ranks, modifying the overall shape of the global income distribution in the process and creating an important global "median" class.'[38] There were two major winners: an emerging middle class

---

[35] Milanovic, *Global Inequality*, p 25. Original version in C. Lakner and B. Milanovic, Global income distribution: From the fall of the Berlin Wall to the Great Recession. *World Bank Economic Review*, 12 August, 2015. doi: 10.1093/wber/lhv039. Also http://elibrary.worldb ank.org/doi/pdf/10.1596/1813-9450-6719

[36] Christopher Lakner, Branco Milanovic, Global income distribution: From the fall of the Berlin Wall to the Great Recession. Policy Research Working Paper, December 2013; No. 6719. World Bank, Washington, DC. Available at: https://openknowledge.worldb ank.org/handle

[37] See particularly discussion in: World Bank, *Globalisation, Growth and Poverty: Building an Inclusive World Economy*. Washington, DC: World Bank, 2002.

[38] Lakner and Milanovic, Global income distribution (2013).

in the Asian countries and the global rich mainly, but not exclusively, in the Western post-industrial societies. There was one major loser: the lower middle and working classes, mainly in the USA and Europe. Here lies the economic and social basis for the rise of 'populism' and the increasing polarisation of interests between Western professional university educated classes and unskilled or semi-skilled employees.

Two major developments have to be considered arising from late twentieth-century globalisation: the changing role of the state in the core capitalist countries, and the challenge posed by rising states to the Western countries at the core of global capitalism. These topics are addressed in the next chapter.

The globalisation balance sheet

Globalisation has been driven by the economic expansion of corporations based in the core capitalist countries that, under neoliberal policies, have been predisposed to search for profits and markets on a world scale. Technologically, the greater connectedness has been facilitated by the rise of communications' technology; economically, by the transfer of investment and relocation of the factors of production through multinational corporations (MNCs); politically, by the hegemony of a dominant core of states, coordinated by international political organisations. It has been legitimated ideologically through notions of electoral democracy and freedom.

Most commentators claim that, whatever its faults, capitalist globalisation has had positive outcomes. The graphs on Figure 9.8 demonstrate the cumulative increase and wider distribution of wealth associated with capitalist globalisation. And it should be recognised that advocates of 'globalisation' recognise that it has faults and needs to be managed,[39] I return to these critics in Chapter 14. Economists contend that the process of globalised free trade enhances the division of labour, brings more efficiency and consequently has promoted an increase in wealth. Following the classical economists, they claim that free trade brings prosperity, democracy and peace to all. Tom Friedman[40] puts the globalist point dramatically when he updates the thesis that 'democracies do not go to war' by contending that nations with McDonald's have never fought each other. This is perhaps an oversimplification. Countries with McDonald's often go to war with what they term 'authoritarian' or non-democratic countries

---

[39] This is the main argument of writers such as Martin Wolf, *Why Globalization Works*. London and New Haven: Yale University Press, 2004 and Jaqdish Bhaqwati, *In Defence of Globalisation*. Oxford: Oxford University Press, 2004.

[40] T. Friedman, *The Lexus and the Olive Tree: Understanding Globalization*. New York: Picador, 1999.

(which also have McDonald's). And warfare can take many forms – particularly economic sanctions which can devastate or weaken some economies, and can politically destabilise others.

Critics would claim that a consequence of global neoliberalism is that some governments have not been disposed (or in some cases have not been able) to protect national interests. In many countries, privatisation and rationalisation of production by multinational companies have led, on one side, to job losses; on the other, for those employed by them, to higher income. Governments, in meeting financial targets set by international institutions (such as the IMF) and regional neoliberal administrations (such as the EU) have reduced public spending and increased the monetarisation of the economy. The European post-socialist countries have been particularly hard hit by greater marketisation, financialisation and de-industrialisation. In countries with low levels of development, such as Africa and parts of Latin America, policies relying on market mechanisms have not resulted in sustainable economic development but have perpetuated non-development. 'Low-income' countries, which are less globalised, have remained low-income countries. Others, in Asia, notably China, which have adopted liberal policies regulated by the state, have prospered.

At the heart of economic, political and cultural globalisation are Western developed countries led by the USA. As summarised by Zbigniew Brzezinski, the USA is the

> geopolitical core of shared responsibility for peaceful global management … That web – woven by multinational corporations, non-governmental organisations, and scientific communities and reinforced by the internet – already creates an informal global system that is inherently congenial to more institutionalised and inclusive global cooperation … Geostrategic success in that cause would represent a fitting legacy of America's role as the first, only and last truly superpower.[41]

In this context, nation states have been weakened as sovereign powers. Global political institutions (the International Monetary Fund (IMF), the Bank for International Settlements (BIS), World Bank, the World Trade Organization (WTO)) and hegemonic states (USA, the EU, Japan) have become the major economic and political stakeholders – with the USA playing a hegemonic role.

All 'developing' or 'rising' countries copy the dominant West – adopt its technology and its popular culture, but only partially or not at all, its liberal

---

[41] Z. Brzezinski, *The Grand Chessboard: American Primacy and its Geostrategic Imperatives.* New York: Basic Books, 1997, p 215.

democratic political institutions and processes. The diplomatic rupture between the USA and China coupled to the Ukraine/NATO war with Russia promises to reverse many aspects of globalisation discussed previously. A new global division of labour brings greater internal differentiation to North and South and thus a new configuration of power relations between core, semi-core and periphery, which will be considered in the next chapter. Economic 'de-colonisation', neoliberal globalisers contend, has improved democracy; internationalisation has extended Western elite and popular culture; and democratic processes and freedoms have enhanced individual well-being. Of great importance is the fact that standards of living have risen and that the process of free trade has led to poverty reduction in the Third World (notably in China, but also in South-East Asia, in countries like South Korea and Singapore). Culturally, it is contended by advocates of globalisation that, among the rising states, the infusion of a Western consumer ethic, products, services, sport, and entertainment is positively accepted.

From this point of view, politically, globalisation has been a positive development promoting beneficial integration between the nations and peoples of the world. It is not conceded that the nation state has lost power. Advocates of globalisation contend that the power, authority and functions of the state have been reconstituted. The nation state must share power with regional and international bodies and is no longer a sovereign self-governing unit. From this point of view, state sovereignty is understood as a bargaining resource for states in a new type of global politics in which global tendencies are mediated by states and local cultures. 'Glocalisation' augments global values and products with local characteristics and features.

Critics claim that these conclusions are far too one-sided. Top managers and executives have experienced enormous hikes in salaries and benefits representing 'what the market' is prepared to pay. Wealth and income inequality have risen. The rise of China and the failure of transition to capitalism in Russia have halted, and reversed, the trend to open globalisation and is likely to continue. The sanctions regime imposed consequent on the Ukraine/NATO–Russia war amplifies this form of deglobalisation – at least for the affected states. The dominant form of capitalist globalisation, championed by the USA, is challenged politically by China. A failure of many commentators on globalisation is to marginalise the more regulated form of internationalisation taken by China, which has selectively chosen from the globalisation menu. I have shown that globalisation trends have been reversed in some areas. However, internationalisation remains at much higher levels than in the late twentieth century and is likely to remain so.

It must be accepted that developments have led to a major rise in wealth in the Asian countries where the mass of the population has been moved out of poverty. The emerging middle class has been a major beneficiary. In contrast, globalisation in the already industrialised countries has disadvantaged the less educated and semi-skilled workers. As we noted in Chapter 7, many previously highly paid semi-skilled and skilled manual jobs have been lost with automation and the outsourcing of production. Concurrently, welfare provision has been curtailed and trade unions have lost bargaining powers. Hence compensatory welfare state measures blunting the effects of capitalistic market competition are no longer as effective as in the past.

Opponents of globalisation, even if they concede some of these positive effects of globalised capitalism, remain sceptical. Benefits of globalisation, they claim, have been grossly maldistributed. Neoliberal globalisation has been particularly advantageous for investors, managers, and higher professionals working in business and financial services which are transnational in scope. Investors and managers have greatly profited from the internationalisation of capital markets through speculation, trading in shares and enhanced dividends. Capitalist globalisation, they claim, perpetuates the hegemony of Western states, which they consider to be harmful. Unjustifiable inequality between and within countries is not significantly decreasing. Democracy is threatened. As Dani Rodrik has put it: 'we cannot simultaneously pursue democracy, national determination and economic globalisation' ('the political trilemma').[42] The fulfilment of excessive 'wants' in the advanced countries leads critics to call for a halt to policies of cumulative economic growth, which exacerbate the exploitation of nature. A green agenda is compromised by neoliberal globalisation.

The globalisation of capitalism has three important implications. First, the structure of the capitalist class includes an international, as well as a national, component. Second, the nation state has been weakened in its responsibility to maintain a social compact with its citizens. Third, in the twenty-first century, the global system is moving towards a bifurcation between the Western core elements and a rising group of states, the 'semi-core'.

The effects of growing hostility between Russia and China and the dominant Western powers, coupled to the imposition of economic, political, and social sanctions by the West have led to regionalisation and 'friendoutsourcing' – consequently, strengthening Russia and China's links with Asia, Africa and Latin America. These development we consider in the next chapter.

---

[42] Rodrik, *The Globalization Paradox*, p xviii.

10

The Changing Global Class
Structure and the Challenge
of the Semi-Core

The role of states in defining foreign and domestic policy is widely believed to have declined with the rise of global capitalism. The ruling classes are reconstituted on a global basis. The power of transnational companies, global agreements transferring power to international agencies, and a reliance on market (rather than political) forces, it is claimed, have weakened the role of states. In encouraging an open competitive playing field, liberalism promotes the unrestricted movement of capital and severely limits state support for national companies – thereby undermining economic ideologies such as Keynesianism and economic nationalism, which are state centric. As a consequence of the displacement of national companies by international ones, governments have less need to negotiate a compromise between their national bourgeoisie and the national working class. The expansion of liberal economic blocs (such as the EU and the Eurasian Economic Union) and the pervasive influence of international organisations draw countries into global and overlapping regional networks. Consequently, social security provided by state full employment policies, welfare state benefits and state-financed old aged pensions are not promoted by national governments. The major concern of national governments is to fulfil the monetary and economic rules laid down by regional (such as the European Union) and international bodies (such as the International Monetary Fund and the World Trade Organization). The onus of social security is put on individuals to make personal provision. These developments are the underlying causes of the decline of social democratic governments that promoted a welfare agenda. Moreover, whereas national economies have democratic oppositions of varying strengths, political classes and elites operating on a global scale are not subject to such countervailing powers. The cause of this disjunction is that all citizens have only one vote in national elections, whereas corporations have as many votes as the size of their capital – money can buy political power.

But the conclusion that nation states have lost their power to an amorphous market is not fully warranted. States retain major powers which include a monopoly over the definition of citizenship, the use of internal lethal weapons and military force, the preservation of national boundaries and the declaration of war. These powers give states considerable powers, at least to some states, in international affairs. Contemporary events – the COVID-19 pandemic, the war in Ukraine, controls over environmental conditions – are regulated by states. The application of sanctions over Russia's military intervention in Ukraine, which negatively affect transnational trade and interpersonal movement, is conducted and applied by states. States retain powers over immigration and, due to political pressure from labour, often restrict immigration – despite the economic rationality of the global market. At a lower level, international companies operating in host countries are subject to their labour and tax laws. The German government, for example, compelled McDonald's to adhere to German labour law to recognise trade unions.

What we can safely conclude is that electoral politics and democracy promotion revolve around control of the nation state, not the global economy. Henry Kissinger puts this distinction clearly '[T]he political and economic organisation of the world are at variance with each other. The international economic system has become global, while the political structure of the world has remained based on the nation-state'[1] Some argue that this divide between nation states and the global economic order is being bridged. The argument here is that the power, authority and functions of the state have been reconstituted. State sovereignty is now understood as a resource for a politics that is embedded in complex transnational networks. In all countries, the legal currency of money, the powers of taxation, popular forms of political representation, extra-legal protest, political parties and politicians – the major articulators and aggregators of political interests – continue to be state based.

These observations have to be modified somewhat as the economic, political and cultural endowments of nation states differ greatly and hence form a hierarchy of states. Some states assume a dominant, even hegemonic position (notably the USA) – and retain their powers – whereas others accept a subordinate role. This is indicated by the trends in the unequal distribution of power, wealth and income between and within states.

---

[1] Henry Kissinger, *World Order: Reflections on the Character of Nations and the Course of History*. London: Allen Lane, 2014, p 368.

The changing structure of the ruling classes

The changing economic structures have important social consequences which in turn shape the pattern of international politics. Some states retain, in attenuated forms, traditional socialist/liberal/nationalist types of political parties, even though their social and economic base has crumbled. The global economy of the advanced societies defines the character of the new ruling classes. The dispersal of ownership through financial instruments weakened the early twentieth-century national bourgeoisies in the Western capitalist countries. The new transnational bourgeoisie includes owners and executives of global companies.

In grappling with the ways in which globalisation has influenced the class structure of contemporary societies, national capitalist classes (those who own and control the means of production) are joined by executives of international organisations (such as the World Bank, WTO, IMF) as well as those who possess cultural capital (administrators of international advisory bodies, 'think tanks' and research institutes). Finance, media, pharmaceutical, weapons and energy corporations have a global character. The new capitalist classes are not only recipients of profits but also receive exceedingly high incomes – economic rents measured in millions of dollars. In the rising states, such as China and Russia, nationally based corporations remain a component of hybrid economic formations.

To encapsulate these changes in actual power relations, the ruling class has to be defined in a wider framework than that of the economic concept of 'relations to the means of production'. Under globalisation a new major player, a transnational capitalist class,[2] based in hegemonic countries with a global reach, has entered the political arena. The implication here is that statist forms of economic coordination and political control come into conflict with globalising developments. The greater spatial interdependence of transnational corporations (TNCs) diminishes rivalry between countries which no longer are exclusive champions of their national companies. The capitalist class has different factions. As we noted, countries differ in the extent and form of globalisation. The national bourgeoisie, the traditional owner of the means of production, retains an important place.

What holds the global system together and what legitimates and drives the propensity for expansion? For the globalisation critics, the answer is competitive capitalism, paralleled by an ideology of popular consumerism. Those who drive and gain most from globalisation are what Leslie Sklair[3]

---

[2] Leslie Sklair, *Globalization: Capitalism and Its Alternatives*. Oxford: Oxford University Press, 2002. Leslie Sklair, The emancipatory potential of generic globalisation. *Globalizations*, 6:4 (9December 2009), pp 525–39.

[3] Sklair, The emancipatory potentia. On transnational capitalist class see pp 528–9.

calls the transnational capitalist class. The constituencies of this class are derived from the character of twenty-first-century capitalism. Sklair defines this dominant class in terms of five major factions, which are interdependent.

At its economic heart is the global (economic) corporate class – the individuals and collective bodies who own and control major transnational financial and non-financial corporations. It should be understood as one faction of the capitalist class on a world scale, as there remain national and international capitalist interests that often conflict. The second faction contains globalising state and regional politicians and officials: state presidents/prime ministers, members of the Commission of the EU. While such leaders are constitutionally representatives of citizens of states (or regions) they have become identified with, and sponsor, policies promoting globalised capitalist interests.

Third, comes the administrative /technical faction, made up of 'globalising professionals' – board-members and executives of the IMF, the World Bank, the WTO, the European Bank of Reconstruction and Development and the Bank for International Settlements. These institutions provide coordinating mechanisms for markets to work on a global basis. While such professionals are not 'capitalists' (they are not part of the process of extracting surplus value), for Sklair, they nevertheless form part of the transnational class.

Fourth, is the ideological faction. This includes members of national and international political think tanks and policy associations, academic bodies (universities and research institutes, particularly in economics), media managers – editors of publishing houses and 'quality' newspapers. Members of this faction articulate, or respond to, an economic ideology of neoliberal globalisation. This faction is particularly important in spreading the culture-ideology not only of economic growth and consumerism but also in interpreting international affairs as defined by the political faction.

The fifth 'consumerist' faction is composed of merchants who promote, and media which gain from, consumerism. The minds of people have been captured not by religion but by the need to pursue the continual consumption of commodities. This faction includes companies in the mass circulation print media, TV, cinema, radio media companies, showbiz and commercialised sport.

Most members of these different factions congregate in such associations as the Davos World Forum, Wittenberg Foundation and International Chambers of Commerce.[4] This approach extends the notion of the dominant capitalist class by including elites of non-economic institutions (such as

---

[4]   For a detailed account see: Kees Van der Pijl, *Transnational Classes and International Relations*. London: Routledge, 1998.

academia, politics, mass media, sport, government) in the global political class. Power is also more widely dispersed. This transnational class is more than a 'capitalist economic class' and I suggest to call it a *global political class* because it is composed of elites who are not 'capitalist' in an economic sense though they are part of the apparatuses of global political power.

In Table 10.1, I summarise the nature of class formations in three different social formations: pre-industrial, industrial and post-industrial societies. Existing states combine elements from each of these formations – a mix of industrial and post-industrial, and some (such as China and India) retain elements from pre-industrial societies. In post-industrial society, the national bourgeoisie and state bureaucracy remain, often in contestation with the global political class, which includes leading politicians and chiefs of global organisations. The industrial working class constituted a subordinate class in industrial society. Its decline in the hegemonic countries entailed the decay of its political forms, the trade union and social democratic/socialist political party. The post-industrial ascendant class is unformed and is likely to rest on the 'creative' class (as discussed in Chapter 11).

Table 10.1: Class formations and geo-political scope: pre-industrial, industrial and post-industrial society

	Pre-industrial	Industrial	Post-industrial
Dominant classes	Aristocracy	National bourgeoisie/ state bureaucracy	Global political class
Geopolitical scope of dominant class	Local	International/ national	Global/ international
Subordinate class	Peasantry	Working class: predominantly manual	Working class: predominantly non-manual
Geopolitical scope of subordinate classes	Local	National	National
Ascendant class	Bourgeoisie	Working class	Not formed ('creative' class)
Geopolitical scope of ascendant class	National	International	Not formed

The challenge of the semi-core

While Sklair's approach, outlined previously, is useful in outlining changes and illustrates how the pattern of 'the core' states of global capitalism has shaped a new global capitalist class, it does not take account of the growing divisions between states and particularly the rise of countries which challenge the hegemony of the core. The grouping of political and economic blocs is illustrated in Table 10.2. The economic core of the world system is composed of a hegemonic bloc led by the USA and other regional powers – the EU, the UK and Japan. The hegemonic bloc has an important military dimension in NATO, which promotes and defends the institutions and values of the hegemonic core. It is in this core that the global political class is to be found.

In the twenty-first century, the dominant powers of the world system in a geo-political sense (often referred to as the 'core') are no longer uniquely formed by the powerful Western states. One must take account of the diversity of, and conflict between, states and regions that have bifurcated the leading world powers. China and Russia have emerged from a state socialist political formation and retain features of state ownership and control quite different from the advanced capitalist countries of Europe and the USA. As components in the world economic system, the rising countries form a 'semi-core' – a counterpoint to the hegemonic countries. These countries exchange with the Western core but politically are not part of it. Conflict arises when the semi-core is reluctant to accept the rules of the international economic order which are set by the economic and political core under the leadership of the USA. A group of countries led by China is in a state

Table 10.2: World capitalist system: core states

CORE	Hegemonic bloc:	Military dimension:
	US, EU, Japan, Australia, UK	US, NATO
SEMI-CORE	Counterpoints:	Military dimension:
	China, Eurasian Economic Union	Russia, China
	Shanghai Cooperation Organisation	

of 'competitive interdependence'[5] – a form of interdependency between the two groups of states that are political and military rivals. They compete for markets with the core Western states and, to their mutual advantage, exchange goods and services, and in doing so they adapt to Western consumer lifestyles (what was described as 'social globalisation'). However, they adopt distinctive features: contemporary China and Russia have developed their own civilisational ideology, their own economic institutions, forms of property relations and military power. They constitute an interdependent but separate semi-core of states.

The semi-core includes countries that are hosts to foreign corporations and concurrently have their own national and international economic corporations. The semi-core includes countries (notably China and Russia) and regional groups whose economic corporations interact, exchange and compete with those of the core. By virtue of their size and the strength of their economies, the nation-state formations are able not only militarily to defend themselves but also socially to ensure reproduction. They constitute political formations in which a class of executives manage state-owned assets and have influence over privately owned companies. The rising states of Russia and China are excluded from the hegemonic capitalist core. These rising states have a different class structure, which contains not only a business class but also powerful nationally based bureaucratic classes. The international conflict between Russia (supported by China) and Ukraine (sponsored by NATO) that erupted in 2022 reflects this division in the constitution of the world economic system. The proxy war between NATO and Russia, is a war about international power and a supposed threat posed to the capitalist core by rising states. The states in the semi-core are less exposed to global capitalist interests and have a potential for internal state-led economic development. The semi-periphery and periphery (not considered here) are made up of states that are less developed and are more dependent on the core and semi-core. They have no globally significant military dimension.

From peripheral dependence to competitive interdependence

What initially brought the new regional actors (the Eurasian Economic Union, the Shanghai Cooperation Organisation, the BRICS [Brazil, Russia, India, China, South Africa]) together was a scepticism, which is not equally shared by the members of these associations, of the political, military and economic policies emanating from the USA and expressed in the policies

---

5   Alberta Sbragia, The EU, the US, and trade policy: Competitive interdependence in the management of globalization. *Journal of European Public Policy*, 17:3 (2010), pp 368–82.

of NATO. Unlike earlier state competitors (notably post-1945 Germany), China (and to a lesser extent Russia) presents not only an economic but also a civilisational alternative. It is heir to an ancient civilisation; it is a continental power with massive human and natural resources.

The changing balance of economic influence may be measured by the decline in the world share of GDP for the Western core states,[6] compared with a new bloc of BRICS. In 1980, the BRICS produced only 11 per cent of world GDP and the EU 32 per cent; by 2007 the BRICS in total equalled the share of the EU, and by 2015, the BRICS accounted for 30 per cent of global GDP – some 12 per cent greater than the EU and 10 per cent greater than NAFTA.[7]

One other robust measure of the declining economic power of the Western core countries is the number of firms listed in the top 2000 world companies. The Forbes List measures the strength of companies in terms of four attributes: sales, profits, assets and market value. By 2015, in Asia, 691 companies were in the top 2000, compared to Europe's 486. China with over two hundred companies had outstripped Japan, and the BRICS combined (370 companies) came to just over 60 per cent of the number of US companies. They included 57 Indian, 27 Russian, 24 Brazilian and 14 South African companies. It must be emphasised that the USA, as a single country, still has a considerable lead – but it is declining. Moreover, China had 5 companies in the top 10 and 13 in the top 100. China has a good spread of firms across the economic sectors including banking, materials, transportation, insurance, utilities, oil and gas, technology and hardware, consumer durables, and food and drink. Table 10.3 shows the top ten countries in Forbes' list of 2000 companies for 2018; five are Chinese.[8]

A strengthening of the semi-core regional economic and political associations is a consequence of the uncertainties unleashed by the global economic crisis following 2008 as well as the more belligerent foreign policy of the USA. The formation of the Shanghai Cooperation Organisation,[9] the Collective Security Treaty Organisation,[10] the Eurasian Economic Community[11] and the Organisation of Central Asian Cooperation,[12]

---

6 NAFTA (US, Mexico and Canada) from 2019, replaced by the US–Mexico–Canada Agreement [USMCA]) and the EU.
7 IMF World Economic Outlook Data Base, 2015. Purchasing power parity (Current international dollars). Available at: https://www.imf.org/external/pubs/ft/weo/2015
8 These leading companies remain fairly constant. By 2020, Wells Fargo had fallen to 17th place, replaced by the Saudi Arabian Oil Company in 5th place.
9 Composed of China, Kazakhstan, Kyrgyzstan, Russian Federation, Tajikistan and Uzbekistan.
10 Armenia, Belarus, Kazakhstan, Kyrgyzstan, Russia, Tajikistan and Uzbekistan.
11 Russia, Kazakhstan and Belarus.
12 Russia, Turkmenistan, Tajikistan, Kazakhstan, Uzbekistan and Kyrgyzstan.

Table 10.3: World top companies, 2018

Company	Country	Sales	Profits	Assets	Market value
ICBC	China	$165.3	$43.7	$4,210.9	$311
China Construction Bank	China	$143.2	$37.2	$3,631.6	$261.2
JPMorgan Chase	US	$118.2	$26.5	$2,609.8	$387.7
Berkshire Hathaway	US	$235.2	$39.7	$702.7	$491.9
Agricultural Bank of China	China	$129.3	$29.6	$3,439.3	$184.1
Bank of America	US	$103	$20.3	$2,328.5	$313.5
Wells Fargo	US	$102.1	$21.7	$1,915.4	$265.3
Apple	US	$247.5	$53.3	$367.5	$926.9
Bank of China	China	$118.2	$26.4	$3,204.2	$158.6
Ping An Insurance Group	China	$141.6	$13.9	$1,066.4	$181.4

Data are in current US dollars (billions).

Source: Forbes Global 2000 for 2018. Available at: https://www.forbes.com/global2000/#63394e41335d.

is evidence of the rise of regional economic and political blocs. Latin American countries, such as Brazil, Cuba and Venezuela (MERCOSUR) constitute another trading area having more the character of peripheral dependency on the hegemonic capitalist core. For countries in the semi-core of the world system, regionalism enables them, through cooperative agreements, to strengthen their position against hegemonic powers. They may erect boundaries and rely on exchange through mutual agreements and treaties. Some commentators regard this development as a new or alternative form of globalisation. Following Xi Jinping, they see a divergence of economic models, with the rising countries led by China promoting a regional form of internationalism.[13] As we note in Chapter 14, Xi Jinping's idea of 'globalisation' includes rights to maintain state boundaries and thus to control the flow of matter – commodities and ideologies.[14]

---

[13] Y. Lissovolik, BRICS-PLUS: Alternative Globalization in the Making? Moscow Valdai Club. July 2017. 69 Valdai Papers. Available at: www.valdaiclub.com/files/14927

[14] See Xi Jinping's speech at Davos World Economic Forum, January 2017. Available at: https://www.weforum.org/agenda/2017/01/full-text-of-xi-jinping-keynote-at-the-world-economic-forum/

The competitive interdependence of the rising economies with core ones has led to significant de-industrialisation of the Western core, and economic development in the previous semi-peripheral countries. China, in terms of national GDP measured in terms of purchasing power, caught up with the USA in 2016 (see Figure 10.1). (China uses a different measure and Chinese statistics in 2018 put it in second place after the USA). When combined, Russia, India and China have considerable manufacturing and military capacity and enormous internal markets. But of the five BRICS countries, only three (Russia, India and China) share common geographical borders. There are also very great differences between their economic wealth and political power. (One could, of course, say the same about the EU, though it does not contain a similar hegemonic state to China – France and Germany equally constitute leading states).

Figure 10.1 shows the gross national income of China and the USA. The picture changes considerably when we consider *per capita* income where China is well behind Western countries. When we take population into account, in 2019 the gross national income per capita measured by purchasing power parity in dollars, came to $16,708 for China and $65,253

Figure 10.1: Gross domestic product (purchasing power parity): China, US, 1980–2020

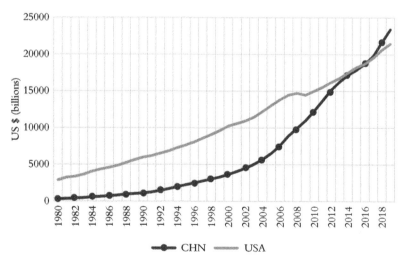

Note: PPP GDP is gross domestic product converted to international dollars using purchasing power parity rates. An international dollar has the same purchasing power over GDP as the U.S. dollar has in the US.

Source: International Monetary Fund, World Economic Outlook Database, October 2020. Available at: https://www.imf.org/en/Publications/WEO/weo-database/2020/October/downl oad-entire-database.

for the USA.[15] The Human Development Index (HDI) – an average of life expectancy, years of schooling and income[16] – is a better measure than GDP to estimate the all-round development of a country. Here in 2019, China came in 85th place, well below Russia (49th), and the USA at 15th place (the top country was Norway). In making a comparison between China and the West, one must take into account the large economies of the states in the EU, as well as Japan and Australia, which when combined with the USA, present a much stronger economic and political bloc.

The United States faces the prospect of a relative economic decline and the loss of its role as a hegemonic world power.[17] The export of value added manufactures is an indicator of economic dynamism. Since 2000, the USA has experienced a steady decline in exports of high technology products (as a proportion of all manufactured exports) in the face Chinese exports. As detailed in Figure 10.2, since the world financial crisis of 2007, China has surpassed the amount (measured in value) of high-tech exports of the USA.

Figure 10.2: High-tech exports: China, US, EU, 2007–2018

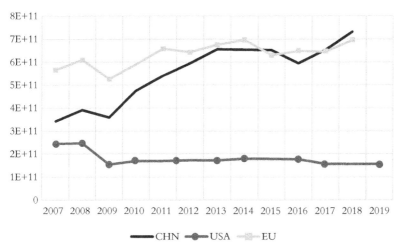

Exports given in current US dollars. The notation in the graph deals with large numbers: i.e. 7E +11 represents 700 000 000 000 or 700 billion US dollars.

Source: World Bank Database. Available at: https://data.worldbank.org/indicator/TX.VAL. TECH.CD.

---

[15] IMF database World Economic Outlook 2020. Available at: https://www.imf.org/en/Publications/WEO/weo-database/2020/October/download-entire-database

[16] UNDP, Human Development Index 2019. Available at: http://hdr.undp.org/en/data. Table 1.

[17] See Z. Brzezinski, The Grand Chessboard. New York: Basic Books. 1997.

Innovation and new product development, of course, are a different story and many qualify China's technological development by pointing to the dependency on the import of foreign hi-tech components.[18] Nevertheless, the USA, has suffered greatly as a consequence of Chinese competition, and its superiority in many fields has been threatened. China's exports have built up significant currency reserves, which have been invested mainly in US bonds. Consequently, by the early twenty-first century, China held around half of US foreign debt, which added another strand to US–China interdependence.[19] What underlies the sanctions proposed against Chinese companies trading in the West (such as Huawei) is the technological threat posed by these companies to Western (especially American) ones. States then take up the cause of 'their' transnational companies. Threats to national security, requiring economic sanctions, are a secondary and more disputable issue.

The balance of economic power is shifting away from the core capitalist countries to a group of rising states led by China. Figure 10.3 illustrates the relative shares in world GDP of the top 11 countries in 1980 and 2020 by geographical areas.[20] Not all members of the various economic blocs are shown here of course but study of the differences between the two figures brings out the significant change in relative positions of the leading world states between 1980 and 2020. The GDP of all countries rose considerably between these dates, but the share of the hegemonic core fell. The ratio of the share of world GDP of the top countries in America, Europe and Japan to other countries came to more than three quarters in 1980. By 2020 this ratio had fallen to less than half. The leading European countries' share had fallen dramatically and is a significant factor underpinning the relentless enlargement policy pursued by the EU to maintain its 'market share'.[21] That the Western dominated liberal international order is confronted by a challenger is widely recognised.[22]

---

[18] See Elizabeth Economy, *The Third Revolution: Xi Jinping and the New Chinese State*. Oxford: Oxford University Press, 2018.

[19] On the trade imbalance see Jenny Clegg, *China's Global Strategy: Towards a Multipolar World*. London: Pluto Press, 2009, Chapter 10.

[20] Top countries by GDP (purchasing power parity, figures in international US dollars) 1980: US, Japan, Germany, Italy, France, Brazil, UK, Mexico, India, Saudi Arabia, China; in 2020: China, US, India, Japan, Germany, Russia, Indonesia, Brazil, UK, France, Mexico.

[21] See J. Borocz, Geopolitical scenarios for European integration. In J. Jensen and F. Miszlivetz (Eds), *Reframing Europe's Future: Challenges and Failures of the European Construction*. London: Routledge, 2014, pp 20–34.

[22] C.A. McNally, Sino capitalism: China's re-emergence and the international political economy. *World Politics*, 64:4 (October 2012), pp 741–76; Kees van der Pijl, Is the East still Red?. *Globalisations*, 9:4 (2012), pp 503–16.

Figure 10.3: World top 11 countries by GDP (PPP), 1980 and 2020, presented by economic blocs

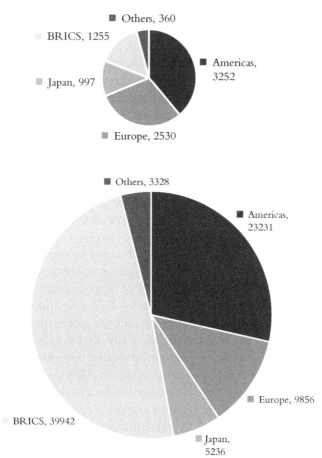

Data measured in purchasing power parity (current international dollars; billions).

Note: First figure 1980, second figure 2020. In the figures the top 11 countries are allocated to one geographical area.

Source: IMF, World Economic Outlook 2016 and 2020, database.

Globalisation in reverse?

Many doubt whether neoliberal globalisation can secure a non-territorial form of power for Western states. By the 2020s, global neoliberalism appeared to be in retreat. The Ukrainian–Russian war led NATO to call for limitations to globalisation but not to capitalism – security of fuel and power supply trumped free trade. The invasion of Ukraine by Russia in 2022 and the sanctions imposed by the Western core countries on Russia, as well as controls over trade with China, have led many commentators to declare a process of de-globalisation. Sanctions have disrupted supply chains. Russian companies and citizens have been cut off from international banking services. Employees and creditors in foreign countries cannot be paid and many companies have closed their foreign branches. Export of commodities and spare parts to Russia are illegal and involve high penalties to Western companies. Russian car manufacturing and energy companies have been seriously affected and exports to Western countries have also been severely restricted – though not to the global South. As for China: here is one example, 'Leading [US] chip equipment suppliers have suspended sales and services to semiconductor manufacturers in China, as new US export controls disrupt the Chinese tech industry and global companies' operations … ASML … has told its US staff to stop serving all Chinese customers while it assesses the sanctions'.[23]

The COVID-19 crisis led state governments to prioritise their own supplies of pharmaceutical products boosting domestic production and demands for state ownership and control of supplies rather than corporate ownership. The fuel crisis which broke in 2022 called into question the corporate ownership of energy supplies and the global market's ability to fulfil human needs. As illustrated by the COVID-19 crisis and the war in Ukraine, under conditions of geopolitical rivalry, dependence on imports from adversaries poses a threat to national security. Withheld supplies of key medical supplies by foreigners can threaten national health. The dependence of some NATO countries on Russian energy, is considered a threat. Even countries that have benefitted from globalisation, notably China and India, have modified foreign trade by maintaining state coordination and controls over interaction with foreigners. Most commentators recognise the need for further regulation, some for a different form of globalisation and others insist on departure from any form of globalisation. The effects of the sanctions and counter sanctions restrict the freedom of trade and thus lead to some form of de-globalisation. However, 'globalised' forms of exchange between 'Western friendly' countries and between Russia/China and their associates will continue. A likely consequence is that regional blocs of countries will form a kind of 'friendshoring' – countries will trade with others that have compatible economic and political regimes.

The sanctions exercised by Western states (the USA, UK) and regional blocs (the EU) indicate quite clearly that political power can be wielded by states independently of global norms and against the interests of international

---

[23] *Financial Times* (London) 15 October 2022.

business. In this context, states still retain power though sometimes not in concert with international corporations. Sanctions enforced in 2022 against Russia affect a very large range of companies with respect to financial services, investments, foreign exchange, a vast range of goods and services, technology transfer, tourism, internet services, transport, immigration.[24] These were not in accord with the interests of European industrial interests, which faced significant supply chain costs when Russian energy supply was curtailed. Transnational companies which have profited from trade with Russia have been severely penalised by the sanctions regimes enforced by the UK and the EU.

What then of the assertion by Colin Crouch that the TNCs are 'right inside the room of political decision-making',[25] do states prevail over corporations? The answer depends very much on which states and which corporations are in the room. President Biden, like President Bush before him, listens to the energy sector companies, which gain from shutting down Russian energy supplies to Europe (they can step in with liquified gas), but not the pleas of importers and retailers of Russian oil and gas. American companies, such as Lockheed Martin, the world's largest commercial arms manufacturer, clearly benefits from the enlargement of NATO. But it is not only military suppliers that gain from war, so do their employees: on 19 October 2022, the British Trade Union Congress voted (narrowly) to increase military spending – to defend jobs in the British armaments industry.

The exercise of sanctions, which often break the norms of international trade and rights of ownership, brings into focus divisions in the international order which disturb the neoliberal global system. In terms of world politics, President Putin and President Xi Jinping oppose the 'unipolar world order' dominated by the USA. The claim here, echoed by many rising states, is that global rules are made by the hegemonic Western core states. In the case of sanctions, rules are broken if they contravene the interests of the USA. Sanctions against Russian energy producers, for example, favour American exports of liquified gas to the European markets. Hence the USA's actions are in concert with their own national (or American-controlled transnational) corporations as well as the political aspirations of some American politicians. One should be cautious, however, in writing off globalisation following the sanction wars of 2022. Wars always have limiting effects on international relations. Both the First and Second World Wars limited trade, development, social and political contacts. But they revived in following years. The technical processes of globalisation – the narrowing of space and time between

---

[24] Sanctions against Russia are listed at: https://www.gov.uk/government/publications/rus sia-sanctions-guidance/russia-sanctions-guidance

[25] C. Crouch, *The Strange Non-Death of Neoliberalism*, p 310.

players – have great advantages to all parties. The restrictions created by COVID-19 and sanctions' wars are likely to be reversed over time.

Conclusion

As globalisation creates international forms of political and economic power, an alternative politics and economics to neoliberalism has to address the international framework in which they operate. Alternative forms of capitalism or alternatives to capitalism may be considered in the ways that states or groups of states are constrained by, and concurrently influence, the world's economic and political systems. Significant changes have taken place in the world economy, which have weakened the relative position of the traditional core members. States have lost many of their powers to regional (the EU) and international organisations (the IMF) though they still retain considerable powers – depending on their economic and political constitution. The global politically dominant classes are composed not only of those who own and control transnational economic corporations but also globalising politicians, professionals from international coordinating organisations, journalists in the ideological faction, ideologues from international policy associations and academia, and merchants promoting consumerism. In the twenty-first century, there is no longer a core and dependent semi-periphery and periphery, but a core, semi-core and periphery. The semi-core is a challenge to the hegemony of the capitalist economic core. China in the period between 1980 and 2007 shifted from peripheral dependence to competitive interdependence.[26] Advanced industrialised states such as contemporary China, and earlier the USSR, developed their own civilisational ideology, their own economic institutions, forms of property relations and military power. They constituted a separate semi-core of states. They compete for markets with the core Western states and, to their mutual advantage, exchange goods and services, and in doing so they adapt to Western consumer lifestyles. President Xi Jinping has defined the world system as one world, two systems. The US remains a hegemonic power, though weakened by excessive ambitions for world hegemony as the leader of the free world. Economic and other sanctions exercised against China and Russia threaten globalisation and are likely to lead to a bifurcation in the world economic and political order. The current challenge of China presages a power transition: a shift of political and economic influence to the east. Its geo-political position makes possible an alternative economy and civilisation – a challenge to global neoliberal capitalism, to which we return in Chapter 15.

---

[26] Sbragia, The EU, the US, and trade policy.

11

Self-destructing Propensities of Global Capitalism

As we noted in Chapter 9, opinion about the effects of global capitalism is divided. Positive evaluations dwell on the ways in which information technology facilitates diverse forms of exchange and on the benefits it brings by reducing costs, widening markets and facilitating access to information, knowledge and services. Opponents view globalisation as a set of negative processes flowing from capitalist structures of ownership and international organisations and associations which are not subject to any form of democratic accountability. For others, globalisation is a consequence of modernity and poses a threat to traditional values.[1] Most criticism is directed at the economic features of globalisation that are embedded in a neoliberal form of capitalism and such critics do not separate the effects of globalisation, which might be positive (or negative), from capitalism, which might be negative (or positive).

Some believe that faults can be corrected without major changes in the world capitalist system; they advocate a democratically regulated form of globalisation which retains capitalist features. Others, in contrast, contend that the benefits of globalisation cannot be achieved without a fundamental move away from the capitalist system and advocate a shift to a post-capitalist or socialist form of globalisation. The latter we consider in Chapter 14. Many look for, or detect, changes already occurring within capitalism and they envisage not only a 'post-global' but an ascendant 'post capitalist' social system. These approaches represent a return to internationalism in which states mediate the reciprocated forms of global exchange. Finally, there remain the critical 'anti-globalisation' and 'anti-capitalism' perspectives, which regard capitalistic globalisation as politically and ecologically harmful. They seek

---

[1]   C. Crouch, *The Globalization Backlash*. Cambridge: Polity, 2019, pp 4–6.

to reverse these tendencies by moving to various forms of autonomy and self-government with democratic forms of control.

Ideological critiques gained momentum after the economic crisis of 2007 and have emphasised contradictions within capitalism rather than globalisation as the major target of change. Opponents condemn the global financial system and transnational corporations (TNCs), whereas anti-globalisation activists are more critical of the environmental effects of excessive growth rates and ecological unsustainability rooted in the production processes of capitalism. The opponent here is industrialism and the social system that accompanies it. Many call for a return to more localised and self-sufficient communities. A major distinction may be made between those who advocate a localised, autonomous and democratic community approach, which would curb economic growth, industrialism and its capitalist underpinnings, and those who accept capitalist globalisation and market relations but call for significant reforms to control the spontaneity of globalisation and its undesirable effects.

Critical appraisals, and implied or associated alternatives, may be linked to four social and political standpoints which are not mutually exclusive. I identify the major thrusts of criticism, which are detailed later in this and the following chapters.

1. Global capitalism of the late twentieth century is held to be in decline and is being replaced by new technologically based forms of production, finance and exchange. The mode of production is moving from hierarchy and markets to de-centralised networks which replace globalisation and capitalism. A mutation is taking place, with a post-capitalist economy in the ascendance. Capitalism is transforming itself and turning into a new social formation – which might, or might not, be a form of socialism, it is referred to as 'post-capitalism'. This theme is considered in this chapter.

2. Capitalistic neoliberal forms of globalisation are harmful. Environmental degradation and climate change resulting from profit-motivated industrial development present a challenge to human civilisation. A strategy to reverse its harmful effects entails the strengthening of democratic forms of spontaneous anti-capitalist and/or anti-globalisation movements. The objectives of transformation for these groups are ambiguous; for some the objective is to reverse globalisation, to revert to a less industrialised economic system; others see advanced technology as the means to create a sharing democratic society. The objective is to achieve environmental sustainability and the protection of nature – objectives that are incompatible with the present form of market-oriented consumer society. These views are considered in Chapter 13. Rather than anti-globalisation, many in this category prefer the label of alter-globalisation

(alternative globalisation). Its campaigners advocate international global social justice and oppose the neoliberal form of economic globalisation.

3. Economic globalisation processes are positive, but significant changes are required – democratic control being the most important. Writers here advocate a 'beneficial for all' type of globalisation. Capitalist globalisation is accepted but the neoliberal model is rejected in favour of a managed global social democratic capitalism. The emphasis is placed on democratic institutions, global in scope, which would curb the excesses of economic liberalism. We turn to consider these proposals in the first part of Chapter 14.

4. Globalisation is beneficial but the capitalist version is harmful. Globalisation represents a technologically advanced level of the productive forces, but the capitalist ownership relations have to be changed. This is something more than the alter-globalisation or social democratic reformed globalisation, defined previously. A socialist form of globalisation transcends capitalism. It entails the replacement of the institutions and processes of capitalism and the substitution of a socialist global economic and political order, which is the subject of the second part of Chapter 14.

These assumptions about desirable economic and political changes are grounded in the critic's political views and understanding of society.[2] The first mode assumes that endogenous contradictions lead to mutations or to a metamorphosis that forms a new social system, which may be neither capitalist nor globalised. The second approach considers the tensions between social institutions and civil society, which generate within system change and alternative forms of globalisation (mode 2). The more conservative approach stresses the embeddedness and resilience of the current social system in which marginal changes are desirable and possible (mode 3). Finally, there are political activists who stress the need for action and seek policies and strategies to ensure a transformation to a different mode of production. Globalised capitalism should be replaced by globalised socialism (mode 4). These approaches are not mutually exclusive and in practice different social forces act simultaneously often with conflicting aims and objectives. Modes 1 and 4, for example, propose a transformation but with different ends.

In this chapter, I discuss the replacement of global capitalism by a post capitalist social formation. In the next chapter I turn to the character of various strands in the 'anti-globalisation' and alter-globalisation movements. In Chapter 13, I turn to ecological critiques. In Chapter 14, I consider social democratic and socialist proposals for embedding globalisation in a different

---

2   E.O. Wright presents an analysis of transformation. See *Envisioning Real Utopias*. See particularly Chapter 8.

political shell. In all these cases, there is overlap of the different propositions for change, sometimes even in incompatible ways.

The coming of post-capitalism

Many sociologists consider that globalised capitalism has already entered its 'post-capitalist' phase. The groundwork for the rise of 'post-industrial', 'informational' or 'knowledge' based societies may be traced back to the 1960s and particularly to the synthetic work of Daniel Bell[3] discussed in Chapter 9. From this point of view, capitalism is experiencing a process of fundamental change similar in character to the shift from pre-industrial to industrial society. Information technology and knowledge-based production create a more advanced society in which globalisation plays a transformative role. For post-capitalist theorists, emphasis is put on contradictions developing within societies predicated on the technological means which underpin globalisation. New economic forms described by these critics are replacing market coordination. Prominent advocates of this position are writers such as Paul Mason, Jeremy Rifkin, Manuel Castells, Richard Florida and Alexander Buzgalin. They identify an ascendant post-industrial social formation. Here analogies are made to 'seeds' of new economic forces or 'embryos' that, when grown, form the economic base of a new society.

Bell's approach has been updated and revised in the light of twenty-first-century developments. In the USA, Jeremy Rifkin and Richard Florida envisage a third industrial revolution which constitutes

> the last of the great Industrial Revolutions and will lay the foundational infrastructure for an emerging collaborative age ... Collaborative power unleashed by the merging of Internet technology and renewable energies is fundamentally restructuring human relationships, from top to bottom, from side to side, with profound implications for the future of society.[4]

Changes in the level of productive forces are the transformative agents.

Continuing this line of approach, Paul Mason[5] claims that developments within capitalism are leading to its breakdown. We move from 'post-industrial' to 'post-capitalist'. He contends that capitalism's earlier success in

---

[3] Bell, *The Coming of Post-Industrial Society*.

[4] Jeremy Rifkin, *The Third Industrial Revolution*. New York: Palgrave, 2011, p 5.

[5] Paul Mason, *PostCapitalism: A Guide to Our Future*. London: Allen Lane, 2015. For a trenchant review of Mason see Christian Fuchs, Henryk Grossman 2.0: A critique of Paul Mason's book 'PostCapitalism: A Guide to our Future'. *TripleC*, 14:1 (2016), pp 232–24. Available at: http://www.triple-c.at

the development of the means of production has ended. The technologies that have arisen in the late twentieth and early twenty-first centuries are 'not compatible with capitalism ... Once capitalism can no longer adapt to technological change, postcapitalism becomes necessary'.[6] For Mason, post-capitalism has arrived due to three 'impacts of new technology' that have occurred in the twenty-first century:

> First, information technology has reduced the need for work, blurred the edges between work and free time and loosened the relationship between work and wages. Second, information goods are corroding the market's ability to form prices correctly. This is because markets are based on scarcity while information is abundant ... Third, ... the spontaneous rise of collaborative production: goods, services and organisations are appearing that no longer respond to the dictates of the market and the managerial hierarchy.[7]

In this approach, globalisation has a positive role because it develops the means of production which ensure its own destruction.

The rise of the 'creative class'

What then of the movers, the dynamics, of political change? Opinions differ about the nature of the ascendant class in post-industrial society: many deny its existence; others contemplate not a conflict between classes but a division between political and economic elites, on the one hand, and a mass society, on the other. Some contend that the embryo of a new economic order is to be found within the creative class – the scientific and intellectual strata. Of great importance here is the 'post-industrial' economy, which makes knowledge, not labour, the prime source of wealth. The logic of this thinking is that the creatariat, the 'creative class', forms an 'ascendant' class in waiting. Discourse moves from the 'post-industrial' to the 'post-capitalist' societies as the capitalist class is redundant and replaced by the creative class. The social basis of the ascendant class, 'a new agent of change in history, [is] the educated and connected human being'.[8]

Elsewhere, however, Paul Mason relies on the state to deliver a transition to a society 'beyond work and beyond carbon'. He insists that 'centralised government action will be required to forcibly alter or shut down some key business models in the private sector and to enforce behavioural change'.[9] To

---

[6] Mason, *PostCapitalism*, p xiii.
[7] Mason, *PostCapitalism*, p xv.
[8] Mason, *PostCapitalism*, p xvii.
[9] Paul Mason, Manifesto for a post-carbon future. *New Statesman*. 19–25 July 2019.

eradicate carbon emissions, which has become the 'animating spirit of the left', 'we need decisive state action and ownership'.[10] The transformation is spontaneous and productive forces brought about by globalisation provide the driving forces.

Further forms taken by these ascendant forces are described by Alexander Buzgalin and Andrei Kolganov. They emphasise developments giving rise to a new 'knowledge based' sector, which is leading to 'a negation of the capitalist system as such and to the birth of a new type of economy'.[11] Market relations are superseded by the extensive redistributive role of the state in providing goods and services in the social and cultural fields. Economic corporations transcend the market by forms of 'partial planning'.[12] This is a theme taken up by Paul Mason who, citing positively the views of Herbert Simon, contends that 'the capitalist system is primarily made up of organisations that plan and allocate goods internally, in ways not directly driven by market forces'.[13] There are contradictory tendencies here – between networks and planning (to which I return later). For Buzgalin and Kolganov, the rise of 'socially responsible business', regulation of companies, and socially based enterprises which function on a 'not for profit basis', all make inroads into market relations. 'Social capital' and self-management enterprises supersede the market. Such socially responsible institutional forms also replace the motivation of monetary gain.[14] Of particular significance is the rise of a 'creative' class predicated on the new technological forms and enabled by the network society. In concert, the ascendant class, socially responsible business, and state intervention combine to create not just a post-industrial but a post-capitalist society. Rather like the ascendant class for Marx, the 'creative class' has the role of transformation. It is composed of 'scientists, engineers, artists, musicians, designers and knowledge-based professionals'.[15] Collective creativity brings with it 'a process of collaborating and exchanging activity' without the production of exchange value.[16]

Post-capitalist society has led to an explosion of networks in the service sphere which have important consequences for the nature of labour. Florida

---

[10]   Mason, Manifesto for a post-carbon future.

[11]   A. Buzgalin and A. Kolganov, Critical political economy: The 'market-centric' model of economic theory must remain in the past – notes of the post-Soviet School of Critical Marxism. *Cambridge Journal of Economics*, 40 (2015), pp 575–98. Quotation p 583. On the importance of knowledge in the new industrial economy see S.D. Bodrunov, *Gryadushchee. Novoe industrial'noe obshchestvo: perezagruzka*. Moscow: Kulturnaya revolyutsiya, 2016.

[12]   Buzgalin and Kolganov, Critical political economy. See footnote p 582.

[13]   Mason, *PostCapitalism*, pp 263–4.

[14]   Buzgalin and Kolganov, Critical political economy, pp 582–3.

[15]   Richard Florida, *The Rise of the Creative Class*. New York: Basic Books, 2004, p xiii.

[16]   Buzgalin and Kolganov, Critical political economy, p 591.

sketches the shift from physical inputs (land and labour), raw materials and physical labour to the post-capitalist stage, based 'fundamentally on human intelligence, knowledge and creativity'.[17] For Florida and like-minded theorists, 'talent, technology, and tolerance'[18] promote economic growth and replace the Marxist concepts of wage labour, profit and exploitation.[19] 'In the new, distributed, and collaborative communication and energy spaces of the Third Industrial Revolution ... the accumulation of social capital becomes as important and valuable as the accumulation of financial capital.'[20]

The new ascendant class is composed of a 'super-creative core', people involved in problem finding and problem solving. The subsidiary part of the class is composed of those who use 'complex bodies of knowledge to solve specific problems'; they use knowledge to 'think on their own'.[21] Creative work is diverse; its actors typically are free agents accepting commissions often on an entrepreneurial basis. They operate through horizontal 'network' linkages between actors rather than occupying the vertical or hierarchical organisational roles of companies and formal types of employment. They create and coordinate services but they lack a permanent and stable work place. Hence, they do not 'sell their labour' in the traditional way. Rather their creative activity is formed through networks sustaining their self-employment. Their work and life styles differ considerably from the relationship between traditional employee and employer.[22] Jeremy Rifkin considers the end of the capitalist era to be 'inevitably' succeeded by the 'Collaborative Commons'.[23] Its decline is propelled by its own contradictions. The cost of production falls to (or near) zero. Products are nearly free, the 'zero marginal cost society' is 'bringing the economy into an era of nearly

---

[17] Florida, *The Rise of the Creative Class*, p xiii.

[18] By *talent* he means those graduating with a college or higher degree, and the number of certified professional and technical workers. *Technology* is measured by the proportion of value added in high technology industries and the number of patents issued per 10,000 of the population. *Tolerance* is measured by the proportion of gays, writers, designers, musicians, actors, painters, sculptors, photographers and dancers in the population (the Bohemian index), the number of people born abroad as well as an index for the diversity of ethnicities and races. See C. Mellander, R. Florida, B.T. Asheim and M. Gertler, *The Creative Class Goes Global*. Abingdon and New York: Routledge, 2014, p 170, and pp 290–1. Measures vary between countries.

[19] He and his followers attempt to show this empirically by a number of studies collected in Mellander et al, *The Creative Class Goes Global*.

[20] Rifkin, *The Third Industrial Revolution*, p 218.

[21] R. Florida, *The Rise of the Creative Class*. New York: Basic Books, 2004, p 69.

[22] See D. O'Doherty and H. Willmott, The decline of labour process analysis and the future sociology of work. Sociology, 43:5 (2009), pp 931–51, particularly 939–43.

[23] Jeremy Rifkin, *The Zero Marginal Cost Society*. New York and Basingstoke: Palgrave, 2014, p 1.

free goods and services into a socialist form of economy'. Therefore profit, the 'lifeblood of capitalism', dries up.[24] For these writers, the major cause of cost reduction is the rise of information and communication technologies[25] and they operate on a global scale. Globalisation continues but in quite different economic and political structures.

Other writers approach post-capitalism in a more structured way. For them neoliberal capitalism is in terminal decline. Aleksandr Buzgalin and Andrey Kolganov[26] adopt an approach based on Marxist methodology.[27] Spontaneous development and innovation in the mode of production are triggered by the dominant forces of contemporary capitalism in the quest for new products; in doing so, however, they undermine it and usher in a 'post-capitalist' future. Here the embryos of the new economic forces, when developed, form the economic base of a new society. They declare that the creatosphere 'negates one of the fundamental laws of the market: the law of value'. In the creatosphere, 'the ownership by everyone of everything ... is also the most precise and complete embodiment of the principle of social ownership [which entails] the goal of emancipating society from private property'.[28]

A similar line of argument is adopted by Aaron Bastani who envisions a future of Fully Automated Luxury Communism (FALC) in which automation, energy, resources, health and food technologies are cohering into the foundations 'for a society beyond scarcity and work'.[29] Not only is the advance of technology, consequent on competition, leading to innovation thus bringing about the end of capitalism, but it also provides the basis for communism. In the post-scarcity society, brought about by advanced technology and artificial intelligence, human labour is replaced by machines. The crises of capitalism (climate change, surplus population, resource scarcity, technological unemployment) undermine capitalism's ability to reproduce itself.[30] The alternative is a communist society in which work is eliminated, scarcity is replaced by abundance, labour and leisure 'blend into one another'.[31] The root causes of developments – the move to communism – is to be found, as Bastani aptly quotes Marx, 'in the economic foundation lead[ing] to the transformation of the whole immense superstructure'.[32]

---

[24] Rifkin, *The Zero Marginal Cost Society*, p 4.
[25] See Rifkin, *The Third Industrial Revolution*, Chapter 7 (Retiring Adam Smith), and p 220.
[26] Buzgalin and Kolganov, Critical political economy.
[27] Buzgalin and Kolganov, Critical political economy, p 582. See also Buzgalin and Kolganov, *Twenty-first-century Capital*.
[28] Buzgalin and Kolganov, Critical political economy, p 592.
[29] A. Bastani, *Fully Automated Luxury Communism*. London: Verso, 2019, p 12.
[30] Bastani, *Fully Automated Luxury Communism*, p 48.
[31] See Bastani, *Fully Automated Luxury Communism*, Chapter 3, quotation p 50.
[32] Bastani, *Fully Automated Luxury Communism*, p 200.

The post-capitalist thinkers make a valid point when they consider that advancements in technology enhance the provision of free goods (at least in the advanced countries). Globalisation furthers these developments, which undoubtedly are important and have latent possibilities. They are undermined and, in my view, overwhelmed by counter developments: the power of TNCs and the role of the state. There is growing commodification of innovation through intellectual property rights, universities and (publicly financed) centres of research and learning which assert their rights to income from their services and products. Monetarisation and financialisation have had significant effects by increasing the commodification of goods and services. The 'creatosphere' is an important part of culture, which is globalised, commercialised and monetarised. It makes profits. The concept of an 'automated communism' is intriguing but its realisation appears unlikely in the near future.

What many of the postcapitalist theorists ignore is the enduring contradiction between the forces of production (the new information technology) and the ownership of productive assets (the purposes of owners of the technology). The post-capitalist thinkers adopt a form of technological determinism. This is quite legitimate in showing how information technology impacts on other parts of the superstructure of capitalism – it shapes the labour process, education, the types of goods produced and the ways they are marketed and consumed. It does not, however, replace the driving forces of modern capitalism – profit-maximising financial and non-financial corporations. As Castells has recognised, 'As the Internet becomes the pervasive infrastructure of our lives, who owns and controls access to this infrastructure becomes an essential battle for freedom'.[33]

The conclusions of the post-capitalism writers need to be qualified. The 'creative' industries are embryonic but are far from being a decisive force. Consider the place of economic corporations in the 'creatosphere' in the ranking of global companies. High-tech digital companies pursue and make profits. But they are by no means dominant economic forces either in the world economy or in national economies. The ranking of companies based on an average of sales, profits, assets and market values provides a good index of the relative power of different sectors. Corporations that would fit into the 'information-based, knowledge-driven sector' are not insignificant. In the 2022 edition of the Global 2000,[34] of the top 15 corporations three were in the 'creatosphere': Apple (ranked 7th), Microsoft (12th) and Samsung (14th). Further down the list were AT&T in 20th place, China Mobile was

---

[33] Manuel Castells, *The Internet Galaxy*. Oxford: Oxford University Press, 2001, p 277.
[34] Forbes, The Global 2000. Available at: https://www.forbes.com/lists/global2000/?sh=72d208f55ac0

31st, Verizon 19th, and Vodafone 479th.[35] The dominant world companies are constituted of financial, energy and manufacturing corporations.

The role of the state

The encroachment of the state on the market, in these theories, is the other crucial element potentially undermining global capitalism. This development was noted by Joseph Schumpeter who, after the Second World War,[36] contended that the rise of large corporations, coupled with bureaucratic and scientific management, would make entrepreneurship obsolete. Capitalism was dying, he declared; the traditional bourgeoisie – national small and medium businesses, the independent professions- was declining in numbers and significance. To manage the new type of capitalism, the state would incrementally replace the market to manage the economy and socialise the costs of capitalism through the welfare state. Greater state involvement would also lead to public participation. Bourgeois values, he thought, were under threat as the capitalist process undermined the 'moral authority' of the bourgeoisie. Just as the credentials of kings and popes have suffered, so would private property 'and the whole scheme of bourgeois values'.[37] Intellectuals and members of the professions, he continued, would be the crucial group turning against capitalism. He anticipated many of the claims mentioned previously recognising the creatariat as the main element of the ascendant class.

Quite unlike those who see globalisation as a process undermining the state, Schumpeter, Buzgalin and Mason all emphasise the important and growing role of the state which they contend is displacing the capitalist market. Mason emphasises that the state makes an 'enormous economic contribution' encompassing some 45 per cent of national GDP across all countries.[38] For Buzgalin and Kolganov, market relations are superseded by the extensive redistributive role of the state in providing goods and services in the social and cultural fields. 'The socio-economic activity of the state is one of the most important forms of transition. Such transitional forms include the embryos of post-market relations and in particular of a conscious, directly social means for the coordination, regulation of the proportions

---

[35] The ranking is an average of sales, profits, assets, market values. Source: Forbes 2000 World Companies for 2017. Data for 2017 available at: https://www.forbes.com/global2 000/list/#tab:overall

[36] Joseph Schumpeter, *Capitalism, Socialism and Democracy* (5th edn). London: Routledge, 1976. See particularly Chapters 12 and 13.

[37] Schumpeter, *Capitalism, Socialism and Democracy*, p 143.

[38] Mason, *PostCapitalism*, p 273.

and distribution (allocation) of resources.'[39] 'State property' in their view is another form which can undermine market-centrism and provide a new economic formation. The state is 'involved in the conscious regulation of economic processes on an all-national (or regional) scale'.[40] All these observations imply that global capitalism is subject to state powers.

Whether such government activity is undermining capitalism is open to challenge. State engagement, when measured in spending as a proportion of GDP, has increased but market forces have not declined. State expenditure is utilised not only for welfare transfers and research but to maintain the state's oppressive powers and ideological functions. Even in welfare states, the creeping transfer of the state's activities to the private sector ensures not only a source of profits but concurrently diminishes the state's ability to act as a countervailing force to capital. Neoliberals endorse state expenditure for the purpose of enforcement of the rules of capitalism and for military defence. Their opposition is to the state as a provider of services and as a hegemonic body, as a competitor to the market and private ownership. States also are sources of contracts for the private enterprise economy – the US has an enormous budget of procurements for its armed forces and promotes financially universities and research institutes, and the electronic, aviation, ship building, armaments, clothing, footwear and food industries.

The fallacy in the argument is to assume that the level of GDP under the state is correlated with an independent state power: a state budget may increase in size but the state's political power over corporations might decrease. Neoliberalism proposes to diminish the role of the state in supplying services and goods. Significant privatisation of public assets has been achieved on a world scale, thereby shrinking the state's productive capacity (the direct provision of goods and services). The role of the state as coordinator and supplier of the factors of production has declined in the face of the free movement of capital, labour, goods and services and the rise of international regulatory agencies.[41] What is true, however, is that neoliberal forces have succeeded in strengthening and extending the state's enforcement powers of liberal market rules. In this case, tensions arise between the state administration and democratically elected representatives.

The exponential growth of transnational acquisitions and mergers has led to the multi-national composition of the boards of transnational companies

---

[39] Buzgalin and Kolganov, Critical political economy, p 584.

[40] Buzgalin and Kolganov, Critical political economy, p 595.

[41] See Colin Crouch, The global firm: The problem of the giant firm in democratic capitalism, in D. Coen, W. Grant and G. Wilson (Eds) *Business and Government*. Oxford: Oxford University Press, 2010, pp 148–72; S. Wilks, *The Political Power of the Business Corporation*. Cheltenham: Edward Elgar, 2013.

shifting power from a national bourgeoisie to a global capitalist class.[42] States vary in their regulative powers. In Russia, Bodrunov, Buzgalin and Konovalov correctly assume that a more independent form of state provision and regulation is growing. This may be a special case, due to the legacy of state ownership and control from the planned economic system. The historical heritage has been reinforced through the incapacity of the post-socialist neoliberal state to function effectively in Russia. A separate stratum of politicians may fill the gap to control the state apparatus to act in ways not compliant with the interests of private global corporations. One must take account of the position of different countries in the world system of capitalism. As I pointed out in Chapter 9, countries are not embedded in the global system to the same degree. They form an international hierarchy derived from the geography of ownership and regional networks of political alliances and communication. The trajectory of development in Russia and China from pre-industrial to industrial has been driven by the state not by a national or international bourgeoisie, and national ownership and control of fundamental assets clearly divides these countries from the core states of the world system. While they are members of international institutions such as the WTO, the United Nations and the IMF, they are kept quite apart from the core's military organisation (NATO) and the symbolic political core of the Group of Seven (France, Germany, Italy, Japan, US, UK and Canada). State regulated societies such as China are less affected by globalised Western corporations and we return to China in Chapter 15. While the state could be a 'new economic force', under current conditions in the core capitalist countries, states do not constitute an alternative form of capitalism.

Ownership of the means of production

While these 'post-capitalist' writers point to significant current developments in the production process and noteworthy changes in social stratification, it may be doubted whether such developments yet constitute the 'embryo' of a new mode of production. The advance of technology has to be considered from two sides: the level of productive forces and the form of ownership. Steam power and mechanical engineering liberated armies of labour from strenuous manual work but concurrently generated surplus value for the owners of the machines. Technology has a positive social function as well as being a means of exploitation. The dynamic of global capitalism is shaped by the level of technology driven by ownership and market relations – the

---

[42] See William I. Robinson and Jerry Harris, A global ruling class? Globalisation and the transnational capitalist class. *Science and Society*, 64:1 (Spring 2000), pp 5380–411; Sklair, *Globalization*; J. Staples, Cross border acquisitions and board globalisation in the world's largest TNCs 1995–2005. *Sociological Quarterly*, 49 (2008), pp 31–51.

opportunity for merchants and shareholders to make profits. Financialisation and speculation are adopted on a global scale because they generate more profits than industrial investment.

The 'creatosphere' is increasingly penetrated by neoliberal developments. Elites in business, politics, media and academia become highly interdependent and disseminate legitimating (and are legitimated by) neoliberal ideology. Places of higher learning are subject to market criteria; intellectual products are evaluated for their contribution to profit oriented production. 'Useful' knowledge is conflated with profitable knowledge. Commercial interests secure property rights over inventions through the ownership of patents. While the emergence of free goods such as Wikipedia, Copyleft and Open Source are indeed non-market activities, one should not ignore the related market structures associated with digitalisation.[43] IT products have to be manufactured and are produced by a work force in low paid precarious employment, usually outside the core post-industrial countries. Call centres employ low-wage employees doing mainly routine and highly controlled service work. Cultural artefacts are dependent on patronage, sponsorship and commercialisation. Software is continually being (often unnecessarily) updated and is not free. Media, such as Google and Face Book, attract colossal levels of advertising, which make profits not only for the media firms but also for advertisers. Google, for example, at the centre of the network global economy, is a highly commercialised and highly profitable company. It is true that there are 'alternative' web platforms run by voluntary labour and supported by donations (such as Diaspora★ and Occupii). But, as Christian Fuchs has pointed out, their users are far fewer than the commercial units: Facebook, in 2012, for example, had 1 billion users, whereas of the non-profits, Diaspora★ had 90,000 and Occupii only 5,303.[44] It is the profit motive and commercial interests that drive the market – not the self-help altruistic commons. Like many platforms it attracts advertising and selects its own messages. The 'post capitalist' economy school emphasises the wide use and relatively free access to media – in doing so, such scholars underestimate, or even ignore, the dominant role of property ownership and commercially driven profit. Any serious discussion of alternatives to capitalism are effectively screened out of the mass media.

Even if alternative networks of production and exchange were to increase, we have no analysis of how the remaining forms of production and distribution, including their control by TNCs, would be changed. Manufacture, finance, as well as consumption, mass leisure, media and sport

---

[43] See Christian Fuchs, *Digital Labour and Karl Marx*. Routledge: New York and London, 2014. Especially Part II.

[44] Data cited by Fuchs, *Digital Labour and Karl Marx*, p 302.

have become commercialised on a global scale. Only in the very distant future could Florida's ideas about autonomous self-centred production and exchange replace globalised production. Similarly, the idea of 'fully automated luxury communism' remains a possible long-term goal, rather than a practical alternative.

The zero marginal cost economy is a long way off. 'Consumerism' is a dominant ideology and growing, rather than declining in significance. Consider, for example, competitive mass sports (such as the Olympic Games, the European/World Football Cup) which are part of the 'super-creative core' of economic activities. These are global events screened through global companies and associations and 'consumed' by a global audience. On the one side, it is true that the marginal cost of viewing these games is near zero, viewing on one's TV is inexpensive – or one can go to the sports bar for free or buy a tonic water, though viewers will be contributing to the income of the bar. All this points to the availability of a 'free service' – but not the arrival of post-capitalism. The success of the English Premier football showbiz league epitomises the competitive market society. It is based on massive audiences facilitated by the internet. The other side is colossal commercialisation, driven by corporate ownership and the profit motive. The screenings are highly commercialised – subscribers pay the media companies; spectators are distracted by flashing advertising on perimeter hoardings. The teams are owned by foreign oligarchs, financed through financial instruments and marketed worldwide through profit making retail and media companies. There are unjustified inequalities in income and conditions for the clubs' employees, notably between players and ground catering and security attendants. While many observers recognise that there are contradictions, they follow Bell rather than Marx to attribute their causes to hierarchy rather than to capitalism. As Mason puts it: 'everything is pervaded by a fight between network and hierarchy'.[45] But the fight for commercial contracts, for the purchase of clubs and franchises for media rights, for contracting players (the very life blood of successful sports' companies) is determined by money.

Moreover, the understanding of the 'creatosphere' is exclusively focused on Western hegemonic countries and ignores capitalism's rising South where the main economic activities continue to be in agriculture and manufacturing. If one conceives of capitalism as a global process, then the distribution of the labour force by 'creative class', working class, service class and agricultural workers takes a completely different form. The employed classes are territorially segregated in global space, unlike the global capitalist class which is integrated globally.

---

[45] Mason, *PostCapitalism*, p 144.

We are far from witnessing the transcendence of capitalism to a higher mode of production. While an increase has occurred in personal well-being for some classes and countries, this is not universally the case. The data collected in Chapter 9 (Figure 9.8) do not show the division between classes in various social categories. We can safely say that the share of income going to labour has declined. Thomas Piketty, for example, also provides data showing a decline in labour's share of income in Britain from 80 per cent in 1970 to 73 per cent in 2010 (data for France are similar).[46] These figures underestimate the extent of decline for unskilled and semi-skilled workers and include (in 'labour's share') professional and executive salaries which have risen at an exponential rate. While changes in the nature of the labour force are important, they have to be contextualised as part of a global capitalism with its own territorial division of labour as well as structures of transnational financial and non-financial companies.

Not all the creatariat are highly paid and the new service and production industries include large numbers of lowly paid semi-skilled employees. A different analysis of labour stratification is put forward by Guy Standing[47] who recognises many of these developments but highlights quite a different category: the precariat. Unlike the traditional working class, the precariat does not have regular employment or even guaranteed hours of work. Remuneration is not linked to trade union or national wage agreements, there usually are no pension or holiday rights and in some places such workers lack access to public health and social provision. The open labour market, promoted by neoliberalism, weakens the position of significant groups of people. A stratum, made up of recent immigrants and young people (many with high educational qualifications) constitutes this underclass. A high proportion of such workers are employed in the low pay health, welfare and personal care sectors. The existence of the precariat illustrates negative features of 'post-capitalism' – quite the opposite to what is enjoyed by the supposed creative class.

Nevertheless, these authors point to significant changes in the occupational composition of the advanced economies. They consider important developments in the ways work is done in post-industrial society and the impact on the system of social stratification. Csaba Mako and Miklos Illessy have detailed the changes that have taken place in Europe in the twenty-first century.[48]

---

[46] Piketty, *Capital in the Twenty-First Century*, pp 200–201.

[47] Guy Standing, *The Precariat: The New Dangerous Class*. London: Bloomsbury, 2011; 2nd edn, 2014.

[48] Csaba Mako and Miklos Illessy, Automation, creativity, and the future of work in Europe: A comparison between the old and new member states with a special focus on Hungary. *Intersections EEJSP*, 6:2 (2020), pp 112–129, doi: 10.17356/ieejsp. v6i2.625 http://inters ections.tk.mta.hu

Based on data collected by the European Working Conditions Survey, they divide occupations into three different categories: Creative Workers, Constrained problem solvers, and Taylorised Workers. In creative jobs, employees have to make use of their cognitive abilities to a large extent and enjoy a high degree of work autonomy. Jobs organised on Taylorean principles involve the least use of cognitive abilities and autonomy. This group is essentially the proletariat envisaged by nineteenth-century socialists. Between these two groups, 'constrained problem solvers' have 'relatively strong expectancies about cognitive learning, and an extremely low level of autonomy'.

The surveys conducted in the EU in 2015 found that 59 per cent of jobs were in the 'creative' category and only 20 per cent in the 'Taylorised'. There are, however, significant differences between countries: Denmark, Sweden, Germany, and the UK had respectively 77, 74, 49, 59 per cent of jobs in the 'creative sector'. Other countries remain more 'Taylorised': Latvia, Hungary and Romania retained a large traditional work force, with respectively only 35, 37 and 35 per cent of jobs being 'creative'. The implications here are quite important for the differentiation and geographical location of the working class.

Robotisation and artificial intelligence will certainly reduce the number of employees in all occupations, including non-manual ones. As Mako and Illessy point out, those in the 'creative' positions are less likely to be threatened by technological innovation and replaced by machines (guided by artificial intelligence) than those in the 'Taylorised' category.[49] A study by PriceWaterhouseCooper found that non-manual jobs as well as manual ones would be subject to automation by the 2030s: 20 per cent in East Asia, 38 per cent in the USA and 25 per cent in Russia. In total, 35 per cent of jobs in administration, 30 per cent in finance, but only 9 per cent in education were under threat. Like Mako and Illessy, the study concluded that those with lower educational qualifications would be the most likely to lose their jobs.[50] This form of stratification has led not to the rise of an ascendant class but to the assimilation of the creatariat into the bourgeois system and the alienation of the lower educated and unskilled who have had little benefit from technological advance. 'Reformed' or 'New Labour' social-democratic parties have cultivated the new 'creative' working class found among 'networked' youth – with little electoral success (see Chapter 6).

---

[49] Mako and Milos Illessy, Automation, creativity, and the future of work in Europe. See pp 120–1.

[50] PwC, Will robots really steal our jobs?. *UK Economic Outlook* (March 2017). Available at: https://www.pwc.co.uk/economic-services/ukeo/pwc-uk-economic-outlook-full-report-march-2017-v2.pdf

Marxist revisions

The discussion of the role of an 'ascendant' class, in the sense of a class predisposed to dispossess the dominant ruling class, poses the problem of how political opportunity is turned into political power. Writers critical of both the Leninist 'vanguard party' and the traditional social democratic party approach adopt what is sometimes called an 'open Marxist' position.[51] A significant revision is suggested by Antonio Negri and Michael Hardt.[52] They echo the widespread acceptance of the adverse effects of bureaucratic control, endorsing Robert Michels's criticism[53] that all types of party hierarchical organisation lead to oligarchy. Their counter argument is predicated on what they consider to be the ways that post-industrial capitalism is creating 'forms of cooperation' that are emerging from the production process. Here they follow writers discussed previously and rely on the development of new forms of technology: 'digital and communicative technologies', which establish a 'new mode of production'. This 'heterogeneous' formation contains elements of previous forms of production.[54] Their proposals advocate the formation of autonomous economic and political formations. Negri and Hardt promote the novel idea of the 'multitude' as a revolutionary actor having emancipatory potential.

Their approach combines a determinist mode of transformation with a more voluntaristic politics. Lenin's organisational form of 'democratic centralism', according to Hardt and Negri, should be reversed.[55] 'Comprehensive long-term political projects should no longer be the responsibility of leaders or the party' but 'should be entrusted to the multitude'.[56] Long-term plans and strategic objectives should be decided by the multitude, and political leadership should be 'limited to short-term action and tied to specific occasions'.[57] Only current tactics should be the concern of leaders. There is a place for leadership, but this is reduced to confrontation with existing institutions, it is temporary and ad hoc and is always subordinated to the multitude.

The approach is a return to the idea that capitalism is subject to a metamorphosis. The alternative being proposed here is not a form of national

---

[51] For an overview see W. Bonefeld, R. Gunn and K. Psychopedis, *Open Marxism. Volume 1, Dialectics and History*. London: Pluto Press, 1992.

[52] M. Hardt and A. Negri, *Empire*. Cambridge, MA: Harvard University Press, 2000 and M. Hardt and A. Negri, *Assembly*. New York: Oxford University Press, 2017.

[53] Robert Michels, *Political Parties*. New York: Hearst, 1915.

[54] Hardt and Negri, *Assembly*, p 145, p 144.

[55] Hardt and Negri, *Assembly*.

[56] Hardt and Negri, *Assembly*, p 291.

[57] Hardt and Negri, *Assembly*, p 19.

collectivist planned economy but an encroachment into capitalist space by autonomous self-governing and self-propelled units. The ascendant mode of production, socialism, will arrive through a mutation taking place within the capitalist form – not through a revolutionary party-led transformation. The agent is not the working class. In their book on *Empire*,[58] Hardt and Negri articulate the idea of the 'multitude' as a revolutionary counterpoint to 'empire'.[59] The multitude is made up of all those who are dominated by the ruling capitalist class – it is much wider than Marx's idea of the working class. Moreover, the 'multitude' spontaneously forms its own self-consciousness. The multitude has the capacity of the 'political entrepreneur'.[60]

This position, however, detaches the movers of change from social class analysis. It moves discussion out of an historical materialist explanation. It is the antithesis of Lenin's party of a new type which brings consciousness to, and leads, the working class. It rejects also the non-Leninist social democratic position of the party representing the working class in an electoral contest for parliamentary power. The multitude is a collectivity of individuals acting in common – a spontaneous expression of the people's interest. Negri defines a strategy of revolution as 'the exodus of the multitude of workers from the modern regime of production and capitalist domination ... [T]he revolutionary process appears as the *exodus constitutive of a new world*, set up by the multitude in opposition to the structure of present day capitalism.'[61] What this statement means is that individuals and groups composing the multitude will make their own living independently of, but in opposition to, the existing capitalist system. These proposals envisage more permanent living and working arrangements than the kinds of popular spontaneous street resistance one saw in the anti-globalisation riots in Seattle in 1999.

Ernesto Laclau illustrates this shift. He sets the complexity of the social structure in the late twentieth century in, what he considers to be, a post-Marxist mould. 'For classical Marxism, the possibility of transcending capitalist society depended on the simplification of social structure and the emergence of a privileged agent of social change [the working class], while for us, the possibility of a democratic transformation of society depends on a proliferation of new subjects of change.'[62] These subjects are groups of people who experience social and political discrimination – quite a different

[58] Hardt and Negri, *Empire*.

[59] See Hardt and Negri, *Empire*; *Multitude: War and Democracy in the Age of Empire*. London and New York: Penguin, 2004.

[60] Hardt and Negri, *Assembly*, p 280.

[61] Antonio Negri, Afterword: on the concept of revolution, in John Foran, David Lane and Andreja Zivkovic, *Revolution in the Making of the Modern World*. London: Routledge, 2008, p 258. Italics in original.

[62] Ernesto Laclau, *New Reflections on the Revolution of Our Time*. London: Verso, 1990, p 41.

group to the creatariat. Such a form of politics predicated on ethnic, racial, caste, generational and gender grievances, however real they may be, is bound to lead to a fragmented form of identity politics replacing classes (see Chapter 7). Nick Srnicek and Alex Williams have pointed out that this kind of approach is a form of 'folk politics' prioritising short-term localised advances which yield only limited results.[63] I would agree that modern capitalism has superseded the conditions that the early twentieth-century socialist activists had in mind, and which now cannot be a yardstick to guide revolutionary strategy. But does this 'new world', envisaged by Negri and Hardt, transcend capitalist society, or is it essentially a form of anarchistic opposition to capitalism and the state involving withdrawal from society?[64]

There are very mixed answers to this question. Slavoj Zizek,[65] John Holloway[66] and Chris Rogers[67] seek to transcend capitalism and move to another form of society, which I turn to later. Like Negri and Hardt they express, disillusion with the Soviet Leninist form of socialism and despair at social democratic governments. Other writers come to pessimistic conclusions. Wolfgang Streeck contends that there is no alternative in sight – there is 'no political-economic formula on the horizon, Left or Right, that might provide capitalist societies with a coherent new regime of regulation'.[68] For Streeck, disorganised capitalism, its 'cumulative decay',[69] will simply destroy itself, without any clear alternative. Leslie Sklair is even more pessimistic when he contends that attempts to transcend capitalism will fail: 'It is easier to imagine the end of the world than to imagine the end of capitalism'. Capitalist hegemony is 'overwhelming': it cannot be overturned.[70]

These writers explicitly turn away from any form of organised political movement to rely on spontaneous bottom-up associations that operate as self-reliant and autonomous communities. Attention shifts from state capture (whether it be revolutionary or social democratic) to carving out self-governing communities which present an alternative to capitalism. The intention of this 'autonomous' spontaneous set of tactics is to widen

---

[63] Srnicek and Williams, *Inventing the Future.*

[64] See the critique of anarchism by S. Choat, Marxism and anarchism in an age of neoliberal crisis. *Capital and Class*, 40:1 (2016), pp 95–109.

[65] Slavoj Zizek, The ongoing 'soft' revolution. *Critical Inquiry*, 30:2 (2004), pp 292–323.

[66] Holloway, *Crack Capitalism.*

[67] Chris Rogers, *Capitalism and Its Alternatives.*

[68] Streeck, *How Will Capitalism End?*, p 58.

[69] Streeck, *How Will Capitalism End?*, p 72.

[70] Leslie Sklair, World revolution or socialism, community by community, in the Anthropocene?. *Journal of World System Research*, 25:2 (2019), pp 297–305, quotations p 300.

'the cracks' which occur in capitalism. By developing local self-organised forms of production, a non-capitalist form of economy and society may take root in 'the cracks'. As John Holloway proposes, 'The central issue is the counterposing of a distinctly different logic ... to the logic of capitalism ... [H]ere and now, we refuse to subordinate our activity to the rule of capital: we can, and will, and are doing something else'.[71] The alternative is to form autonomous enclaves meeting the needs of a sustainable standard of living; de-growth of capitalism should be pursued – and would replace the consumer society (we return to this topic in the next chapter).

Self-destruction, consequent on the exploitation of nature, leads to the destruction of the planet and civilised life and has replaced the more positive vision of twentieth-century Marxists. There is a danger here of 'overweening and fantastical predictions about capitalism's coming to an end ... Left politics is immobilized ... by the idea ... of catastrophe and salvation'.[72]

Conclusion

I have outlined the views of writers who contend that spontaneous social activity furthers the self-destructing propensities of globalised capitalism. Influenced by Marxist thinking, there is an assumption that, as in nature, a self-induced metamorphosis makes capitalism mutate into something else, either post-capitalism or socialism. Others, rather pessimistically, envisage collapse with no clear outcome. The new social forces under global capitalism are driven by knowledge and creativity in the form of a 'creative class' that favours collaborative production rather than competition. While the seeds of change are to be found in the productive forces and can give rise to an ascendant class, they currently remain in an emergent state awaiting development. The methodology, as utilised by these post-capitalist thinkers, has a determinist dimension. There is a spontaneous development of the productive forces challenging and replacing competitive market capitalism. The problem here is that embryos may not grow or may be subjected to abortion. Seeds may wither and die, they may be stifled by weeds or destroyed by pesticides. In other words, the self-destruction of capitalism might lead to something worse – a regression to a society with a much lower level of productive forces giving rise to life that is nasty, brutal and short. Or self-destructive tendencies may be corrected.

Critics of this position claim that such ascendant forces could find a place alongside the bourgeoisie rather than being a challenge to it. Globalised capitalism of the twenty-first century has witnessed the growth and

---

[71] Holloway, *Crack Capitalism*, p 26.
[72] Clark, For a Left with no future, p 54.

development of transnational companies and the integration of business, government, media and ideological elites. There has been no antithesis from the working class. A transformation to a new type of society (a mode of production) requires not only economic and ideological prerequisites but also human agents to promote social change, to dismantle institutional blockages, and to neutralise opponents; in short, to create a better world. Unlike the vision of early twentieth-century socialists, there is no clear vision of a socialist or an alternative future.

Another group of critics encourages the formation of pockets of resistance to create islands of alternative economies and life styles. Community action and collective activity are promoted to undermine capitalism by forms of direct action. By developing local self-organised forms of production, a non-capitalist and non-hierarchical form of economy and society could be organised. The motivating factor in this approach is the conscious desire of individuals to exit from capitalism and to form something else. If multiplied, such forms would replace global capitalism.

I accept that self-provision might constitute a different social formation; it would abandon modern production. But it is questionable whether, without industrial production and increases in labour productivity, it would be sustainable. In my view, a more realistic vision of a 'left modernity' is to be found in movements that promote the 'maximum provision of the basic resources needed for a meaningful life'.[73] The way forward is to promote the development of the productive forces to enlarge the provision of the goods and services outside of the price system – the collective provision of health, housing, transport and internet access. Increasing automation can lead to a shorter working week and an increase in leisure time. Post-industrial societies are rich enough to provide a basic income for all. The underlying technological developments lead to the growing abundance of products and services brought about by new technology, robotisation and artificial intelligence. What the writers, considered in this chapter, neglect is the role of leadership, of alternative parties and channels that will bring about a major change. I return to these issues in the final chapter of this book.

In the next chapter, we turn to critics of post-capitalism who recognise that political action is required to reverse and/or replace globalised capitalism. The 'anti' movements are a call to arms, for political action. Anti-capitalist and anti-globalisation movements blossomed under the austerity regimes following the world economic crisis of 2007. They are also fuelled by environmental concerns, global warming and the ecological crisis that I turn to in Chapter 13.

---

[73] Srnicek and Williams, *Inventing the Future*, p 80.

12

The 'Anti-Capitalist' Critique

While the critics of globalised capitalism considered in Chapter 11 considered that capitalism would be replaced through a metamorphosis or could be undermined by autonomous parallel developments, others adopt a more combative stance. Capitalism, they maintain, must be confronted, dismantled and, importantly, an alternative type of society put in its place. Political movements that have adopted 'anti-globalisation' and 'anti-capitalism' appellations are directed against different parts and functions of global and national capitalist arrangements. They are ideologically, socially and politically heterogeneous and include individuals and associations with democratic, socialist, liberal and anarchistic outlooks.[1] The consumption-driven world system promotes environmental harm which poses an existential threat to civilisation. They all agree that globalisation is harmful. Such critics seek to reverse globalisation and strengthen local economies by developing sustainable autonomous economic, political and social units (communities, production and consumption collectives). Rather than a focus on replacing globalised capitalism with a different type of industrial or post-industrial society, these movements envisage changes at a more micro level which lead

---

[1] For an overview see Rogers, *Capitalism and its Alternatives* and Alex Callinicos, *An Anti-Capitalist Manifesto*, Cambridge: Polity, 2013; Lara Monticelli, Embodying alternatives to capitalism in the 21st century, *TripleC*, 16:2 (2018), pp 501–17; Holloway, *Crack Capitalism*; Paul Mason, *Why It's Kicking Off Everywhere: The New Global Revolutions*. London: Verso, 2012; Astra Taylor et al (Eds), *Occupy! Scenes from Occupied America*. London: Verso, 2011; Occupy Wall Street (2011), 'Declaration of the Occupation of New York City', www.nycga.net/resources/documents/declaration; World Social Forum (2013), 'World Social Forum Charter and Principles', www.fsm2013.org/en/node/204; E. Bircham and J. Charlton (Eds), *Anti-Capitalism*. London: Bookmarks, 2001; C. Hines, *Localisation: A Global Manifesto*. London: no publisher, 2000. On ecological crisis see: Lechner and Boli, *The Globalisation Reader*, pp 438–48; Manuel Castells, The crisis of global capitalism: Towards a new economic culture?, in Craig Calhoun and Georgi Derluguian, *Business as Usual*, pp 185–210.

to a qualitatively distinctive form of a democratic and just society. Leslie Sklair, for example, makes a call for 'exiting capitalism and the system of hierarchic so-called nation states' in favour of 'the creation of smaller scale human settlements, rather than huge cities and world revolution'.[2]

Autonomists reject state capture as a means to secure their objectives.[3] Scepticism stemming from the failures of state socialism and the inadequacies of social democracy has led to the denunciation of state power, which has failed to achieve democracy and to stop environmental degradation. Anger is focussed somewhat indiscriminately at international bankers, the international system, industrialisation, globalisation and capitalism in general. As political power is global in character, the movements regard formal electoral politics as futile. Such opponents, therefore, rely on elemental, often spontaneous, movements seeking to reverse current trends to globalised capitalism. Their discourse is less theoretical and academic and more activist. They want action, not words. Lara Monticelli has called these movements 'prefigurative' in the sense that they 'embody their ultimate goals and their vision of a future society through their ongoing social practices, social relations, decision-making philosophy and culture'.[4] In other words, they seek to put into effect *now* elements of the 'desired future', which in total cannot be attained. These movements are anti-hierarchy and strongly committed to collectivist democratisation.

Russell Brand[5] can be used as an example of an articulate and popular advocate of revolutionary anti-globalisation. He proposes a transition from a society, based on competition and domination, to one of symbiosis and cooperation, a shift from greed to altruism. Following a revolution, society will be organised on 'the principles of equality, non-violence and ecological responsibility'.[6] A major objective is to localise food production and farming: 'life over profits' is prioritised. The major demands of the anti-globalisation movement rest on pleas for self-government, decentralisation of power, cancellation of unfair debt and the removal of 'the physical and psychological tools of the powerful'.[7] A 'green agenda' figures prominently in the objectives.

Political change through competitive elections is rejected. An alternative system cannot be achieved through 'the infertile dung-heap of gestural democracy' [parliamentary democracy] which is 'a hollow, predefined ritual'.[8]

---

2 L. Sklair, *Second Thoughts on Capitalism and the State*. Newcastle: Scholars Press, 2022, p 18.
3 On autonomism see Bircham and Charlton, *Anti-Capitalism*.
4 Monticelli, Embodying alternatives to capitalism, p 509.
5 Russell Brand, *Revolution*. London: Century, Random House, 2014.
6 Brand, *Revolution*, p 98.
7 Brand, *Revolution*, quotations pp 89, 171.
8 Brand, *Revolution*, p 77.

Russell Brand is confident that revolution is possible and can be brought about by peaceful means. Using the analogy of the successful campaigns for equal rights for gays, lesbians, bisexual and transgender issues (LGBTQ+), he concludes that if one can change gender relations then one can change others too. The Occupy Movement is one way in which these ideals may be attained.

The Occupy movement

The Occupy movements mushroomed in 2011 under the slogan: 'We are the 99 per cent'[9] – this distinction was first made by Joseph Stiglitz who defined the top 1 per cent who monopolised wealth and power. Groups of disaffected people 'occupied' public buildings as an act of protest: Occupy Wall St, Occupy the Stock Exchange, Occupy St Paul's [Cathedral]. Within the anti-capitalist and Occupy social movements, one finds people who are alienated by the modern competitive capitalist system and see no future for themselves within it. Some are homeless, penniless and without a future. To paraphrase Marx, they find themselves in a heartless world. Others are from well-educated affluent families. Noam Chomsky regards the movement as positive and significant, he claims that 'Occupy is the first major public response to thirty years of class war'. It has moved from 'occupying tent camps to occupying the national conscience'. The movement put the 'inequality of everyday life on the national agenda'.[10] The direct action of literally thousands of people was an expression of anger against the system[11] by people who were being crushed by it.

Chomsky views the movement as an expression of people's dissatisfaction, though it lacks a clear political agenda. As one participant in an Occupy squat put it:

> We still don't know exactly what [our] demands are. One of the members of our group, in discussing the criteria for a good demand, noted that Americans like to 'get something' out of a political action. Repeal, enact, ban. We want visible, measurable outcomes. But we have no Mubarak, no Qaddafi. We are the country that re-elected Bush, that bailed out the banks, that has stalemates in Congress about paltry tax increases. Our partial joblessness and alienating democratic system may be very real, our reasons for congregating concrete, but

---

[9]   See D. Graeber, *The Democracy Project*. New York: Spiegel and Grau, 2013.

[10] Noam Chomsky, *Occupy*. London: Penguin Books, 2012, p 9. Chomsky, cited in editorial preface.

[11] Chomsky, *Occupy*, p 10.

the precise causes of our distress are still far off, the specific solutions perhaps further.[12]

Russell Brand echoes such sentiments when he reflects on the widespread feelings of 'inadequacy, isolation and anxiety', which he attributes to the 'concerted effort[s]' of those with power in society.[13] These ephemeral movements embrace an assembly of people presenting very disparate challenges.

There is an absence of a political agenda and constructive mechanisms for change. Like mushrooms, they rise quickly, have a prominent presence, then disappear. Where the tactics are more relevant and practical is in countries where landless peasants are successful in seizing land to work themselves. They have positive effects in defending, restoring and creating new spaces.[14] The Zapatista movement in Mexico is an example of this form of anti-capitalism.[15] In the industrialised countries, however, such movements – epitomised by the 'Occupy' seizures of property – quickly have fizzled out and became forgotten. By 2014, the earlier encampments of people, often over 1,000 in size and located in 80 countries, had disappeared.[16] The significance of these popular insurrections has been addressed by many social scientists. Changes in the class structure (particularly the emergence of a middle class 'precariat'), the rise of social media (the effects of Twitter, Facebook and the opportunity for grass roots mobilisation) and the decline of effective parliamentary-types of political contestation are seen as underlying causes.[17]

Some commentators, however, have detected a shift in political emphasis within the anti-globalisation movements from a focus on forms of identity and democratic pluralism – gender, ethnicity, generation, equality of consideration – to more social class related issues such as the domination by financial interests and the separation of a political class from democratic politics. In Chomsky's view, 'Occupy embodies a vision of democracy that is fundamentally antagonistic to the management of society as a

12 Astra Taylor and Keith Gessen (Eds), *Occupy: Scenes from an Occupation*. London: Verso, 2011, p 6.
13 Brand, *Revolution*, p 25.
14 Monticelli, Embodying alternatives to capitalism, p 510, spells out these aspects of 'prefiguration'.
15 For a positive evaluation see Rogers, *Capitalism and Its Alternatives*, pp 141–2.
16 See discussion in Mark Chou, From crisis to crisis, crisis and the Occupy movement. *Political Studies Review*, 13:1 (2015), pp 46–58.
17 For further interpretations see: S. Zizek, *The Year of Dreaming Dangerously*. London: Verso, 2012; Chomsky, *Occupy*; D. Harvey, *Rebel Cities: From the Right to the City to the Urban Revolution*. London: Verso, 2012; Fuchs, *Digital Labour and Karl Marx*; Mason, *Why It's Kicking Off Everywhere*.

corporate-controlled space that funds a political system to serve the wealthy [and to] ignore the poor'.[18] Christian Fuchs goes even further: 'The importance of the Occupy movement is that it shows the topicality of capitalism, exploitation and class and that it has put the need for a discussion about a commons-based society as an alternative to capitalism on the agenda'.[19] The symbolic focus is to 'occupy' areas of financial and capitalist power – Wall St and the Stock Exchange.

The social movement is driven by, and composed of, the urban middle class. According to the Occupy Research General Survey,[20] 39 per cent of participants defined themselves as working class or lower middle class, 29.3 per cent as middle class, 10.9 per cent as upper middle or upper class. It is dominated by a core of university-educated middle-class people. Education is a reliable guide to objective social class: 70.9 per cent have university education, though only 31.6 per cent had full time jobs. These results are confirmed by Manuel Castells who has estimated that around a half of participants had a full-time job. Of those employed, their income was around the median income of Americans.[21] Christian Fuchs points to the considerable number of participants who might be 'described as precarious and proletarianised knowledge workers'.[22] While one might concede, as suggested by Fuchs, that the Occupy movement is more related to 'class structures' and less to 'individual liberties', whether the movement is 'motivated by socialist interests' is highly questionable.[23] Dividing the population into a dominant 1 per cent and the remainder 99 per cent ('We are the People') does not in itself lead to a coherent political opposition. The 99 per cent is a good rallying cry, but sociologically the 99 per cent are politically divided, they do not see the world in binary terms and by far the majority of Americans relate to the political Party system. For many Americans, the 'other 1 per cent', could as well be the 'anti-Wall St' demonstrators.

The objectives of many in the these movements were to be achieved through a revitalised American democracy. [24] The call of the demonstrators in Manhattan, on 17 September 2011, to President Obama was to end the influence of money over elected representatives. The slogan was: 'Democracy not Corporatocracy'.[25] Rather than a movement of socialism against

---

[18]   Chomsky, *Occupy*, pp 15–16.
[19]   Fuchs, *Digital Labour and Karl Marx*, p 323.
[20]   See http://occupyresearch.wikispaces.com. Cited by Fuchs, *Digital Labour and Karl Marx*, pp 319–20.
[21]   Cited by Manuel Castells, *Networks of Outrage and Hope: Social Movements in the Internet Age*. Cambridge: Polity, 2012, pp 166–7.
[22]   Castells, *Networks of Outrage and Hope*.
[23]   Fuchs, *Digital Labour and Karl Marx*, p 320.
[24]   Castells, *Networks of Outrage and Hope*, p 161.
[25]   Cited by Castells, *Networks of Outrage and Hope*, p 160.

capitalism, it postulates democracy against corporate domination. The participants originated from 'a large majority of democratic [Party] voters, as well as politically independent-minded people'.[26] Important in the mobilisation process is the use of social media to organise demonstrations. 'Occupy Wall Street was born digital.'[27]

Paul Mason[28] relates these popular protests to developments on a world scale. In discussing the period 2009–11, he likens the upsurge of street demonstrations in Europe (notably Greece and the various Occupy movements), the Middle East and the USA to a revolutionary movement. According to Mason, a revolution, which he believes we are living through, has been caused 'by the near collapse of free-market capitalism combined with an upswing in technical innovation, a surge in desire for individual freedom and a change in human consciousness about what freedom means'. Echoing the sentiments of the autonomy movement, he suggests that competitive democratic politics has become 'gestural', the present anti-capitalist movement is 'about action ... about the symbolic control of territory to create islands of utopia'.[29] At best these movements might be 'prefigurative' signifying an 'emancipatory potential' – a view shared by commentators such as Sklair, Brand and Monticelli. The danger here is that the prefigurative movements not only make islands, but become islands, and their inhabitants remain isolated from the wider population.

The coordination of economies may be achieved through markets, hierarchy (planning), networks, barter or combinations of these processes. What the Occupy groups share with many social movements is a belief that informal networks of associated producers or consumers are the way forward to achieve a more humane society and a sustainable economy. The scope of the movements is at the micro, local or communal level. The mechanism for their actions is provided by the interactive, multidirectional communication on the internet, and by wireless communication networks.[30] Ironically perhaps, anti-globalisation is made possible by the technical tools of globalisation.

The various movements seek 'the conquest of space *within* the system rather than to replace the system'.[31] Personal politics, reclaiming symbolic space (Wall St, St Paul's, Tahrir Square) become a form of release rather than the constitution of the collective politics of socialist parties. Informed by

---

[26] Castells, *Networks of Outrage and Hope*, p 170.
[27] Castells, *Networks of Outrage and Hope*, p 171.
[28] Mason, *Why It's Kicking Off Everywhere*.
[29] Mason, *Why It's Kicking Off Everywhere*, p 3.
[30] See Castells, *Networks of Outrage and Hope*, p 220.
[31] Mason, *Why It's Kicking Off Everywhere*, p 85. Italics in original.

'info-capitalism' and connected by social media, emancipation is possible.[32] Mason looks for the seeds of change within capitalism:

> [The] networked movements are evidence that a new historical subject exists. It is not just the working class in a different guise; it is networked humanity ... It is the networked individuals who have camped in the city squares, blockaded the fracking sites, performed punk rock on the roofs of Russian cathedrals, raised defiant cans of beer in the face of Islamism on the grass of Grezi Park, pulled a million people on to the streets of Rio and Sao Paulo and now organise mass strikes across southern China.[33]

Networked people are the base of 'Twitter' revolutions. These actions, however, lack a coherent focus and one should be sceptical of whether they will lead to significant political or economic change. While the movements share some form of popular mobilisation, they relate to different causes and have diverse political and social objectives. As Nick Srnicek and Alex Williams contend, their proposals are 'fetishisms of local spaces, immediate actions, transnational gestures and particularisms'.[34] While they should not be dismissed as compelling theatrical street performances, they do not present a fundamental alternative to globalised capitalism.

The 'networked' society

The 'network society' facilitated through digital contacts is widely regarded as a decisive instrument of alternative social movements. Manuel Castells writes: 'The characteristics of communication processes between individuals engaged in the social movement determine the organisational characteristics of the social movement itself ... The networked social movements of the digital age represent a new species of social movement'.[35] Mason and Castells emphasise the mobilisation effects of communication through the internet, which connects people to ideas, and mobile phones, which can coordinate mass protests. Digital networks are certainly tools for mobilising and organising, and internet communication channels are a new and important phenomenon. They allow for the mass dissemination of information to form an alternative politics. However, one should be wary of the claim that the internet itself creates protests; rather, communication enables people to

---

[32] See Mason, *Why It's Kicking Off Everywhere*, p 211.
[33] See Mason, *PostCapitalism*, p 212.
[34] Srnicek and Williams, *Inventing the Future*, p 3.
[35] Castells, *Networks of Outrage and Hope*, p 15.

respond to 'calls to action'. Movements are 'not created by the Internet, but from the antagonistic economic, political and ideological structures of society … it has no inbuilt effects or determinations'.[36] The calls to action are articulated by the informal leadership of social movements. Christian Fuchs has cogently examined the potentialities as well as the limits of 'Twitter revolutions'. 'Protests are not created online but by the social relations of activists that communicate with each other and connect with others.'[37] Hence 'Twitter' revolutions are dependent on an ideological critique as well as leadership, which can lead in diverse directions. These movements of protest may engender reform as well as revolution. Paradoxically, they may be orchestrated by authoritarian movements seeking to bring down democratic governments and by Western-sponsored democratic movements to replace 'populist' or anti-capitalist governments (such as Venezuela). The 'coloured' revolution phenomena are instances of this kind of social media mobilisation.[38]

The anti-globalisation movements, however, do not pose an institutional alternative to modern capitalism and some are quite compatible with different forms of capitalism. The constituent parts of the 'anti-globalisation' movements seek to change the domination of global capitalism, though the target is usually globalisation rather than capitalism.[39] The thrust of reform for many of the groups is to restore the sovereignty of 'the people', sometimes at state level but more often at that of the local community. Globalisation is considered responsible for the demise of the nation state which, it is contended, makes elected parties powerless in their own country. This general outlook is shared by The World Social Forum, which is a grouping of social forces composed of 'Unions and NGOs, movements and organisations, intellectuals and artists', which seek to build 'a great alliance to create a new society … where human beings and nature are the center of our concern'.[40] The struggle is 'against the hegemony of finance, the destruction of our cultures, the monopolisation of knowledge, mass media, and communication, the degradation of nature and the destruction of the quality of life by multinational corporations (MNCs) and anti-democratic policies'.[41]

---

[36] Fuchs, *Digital Labour and Karl Marx*, p 328.

[37] Fuchs, *Digital Labour and Karl Marx*, p 341.

[38] See D. Lane and S. White (Eds), *Rethinking the 'Coloured Revolutions'*. London and New York: Routledge, 2010.

[39] For an overview see Callinicos, *An Anti-Capitalist Manifesto*.

[40] World Social Forum, Porto Alegre call for mobilisation, in Lechner and Boli, *The Globalisation Reader*, p 435.

[41] World Social Forum, Porto Alegre call for mobilisation, p 435.

The objective of the World Social Forum is 'to achieve peoples' sovereignty and a just world'.[42]

The alter-globalists fit into this space, they accept internationalism in the form of a 'decentralised network model based on collective and divisible agents who make decisions through consensus'.[43] The emphasis is on reviving a people's form of democracy. In J.K. Gibson-Graham's view, society is pluralist and diverse and contains many kinds of transactions, forms of labour and practices that are usually excluded or minimised not only by mainstream economics but also by historical materialism. There is, they contend, no 'singular capitalist system or space' but zones or 'cohabitation' in which 'flourish contestation between multiple economic forms'.[44] Gibson-Graham draw attention to the fact that even in capitalist modes of production, only just over 40 per cent of labour hours are worked in commodity production, non-waged 'unpaid labour' in the household economy and community is of great importance.[45] Moreover, 'non-market' transactions include state allocations and appropriation, prison labour, barter and theft. Gibson-Graham contend that the objective to end capitalism should involve the development of the non-capitalist sector. The 'community economy' in which new kinds of economic subjects should be developed: small-scale, cooperative, dispersed, autonomous, local market-oriented, community-owned, led and controlled, self-reliant, interdependent forms of economy are the seeds of the alternative to capitalism. Alternatives to wage labour include self-employment, exchange of labour, barter, state enterprise, non-profit organisation, share-food, child-care sharing and charity. Their proposals are illustrated by reference to numerous cooperative associations and corporations. Mondragon, for example, is a self-governing participatory business employing 81,000 people (data for 2019) with financial assets of 24,725 billion euros in 2015; in 2011 it was Spain's fourth largest industrial and tenth largest financial group.[46] While these proposals present an alternative, they remain developments on the periphery of the capitalist system, islands of cooperative self-government and self-development in the global sea. As Leslie Sklair has noted, the Mondragon venture is closer to 'caring capitalism, perhaps even caring capitalist globalisation ... [than] an exemplar of a revolutionary socialist globalisation'.[47] They are part of what Nick Srnicek and Alex Williams

---

[42] World Social Forum, Porto Alegre call for mobilisation, p 437.
[43] M. Maeckelbergh, *Will of the Many: How the Alterglobalisation Movement Is Changing the Face of Democracy*. London: Pluto, 2009, p 225.
[44] Gibson-Graham, *The End of Capitalism*, p xxi.
[45] Gibson-Graham, *The End of Capitalism*, Chapter 3, see p 68.
[46] Data taken from Wikipedia, https://en.wikipedia.org/wiki/Mondragon_Corporation. Other examples are given by Gibson-Graham, *The End of Capitalism*, p 187.
[47] Sklair, *Second Thoughts*, p 162.

consider to be a politics that privileges the local, favours the small community, rejects hegemony and values withdrawal and exit.[48]

While these movements show that alternative cooperative non-monetary forms of economy are perfectly viable at a local level, they have not made any significant challenge to globalised capitalism and are likely to remain peripheral parallel developments. Localised alternatives have been part of capitalism for a long time and include ventures in the nineteenth century, such as Robert Owen's initiatives, self-sufficient societies, such as the Amish community in Pennsylvania and the welfare efforts of trade unions. Economically, they neglect the productivity gains that have been the hallmark of capitalism and that have been the basis of liberation from poverty, and the promise of an economy of plenty. The 'autonomous' associations are dependent on the national economy for supplies of cultural and health services. as well as physical commodities such as large manufactured goods (for example, trains and fertilisers). Without the supplies of a modern economy, they would wither and probably die.

What is noteworthy is that anti-capitalist and anti-globalist street protests have been organised outside of, and unsupported by, the major political movements and parties. While leftist political leaders of electoral parties (Jeremy Corbyn, when leader of the British Labour Party) have defended the demonstrators, no major political party has had a significant presence.

The outlook of such movements is highly heterogeneous, though there are some common theoretical and policy orientations, as outlined previously. They concurrently call for autonomous production and distributive units, as well as for the reform or disbanding of global institutions. Some of these views reflect disenchantment not just with capitalism but with industrialism in general, with relentless economic growth and the consequent consumptionist culture. The quest for autonomy and self-sufficiency shades into calls for a return to a simpler agriculturally based economy. Reliance is placed on networks and the institution of people's democracy, rather than on markets and hierarchies. Others, in contrast, emphasise and oppose the capitalist nature of globalisation.

Reformist perspectives

Most of these counter movements address single issues. 'Anti-Wall St' and 'Occupy the Stock Exchange' condemn the financial system and demonstrate disapproval. But they do not suggest what kind of alternative financial system or form of ownership should take their place. Castells points out that the Occupy Wall St movement is not anti-capitalist but can lead to reform

---

[48]   Srnicek and Williams, *Inventing the Future*, p 11.

of capitalism.[49] A study by the Pew Research Center found that of those who supported 'Occupy Wall St', 45 per cent were 'positively' disposed to the capitalist system and 39 per cent were positive to socialism.[50] Paul Mason's proposal is not to 'transcend capitalism' but to 'save globalisation by ditching neoliberalism'.[51] His vision is for 'postcapitalism' – a reformed type of capitalism combining the market with a network society. He expresses fears that globalisation may 'fall apart' and lead to conflicts between states. Alternatively, globalisation will be partially saved at great cost through austerity programmes.[52] By dismantling neoliberalism, he argues, society can supersede capitalism and move to postcapitalism[53] – not socialism. Writers like David Harvey[54] identify the function of occupying civic space. But what the occupants do when (and after) they the occupation is not defined.

Social movements in opposition are useful in addressing, and bringing public attention to, certain issues – such as the impact of financialisation, the fraudulent practices of banks, links between globalisation and inequality, between gender and inequality, between financial crisis and austerity, and between green issues and energy extracting companies. Critical writers highlight injustices and malpractices and call for reforms, even revolution. But the suggested 'alternatives' apply to a limited number of aspects of capitalism and lack a theory of society. These viewpoints have positive features in criticising some of the failings of neoliberal capitalist globalisation, but are unlikely to have wider systemic effects under the conditions of contemporary politics.

Conclusion

These critical approaches to global capitalism provide strategies for moving away from the current neoliberal capitalist ways of doing things, and all point to the evolution of collectivist entities which produce goods and services for use – rather than for market exchange. Such perspectives have in common calls for action in ways outside traditional electoral politics. They share a commitment to participatory democracy and justice and opposition to authority and hierarchy. They advance objectives that promote a world system based on justice, democracy, equality, environmental sustainability and peace.

---

[49] Castells, *Networks of Outrage and Hope*, p 197.

[50] Pew Research Center, Little Change in Public's Response to 'Capitalism', 'Socialism'. Available at: www.people-press.org/2011/12/28little-change-in-public-response-to-cap italism

[51] Mason, *PostCapitalism*, p xi.

[52] See Mason, *PostCapitalism*, p x.

[53] Mason, *PostCapitalism*, p xi.

[54] Harvey, *Rebel Cities*.

Most of the proposals for institutional reform call for localised autonomous associations coexisting with global organisations. Others demand the installation of a new social order promoting ecological sustainability and de-growth, which we consider in the next chapter. Such critics have an optimistic vision of a non-consumptionist economic culture. This shift to a self-sustaining subsistence economy could lead to a barter form of economic coordination coexisting with global capitalism.

Reflecting these diverse political objectives, the means to achieve them range from direct action to demonstrations calling for international system change. Networks and participatory democracy, rather than hierarchies or markets, are the favoured organisational alternatives. Micro, rather than macro, changes involving individual and group autonomy are the behavioural frames of reference. The post-capitalism theorists considered in this chapter count on the demands coming from below, from civil society associations. However, the strategy of using civil rights (as proposed by Russell Brand on the model of LGBTQ+, or sexual liberation) appears to me to be an implausible strategy to change global capitalism. Civil rights may be achieved within a pluralist political system but transforming global capitalism calls for major changes in economic and political institutional structures, as well as in the processes of the contemporary global economy. Curbing legal rights to corporate property on which class relations are based is a high order of political and economic transformation. The social movements, 'Occupy Wall Street', 'Black Lives Matter', 'Extinction Rebellion', lack a sociologically informed vision comparable to historical materialism. These are boats with very large rhetorical sails and light theoretical ballast. They identify injustices and inequalities but lack a vision of how to move to a new post-capitalist way of life. The demonstrations that have taken place in localities like Seattle and St Paul's, London, have not resulted in any significant structural changes, though there have been some short-term effects. The 'Occupy' movements, lacking any hierarchical organisation and coherent ideology, have melted away. A similar fate, I suggest, will fall to the Extinction Rebellion movement. The prefigurative idea of 'creating now' the kind of society that is intended for the idealised future will fail without changes in the global economy.

The anti-globalisation movements are an expression of the discontent which has grown out of the changing occupational structures shaped by neoliberal globalisation. The international division of labour has produced a capitalist class, a large middle class and a creatariat in the core countries; an industrial working class and agricultural precariat have grown in the rising semi-core. Social instability has been triggered by under-employment and unemployment in the advanced countries. Many of the writers cited in this chapter acknowledge that international action of some kind is necessary to unseat the dominant globalised political and economic classes to install a new system, but they retreat to, or even fall into, the 'cracks' of capitalism.

Such critics have a constructive vision of a non-consumptionist economic culture predicated on the production of use-values. They begin to fill in the 'spaces between capitalism and socialism'.[55] But their emphasis on the micro and local levels does not connect to the forces of corporate and state power driving the political economy of neoliberalism. 'Educated and connected human beings' and 'networked humanity'[56] do not make a political movement in any way comparable to the socio-economic forces which have driven the movement from feudalism to capitalism, or more recently, the transition from state socialism to capitalism. Moreover, such economic communities are incapable of replacing the current mass production of national and global corporations. They remain small communities of mutual production set in globalised capitalist economies. They present islands of dissent, cut off from the worlds inhabited by the wider population.

An alternative approach is to consider policies that promote economic and political advances and that modify or transcend neoliberal capitalist institutions. What must be addressed are macro developments: financialisation, multi-national corporations, destatisation and deterritorialisation of the nation state, which (with the exception of some major powers with strong self-sustaining economies, such as China and the USA) have weakened political control over national economies. Recent history shows that states and international agencies remain the principal agent by which collectivities can change forms of property ownership and influence politics on a regional and international scale. A major transformation of the European state socialist societies was carried out in a decade by states and international organisations, though at considerable social cost. Human agency and active political intervention are drivers of transformation. Securing the power of the state, either by electoral or other means, remains the most realistic method to achieve any significant political and economic transformation.

Rather than pursuing long-term 'emancipatory potential', one should consider policies that are amenable to implementation within a realistic time span. The state, or state sponsored, institutions are the principal forms of organisation able to contest the powers of modern global economic corporations. Some post-capitalist writers point to statist developments that not only undermine capitalism but also represent ascendant forces. Paul Mason, for example, while denying the state a major coordinating role (as under central planning), concedes that national governments and multilateral agreements are necessary[57] to promote transformation. He concludes that: 'Whatever micro-level actions we take to alleviate these risks,

---

[55] Sklair, *Second Thoughts*, p 161.
[56] Mason, *PostCapitalism*, p 212.
[57] Mason, *PostCapitalism*, p 274.

only national governments and multilateral agreements can actually solve them'.[58] This invocation of state intervention coexists with autonomous spontaneous developments. I would propose to adopt a range of political strategies employing market, state-based hierarchy and planning. In this scenario, the state would introduce some form of ex-ante planning, instead of ex-post reaction. Policy would be constructed to meet human needs and concurrently to address the question of sustainable economic development.

Alternative policies calling for a challenge to global capitalism on a regional or transnational basis require movements on a continental or international-wide scale. Ironically perhaps, Margaret Thatcher recognised the necessity of a global solution to global problems. In her memoirs she points out that: 'Clearly no plan to alter climate could be considered on anything but a global scale, it provides a marvellous excuse for worldwide, supra-national socialism'.[59] Indeed. Ecological unsustainability is a major issue addressed by the anti-capitalist and anti-globalisation movements. Moreover, the ecological movement poses the wider question of ecological catastrophe and an alternative ecological civilisation, which we turn to in the next chapter.

---

[58]   Mason, *PostCapitalism*, p 274.
[59]   Cited in *Ecologist*, 17 October 2018. Available at: https://theecologist.org/2018/oct/17/who-drove-thatchers-climate-change-u-turn

13

Ecological 'Catastrophe'

Ecological unsustainability[1] and environmental 'catastrophe'[2] are current dilemmas leading to polarised political positions. Karl Polanyi[3] was one of the first writers to recognise that, if unchecked, 'leaving the fate of soil and people to the market would be tantamount to annihilating them'. While political movements can be organised to resist the actions of the market for labour, there is no comparable movement which can resist the exploitation of nature. The supremacy of human beings, enabled by the capitalist mode of production, has led to human domination over nature.[4] Various environmental groups acting, as it were, on behalf of nature, seek to redress the balance between human beings and nature. Their objectives vary: some oppose the assumption that economic development is positive and question whether economic growth promotes human well-being; others seek to limit the harmful effects of industrialism in the exploitation of nature. The Marxist position is that the capitalist form taken by industrialisation is at fault. Environmentalists address the problem of how global capitalism can resolve the problem, or whether it should be replaced by some other form

---

[1] For an overview see Michael Mann, The Sources of Social Power. Volume 4, Globalization 1945–2011, Cambridge: Cambridge University Press, 2013, Chapter 12; Sklair, *Globalization: Capitalism and its Alternatives*, pp 53–7; John Bellamy Foster, *The Return of Nature: Socialism and Ecology*. New York: Monthly Review Press, 2020; John Bellamy Foster, *Materialism and Nature*. New York: Monthly Review Press, 2000; Andreas Malm, *Fossil Capital: The Rise of Steam Power and the Roots of Global Warming*. London: Verso. 2016; M. Bookchin, *The Ecology of Freedom*. Palo Alto: Cheshire Books, 1982.

[2] See Held et al, *Global Transformation: Politics, Economics and Culture*, Chapter 8.

[3] Polanyi, *The Great Transformation*.

[4] See Murray Bookchin, *The Murray Bookchin Reader*. J. Biehl (Ed), Montreal and London: Black Rose Books, 1999; see introduction p 9. Available online at: https://theanarchistlibrary.org/library/murray-bookchin-janet-biehl-the-murray-bookchin-reader. See also Murray Bookchin, *Towards an Ecological Society*. Mantred-Buffalo: Black Rose, 1986.

of production that would recreate a harmonious balance between mankind and nature.

The political problem is that economic and commercial activities in one country have unintended, uncontrollable and deleterious effects on a global scale. Some are confident that changes within the existing economic framework can reduce carbon emissions and thus significantly reduce the threat; others seek a more fundamental change in the basis of industrial globalisation. Ways to resolve the environmental threat depend on what activists and politicians believe to be the causes. An environmentalist approach seeks to curb the effects of the industrial revolution, which have led to the use and misuse of the Earth's resources; others attribute unsustainability not to the industrialisation process but to the rapacious nature of the capitalist form of production.

The term 'Anthropocene'[5] has been coined to describe the ways that lead to breakdown of the ecological system. It refers to the impact of human activity on the planet and includes all the interacting 'physical, chemical, biological and human processes which affect the environment'.[6] The consequences of this rift in the Earth system threaten 'the entire realm of human civilisation, in the sense of an advanced, ordered society, it could potentially undermine the conditions of human life itself, as well as that of innumerable other species'.[7] Many use the term in an apocalyptic way to describe the effects of human activity which is not only threatening the planet, but, if left unchecked, will destroy it. Economic growth and development, according to this school of thought, must be curbed to preserve nature through policies of environmental sustainability. Some go even further and call for a completely different relationship between human beings and nature, which would abandon a civilisation based on industrialism and would put an end to capitalism. This approach calls for 'degrowth' – to reverse industrial activity. Global capitalism, would be replaced by an anarchistic, decentralised, mutualistic, non-hierarchical civilisation[8] – only such a society is able to prioritise environmentalism. Others accept the advances that an industrial civilisation brings to human civilisation: the remedies are found either by curbing the excesses of global capitalism – through market mechanisms or state regulation – or

---

[5] Ian Angus, *Facing the Anthropocene: Fossil Capitalism and the Crises of the Earth System*. New York: Monthly Review Press, 2016.

[6] See Julia A. Thomas, Why the Anthropocene is not 'climate change'. *Climate and Capitalism* (31 January 2019). Available at: https://climateandcapitalism.com/2019/01/31/why-the-anthropocene-is-not-climate-change-and-why-that-matters/

[7] J.B. Foster, The Earth-system crisis and ecological civilization: A Marxian view. *International Critical Thought*, 7:4, pp 439–58, quotation p 439.

[8] Bookchin, *The Murray Bookchin Reader*, p 14.

through replacing global capitalism with a system of socialist planning. Before I turn to outline these various proposals, I consider the facts, what is the danger?

Ecological catastrophe

The Intergovernmental Panel on Climate Change (IPCC) in its report of October 2018 predicted that without significant reductions in carbon emissions by 2030, global warming would result in global catastrophe. Changes in sea temperatures leading to rising sea levels, melting ice caps, climatic events, soil degradation and other threats to the global ecosystem are attributed to global warming, which in turn has been caused by increases in gas emissions. Climate change has many causes: natural as well as human-made. The latter include the effects of industrialisation leading to the exploitation of natural resources and transcontinental transportation. Even critics of current eco-policies, such as Steven E. Koonin, agree that 'humans are influencing the climate'.[9] The question is about the relative contribution of human activity (compared to natural changes) that is taking place. Koonin contends that human influences are physically small in relation to the climate system as a whole. He points out that 'human additions to carbon dioxide in the atmosphere by the middle of the twenty-first century are expected to directly shift the atmosphere's natural greenhouse effect by only 1% to 2%'.[10] The validity of these arguments is outside the parameters of this book, though Koonin's opinion must be taken seriously.[11] Given that there is a problem, we are concerned with what kinds of political and economic mechanisms may control energy use. Globalised capitalism is widely recognised by environmentalists as a cause of pollution, but it is not the only cause.

The problem to be addressed is whether or not global capitalism may solve the problems through market mechanisms (the liberal economists's answer) or whether the system requires a fundamental transformation. The significance of 'sustainable development' is that economic progress should

---

[9] S.E. Koonin, *Unsettled: What Climate Science Tells Us, What It Doesn't, and Why It Matters.* Dallas: BenBella Books, 2021. For another critical approach see: Bjorn Lomborg, *False Alarm: How Climate Change Panic Costs Us Trillions.* New York: Basic Books, 2020.

[10] See his calculations reference 1, p 2 in: S.E. Koonin, Climate science is not settled. *Wall St Journal*, 19 September 2014.

[11] He is a physicist having worked for BP as Chief Scientist He has been the director of the Center for Urban Science and Progress at New York University, and between 2009 and 2011, he was Under Secretary for Science, Department of Energy, in the Obama administration.

take into account disproportions between rich and poor areas, and the needs of future generations.[12]

The market solution

The 'market solution' contends that policy makers can resolve the problem within the parameters of global capitalism. Problems created by environmental despoilation are recognised by the dominant political and economic elites who propose market mechanisms to curb the detrimental effects. The assumption here is that the market through financial incentives will find a solution. Economists, such as Jeffrey Sachs, believe that, if there is sufficient demand, new technology (such as wind power or converting sunlight) can replace fossil fuels. The market can be utilised to price out pollution, and the market will stimulate innovation and invention. Policies for 'greening the economy' are proposed. In 2007, for example, the meeting of the Business Forum under the UN Framework Convention on Climate Change (attended by 450 companies from 65 countries) was convened to 'advance the power of sustainable business'. The C4C website declares: 'Business leaders around the world realize that climate change and environmental degradation pose important new risks and opportunities for their companies' competitiveness, growth and development. Through innovation and long-term investments in energy efficiency and low-carbon technologies, business has the solutions to turn the climate challenge into market opportunities'.[13] Here we observe the neoliberal policy response to environmental problems.

The major mechanism to ensure environmental policies comes from international agreements, concluded by the United Nations' Climate Change Conferences (COP) (formulated as the Kyoto Protocol and the Copenhagen Accord) to limit environment despoilation, and to manage the risks. The Glasgow COP26 (November 2021) reached agreements by heads of states to reduce global emissions by specified dates. Such proposals call for government regulation of gas discharges. Working within the current system of globalisation, other measures include: the reduction of carbon emissions, moving away from meat production, promotion of green policies ('greenwashing') and 'sustainable investing'. In addition to reduction of emissions, COP meetings promote the transfer of finance from the richer

---

[12] World Commission on Environment and Development, *Our Common Future*, 1987. Available at: https://sustainabledevelopment.un.org/content/documents/5987our-common-future.pdf

[13] Cited by G. Di Chiro, Care not growth: Imagining a subsistence economy for all. *British Journal of Politics and International Relations*, 21:2 (2019), pp 303–311, quotation p 305.

countries to poorer ones to cope with the effects of climate change. They also sponsor private sector investment and loans in green technology.

Many green proposals, if robustly carried out, would change life as we currently live it: motor and air transport would be drastically reduced to burn less fuel; fossil burning power stations would be closed down, houses would be redesigned to reduce heat loss and trap non-carbon forms of heating, manufacturing would be reduced and local production (particularly for food and consumables) would replace transported commodities. Some critics propose that urban industrial civilisation would be transformed into an ecological civilisation – an economy based on market derived wants, would be replaced by one predicated on the maintenance of nature to meet human needs. One problem here is the imbalance in world production: industrialising countries, such as China and India, are dependent of cheap sources of energy, whereas rich post-industrialised countries can rely on imports of manufactured goods and are able to finance reductions of emissions.

'Save the planet'

By 2020, the activist environmentalist movement had moved to the centre of extra-political opposition. 'Saving the planet' became the major issue for supporters of the Extinction Rebellion movement, which organised protests of some 1.5 million students in 2019 drawing attention to the dangers of climate change. For Extinction Rebellion, the world faces the probability of the destruction of human life; economies must move away from economic growth. The alternative is a terminal state for human civilisation.[14]

These popular movements do not challenge capitalism as such, but propose a non-carbon footprint for industrialisation. Sustainable development, they argue, should be at the centre of policymaking. Their activity is to pressurise governments to 'do more' to reduce carbon emissions. The Extinction Rebellion movement is not predicated on any theory of capitalism or industrial society to attain sustainable development. The proposals are to reduce completely carbon emissions, which would lead to a severe contraction of industrial production, including machinery and chemicals used in agriculture. Such developments would seriously affect contemporary ways of life, and there would be some harmful effects: food production, for example, would decline due to reduction in the use of fertiliser. The moral dilemma here is that people in poor countries are dependent on fossil fuels (essential for heating, power, and food production) which produce greenhouse emissions.

---

[14] S. Alexander, *This Civilisation is Finished*. London: Simplicity Books, 2019.

What complicates policy issues, is that the distribution of pollution is a global issue. According to calculations made by the Global Carbon Budget Project,[15] major polluters are in the non-industrialised countries which, in 2017, accounted for 6,027 million tonnes of carbon per year; OECD countries for 3,455 (those in the EU 967, Africa 363, Asia 4,617, North America 1,729) out of a world total of 9,867 million tonnes. Major pollution comes from Asia, which is greater than that of the EU and North America combined. Deduction of carbon emissions consequent on major changes in forms of production and life styles in countries like the UK would have very little effect on global warming. In 2017, the UK's total emissions came to 105 million tonnes of carbon per year, Germany's to 218, Japan's to 329, Russia's to 462, India's to 673, and the largest polluters were the USA with 1,438 and China with 2,685 million tonnes (China's level is nearly three times that of the EU). Here we may note that greater environmental demands put on India and China, as they catch up with the industrialised West, would involve unjust discrimination as these countries seek to raise the standard of well-being. India and China have large populations with relatively low emissions per head. In 2015, the USA's emission of carbon per capita (measured in metric tons) was 17.5 metric tons, China's 6.18 and India's only 1.64; the figures for European countries (UK 7.96 and Germany 9.06) were higher than China in per capita terms.[16] Ranking of countries by level of carbon emissions per head put China in 47th place and the USA, 11th in 2017.[17] However, Asian countries are industrialising rapidly and one can expect their carbon footprint to increase.

Blanket restrictions on fossil fuel use would therefore severely penalise the poor in India and China. To take such issues into account, political policy has shifted to restrict 'luxury' emissions, which do not threaten human life, while allowing 'survival' emissions.[18] One proposal is to move to a system of 'climate justice' in which human needs (for shelter, food, medicine, education) are met while emissions created to meet 'unnecessary' market generated wants (luxuries) are reduced. This distinction is expressed by Henry Shue: 'The central point about equity is that it is not equitable to ask some people to surrender necessities so that other people can retain luxuries'.[19] While the distinction between needs and wants is socially conditioned, it

---

[15] Available at: http://www.globalcarbonproject.org/carbonbudget

[16] UN, *Millennium Development Goals Indicators*. Available at: http://mdgs.un.org/unsd/mdg/SeriesDetail.aspx?srid=751. Data for 2015.

[17] Cotap.org. Based on UN statistics. Available at: https://cotap.org/per-capita-carbon-co2-emissions-by-country/?gclid=CjwKCAjwtO7qBRBQEiwAl5WC29zRUZeC-IAi4Tx4E1gT0SM31do_Uoq_OquTjqN2xfvUbQ6tsGg1bhoCEu4QAvD_BwE

[18] H. Shue, *Climate Justice: Vulnerability and Protection*. Oxford: Oxford University Press, 2014.

[19] H. Shue, Subsistence emissions and luxury emissions. *Law and Policy*, 15:1 (1993), p 56.

does provide a basis on which policy can discriminate between different end-uses and avoids penalising the populations of late developing countries. Applying this distinction would give preference to allow emissions of methane to enable poor people to have a life-promoting diet ('subsistence emissions') while denying other people the right to have steak dinners ('luxury emissions'). Poverty reduction and human well-being cannot be ignored when considering measures for dealing with climate change and eliminating pollution. Some pollution is inevitable but could be reduced. The problem is how to carry out such policies – how to control or replace global capitalism.

Political enforcement of agreements is hampered by the uneven distribution of wealth and power between, and within, countries. Relatively well-off people in rich countries will not vote for austerity policies which a non-growth economy implies. 'Subsistence' is also socially defined and in the advanced developed countries includes much more than a minimum set of physical 'needs'. Civilisations change and create different sets of 'wants' and 'needs'; currently in modern societies people have a 'need' for higher education, a 'need' for international travel, a 'need' for hi-tech communication – these needs require machines, books, moving carriages. Under capitalism, many claim a 'need' to own and use their own private property. To avoid the elitism of politicians and philosophers, who are prone to assume that they know what people 'really need', one has to rely on democratic procedures to make the distinction between needs and wants. The dilemma for environmentalists is that democratic choice is likely to opt to continue pollution if 'green' policies threaten current life styles. Proposals for reducing emissions come into conflict with policies of governments and political parties which encourage economic growth and consumption to meet consumers' wants. A significant reduction in emissions would effectively lead to 'austerity' economies – quite the opposite of more growth and jobs, which are proposed by contemporary domestic political parties in both developing and developed economies. Hence domestic pressures on governments – to maintain a 'modern' way of life, to preserve employment in the domestic coal industry, and opposition to costs involved in replacing polluting heating in homes – make them reluctant to move decisively to cut emissions.

Control over the extractive and production process is quite compatible with capitalism if it can promote extractive processes that are cleaner and more eco-friendly. State sponsored policies, such as the Green New Deal[20] are attempts to reduce global warming. They include the promotion of

---

[20] See for example, Naomi Klein, *On Fire: The (Burning) Case for a Green New Deal*. New York: Simon & Schuster, 2020.

carbon tax policies and administrative measures (phasing out fossil fuels), shifting from coal and oil to renewables, reducing carbon-based transport, discouraging meat production and subsidising renewable home heating. These measures no doubt lead to rearrangements of production and types of consumption of current practices; they challenge unrestricted globalisation by insisting on state agreements over production and a preference for environmental protection over efficient production. They present a form of 'green' capitalism rather than its replacement.

The Marxist critique

There is a significant difference in the ways that such environmentalists and Marxists understand the problem. Environmentalists seek to limit the effects of industrialism by controlling the levels of extraction and consequences of industrialism. They focus on the exploitation of nature and seek solutions to control the effects of industrialism, whereas the Marxist analysis of capitalism is predicated on the exploitation of labour and production for profit[21] which, through the increase in production, has had positive liberating effects. John Bellamy Foster[22] unambiguously considers that capitalism – acting for profit though the market – is responsible for environmental degradation. Capitalism is the driving force in the overuse and misuse of resources, and its destructive forces cannot be curbed.[23] The remedy is to replace capitalism by socialism to restrict the excesses of industrialisation and concurrently to improve conditions for the growing population of the world. Following Paul Sweezy, Foster contends that socialist societies do not have the same '*inner* drive' for capital accumulation and that planning could successfully address these problems.[24] Nevertheless, while the state under socialism has the power to act in an environmentally friendly way, in the transition to socialism, such policies also have social costs. Industrialism is a positive development because it raises human productivity and the quality of human life, and the leadership of socialist states has been unwilling to sacrifice industrial advances to promote environmentally friendly policies. Communist China has become the centre of this debate.

---

[21] T. Benton, Marxism and natural limits: An ecological critique and reconstruction, *New Left Review*, I:178 (November/December 1989), pp 51–88.

[22] Foster, *The Return of Nature*; J.B. Foster, *Against Capitalism*. New York: Monthly Review Press, 2002; J.B. Foster and R.W. McChesney, *The Endless Crisis*. New York: Monthly Review Press, 2012.

[23] Foster, The Earth-system crisis and ecological civilization.

[24] Foster, The Earth-system crisis and ecological civilization, p 442. Italics in original.

An 'ecological civilisation'?

Though the People's Republic of China produces environmental hazards, the Chinese government proposes to reduce environmental pollution as its advance to socialism materialises.[25] Under President Xi Jinping, in 2017, the Chinese political leadership has added to the country's Constitution the concept of a 'socialist ecological civilisation'. China has been confronted by the need to improve the living conditions of the population while concurrently addressing problems of pollution and environmental unsustainability. A 2015 Communist Party document ('Opinions of the Central Committee of the Communist Party of China and the State Council on Further Promoting the Development of Ecological Civilisation'[26]) recognises the need for a shift of priorities from economic growth to sustainable development:

> [N]ature should be respected, adapted to, and protected; ... lucid waters and lush mountains are invaluable assets; [we must] uphold the principle of prioritizing resource conservation and environmental protection and letting nature restore itself; and take a positive path to development that ensures increased production, higher living standards, and healthy ecosystems. The Party shall strive to build a resource-conserving [society].[27]

The government has sought to introduce measures for environmental protection, including reduction of noxious emissions, increasing the use of renewables, promoting a 'circular economy' and generally sponsoring a 'green and low-carbon development'.[28] China has supported world initiatives such as the 2030 Agenda for Sustainable Development and the Paris Agreement on Climate Change (2015). However, following the previous line of argument, China has continued its policy of industrialisation and rates of pollution have not significantly diminished. The Chinese concept of an ecological civilisation embeds environmentalism within the context of a market industrial society driven by the communist state. The Chinese idea of an ecological civilisation is devised in the context of state led development of the productive forces to improve human welfare.

---

[25] If they are successful, they would vindicate Sweezy's conclusions. P.M. Sweezy, Socialism and ecology. *Monthly Review*, 41:4 (1989), pp 1–8, see p 8.

[26] Cited in Berthold Kuhn, Ecological civilisation in China. Dialogue of Civilisations Research Institute (DOC)(Berlin). September 2019. Available at: https://researchgate.net/publication/335661761_Ecological_civilisation_in_China.

[27] Constitution of the Communist Party of China, adopted at the 19th Congress of the CPC, 24 October 2017, quotation p 6.

[28] Citations taken from Kuhn, Ecological civilisation in China.

Whether China will follow a 'liberal' or an 'authoritarian' environmentalism is a disputed political agenda. Writers such as Steven Bernstein[29] have argued that in fact liberal environmentalism is being promoted in China and achieves only limited results. Berthold Kuhn has concluded that 'the party state not only relies strongly on cooperation from a variety of stakeholders, including scientists, experts, and the business community, but also on private investments, technological innovations, and creative designs for liveable environments. It needs stakeholders outside the realm of the party state to promote its vision'.[30] The present indications are that Chinese industrialisation will continue and that priority will be given to improving living standards with the government promoting environmental safeguards wherever possible. Adopting an ecological civilisation would involve moving away significantly from a consumer society that currently in China has wide social support. The challenge to global capitalism of an ecological society or civilisation is how it may promote a rational coherence between man and nature, not an 'irrational incoherence'.[31]

A non-consumptionist economy

One alternative is the adoption of a 'non-consumptionist' economic culture which moves in the direction of economic autonomy outlined in the previous chapter. Manuel Castells envisages the development of a three-tier economy that involves: a 'revamped informational capitalist economy'; an enlarged public and semi-public sector and a smaller market sector with tighter regulation of financial institutions; and a use-value economy.[32] Barter networks and non-monetary exchange through the internet would replace the market. Urban farming would significantly increase self-production (he recommends following Michelle Obama's cultivation of tomatoes and vegetables on the White House lawn), and he points out that transportation in cities could be transformed if we made more use of cycles, skateboards and walking. As Castells puts it: the 'decisive battle against capitalism may not be about the means of production but about the means of consumption'.[33] He foresees a confrontation between different economic cultures based on communal and capitalistic production. The kinds of autonomous units mentioned previously would coexist with global capitalism. The influence of the internet is a major factor in these approaches. Digital cultural sharing

---

[29] S. Bernstein, Liberal environmentalism and global environmental governance. *Global Environmental Politics*, 2:3 (2002), pp 1–16. Cited by Kuhn, Ecological civilisation in China.
[30] Kuhn, Ecological civilisation in China.
[31] Bookchin, *The Murray Bookchin Reader*, p 232.
[32] Castells, The crisis of global capitalism, p 205.
[33] Castells, The crisis of global capitalism, pp 207–9.

and open-source innovation in the computer world would be another area contesting production predicated on the profit motive. These proposals address environmental concerns by limiting and controlling the amount of production at the micro level, rather than by top-down processes of socialist planning that accept industrialism and the introduction of state ownership and control. These community-based measures have similar shortcomings as those described in Chapter 12.

Convivial de-growth

Leslie Sklair takes a similar approach, but comes to rather different conclusions. He affirms that ecological unsustainability leading to ecocide is driven by the productive capacity of capitalist globalisation and the culture-ideology of consumerism.[34] Sklair proposes a form of autonomism; he contends that a socialist globalisation which would be achieved through 'networks of relatively small producer-consumer cooperatives cooperating at a variety of levels to accomplish a variety of societal tasks'.[35] Such associations would 're-connect with nature' and would provide the necessities of life: they would provide for human needs, rather than market generated wants. They would not, however, involve a regression to a barter economy. The reason is that digital technologies allow small networking associations to attain a high standard of living and can promote a modern civilisation. These network associations would be high-technology based. They would provide 'reconstructed political communities', which would create 'more genuinely democratizing forms of economic, social and political organisation', which would be a haven for 'those wishing to escape the capitalist market and the hierarchic state'.[36]

Some of these writers are confident that such developments will gradually undermine the logic of the market and the hierarchical state: 'capitalism and states will eventually wither away'. Following writers like Nathan Barlow,[37] 'convivial degrowth' would represent a retreat from capitalist globalisation as well as the developmental state.[38] Policies of de-growth, driven from below by climate and environmental justice, and indigenous social movements, would secure ecologically sustainability and socially just outcomes. Non-hierarchical social movements are envisaged to 'reshape the existing institutions' to secure degrowth.[39] The focus of the Western anti-globalisation

---

[34] Leslie Sklair, World revolution or socialism, community by community, in the Anthropocene? Chapter 11 (pp 244–60) in *Second Thoughts*.
[35] Sklair, World revolution or socialism, p 246.
[36] Sklair, World revolution or socialism, p 258.
[37] N. Barlow et al, *Degrowth and Strategy*. Mayfly Books, 2022.
[38] Sklair, World revolution or socialism, p 260.
[39] Barlow et al, *Degrowth and Strategy*.

movements turns away from concerns for promoting economic growth to an involvement with the threat of ecological degradation consequent on industrialisation. However, the capitalist system would not, at least in the short run, be dismantled and the labour market would continue alongside these progressive alternatives. The idea that there can be an alternative directly challenging the market economy is considered to be unrealistic and should be abandoned.[40] Instead, an alternative is to negate and avoid capitalism by developing parallel institutions and processes. A hybrid system by creating parallel worlds allows some to escape global capitalism and its discontents, but it does not transcend it.

The enemy of environmentalism is not only global capitalism but also modern consumer civilisation which, as we noted earlier in the case of China, would not be negated by a contemporary socialist alternative. State controls of market and planned societies can promote environmentalism, but there are social costs, which raises the question of who makes the sacrifices. Western civilisation has provided positive advances and has 'enormous potentialities' for freedom[41], which should not be abandoned. An ecological approach has to combine modern civilisation with a more humanistic, cooperative form of community; an ecological society 'must itself constitute an advance toward civilisation and progress or it will not have been an endeavour worth making'.[42] An ecological society, from this point of view, would seek to reconcile the potentialities of industrialisation with the preservation of nature. One dilemma is that major sources of pollution are found in Asian countries that are poor, and the hasty reduction of fossil fuel use would have grave consequences for the well-being of the poor. The industrial and post-industrial revolutions cannot be reversed without a significant deterioration of what people currently expect from human life. State activity organised on an international scale is likely to be the most successful way to curb rising toxicities. In the next chapter, I consider two political perspectives, social democracy and socialism, involving state regulated markets, which seek to replace global capitalism. In doing so, they provide further environmentally friendly policies.

---

[40] Sklair, World revolution or socialism, p 248.
[41] Bookchin, *The Murray Bookchin Reader*, p 168.
[42] Bookchin, *The Murray Bookchin Reader*, p 226.

14

Social Democratic and Socialist Perspectives

Politicians and policy makers recognise that capitalist globalisation needs some form of regulation. What is problematic is what kind of regulation can be introduced to retain the benefits of globalisation while curbing its excesses. The social democratic approach accepts globalising tendencies but seeks to regulate them. By social democratic, I refer to electoral political movements (including self-defined democratic parties) that advocate greater social equality and more state provided public welfare. Social democrats frame globalisation in a benign way by decoupling globalisation from capitalism. The issues were raised in Chapter 9 by Dani Rodrik who noted the 'political trilemma' between democracy, national political interest and economic globalisation.[1] Economic globalisation (exchanges without borders) undermines state coordination and democratic processes. The boundaries of democratic choice encompass states, whereas the economic processes of globalisation transverse states.

The social democratic approach seeks to strengthen the democratic component of this trilemma. It may be resolved at two levels: first, by creating a new global democratic system of rulemaking – global democracy; second, by strengthening the powers of the nation state against global trends by limiting global reach. Both these approaches propose to modify market power and political influence exercised through globalisation. Writers like David Held, Anne Case and Angus Deaton adopt the first approach: globalisation can be 'tamed' by making it more responsible and democratic.[2] Such proposals

---

[1] Rodrik, *The Globalization Paradox*. See pp xviii–xix. Quotation p xviii.
[2] Anne Case and Angus Deaton, *Deaths of Despair and the Future of Capitalism*. Princeton: Princeton University Press 2020; David Held, Global social democracy, in David Held, *Global Covenant: Social Democratic Alternative to the Washington Consensus*. Cambridge: Polity, 2004, p 13.

accept the processes of globalisation but remedy their worst features by making institutions more democratic. Colin Crouch adopts the second approach by limiting the powers of global entities, strengthening the state and by promoting 'democratic assemblies at world-regional level'.[3]

These writers favour a form of internationalisation in which democratic regulation controls the globalisation process.[4] State sovereignty is limited and is 'shared with', not lost to, regional and international bodies. A related theme is to limit the powers of global corporations through requirements of social responsibility, which must take into account the public interest. This widens democracy by calling on corporations to act democratically[5] and to consider the interests of relevant stakeholders and thus dilute the capitalist drive for profit. In this chapter, I illustrate the social democratic position approach, then turn to discuss ideas of corporate social responsibility (CSR). In the second part of the chapter, I outline the deeper socialist approach, which pays greater attention to public ownership and state planning.

Globalised social democracy

Globalisation, social democrats contend, has to be regulated and global democracy provides one means to do so. This political standpoint views globalisation in a technical sense having positive features but requires democratic participation and control. Global democracy is described as 'a basis for promoting the rule of international law; greater transparency, accountability and democracy in global governance; a deeper commitment to social justice; the protection and reinvention of community at diverse levels; and the transformation of the global economy into a free and fair rule-based economic order'.[6] To achieve these goals a 'progressive transformation of global affairs' is required.[7] The vision here is of a new global social democracy predicated on the 'guiding ethical principles' of 'equal moral worth, equal liberty, equal political status, collective decision-making about public affairs, amelioration of urgent need, development for all, [and] environmental sustainability'.

The neoliberal global free market needs to be severely curtailed. Measures include 'taming global markets', 'market correction' (mandatory global

3   Crouch, *The Globalisation Backlash*, p 92
4   Crouch, *The Globalisation Backlash*. See Chapter 4.
5   Crouch, *The Strange Non-Death of Neoliberalism*. See pp 125–143. See also A. Crane, D. Matten and J. Moon, *Corporations and Citizenship*. Cambridge: Cambridge University Press, 2008.
6   David Held, Towards a global covenant, in David Held, *Global Covenant*. See discussion, pp 161–169.
7   Held, Towards a global covenant, p xv.

labour and environmental standards), and market promotion (privileged market access for developing economies). In politics, the call is for the democratisation of supra-state governance, the establishment of an international human rights court with strong supporting regional courts and the establishment of permanent peace-keeping forces.[8] Such writers acknowledge the infringement of the capacity of the state, which has to share power in the context of 'collaborative mechanisms of governance at supra-national, regional and global levels'.[9] There is an important shift in this way of thinking – from reconstituting and strengthening the nation state (as advocated by nationalist anti-globalisers) to the formation of supra-state institutions.

The structural problem of global democracy has been articulated by Robert Dahl, who contends that international institutions and organisations are too big to allow 'the ordinary citizen to participate effectively in the decisions of a world government'.[10] However, the way forward for the previously discussed theorists is not that of the alter-globalisers (discussed in Chapter 12) but the adaptation of existing institutions. A move to democracy would come about through 'a coalition of political groupings … comprising European countries with strong liberal and social democratic traditions, [and] the United States [through liberal democratic groups] that support multilateralism and the rule of law in international affairs'.[11] This kind of approach relies on countervailing forces from global civil society acting through international organisations. Positive participation is encouraged from nongovernmental organisations (NGOs) and transnational social movements. The major institutional goals are to establish the rule of law, democratic politics, global social justice, and global ecological balance. Priorities are to regulate global markets, to promote development and to abolish debt for indebted poor countries. To enhance political and democratic control of regional and international bodies, a major role for the United Nations' Security Council is proposed. The UN would have the powers to control and regulate the arms trade, and to further global poverty reduction.

Colin Crouch echoes Dahl's critique: 'Democracy separated from the nation state … implies global democracy, which is impossible to achieve'.[12]

---

[8] Here I have summarised the main points. For details see Held, *The Global Covenant*, pp 164–5.

[9] Held, *The Global Covenant*, p 15.

[10] Robert A. Dahl, Can international organisations be democratic? A sceptic's view. In Held and McGrew, *The Global Transformation Reader*, p 532.

[11] See for example, David Held and Kevin Young, Crises in parallel worlds: The governance of global risks in finance, security, and the environment, in Calhoun and Derluguian, *The Deepening Crisis*, p 41.

[12] Crouch, *The Globalisation Backlash*, p 110.

His solution is greater regulation of international agencies, such as the World Trade Organization (WTO), which should be subject to democratic pressure. States can also regulate globalisation by limiting deleterious effects on their economies. Crouch endorses the development of regionalism (such as in the EU) in which states 'pool their sovereignty'.[13] Thus, states retain powers of local economic development and the provision of welfare through a process of subsidiarity.

The problematic element lies in confrontation with interests linked to transnational companies and international organisations. Globalisation has reshaped 'state institutions, laws and governance processes in accordance with global priorities, regulatory standards and action plans'.[14] Institutions such as the WTO enforce global rules. The balance of power has moved to those interests that are able to define 'global priorities', 'standards' and 'action plans'. Global civil society may be too weak to counter global liberal market policy promoted by international organisations and transnational corporations (TNCs), especially when they have the support of leading neoliberal states.

Only a few states have the power to reshape the rules or to ignore the rules. Under Donald Trump's presidency, the USA promoted its own version of global rules. Economic sanctions exerted by the EU, the UK and US against Russia in the 2020s clearly indicate that states and groups of states can make the rules that undermine globalisation. National security, in this case, trumps free trade.

Nongovernmental organisations (NGOs) on which much reliance is placed by democratic reformers are in an ambiguous position. Neoliberal strategy is to diminish the state by fortifying civil society organisations consequently weakening local as well as national government. NGOs are not responsible to elected representatives (as in national and local government) but to sponsors who represent interests having their own political agenda. Sponsors' goals may conflict with the kinds of changes proposed by local interests. In a wider sociological sense, neoliberalism promotes markets, the financialisaton of services and the privatisation of public welfare. Attempts to introduce state or regional regulation come into conflict with the principles of the free movement of capital and labour. As I illustrate later, when in power, social democratic parties have compromised with the dominant global political elites and a sceptic might suggest that social democratic politicians (Blair, Obama and Biden) were, or are, part of the global elites. (They are part of the problem, not the solution). The social democratic project has moved the

---

[13] Crouch, *The Globalisation Backlash*, p 111.
[14] S. Hameiri and L. Jones, Global governance as state transformation. *Political Studies*, 64:4 (2016), pp 793–810, quotation p 793.

discourse from the level of the nation state to an international one, though social democratic parties (not their leaders) remain embedded in national politics. While the pictures drawn by David Held and Colin Crouch display the face of democracy comfortably nestled in democratic nation states and responsive international institutions, in practice national governments are confronted by powerful corporations and international organisations which promote their own interests. The Democratic Party in the USA as well as social democratic parties in the EU have backed economic sanctions even if they break WTO rules. Following the disruption of production chains during the COVID-19 emergency, and the consequences of Western sanctions exercised by NATO countries over the Russian invasion of Ukraine, moves towards greater economic self-sufficiency have grown.

Social democratic parties in power

Consider the policy of the British Labour government under Tony Blair and Gordon Brown. The Labour Party advocated a market-led state within the EU and provided no sustained critique of globalising tendencies. The Labour Party's 2010 Manifesto, for example, had chapters on the British economy, living standards, education, health, crime and immigration, families and the old, communities, green issues, democratic reform. It had one section on how Britain could meet the challenge of a global age, which largely covered domestic concerns about the defence review, combating international terrorism, the need for a strong (and enlarged) EU and commitment to western forces in Afghanistan.[15] The leadership of the Parliamentary Labour Party was co-opted into the global political class: the Labour government participated in the neoliberal EU, the American Alliance and NATO. It proposed within system changes: extension of the powers of the G8 (now G7), the World Bank was requested to 'focus on low-carbon development and the IMF to focus on financial stability, with both becoming more inclusive'. The UN and the British Commonwealth were to be strengthened.[16] Privatisation, financialisation, the opening up of markets globally and the down-sizing of the state were generally accepted, as was the institutional architecture of the IMF, BIS, the EU, and the assumptions on which they were built – the free movement of labour, goods, services and capital.

Prime Minister Gordon Brown's[17] notion of a 'London Consensus' was to strengthen international control of the world financial system, the

---

[15]   Labour Party 2010 Manifesto, Available at: www.labour.org.uk/manifesto
[16]   Labour Party 2010 Manifesto.
[17]   Chancellor of the exchequer until June 2007 when he became prime minister.

corollary of which would be weakening at the state level.[18] There were no proposals for supervision of transnational corporations (TNCs). Controls over financial companies were not possible as the global architecture was not set up to regulate financial markets and financial companies. Brown's proposals were part of the process of the creation, or strengthening, of supranational organisations (the Bank for International Settlements, the Financial Stability Board and IMF). They had positive elements and signalled a reinforcement of global institutions governed, at least notionally, by international laws and enforced through international agencies and the EU. The London Consensus strengthened the technical coordinating factions of the global political class.

Brown followed earlier proposals for reform, such as the World Bank's, The State of a Changing World (1997), which was designed to provide a regulative framework in which states would work under the leadership of bodies such as the IMF and WTO. Such intervention does not curb the private sector but calls for downsizing the state, cuts in public services (to facilitate control of public expenditure) and privatisation of state assets (to promote competition) – policies in line with neoliberal sentiments. The IMF is an important institution in the evolving global capitalist regulatory formation. Its regulatory role, however, relates to states, many of which have been burdened with the costs of defaults by financial and banking corporations. It lacks authority over global financial corporations. The Bank for International Settlements provides coordination and promotes financial stability but has no effective powers over its members (central banks of sovereign states). Thus Brown's proposals for reform were welcomed by transnational capitalist interests as they provided stability through a regulatory framework. As represented by social democracy in power, the Labour Party's policy accepted the fundamental features of neoliberal globalisation. Its proposals amounted to desirable adjustments to curb inequalities and financial instability but the Party, when in power, lacked a coherent policy of containing globalisation in the context of its national policy.

While the leadership under Corbyn certainly turned policy significantly away from New Labour, there was little economic and political analysis of neoliberal globalisation. The policy outlined in the Labour Party Manifesto of 2017 did not engage with globalisation; policy was essentially a list of proposals safeguarding Britain's position following exit from the EU within the context of the World Trade Organization – whose principles it supported. Corbyn's policies, if implemented, would have been contained within the institutions of competitive global capitalism.

---

[18] At the G20 summit meeting in April 2007, Brown spelled out his policy. See 2007 G20 Summit. Available at: www.pressrun.net

Social democratic parties competing through elections for political power are bound into the nation state system of politics. Politics and debate on a broad front are conducted in terms of national economic needs. A socialist party in power in an electoral democracy finds itself in a quandary: significant moves to public ownership (say nationalising financial companies in the City of London) could lead to economic sanctions and economic dislocation – and consequently likely rejection at the polls. Whereas, marginal changes (enhancing the welfare state, mandating employees to boards of companies) over time lead to assimilation into, and give even greater legitimacy to, the capitalist system. The values of the ethics of capitalism and the market as a way of life are very deeply ingrained and contest the realisation of socialist values and policies. Without a competing and well-grounded alternative socialist ideology, any significant reform of global capitalism is unlikely and makes the British Labour Party a 'crippling illusion'.[19] Overcoming this illusion is, as Panitch and Leys put it, 'the central dilemma for democratic socialists, not just in Britain but everywhere'.[20] I suggest some ways this can be achieved in the final chapter of this book.

The failings of politics as a mechanism of change has led to an alternative social democratic approach, the objective of which is to 'democratise' the institutions which have economic power: financial and non-financial corporations. The issue here is the extent to which power has already passed from the formal political domain – the state, political parties, electoral politics – to transnational economic corporations and global coordinating institutions. As Colin Crouch has explained:

> The representatives of today's Trans National Corporations are not in the lobby, outside the real decision-making space of government, at all. They are right inside the room of political decision-making. They set standards, establish private regulatory systems, act as consultants to government, even have staff seconded to ministers' offices ... These corporations exist out there *alongside* the international and transnational agencies, not generally subordinate to them.[21]

One needs to add here, what happens in the 'room of decision-making'? Powerful states, such as the USA, UK and France, might overrule some transnational interests and favour others. American politicians may hear European transnational corporations (TNCs), but listen to, and act on, the advice of American corporations. As we noted in Chapter 10, economic

---

[19] Ralph Miliband, Moving on, Socialist Register. London: 1976, p 128.
[20] Panitch and Leys, p 255.
[21] Crouch, *The Strange Non-Death of Neoliberalism*, pp 131, 133. Italics in original.

sanctions on Russia and China negatively affect some TNCs, as well as their customers and shareholders, but others have benefitted.

One other social democratic strategy is to shift national and TNCs away from profit maximisation, and to act in a paternalistic and more responsible way. Shareholders would become one of many stakeholders and corporations would promote Corporate social responsibility (CSR).

Corporate social responsibility

Corporate social responsibility is endorsed as a means by which firms accept some of the obligations normally performed by governments. It involves a pattern of managerial behaviour that takes into account broader social obligations of companies. In August 2019, the American Business Roundtable declared: 'While each of our individual companies serves its own corporate purpose, we share a fundamental commitment to all of our stakeholders – customers, employees, suppliers, communities and – last in the list – shareholders.'[22] This statement epitomises the ideas underpinning CSR: companies have an obligation to the wider community to protect the environment, to fulfil social and economic commitments and to recognise the rights of employees and others who have a 'stake' in the company. Firms have to exercise rights as citizens in a global context. In social democratic analysis, stakeholders have rights to representation on the boards of companies; and boards have a responsibility to local communities.

Companies can be constrained by values other than profit maximisation, and these values influence company policy independently of global markets or state pressures. Corporations should accept social responsibility and thereby counter criticisms that globalisation leads solely to profit maximisation and to a weakening of social welfare. Non-business social activity, it is claimed, can have advantages to the company: it may reduce social costs (cut pollution, eliminate discrimination, limit redundancies) and encourages investments to further welfare (support of health projects, charities, local public works, educational initiatives). It is democratic in the sense that companies respond to stakeholders and public demands. Campaigners become important sources of pressure, which can adversely affect companies if they do not comply. This kind of policy moves significantly away from neoliberal market economic philosophy.

The problem here is that companies, to operate efficiently, have a duty to promote shareholder value. As Milton Friedman puts it:

---

[22] Cited by Andrew Hill, The limits of the pursuit of profit. *Financial Times*, 24 September 2019.

The social responsibility of business is to increase its profits ... In a free-enterprise, private-property system, a corporate executive is an employee of the owners of the business. He has direct responsibility to his employers. That responsibility is to conduct the business in accordance with their desires, which generally will be to make as much money as possible while conforming to the basic rules of the society, both those embodied in law and those embodied in ethical custom. Of course, in some cases employers may have a different objective. A group of persons might establish a corporation for an eleemosynary [charitable] purpose – for example, a hospital or a school. The manager of such a corporation will not have money profit as his objective but the rendering of certain services.[23]

For Milton Friedman, CSR is a form of window dressing, which is not only unnecessary but actually harmful as it prevents the market from working. The essence of the liberal economic approach is that competition through markets should operate without outside interference. Should society want the services of corporations to be diverted for the public good then, he argues, governments should be persuaded to tax corporations. CSR, he contends, is a perverse form of collectivist activity: 'professing to believe that collectivist ends can be attained without collectivist means'. This is precisely what CSR proposes. Friedman, however, does not take into account the need for corporate capital to legitimate itself in a global environment. The growth of corporate transnational companies has left a political vacuum and has led to protests about the unconstrained activity of companies, especially energy corporations such as Shell and BP. As Friedman recognises, corporations are subject to 'the basic rules' of society. The argument of CSR is that 'basic rules' could be introduced which constrain profits for the benefit of the public good. Global companies adopting CSR could legitimate such expenditures on the basis of enlightened self-interest. They improve their brand image (by supporting local sports), they minimize the risk of public protest (by financing environmental infrastructure) and, by paying over the minimum wage, they improve personnel relations. One would expect that countries with many transnational corporations would have more corporate social responsibility.[24] From this point of view, CSR would appear to legitimate globalisation and those who benefit from it.

---

23   Milton Friedman, The social responsibility of business is to increase its profits. *New York Times Magazine*, 13 September 1970. Available at: http://www.colorado.edu/studentgro ups/libertarians/issues/friedman-soc-resp-business.html

24   See Maria Gjolberg, The origin of corporate social responsibility: Global forces or national legacies? *Socio-Economic Review*, 7 (2009), pp 605–37, especially p 608.

Maria Gjolberg suggests that political culture can have a substantial influence over company behaviour. A strong civil society with vigorous public debate will encourage the development of CSR.[25] Public campaigns (Extinction Rebellion), press coverage, government action (for example, against oil spills by BP in US) can influence the rules that constrain the behaviour of global companies. However, even virtuous civil society associations currently are incomparable to global corporations in the power they can wield. There is a limit to which any company will act in the public interest: corporations are driven by the need to make profits and to expand business.

One might also question whether global companies are the best organisations to make decisions about the public interest. To make CSR effective, corporations would need regulation; legislation would have to be introduced to require public companies to fulfil criteria laid down in their charters.[26] It is under conditions of political capitalism (see Chapter 15), such as in contemporary Russia and China, that non-market values can be exercised by companies controlled by the state. From a reformist social democratic perspective, CSR, if successfully implemented, offers some important modifications to global capitalism. Stakeholders could have a legally prescribed role in the governance of companies: CSR could also be a requirement written into company laws to promote public welfare. Such proposals are positive ways forward and we return to them in Chapter 16. Sceptics would reject these piecemeal measures mainly on the grounds that under capitalism shareholder value would remain the predominant objective and they call for more radical policies.

Under current conditions, the reformist social democratic agenda considered previously is limited. Consider Greece. Following the 2007 economic crisis, the country had run up 320 billion euros in debt, the electorate voted not to accept the austerity conditions imposed to clear them by the EU, the European Banks and the IMF. However, there was no political or financial way to change the conditions. The state was overwhelmed by the power of the supranational bodies and there was no acceptable alternative to the conditions they had declared. Economic power trumped democratic capacity. National electoral systems, when confronted by the agents of the dominant global capitalist interests, are limited as vehicles of public choice.

---

[25] Gjolberg, The origin of corporate social responsibility, p 611.
[26] Will Hutton, *How Good We Can Be*. London: Little Brown, 2015.

Socialist perspectives: a shift to socialist globalisation?

Socialist perspectives provide a critique of the antagonistic forces of capitalist accumulation and military power located in the core capitalist states.[27] In the 1950s, C.W. Mills coined the term 'power elite' composed of the military, political and economic elites which formed a unitary social and political bloc advancing the interests of the American political class. For Mills, the power elite was national in scope and defined in the context of American society. Democratic processes, for Mills, simply did not have the capacity to overcome the national power elite. Even in the 1950s, when he wrote, the international linkages were given insufficient attention, by the twenty-first century, national power elites coexisted with global elites (discussed in Chapter 9). The focus of power has shifted from the state level to the division of power in a global perspective. Consequently, the proposals of social democrats, as described previously, are likely to remain ineffectual in curbing global political forces.

Donald Trump, on his election to president of the USA, brought out the transnational nature of the power elite. His criticisms of NATO and US foreign policy in Syria and Afghanistan brought swift retribution from what Trump referred to as the 'deep state': the US media and the security institutions – the Pentagon, the CIA. Their opposition effectively blocked Trump's attempt to improve relationships between the USA and Russia and he failed to bring President Putin back into the Group of Seven major states. Mills's power elite now includes not only the political elites of Congress, the military elite in the Pentagon and the corporate elites, but also the Central Intelligence Agency, the leading print and media corporations, most academic 'think tanks' concerned with international relations. All these institutions have a global, not a national reach. NATO is a military instrument of American power.[28] 'Socialist globalisation' proposes to change the international power structure but retain the advantages of globalisation. Globalisation under the right conditions is emancipatory. But the current global system is faulted by its embeddedness in the class and related institutional structures of global capitalism.

One may make an analogy with the industrial structures of the nineteenth century. Changes in the productive forces (the advent of the steam engine, the division of labour and mass production) had long-term beneficial effects, but their full possibilities for human emancipation were limited by their

---

[27] Callinicos, *An Anti-Capitalist Manifesto*, Chapter 1, pp 64–65; William I. Robinson, *Promoting Polyarchy: Globalisation, US Intervention and Hegemony*. Cambridge: Cambridge University Press, 1996.

[28] A. Cockburn, *The Spoils of War: Power, Profit, the American War Machine*. London: Verso, 2021.

capitalist forms. The transnational corporation (TNC) is the dominant economic institution that shapes the character and defines the transnational capitalist class. I would add that in its neoliberal form it adopts a global perspective backed, when market competition fails, by economic and military sanctions. This line of thinking has been generalised as a form of 'surveillance capitalism' in which internet providers are able to exert a form of 'totalitarian control' over people.[29]

Socialist globalisation

Leslie Sklair identifies a form of generic globalism, which potentially has universal human benefits, but which can only be achieved under socialism. Leslie Sklair endorses generic globalisation namely, the electronic revolution, transnational social spaces, and cosmopolitanism; he contends that these phenomena offer 'tremendous emancipatory potential over a wide range of economic, political, and social issues'.[30] We might note four fundamental differences between socialist and capitalist globalisation: the economic, political, ideological, and socialisation through media and education. The major components are illustrated in Table 14.1. In place of profit, electoral democracy, and a psychology and ideology of consumerism, the socialist form of globalisation promotes ecological sustainability, participatory democracy and human rights.

As noted in Chapter 10, the global capitalist class structure is constituted by economic interests (TNCs), political institutions – neoliberal governments in hegemonic states (US, the EU), and international global organisations (IMF, BIS, World Bank and WTO). Sklair's proposal is to shift from a global economy dominated by the interests of those who own, control and represent TNCs to an economy organised around global networks of producer-consumer cooperatives. Here his ideas are similar to the pluralistic autonomy argument discussed earlier. The provision of employment would be a major objective of a globalised socialist system. It would take a direct democratic participatory, rather than a representative, form and would transcend state boundaries. Deputies would be subject to immediate recall. The dominant military forces maintaining world order, dominated by NATO, would be replaced by the United Nations.

The culture-ideology of consumerism, which prioritises the provision and consumption of goods and services, provides an inducement to work and is a source of social differentiation and satisfaction, would be replaced. An alternative would be an ideology of rights and responsibilities. In other

---

[29] See particularly Z. Zuboff, *The Age of Surveillance Capitalism*. London: Profile Books, 2019.
[30] Sklair, The emancipatory potential. See also Harris, *The Dialectics of Globalisation*.

Table 14.1: Capitalist and socialist globalisation

	Capitalist globalisation	Socialist globalisation
Scope	Global economy, subject to economic rules and national laws	International economy, subject to national interests
Economic	Wealth creation, accumulation of profit	Wealth creation, creation of employment, ecological sustainability
Political	Electoral democracy, nation state base	Participatory democracy, at international, national and local levels
Culture-psychology	Freedom, consumerism	Equality, human rights/ responsibilities
Military	Enforcement of Western values and interests	Values of peace
Socialisation (media and education)	Ideology: promoting the above	Ideology: promoting the above

Source: Derived from Leslie Sklair, The emancipatory potential of generic globalisation, *Globalizations*, 6:4: (December 2009), pp 525–39, table adapted from p 534. Rows on socialisation and military added.

words, consumption needs are tempered by responsibilities in the economic and political sphere – particularly in the preservation of the environment. Ecological concerns would be measured against other objectives, such as providing employment and the promotion of life. The current oligopolistic structure of national and transnational companies would be replaced by more pluralistic structures and more decentralised and autonomous organisational forms – such as those discussed in earlier chapters.

Socialist globalisation could be supplemented by traditional national socialist measures, some advocated by social democratic leaders have been outlined. Economic policies, for example, could be adopted to enlarge the public sector, widen the welfare state, and bring key sectors under public management. State control could be extended to include the major private banks. There would be a move to a state-led mixed market socialist economy. Such a structure, moreover, could promote the role of autonomous economic actors which would occupy a niche in the mixed economy.

A socialist form of globalisation goes much further than current social democratic proposals. The vision is one of economies operating on a global scale though not in the same way as globalised neoliberal economies. At a national level, the governance of private and public companies would include stakeholders, as discussed – a development of corporate responsibility. Such stakeholder socialism would reverse the plundering of national resources. It could involve stakeholder control of TV, newspapers and professional sports clubs and show business, thus transforming the mass media into a more pluralistic democratic form. Employment would become a major policy objective, a Ministry of Employment could be set up to devise and administer full employment policies, to mitigate the effects of robotisation and automation. It would put into effect proposals for meaningful work.[31] Such measures would significantly reduce the emphasis on private profit as well as having positive effects on income and wealth distribution. The culture-ideology sector would be transformed from profit maximising to happiness development (there could be policies to combat loneliness, for example). International affairs would be structured around the United Nations. There is a vision here of a socialist alternative.

Socialist coordinated economies on a world scale

Any attempted regulation of the existing system is likely to fail unless significant changes are made to its structural forms. Moreover, reforms at the level of the nation state are limited unless complimented on a global scale. Alex Callinicos has argued that only 'a revolutionary transformation that establishes a new global economic system based upon social ownership of the main productive resources and democratic planning' can lead to a genuine universal emancipation.[32] For Callinicos, an alternative form of internationalism consists of democratically planned national economies coordinated on a world scale.[33]

While these kinds of democratically planned economies might be desirable, problems multiply when applied to the world economy. If a globalised system is to continue, it would require a new institutional framework – though some of Callinicos's proposals could be initiated by national governments.[34] The notion of a democratically planned global economy is a very long-term goal. To be put into practice, it would require a transformation of institutions such as the WTO, BIS, IMF and the World Bank, as well as regional neoliberal blocs such as the EU. A global economic policy would also have to include ways to promote the development of poor countries and to reverse their decline.

The problem with the approach (like so many in the critical field) is not so much the desirability of the aims and objectives but ways of realising

---

[31] Srnicek and Williams, *Inventing the Future.*
[32] Callinicos, *An Anti-Capitalist Manifesto*, p 148.
[33] Callinicos, *An Anti-Capitalist Manifesto*, p 123.
[34] Callinicos, *An Anti-Capitalist Manifesto*, pp 132–8.

them. However, as Milton Friedman has pointed out (Chapter 1 in this book), as situations change, the theoretically desirable can become the politically possible. During a political or economic crisis, alternative ways of understanding or doing things, can be taken up as policy options. There is a tendency in social science analysis to over-determine future pathways by excessively narrowing possibilities to existing institutions and norms. Even in the last quarter of the twentieth century, social and political scientists would not have predicted the dismantling of the USSR by its own political leadership, the rise of China as a major industrial and political power, the exit of the UK from the EU, and the war between Russia and NATO/Ukraine.

Political mobilisation

Both Alex Callinicos and Leslie Sklair have a vision of an alternative future. How to get there, and how to implement it, Sklair considers to be the tasks of social science tempered by political realities. He suggests that socialist globalisation can be achieved through the agency of '[c]ommunities, cities, subnational regions, whole countries, multi-country unions, and even transnational cooperative associations [which] could all in principle try to make their own arrangements for checking and reversing class polarization and ecological unsustainability'.[35] Political movements are envisaged to drive political change and are wider than political parties. Transformation comes not from counter elites in the form of political parties but from below, from localisation advocated by writers like Castells (see Chapter 11). There would eventually be international networks of producer-consumer cooperatives and a more decentralised system of exchange. But how to replace the transnational companies and their related developed global production chains is not given sufficient attention by these proposals.

The problem confronting a socialist form of globalisation is how it can be achieved. Ideological, political and economic power is weighted against the proposed transformations. The resources of Greenpeace, for example, are infinitesimal compared to those of energy companies such as BP. The variegated groupings of NGOs, liberals, democrats, anarchists and socialists might have local political impacts but are not adequate for effective international action.[36] There is also the important issue of coming to agreements on a common programme. Democratic decisions might well reject many of these proposals – especially where employment and consumerism are put under threat, and citizens in the global South may

---

[35] Sklair, The emancipatory potential, p 538.
[36] See David Laibman, Marxist-anarchist dialogue: A two-way learning curve, *Science and Society*, 80:3 (2016), pp 414–18.

be expected to have different objectives from those of the global North. Direct action movements, such as Extinction Rebellion, reject majoritarian democracy and rely on direct action which have little public support.

Within system reforms

One other source of change might come from existing international organisations that form part of the global capitalist class. They have potentialities for different policies, as they are responsible to, and funded by, state governments. A major shock, in the form of a severe and prolonged economic crisis discrediting liberal ways of doing things, might transform the policies of Bretton Woods' organisations such as the IMF and the World Bank. These organisations are servants of governments, and policies can be changed by them. Indeed, since the beginning of the twenty-first century, the IMF and World Bank have been more responsive to stakeholders' interests with respect to inequality issues.

Following the world economic recession of 2007/08, elites as well as publics in the West have been sceptical about the benefits of globalisation. China's leader, Xi Jinping, has come to its defence, notably in a speech at Davos in January 2017. China has been a major beneficiary of the globalisation process. Jinping differentiated between the generic virtues of globalisation and many of its current practices. The major differences are summarised in Table 14.2: many of the 'Chinese characteristics' follow proposals discussed previously. Xi Jinping endorsed free trade and the free movement of capital but advocated moving away from its neoliberal form. He noted that it had furthered modernisation in China and secured significant improvement in living conditions for all the population. He called for 'reform of the global governance system' and greater benefits for emerging nations. The differences between liberal and Chinese ideas of globalisation are shown in Table 14.2.

The Chinese approach goes some way to meeting the objectives of Held, Crouch and Sklair. Xi Jinping has called for greater regulation and a new balance between 'efficiency and equity to ensure that … all share in the benefits … [of globalisation]'.[37] The claim here is for globalisation to be set in the laws and cultures of nation states. Such proposals involve a move to internationalisation which involves the monitoring of international exchanges by states and entails the hegemony of the party-state in China – opposed by Western political elites. In Xi Jinping's view, there should not be one set of universal rules set by the current hegemonic states. Dependent

---

[37] Xi Jinping, Davos speech. Available at: weforum.org/agenda/2017. https://www.weforum.org/agenda/2017/01/full-text-of-xi-jinping-keynote-at-the-world-econo mic-forum/

Table 14.2: Neoliberal and Chinese forms of globalisation

	Capitalist globalisation	Chinese globalisation
Scope	Global market promoted	International exchange, monitored by states
Economic	Wealth promotion, market coordination, accumulation of profit	Promotion of all-round development and full employment State coordination of market
Political	Electoral democracy, universal laws, nation state base	Recognition of national interests and laws, Party-state leadership, reform of global governance
Culture-ideology	Freedom, consumerism, ecology	Recognition of national civilisations, consumerism, ecology
Socialisation (media, education)	Promote above in context of neoliberal norms	Promote above in context of Socialism with Chinese characteristics

states are able to protect their economic and political interests and cultural traditions by regulating the effects of globalisation. Globalisation becomes a form of internationalisation coordinated by international bodies but subject to the interests of state actors.

Conclusion

The alternative scenarios to capitalist globalisation encompass three major strategies. In Chapter 12, I outlined movements based on spontaneous evolution, concurrent with a move to local self-governing autonomous units. In this chapter, I have considered another two other approaches based on social democratic and socialist approaches. The first proposes to keep the major institutions of capitalism and to reform the practices of globalisation – involving greater democratisation of global political organisations and institutions, and a sharing of sovereignty (subsidiarisation) between nation states. The second envisages the retention of global mechanisms with greater state mediation and the institution of (global) socialist institutions, the emphasis here is on supplanting capitalist institutions with socialist ones.

Social democratic proposals for action through the nation state are, in my view, the most realistic form in which major changes can be achieved. Capturing the nation state is possible through the electoral process. Reform would take the character of alternative strategies at national levels to modify neoliberal policies and to use the state's powers to influence policies in international organisations such as the IMF, the World Bank and the WTO.

These organisations are currently responsible to state politicians who are enamoured by neoliberal thinking and ways of doing things. The leadership of states would have to adopt more national related policies and in turn influence the policies of global coordinating organisations. The state is the only realistic instrument through which opponents of global capitalism can effect reforms. That they have not done so is due to the acceptance by established political parties of neoliberal globalisation. Such changes may be led by states that differ in their attitudes to global capitalism. Some are more entwined in global networks than others and have more to lose if the neoliberal system would be dismantled.

Alternative policies here would strengthen the state, reverse privatisation, and institute stakeholder interests in national forms of governance. In practical terms, it would mean supporting movements in favour of weakening the neoliberal policies in nation states and in international organisations such as the IMF, WTO and World Bank. While in some respects these organisations can be changed, in others (such as financial services) it may be politically more feasible to move out of their orbit to set up alternative institutions. A current example is the Chinese-sponsored Development Bank. In many countries, dependence on foreign global capital has little domestic democratic political legitimacy though under present conditions many countries favour foreign investment as a means to promote development. The real possibility here is for a revitalised statist form of social democracy. Social democracy predicated on Keynesian policies of national development, promoting high levels of employment and national welfare, command considerable electoral support. David Edgerton has shown that in the post-war period, until the 1980s, the UK was largely self-sufficient in infrastructure, manufacturing and food; opening up the UK economy led to foreign trade and to the purchase of British financial and non-financial companies, and consequently the net import of manufactures and food.[38] Economic nationalism could lead to British companies developing in high-tech areas such as computing, bio-tech and green technologies. Such policies would move away from current globalisation trends.

WTO rules might be qualified on the basis of democratically agreed preferences expressed through nation states.[39] As Rodrik puts it: 'democracies if superior to globalisation will make globalisation more stable'[40] and, one might add, globalisation will not only be more acceptable but also more effective. National interests may be safeguarded through states insisting on environmental, financial, labour and consumer standards. Such developments

---

[38] David Edgerton, *The Rise and Fall of the British Nation*. London: Penguin Books, 2019.
[39] See Rodrik, *The Globalisation Paradox*, chapter 12.
[40] Rodrik, *The Globalisation Paradox*, p xix.

would move what is now considered as globalisation to internationalisation. Negotiation between states and international regulatory bodies, such as the WTO and IMF, would be one way in which the proposals of academics such as Held and Crouch might be furthered.

One other alternative strategy is a revival of the nation state in a more national populist rather than in a social democratic form. National corporatism, based on a political consensus between big business, organised labour and party politics, is a clear possibility – and an alternative to socialism. Such developments are alternative forms of capitalism – rather than alternatives to capitalism.

Major political change may come about through the formation of constellations of countries adopting different forms of economic and political coordination. Most of the discussion of 'alternatives' is predicated on Western core societies. Global capitalism is weaker in the semi-core and the semi-periphery. The formation of regional blocs, such as the BRICS, the Eurasian Economic Union and the rise of statist economies, such as China, present possibilities of an alternative 'developmental state' taking the form either of state-capitalism or state socialism, which I consider in the next chapter.

How global capitalism will develop in the future depends not only on the political complexion of different countries and regions but also on the size and level of development of their productive forces. The global economy has different components and one should distinguish between them. Only large states, with strong widely based economies, confident political leaders and alternative ideologies or challenging civilisations, can resist or reshape the current dominant Atlanticism and its economic and political culture. Even in countries that challenge the current dominant world order, Western-type cultural trends are likely to continue: these include Western material consumerism in life styles, sport, fashion, arts; as well as developments in knowledge, science and popular and elite leisure use. The US, China, the Eurasian Economic Union and the EU are economic regions that have sufficient economic mass to survive independently. To promote their economic and political sovereignty involves a shift to internationalisation, in which states can act as gatekeepers to global flows. The response of states to the COVID-19 crisis, the energy crisis and the consequences of the war in Ukraine is likely to strengthen regionalism and internationalisation.

15

The Challenge of State Capitalisms

A political formation of 'state capitalism' presents the most frequently posed alternative to liberal capitalism. The concept, however, is not only complex but ambiguous. In this chapter, I clarify and refine its different meanings. The term state capitalism (without a hyphen) is a generic term applied to all its forms and concepts. I distinguish between three distinct types of political economy in which the state has a predominant role: state socialism, state-capitalism (with a hyphen), and state-controlled capitalism. All three present theoretical alternatives to liberal capitalism. In the light of these definitions, I discuss the ways scholars use them with respect to socialist societies. I pay particular attention to the ways in which the Soviet Union was, and contemporary China is, 'state capitalist'.

State capitalism

All states, to varying degrees, since the beginning of capitalism have exercised control over the economy. Historically, the state has enforced laws on the preservation of property and organised policing necessary to maintain laws and public order and to raise taxes. The state has regulated the economy to sustain the value of money and determine the terms of trade and relations with other states. In its neoliberal form, free enterprise capitalism relies on the state not only to make and enforce a legal and political framework but also to extend its geographical reach. Other current practices of states include investment in sovereign wealth funds, raising money through taxes and support of private corporations through selective state ownership.[1] The

---

[1] For an overview of this literature see, I. Alami and A.D. Dixon, State capitalism(s) redux? Theories, tensions, controversies. *Competition and Change*, 24:1 (October 2019), pp 70–94; M. Wright, G.T. Wood, A. Cuervo-Cazzurra, P. Sun, I. Okhmatovskiy and A. Grosman (Eds). *The Oxford Handbook of State Capitalism and the Firm*. Oxford: Oxford University Press, 2022; J. Kurlantzick, *State Capitalism: How the Return of Statism is Transforming the World*.

exercise of these kinds of supervisory roles over a capitalist economy is not usually referred to as state capitalist. The term 'state capitalism' is used in a generic sense to describe economies having a modern capitalist system of production in which the state plays a coordinating role over the economy with an active economic presence, usually (but not necessarily) based on significant ownership of productive assets. Joshua Kurlantzick, for example, includes economies where the government has a stake in 'more than one-third of the five hundred largest companies, by revenue in that country'.[2] Such a definition includes a very wide range of economies and types of regimes, including not only Russia, but also Thailand, Brazil, Turkey, Egypt, Singapore, Venezuela and Norway.

The term 'political capitalism' is often used interchangeably with state capitalism, and often refers to any form of state power which is exercised to procure economic assets and wealth. It has also been applied to earlier, pre-modern forms of what Weber called colonial capitalism or 'booty' capitalism[3] (the profit derived from political prerogatives over conquered territories, which are not our concern). These forms of state capitalism focus on the state as a controlling or guiding agency operating in different forms of capitalist economies.

State socialism

In the socialist states the idea of state capitalism arose in opposition to the official self designation of socialism. The early twentieth-century Marxist approach was to define the mode of production by the nature of ownership relations (which defined classes) and the level of productive forces, composed of the capital used in production, and the labour process. In this model, the state combines state ownership, administrative coordination of the economy guided by a plan, and allocation of economic surplus to provide for economic growth and public welfare. The state owns economic assets and has direct control over the allocation of surplus, which is used for the renewal of society or for the formation of capital. Marxists contended that with socialist state ownership there would be no place for the benefit to a class or elite accruing from the 'profits of enterprise'. Any diversion of economic surplus to those allocating it is illegitimate – a form of corruption. As we noted in Chapter 5, socialism is ensured by the replacement of the capitalist class by the working class – the ownership and control of productive forces

---

New York: New York University Press, 2016. For current Western economists' views see G.W. Kolodko, *China and the Future of Globalization*. London: Tauris, 2020, pp 78, 112–3.

2   Kuriantzick, *State Capitalism*, p 9.
3   See Gerth and Wright Mills, *From Max Weber*, pp 66–7.

by the Party-state – on the one side, and the advanced level of productive forces, on the other. This approach legitimated the construction of the economic basis of socialism consequent on the destruction of the capitalist class. The form of economy is defined as socialist because the motivating values are predominantly collectivistic, driven by the socialist Party, rather than individualistic, driven by profit.

I have called this formation 'state socialist' because the state, in Russia, played a dominant role in creating the post-feudal productive forces. It was a state led by the Communist Party, which defined its goals and organised its processes. As Article 6 of the 1977 Constitution of the USSR decreed:

> The Communist Party of the Soviet Union is the leading and guiding force of Soviet society and the nucleus of is political system, of all state and public organisations ... The Communist Party armed with Marxism-Leninism, determines the general perspectives of the development of society and the course of the home and foreign policy of the USSR, directs the great constructive work of the Soviet people and imparts a planned, systematic and theoretically substantiated character to their struggle for the victory of communism.[4]

Sociologists, such as Wlodek Wesolowski,[5] contended that these conditions entailed the elimination of the appropriation of surplus value by a capitalist class.

Such a social formation, Marxist-Leninists claimed, was the first stage of socialism. The class relations define the mode of production as socialist because the workers' state owned the means of production, which is administered by the dominant socialist party, and exercised a monopoly of political and economic power, in the interests of all members of society. *State socialism* is defined as an economic system in which the state is the principal owner of the means of production and a dominant socialist party regulates the economy and extracts surplus value for further investment and the renewal of society. The Marxist state-capitalist critique, however, rejects this reasoning.

State-capitalism

What distinguishes state-capitalism (with a hyphen) from other forms of capitalism is ownership by the state of productive economic assets and control

---

[4] Article 6. 1977 Constitution of the USSR, adopted 7 October 1977.
[5] Wesolowski, *Classes, Strata and Power*, p 120.

of the economic surplus by state officials who can direct it to different purposes: not only to variable capital and constant capital, but also to the profits of enterprise. Where the approach differs from state socialism lies in the character of the state bureaucracy, which is driven to make surplus value, part of which – the profits of enterprise - is utilised for its own economic or political benefit. Such benefit constitutes the process of exploitation that, according to this critical Marxist interpretation, defines the class structure. Such Marxist scholars contend that the Soviet Union and contemporary China are state-capitalist in this sense.

State-capitalist forms have arisen as political formations under specific historical circumstances. The uneven world development of capitalism led to economies with agrarian pre-capitalist productive forces and the absence of a bourgeois class. Such societies, in order to transit to capitalism, are subject to autocratic state development. This argument was used by Marxists (principally the Mensheviks) to deny that socialism could develop out of Tsarist Russia in 1917. Socialism cannot be built, they argued, on the foundations of a crumbling feudal society which lacks a mature working class and the infrastructure of developed capitalism. The capitalist mode of production has to be built first – socialism follows. A socialist government would have to utilise the state to build the economic foundations of the capitalist mode of production in the sense of raising the level of productive forces to that of an industrial capital-intensive economy. State-capitalism, they contended, is what would result. The economy would remain capitalist because the exploitation of labour would benefit those controlling the state apparatus who would extract an economic surplus and constitute itself as a capitalist class. The critical Marxist conception of *state-capitalism* might be defined as a modern economic system in which the state is the principal owner of the means of production and in which the extraction of surplus value takes place for the benefit and purposes of an executive state ruling class which has effective control over the means of production.

The Marxist state-capitalist critique of the Soviet economy

The Marxist state-capitalist critique addresses the state-owned and planned economy constituted in the Soviet Union and later in the post-Second World War socialist states of Eastern Europe. While these writers vindicate socialist revolutions in pre-capitalist economies, such as Soviet Russia, the practices of the new incumbents of power are condemned. State-capitalism became defined in critical Marxist circles not, as by the Mensheviks, in terms of the level of productive forces or forms of ownership but by the exercise of political *control* over the labour process, which led to the appropriation of surplus value, of which a significant proportion was channeled to a state based capitalist class.[6]

Control of the means of production is the source of exploitation and profit. Capitalism is defined by the form of exploitation in the labour process that delivers economic surplus to the bureaucratic class. These ideas have been popularised by writers such as Stephen Resnich and Richard Wolff,[7] Raya Dunayevskaya,[8] M. Postone,[9] Tony Cliff and more recently by the Aufheben Collective. Resnich and Wolff contend that state-capitalism is formed by the 'capitalist processes of producing, appropriating and distributing surplus [which] coexist and interact with processes that place state officials (rather than private individuals) in the class position of appropriators and distributors of the surplus'.[10] Robert Brenner takes a similar position defining modes of production as 'modes of labour control'.[11]

As the writers in the Aufheben collective put it:

> the USSR was essentially capitalist in that it was based on wage-labor. The workers in the USSR were divorced from both the means of subsistence and the means of production … Hence like their counterparts in the West, the Russian workers were subordinated to a process of production that was designed and developed to maximise production with scant regard to the living experience of the worker in production.

The relations of production were those of 'self-expanding alienated labour' which were 'the productive relations of capital'.[12] Tony Cliff says quite simply: ' "state capitalism" … denotes the stage in which the capitalist state becomes the repository of the means of production'.[13] This kind of reasoning has very important political implications.

---

[6] See K. Marx, *Theory of Surplus Value*, internet edition. Available at: https://www.marxists. org/archive/marx/works/1863/theories-surplus-value/, p 261; on the profit of enterprise, *Capital* Vol 3, Chapter 23.

[7] S.A. Resnich and R.D. Wolff, *Class Theory and History*. New York: Routledge, 2002, Chapters 3 and 4.

[8] Raya Dunayevskaya, *The Union of Soviet Socialist Republics is a Capitalist Society*. (1941). Available at: https://www.marxists.org/archive/dunayevskaya/works/1941/ussr-capital ist.htm

[9] M. Postone, *Time, Labor, and Social Domination: A Reinterpretation of Marx's Critical Theory*. Cambridge: Cambridge University Press, 1993.

[10] Resnich and Wolff, *Wolff, Class Theory and History*, p 86.

[11] Robert Brenner, The origins of capitalist development, *New Left Review*, 104 (1977), pp 25–72.

[12] *Aufheben Collective*, Issues 6–8, What was the USSR? Pattern Books (No place of publication), 2020. Quotations pp 242–3.

[13] T. Cliff, *Russia: A Marxist Analysis*. London: International Socialism Publishers, nd [1964], p 154. See also Aufheben Collective, Issues 6–8, What was the USSR?

The arguments are used by critics to label the state socialist societies as totalitarian. Alvin Gouldner articulates this position: The bureaucracy is 'a new ruling class' a 'new, many times worse, [form of] domination' [than capitalism].[14] Such writers emphasise not solely the apparatuses of control but also reliance on complete political domination.[15] The determinant factors are the extraction of surplus value enabled by the dominant Party-state apparatuses. In this analogy, the Communist Party represents the major shareholders, and the state management, the capitalist managerial class. The nature of exploitation entails a confrontational class structure composed of a state capitalist ruling class and an exploited working class. From this point of view, the party-state, whatever its stated prescriptions, does not function in the interest of the working class. The essential point is that exploitation by a bureaucratic class takes place through the labour process constituting a statist form of capitalism.

An assessment of the state-capitalist paradigm

In this approach, the issue of the capitalist nature of the ruling class revolves around the ownership of assets and allocation of surplus. A distinction must be made between, on the one side, administrators and executives employed by the state, who may control but do not own and cannot sell the means of production and, on the other, capitalists who own, control, benefit from, and can sell *their* assets. The question is whether, in the absence of de jure property rights, such a bureaucratic class exercises similar de facto rights over property, extracts surplus value and then acts as a bourgeois class. Ernest Mandel presents the case against:

> The bureaucracy is not a new ruling class ... It is a privileged layer which has usurped the exercise of administrative functions in the Soviet state and economy, and which uses its monopoly of power to grant itself big advantages as consumers ... [On the other hand], capitalism is a specific system of class domination, characterised by the private ownership of the means of production, competition, generalised commodity production, the transformation of labour power into a commodity, the necessity to sell all produced commodities before the surplus value contained in them can be realised, the inevitability of periodic crises of generalised overproduction. None of these fundamental characteristics can be found in the Soviet economy.[16]

---

[14] A. Gouldner, *The Two Marxisms*. London: Macmillan, 1980, p 382.

[15] Postone, *Time, Labor, and Social Domination*.

[16] Ernest Mandel, *From Class Society to Communism*. London: Ink Links, 1977, pp 111–12.

The state-capitalist approach emphasises the exploitative role of the political class or political elite in appropriating surplus. I would agree with Mandel that it ignores other constitutive features of socialism: the collective form of ownership, the dominant socialist values of the society, the absence of economic crises and, most important of all, the developmental economic ends to which the state allocates surplus. Administrative forms of illegitimate use of political power are real enough and cannot be denied. The excessive earnings or bureaucratic privilege of officials are certainly unjustified, and acts of repression, coercion and persecution under Soviet power were indefensible crimes. However, they were expressed in the Soviet Union as forms of political domination and excessive bureaucratic power, rather than the structural condition of class exploitation of labour. To distinguish state-capitalism from state socialism, we need to know what proportion of surplus goes to public development including capital accumulation and what is channeled for personal and family benefit and for the political privileges of officials (the Russian chinovnik class). A weakness of current versions of state-capitalism is that its advocates do not measure the extent to which surplus value is used by an exploiting class. The Soviet elite was unable to amass capital either domestically or to purchase capital abroad. Inheritance of personal property was allowed but not of productive capital, and political position was circumscribed by the nomenklatura system of appointments controlled by the Communist Party apparat. The capitalist class system was unformed.

The bureaucracy class, in my view, is better understood as a political class, following Gaetano Mosca's conception, rather than an economic class as defined by Marx. Members of the bureaucracy may receive excessive salaries and other benefits of office (foreign travel, superior accommodation and health benefits), but these are privileges of consumption, they do not specify class position in a Marxist sense. The privileged groups are dependent for their livelihood on an employment status supported by professional credentials or political position. Unlike shareholders, whose wealth is derived from ownership of assets, state officials have no legal rights over productive assets or the produce of economic enterprise.

Lenin's version of state capitalism

Lenin is often invoked as an early advocate of 'state capitalism'. Lenin used the term 'state capitalist' to describe Soviet Russia's New Economic Policy (1921 to 1928). What Lenin had in mind, however, was not state-capitalism as defined previously, but the socialist state's control over capitalist enterprises operating in the state. In the period following the October Revolution, in April 1918, the Bolsheviks recognised that there was 'a role for state capitalism in building socialism in a peasant country'.[17] Lenin uses the term in a generic sense, as defined earlier in this chapter, not as state-capitalism.

The transitional form of economy allowed privately owned enterprises to enjoy free-market operations. Private ownership (allowed for units employing up to 20 people) and profit of enterprise were measures intended to restore the economy from the ravages of civil war to maintain the Bolsheviks in power. It was justified by the Party's leadership because it enabled the market and private enterprise to operate to satisfy public needs under conditions controlled by the socialist state. As Lenin put it: 'a free market and capitalism, both subject to state control, are now being permitted and are developing'.[18] Lenin justified this development as the Communist Party was taking 'the first steps in the transition from capitalism to socialism'[19] in which the market and private enterprise were subject to socialist state regulation. Lenin considered that such a form of dual economy would be necessary for a relatively short period of time after the period of War Communism. He recognised that there was no direct transition to socialism from feudalism, the economic basis of a capitalist mode of production had to be constructed. In this initial period, the state under the Communist Party did not build socialism but exercised control over enterprises trading produce on the market for profit, many of which were owned and managed by capitalists.

The extraction of profit and elements of private ownership did not constitute state-capitalism as I have defined it. Profits (surplus value) from private business went to their owners, who constituted a capitalist class. The private sector was dependent on the communist party-state, which exercised control over the economic, political, mass media and legal institutions and processes. Concurrently, large-scale industrial enterprises remained in state ownership and management and surpluses earned by state enterprises were returned to the state treasury. Lenin presided over a transitional social formation, a mixed economy with a socialist political leadership. State capitalism, as described by Lenin, is a dual economy, and should be defined as state-controlled capitalism. *State-controlled capitalism* might be defined as a dual political and economic system in which privately owned enterprises produce for profit and receive 'rewards for enterprise' subject to moral, political, economic and coercive controls exercised by dominant state mechanisms and institutions. The duality in Russia during the New Economic Policy,

---

[17] Lenin's policy in 1918 is outlined in: V.I. Lenin, The New Economic Policy and the Tasks of the Political Education Departments. 17 October 1921. *V.I. Lenin, Collected Works*, vol 33. pp 60–79. Available at: https://www.marxists.org/archive/lenin/works/1921/oct/17.htm

[18] V.I. Lenin, Draft theses on the role of trade unions. Written 30 December 2021. Available at https://www.marxists.org/archive/lenin/works/1921/dec/30b.htm

[19] Lenin, Draft theses on the role of trade unions.

however, was unstable and constituted a temporary formation preceding socialism. Lenin's conception marks a revision of Marxism: the political is not dependent on the economic; when a revolutionary socialist government assumes power, it is the other way around.[20]

The Leninist form of state-controlled capitalism is often endorsed by socialist scholars as a mechanism to transit from feudalism to capitalism. Samir Amin has remarked:

> [T]he establishment of a state capitalist regime is unavoidable, and will remain so everywhere. The developed capitalist countries themselves will not be able to enter a socialist path (which is not on the visible agenda today) without passing through this first stage. It is the preliminary phase in the potential commitment of any society to liberating itself from historical capitalism on the long route to socialism/communism. Socialisation and reorganisation of the economic system at all levels, from the firm (the elementary unit) to the nation and the world, require a lengthy struggle during an historical time period that cannot be foreshortened.[21]

This way of thinking can be found in the views of Deng Xiaoping who, at the Chinese Communist Party's 14th national congress in 1992, pointed out that it might take 100 years to advance to full socialism from the initial stage. In this process capitalist forms of organisation had to be utilised by the communist state – though Deng Xiaoping did not envisage or refer to his proposals as 'state capitalism'. The alternative to the liberal form of development, based on private property and market competition, is replaced, not by a socialist system, but by a developmental state predicated on the extraction of economic surplus for state development exercised by a ruling socialist Party. The private sector would allow for personal profit – hence it would be capitalist, but the state would control its level and would guide the society to socialism. For state capitalist theorists, China, since the market reforms, presents a more complicated case than the Soviet Union: it has rising private ownership immersed in a powerful Communist Party controlled state. Unlike under the New Economic Policy

---

[20] For a more detailed development of the state-economy-market nexus see: G. Arrighi, *Adam Smith in Beijing*. London: Verso. 2007. The political formation of state-controlled capitalism need not be socialist, it could be populist or national capitalist, in which case state it would not be predicated on any ideology leading to socialism. 'National-socialist' regimes as in Germany and Italy between the two world wars are such economies. This line of enquiry will not be considered here.

[21] Samir Amin, China 2013, *Monthly Review*, 64:10 (2013). Available at https://monthlyrev iew.org/2013/03/01/china-2013/

in Russia, there is no limit to the size of corporations that can be corporately owned, though foreign ownership is regulated.

The Chinese variant: a socialist market economy

In 1978, the Open Door Policy exposed China to the global economy. Liberal norms were introduced into the internal economy. The success of the General Agreement on Tariffs and Trade and World Trade Organization (GATT/WTO) in opening up world trade greatly benefitted China. The country under Zhou Enlai, moved towards economic hybridisation, combining state planning with marketisation. Unlike the European post-communist countries, it maintained the hegemony of the Communist Party and retained strong economic controls, often ignoring the advice of liberalising institutions such as the IMF.[22] The changes released surplus labour and, unlike in the former European state socialist economies, China experienced high levels of economic growth. The state, under the direction of the Communist Party leadership, directed overall macro planning as determined in the five-year economic plans. Allocative distribution of investment remained largely with the planners. The idea was, in the words of reformer Chen Yun, 'to set free the market bird inside the cage of central planning'. In this policy the leadership was influenced by the other south-east Asian economies (the four dragons – Hong Kong, South Korea, Taiwan and Singapore) which had all pursued successful economic reforms under authoritarian rule. Gradually, China moved from pupil to master, and from disciple to competitor.

The state's direct productive role was maintained but significantly reduced: the non-state sector in industry accounted for under a fifth of industrial output in 1978, it rose to 45 per cent in 1990 and to 61 per cent in 1992.[23] This increase initially took place in the rural sector where quasi-private industries were set up after the de-collectivisation of agriculture. Significant changes in property rights were introduced and the state relinquished considerable areas of control to entrepreneurs. In 1988, for example, there were 18.882 million independent rural enterprises[24] and, by the late 1980s, only a third of construction employment remained in the state sector. In transportation and communication, the government maintained a monopoly. In retail trade, market relations became widespread: by the late 1980s, fewer than 40 per cent of retail sales were transacted in the

---

[22] Stiglitz, *Globalization and its Discontents*, p 63.
[23] Nicholas R. Lardy, China: Sustaining development, in Gilbert Rozman (Ed), *Dismantling Communism: Common Causes and Regional Variations*. Johns Hopkins University Press, 1992, p 208.
[24] Lardy, China, p 208.

state sector.[25] By 1991, 85 per cent were determined by market prices.[26] Distributive allocation had shifted to the market with positive results.

The state banking sector became an important source of financing. From 1979, the state banks were given the right to allocate and regulate credit. They became more profit orientated and monitored the activity of borrowers. In this way, financial and economic criteria became more important in industry and commerce. However, economic control was not lost by the government as the planning mechanism still had considerable power of directing the economy, and the banks were state owned and controlled. Allocation was subject to government planning, and distribution was exercised by market mechanisms. The market was given a legitimate and important place and the consequent greater income differentials between sectors of the economy and between different groups of employees were acceptable to the communist leadership. Not only was the market recognised as an internal distributive institution but also the international market was acknowledged as beneficial. In October 1993, China officially became a 'socialist market economy'.

Foreign investment and the internationalisation of the economy were of considerable economic benefit. Between 1979 and 1991, China received $80 billion in foreign capital and imported $24.6 billion in foreign technologies. Initially, the economic reforms were instituted at the edges of the economy: private farming, and village enterprises were introduced, individual entrepreneurship was encouraged and special economic zones were set up.[27] Foreign investment, as we note in Figure 15.1, peaked in 1994, but since then its share of internal investment has significantly declined; fixed capital formation is largely dependent on domestic funding. FDI during the whole period increased, of course, but domestic capital investment was infinitely greater. The trend indicated by Figure 15.1 shows that China was moving from being in a state of peripheral dependence on the West to the status of competitive interdependence. By 2018, China's FDI inflow as a proportion of gross fixed capital formation (2.7 per cent) was not only lower than the average for developed countries (5.4 per cent) but also less than that of developing economies (7.4 per cent).[28] By 2010, China had relatively little dependence on FDI.

---

[25] Lardy, China, p 219.

[26] Zheng Qian, *The Road to Socialism with Chinese Characteristics*. Reading: Paths International, 2018, p 257.

[27] R. Coase and N. Wang, *How China Became Capitalist*. Palgrave: Basingstoke and New York, 2012, p 104.

[28] UNCTAD, World Investment Report 2015. Table 7.

Figure 15.1: China: FDI inflows as a percentage of gross fixed capital formation, 1990–2018

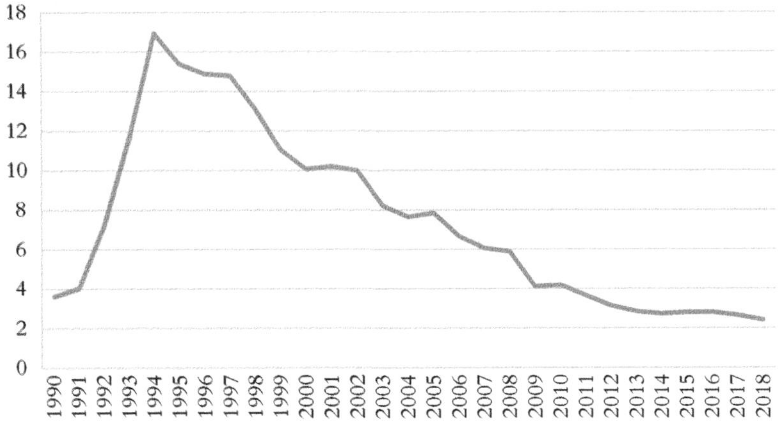

FDI as percentage of Fixed Capital Formation (Inward).

Source: Unctad Statistics. Available at: Unctadstat.unctad.org/wds/TableViewer/ TableViewaspx.

The differentiation of ownership

The ownership and control of economic enterprises are crucial to the nature and character of any economy. In China, the reforms led first, to the installation of different forms of state enterprises and second, to the introduction of diverse kinds of ownership. Before the reforms, state ownership was direct and enterprises were administratively controlled. In the Soviet form of central planning, the assets of enterprises were owned by the state and management was responsible ultimately to government ministers (who in turn were responsible to the Council of Ministers and the Soviet government). Finance, wage differentials, product prices and the product mix were determined by the state plan. Following the reforms, collective enterprises were set up where capital was owned by 'collectives' (mainly lower levels of government). Limited liability corporations were also set up: these were state-owned corporations whose liability to debts are limited to the total assets of the firm; they traded goods or services on the market. Their assets, however, were state owned. Foreign subjects (individuals and companies) were also able to invest in state corporations and those with over 25 per cent of the assets (limited to 49 per cent) owned by foreigners are listed as 'state corporations with foreign investment'. There were also cooperative, joint ownership and private enterprises.[29]

---

[29] State-owned enterprises are non-corporation economic units where the assets are owned by the state. Collective-owned enterprises are units with the assets are owned collectively.

276

Figure 15.2: Number of corporate enterprises by type of ownership, 2017

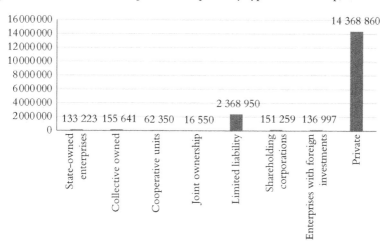

Source: China Statistical Yearbook 2019. Table 1–8. Corporate Enterprises by status of Holdings.

Private ownership and enterprise in China is vast and has been increasing in the twenty-first century. Figure 15.2 show the enormous size of the private sector in 2017.

Figure 15.2 shows that state-owned and collectively owned enterprises are quite numerous (133,223 state owned in 2017), roughly the same as those with foreign shareholders (136,997). Cooperative enterprises (a total of 62,350), owned by employees (and others) in the form of shares and operating on a profit and loss basis, were less numerous. What is striking is the enormous number of small private business enterprises: their numbers had risen to over 14 million (14,368,860) in 2017 and the number of mainly state-owned limited liability companies trebled to 2,368,950; foreign-owned enterprises and share-holding companies also increased but remained rather similar in number to state-owned enterprises. Foreign investment,

---

Cooperative enterprises are forms of collective economic units where capital is come mainly from employees, some from the outside, production is an independent operation, with democratic management. Joint ownership enterprises are established by two or more corporate enterprises or corporate institutions of the same or different forms of ownership. Shareholding corporations are economic units with capital raised through issuing stocks. Private enterprises are profit-making economic units established by persons, or controlled by persons employing labour. Limited liability corporations are economic units with investment from 2–50 investors, each investor bearing limited liability to the corporation depending on its share of investments. Definitions taken from explanatory notes in China Statistical Yearbook 2019.

Figure 15.3: Average number of employees in state-holding industrial enterprises and private industrial enterprises, 1998–2018

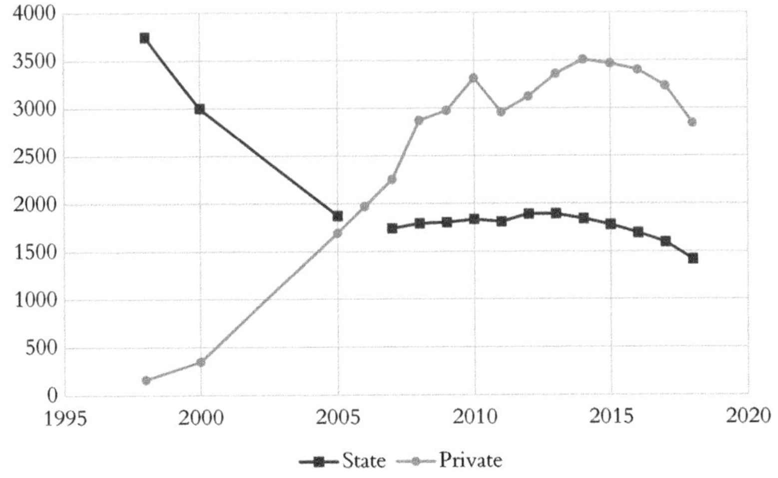

Units 1 = 10,000 persons. No state-holding data for 2006.

Note: The space in the State line indicates that no data were given at this time.

Source: China Annual Statistical Yearbook 2019. Table 13.5 (state sector) and Table 13.7 (private sector).

shareholding corporations. and limited liability companies give a significant demographic density to market orientated and profit-making enterprises.

However, many of these enterprises, especially those defined as privately businesses are small. Study of the number of employees in industrial enterprises gives another indication of the balance between the private and public sectors. In terms of total employment, the private sector accounts by far for the bulk of the industrialised work force. As we note in Figure 15.3, employment in the private sector increased exponentially in the twenty-first century and by 2006 exceeded that of the public sector.

Is China 'state-capitalist'?

The state-capitalist interpretation of the Soviet Union was predicated on the bureaucratic political class extracting surplus in the labour process in the state-owned economy. In China, however, there is also a separate business class with private ownership rights legitimating profits. Simon Gilbert labels this dual development as state capitalism. He equates the state bureaucracy to the individual property owning class with which it is intertwined.[30] In

---

[30] Referring to China, he writes: 'The higher echelons of the state bureaucracy, wealthy private capitalists and the murky mixture of the two that lies between are best understood

this interpretation, there is a shift from Lenin's outlook. For Lenin, the socialist state retained control over the privatised economic sector: politics was in command. For writers like Gilbert, there is a fusion of the two class factions (the state political class and the private capitalist class) to constitute the bureaucratic ruling class. These state capitalist theorists define the major cleavages in China between class groups: on the one side, Party officials, state officials, private corporate business and on the other, the working class. The former all receive surplus value.

Other Western commentators bring out this distinction without the Marxist theorising. 'The major characteristic of Sino-capitalism is the juxtaposition of state-led developmental institutions top-down, and private entrepreneurial networks bottom-up, often resulting in contradictory incentives and friction'.[31] Sino-capitalism, Christopher McNally claims, is a hybrid system based on interpersonal relationships utilising Chinese cultural norms in which the state fosters and guides capitalist accumulation. It is part of a globalised system in which dominant Anglo–American values and institutions are accepted: it presents a 'market-liberal form of state capitalism'.[32] Private capitalism, from this point of view, is embedded in the Chinese party-state; a duality of Leninist state control and private capital accumulation.[33] As Chinese industrial development occurred under conditions of neoliberal globalisation, foreign capital is more accessible and so are global markets. Established flexible labour markets[34] and WTO agreements made China more globalised in terms of trade which gave it the advantage of mobility of capital movements. But the dominance of state politics, led by the Communist Party of China, interpersonal connections and the absence of a Western-type of law-based economic system, put China outside the 'rules-based international order'.[35] From this viewpoint, the Chinese system is indeed an alternative to neoliberal globalisation and, for these critics, an undesirable one.

Branco Milanovic, writing about China, as well as Vietnam and Singapore, adopts the Weberian notion of political capitalism. By this he means 'acquisition of wealth by force, political connection, or speculation'.[36] In China, the bureaucracy, he claims, is 'clearly the primary beneficiary of the

---

as constituting a single ruling class'. Simon Gilbert, Class and class struggle in China today, *International Socialism*, 155 (June 2017). Available at: http://isj.org.uk/class-and-class-struggle-in-china-today. No page in internet edition.

[31] McNally, Sino-capitalism, p 747.
[32] McNally, Sino-capitalism, p 750.
[33] Bruce J. Dickson, *Wealth into Power.* Cambridge: Cambridge University Press, 2008
[34] McNally, Sino-capitalism, p 756.
[35] McNally, Sino-capitalism, p 765.
[36] Milanovic, *Capitalism, Alone*, p 91.

system'[37] and legitimates itself by realising a high rate of economic growth. It exercises, unconstrained by law, its political power over the private sector. This system ensures economic growth concurrently with the enrichment of the bureaucratic class. Milanovic, following Bruce Dickson[38] shows that, as far as the distribution of income and wealth is concerned, the tendency in China since the beginning of the reforms, is for the business and professional classes to become more powerful as a component of the new ruling class.

While private capitalists enrich themselves, the party-state still exercises control over the means of production.[39] Hence while the system is called political capitalism by Milanovic, I would prefer the term state-controlled capitalism. Milanovic has the virtue of quantifying the extent of private profit (economic surplus). With increasing privatisation, the significance of capital income has greatly increased and studies show that the share of capital income in the top 1 per cent of incomes has risen to 37 per cent – making the source of income from capital similar to that found in the USA[40] With the growth of non-state business, the status and income of government officials has declined. The portion of government officials in the top 5 per cent of income recipients fell from 25 per cent in 1988 to 6 per cent in 2013.[41] Milanovic opines that the new capitalist business class remains a 'class by itself' and lacks class consciousness.[42] He contends that, as long as it can amass wealth, the Chinese bourgeoise class will not seek to exert political power.[43]

In China, the new class is able to own and to turn economic surplus into assets and hence has the characteristic of a capitalist class. The direction of the economic system, for Milanovic, is to consolidate a form of political capitalism in which the political elite maintains control, rather than to follow the post-Soviet Union's example of a transition to liberal capitalism. The socialist party-state remains in formal control over an economy in which the business classes operate to maximise profit on the market. Any analogy with Lenin's state capitalism must be faulted, as Lenin did not admit the bourgeois classes to the Party, and the New Economic Policy was intended, and only lasted for, a short transitionary period.

Samir Amin and David Harvey also concede that in China the relations to the means of production have similarities with modern capitalism. For

---

[37] Milanovic, *Capitalism, Alone*, p 91.
[38] Dickson, *Wealth into Power*.
[39] Milanovic, *Capitalism, Alone*, p 106.
[40] Milanovic, *Capitalism, Alone*, p 104.
[41] Milanovic, *Capitalism, Alone*, Figure 3.7, p 106.
[42] Milanovic, *Capitalism, Alone*, p 105.
[43] Milanovic, *Capitalism, Alone*, p 105.

Amin there is 'submissive and alienated labor, extraction of surplus labor'.[44] Harvey, in discussing neoliberalism, claims that: 'In so far as neoliberalism requires a large, easily exploited, and relatively powerless labour force, then China certainly qualifies as a neoliberal economy' though he adds 'albeit "with Chinese characteristics"'.[45] For Amin, the crucial factor lies in the role of the Communist Party's control of the state apparatus and he considers that surplus is utilised predominantly for economic and social development. It is used 'to construct an integrated and sovereign modern industrial system'. It is in my classification a socialist state-controlled form of capitalism.

In contrast to the leadership of the Soviet Union, China's political leaders have integrated the country into the world economic system.[46] Private capital and the market are utilised to this end. Mark Knell and Martin Srholec have shown that in terms of the 'varieties of capitalism' approach, China has adopted many characteristics of the neoliberal model but remains a state coordinated economy.[47] Taking multiple indicators to measure social cohesion, labour market regulation and business regulation, they show that up to 2004, China was less coordinated than France or Germany (see Figure 15.4). Since 2004, neoliberal developments have increased. China has relatively high income inequality and low labour market and business regulation. However, one must bear in mind that China has a dominant Communist Party, which operates on a scale far greater than parties in Western economies. On the basis of these data, the Chinese economy does have neoliberal features, but it is quite incorrect to equate the Chinese economy with neoliberal ones such as the USA, the UK and Russia.

Data published by the Shanghai Stock Exchange on Chinese listed companies give some indication of the considerable and growing levels of surplus value which is utilised as reward for capitalist enterprise. For listed companies, the share of dividends as a proportion of net profits averaged 35 per cent for the years 2007 to 2011. In 2011, the total amount payable was 5,983 hundred million RMB. Dividend yield (for those receiving dividends) averaged just over 1 per cent for the same period. The average number of firms paying dividends per year rose from 51 per cent in 2007 to 76.3 per cent in 2011.[48] While the point must be taken that some two-thirds of net profits was used for renewal and formation of capital, a considerable share

---

[44] Amin, *The Implosion of Capitalism*, p 71.

[45] Harvey, *A Brief History of Neoliberalism*, p 144.

[46] Amin, *The Implosion of Capitalism*, p 72.

[47] Mark Knell and Martin Srholec, Diverging pathways in Central and Eastern Europe, in D. Lane and M. Myant, *Varieties of Capitalism in Post-Communist Countries*. London: Palgrave, 2007, pp 40–62, quotation pp 46–7.

[48] Qingsong An, Research on the current status and trend of dividends of Chinese listed companies (in Chinese), *Securities Market Herald*. Shenzhen Stock Exchange, 2012.

Figure 15.4: Index of coordinated and market regulation: various countries, 2004

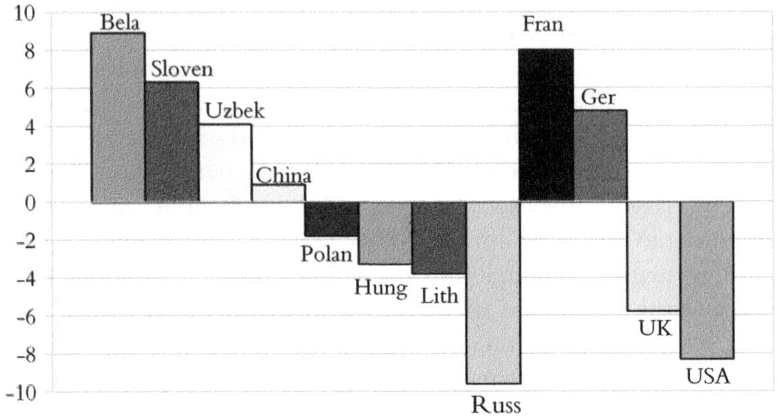

Note: The lower the index, the greater the role of the market, the higher the index the greater the role of state regulation.

Source: Figure created from data in Lane and Myant 2007, pp 40–62.

was enjoyed by owners. Though Samir Amin acknowledges that there are contradictions and that the rising business and state classes could lead to a form of liberal capitalism, he believes that it will take a socialist not a capitalist path.[49] This contrasts with the evaluation of Milanovic who considers that it already has moved along the route to capitalism.

Whether China will transit to a socialist society is contentious. A strengthening of the marketised and privately owned economy invites the formation of a capitalist class consciousness which would destabilise the socialist state. This is the argument proposed by the socialist opponents of introducing the market system in the first place. Already, as noted, capitalists in the private sector can and do amass wealth – they own financial and physical assets. Economic surplus is increasingly channelled to a capitalist class which can use income to purchase assets abroad.

While the structure of power in China is shaped both by corporate ownership of assets and by bureaucratic position, the ruling groups are constituted from different elites (party, government, regional, military, economic, media, academic) with each group containing varied political preferences. The Party organisation is hegemonic and, in a transitionary social formation, it can bring its power to bear against capitalistic practices.

---

[49] For different Leftist positions see, R. Ruckus, *The Communist Road to Capitalism.* Oakland, CA: PM Press, 2021, pp 165–92.

The Party maintains crucial controls over ideology, law, the mass media and, in the economy, control over the banks and the amount and direction of investment as well as considerable state ownership of property. There are also informal controls over private corporations. As writers such as Arrighi[50] have emphasised, in states moving from autocracy and in the early days of capitalism, the political has considerable direct and indirect powers of control over economic life, including private corporations. The powers of Party intervention in the economy are crucial to enforce Party policy and is a means by which the Party-state can legitimately intervene to direct corporations irrespective of their self-interests.

Hence, the contemporary Chinese economy is a form of state-controlled capitalism retaining socialist characteristics. To the extent that surplus value is extracted and used for private purposes, the economy has capitalist features. The increase in private ownership of productive assets which, in recent years, has increased in China, raises the level of extraction of surplus and to this extent reduces what is available for public use. What then the future direction of China?

Future scenarios for China

Branco Milanovic envisages a convergence of political capitalism to liberal capitalism; 'economic power ', he claims, 'is used to conquer politics'.[51] It is a one way convergence: China moves to capitalism. His envisaged pathway is a version of Marxism emphasising the superiority of economics over politics. Milanovic concludes that 'The domination of capitalism … seems absolute'.[52] There may be alternative capitalisms but there is no alternative to capitalism.[53] This conclusion, in my view, is overdetermined. China is essentially a state-led market economy regulated by a politically ordered economic plan. The Party maintains crucial controls over ideology, law, the mass media and, in the economy, supervision over the banks and the amount and direction of investment as well as considerable state ownership of property. In this context, capitalist entrepreneurship and neoliberal processes have been adopted to promote economic growth. The domestic objective of catching up with the West has led to Party-led forms of economic control as well as to a successful private market sector: all have benefitted, and many in the business sector much more than others.

China does not present a political or economic threat to American hegemony. It does not contest the right to private property, or the globalised

---

50   Arrighi, *Adam Smith in Beijing*.
51   Milanovic, *Capitalism, Alone*, p 217.
52   Milanovic, *Capitalism, Alone*, p 196.
53   Milanovic, *Capitalism, Alone*, p 185.

system of production, or American leadership of the Western liberal international order. China presents itself as a political order promoting public welfare and international peace and denies that global markets working through Western imposed laws of globalisation can lead to comprehensive economic development. Convergence to a liberal form of capitalism is unlikely to be promoted by US foreign policy, which considers China to be a threat and has instituted a sanctions regime. State–controlled capitalism (with socialist characteristics) is an ideological alternative to neoliberal capitalism and presents a set of policies designed for an economy emerging from an autocratic form of feudalism. It does not claim to be a model for the advanced economies, and the conditions in which it arose restrict its universal applicability. Competitive interdependence has led to the rise of a multipolar world order that provides alternative foci to current US hegemony.[54] The opposition to Chinese developments in the West is likely to lead to a strengthening of the economic semi-core and a countervailing power to the American dominated core of the world system (as noted in Chapter 10).

---

[54] See Clegg, *China's Global Strategy*.

16

Regulated Market Socialism

By the beginning of the twenty-first century, the political, economic and moral order of neoliberalism had no effective competing ideology or alternative political praxis. Francis Fukuyama, though widely criticised, remains an iconic advocate of 'the goodness of liberal democracy, and of the principles on which it is based'.[1] He concedes that liberal democracies 'are plagued by a host of problems'[2] such as unemployment, drugs, pollution and crime, and he recognises that discontent arises (from both Left and Right) over the 'continuing tension'[3] between liberty and equality. Yet, he follows earlier writers, such as Daniel Bell,[4] to contend that there is agreement on ends, that there are no 'large causes for which to fight'.[5] Neoliberal capitalism has provided not only the keys to how economies could, and should, be coordinated on a world scale but it had also captured the public imagination. It had become the common sense of public policy applicable not only to the ways that economies should be coordinated, but more generally to how societies should be managed and organised.

That said, I have identified systemic faults that are more than secondary problems. These are: the recurring economic crises of capitalism; the unjustifiably unequal levels of wealth and income both within and between countries; the social disruption caused by market processes, particularly unemployment, underemployment and migration; the deficiencies of democratic government; environmental unsustainability and ecological

---

[1] F. Fukuyama, *The End of History and the Last Man*. New York: Avon Books Edition, 1992, p 287.

[2] Fukuyama, *The End of History*, p 288.

[3] Fukuyama, *The End of History*, p 292.

[4] D. Bell, *The End of Ideology: On the Exhaustion of Political Ideas in the Fifties*. Glencoe, IL: Free Press, 1960. Bell's contention is that the major ideologies confronting liberalism (communist and fascist) are exhausted.

[5] Fukuyama, *The End of History*, p 311.

destruction; economic and political conflicts between the core, semi–core and periphery of the world system, and deficient mechanisms to maintain peace and prevent war. Any alternative to the neoliberal approach has to address these systemic problems. One should not, however, attribute all the world's shortcomings to 'global neoliberal capitalism'. Many dilemmas pre-date, or are independent of, neoliberalism or globalisation. Any alternative may not be able to address all of these issues, and solutions not only take time but often give rise to other problems. Global capitalism, nevertheless, is the political and economic casing in which crises occur.

In earlier chapters I outlined liberal capitalism and five alternatives – self-sustaining communities, social democracy, state-capitalism, state-controlled capitalism, and state socialism. Appendix 16A summarises and compares the six economic formations. These models illustrate the major characteristics of these social formations. Real existing economic formations are in practice mixtures of these components and embedded in societies with unique histories. In this chapter, I summarise these alternative scenarios, and I outline another preferred option: regulated market socialism.

Five alternative economic formations

Liberal capitalism is an economic system predicated on market exchange, private property and profit for enterprise. Under liberal capitalism, the form of utilisation of surplus value, which sustains a capitalist class, is minimally regulated by the state through taxes. The 'minimal' state provides crucial coordinating and legal enforcement functions. *State socialism* (Soviet-type central planning) had a minor role for the market and property was publicly owned. The state administration completely directed the use of surplus product. A major economic objective of the socialist state is the enlargement and utilisation of surplus product for renewal and cumulative development of the productive forces – a developmental state. There is no payment (profit) to state functionaries as a 'reward for enterprise'. *State-capitalism* has a similar structure to state-socialism: the state legally owns and controls economic enterprises. While the state extracts surplus for renewal and investment, surplus is also used for the benefit of, and interests directed by, a bureaucratic stratum or class. The extent to which this benefit gives rise to a ruling class defines the formation as state-capitalist and distinguishes it from state socialism. *State-controlled capitalism* is a form of capitalism with private and state ownership. It is a hybrid multi-levelled market economy in which profit accrues to an entrepreneurial class. The state exerts authority over the non-state sector through the apparatuses of state economic management, which utilises administrative means, coercion, socialisation and persuasion.

State-controlled capitalism, state-capitalism and state socialism all have state bureaucratic forms of coordination. The difference is that under state-controlled capitalism, private corporations receive and distribute economic surplus, some of which is 'reward for enterprise.' Under state-capitalism, a significant part of economic surplus is appropriated by a bureaucratic class. Under state socialism, there is no such reward.

In addition to these state centred paradigms are other forms of coordination. At the other end of the scale, an autonomous *self-sustaining economy* is predicated on collective ownership, extraction of surplus solely to meet collective needs; there is neither state nor market coordination, the collective is coordinated on self-governing democratic principles. This social formation contracts out of the global and national market economy with which it interacts. *Social democracy* proposes a hybrid system of public ownership and private corporations operating through market mechanisms, subject to partially regulated extraction of economic surplus and state provision of welfare services embedded in a market system. There is division between those, on the one side, who see socialism as embodied in the achievement of certain policy goals – reducing levels of income inequality, securing equality of opportunity, providing universal social security (including provision of employment). Capitalist ownership relations remain relatively untouched. On the other side, are those who advocate institutional changes – the replacement of private ownership by public ownership and democratic decision-making. In this version, market socialism retains the economic market set in public property under different forms of democratic state coordination.

The major alternatives to liberal capitalism, presented in the first half of the twentieth century, arose in a social and economic world considerably different from that confronting political movements today. State socialism and post-Second World War European social democracy were reactions against a nationally-rooted class-based form of industrial capitalism. These were class-based movements. In the second and third quarters of the twentieth century, state socialism proved an effective form of state sponsored growth and modernisation for developing countries. Later, its underlying political, organisational and ideological foundations no longer responded effectively to the conditions of twenty-first-century global capitalism.

Social democracy in Western Europe provided a political shell for a state-led recovery from the devastation of the Second World War and social support for the population in the form of a welfare state. By the final quarter of the twentieth century, the factory-based proletariat had moved from the industrialised North to the global South. Globalised capitalism mutated into a more developed and complex form that weakened socialist political challenges. In the developed Western societies, the work force became more heterogeneous both occupationally and socially; national trade-union movements and national social democratic parties shrunk like plants without water. The Western working class has become assimilated into consumer capitalism; an acquisitive individualism replaces class identity.

Twenty-first-century capitalism possesses an asymmetric form of class consciousness: a strong awareness of class identity and organisation by the capitalist class, though with dual global or national frames of reference, whereas the middle and lower non-manual and manual classes have dwindling levels of organisation and self-awareness and consequently present a weak challenge to capitalism.[6] Politics is shaped by neoliberalism (as a social and economic theory) and globalisation (technological processes which compress time and space). The rules of national politics are increasingly shaped by global political institutions such as the International Monetary Fund, the World Bank, the World Trade Organization and, to a lesser extent, by the United Nations. Global politicians and officials from international and regional organisations enforce global norms, which are legitimated and propagated respectively by think tanks, global civil society associations and the mass media. But there are countervailing tendencies presented by rising states and articulated by Russia and China.

Concurrently, transnational financial and non-financial corporations undermine national capitalisms. But not completely, as political institutions (political parties, electoral procedures) and political identities continue in an attenuated form within a national shell. Citizenship, giving national democratic rights, is determined by states – not conferred by global actors. The dilemma presented by globalisation is that economic decisions are increasingly framed and implemented at international levels while political parties, which articulate citizens' interests, remain at the national level. States, even if weakened, remain important entities. They protect and enforce property rights, levy enormous amounts of taxes, have a monopoly over the ownership and use of heavy lethal weapons, and declare war.

The interconnectedness of politics and economics, concurrent with the hegemonic role of the US, have made the capture of state power by anti-neoliberal movements not only more problematic but, even when achieved, less effective. With the exception of the dominant world powers, capturing the state leads to the possession of a half-empty shell. Countervailing powers may arise, such as Brexit, but the national political base for any form of alternative to globalised capitalism is restricted. Brexit called for a different more regulated national form of globalisation, not its transformation. Though subject to national laws in host countries, transnational corporations (TNCs) are not acquiescent to national political control and are very difficult for some, and impossible for most, national governments to regulate. The military/political/ideological actions of the hegemonic capitalist states (led by the USA) strongly oppose socialist or nationalist challenges for political power; and the dominant world powers can harness civil society forces to

---

[6]   Mann, *The Sources of Social Power*, p 414.

defeat opponents through 'democracy promotion'. Democracies, defined in neoliberal terms, confront autocracies, defined in other terms. Counter ideologies – socialism, communism, fascism, 'populism' and Islam – have become sidelined and even suppressed in the core states of the international system. It is as though the population, through socialisation, has been subjected to some form of mass herd immunity to alien ideas, only to surface occasionally through disaffected protest groups.

Mechanisms and movements for social change

What then are the mechanisms and movements for social change? Two major approaches have been outlined in previous chapters. First, the belief that the capitalist or industrial system through its own contradictions or developments mutates into a new mode of production or social order. Second, that human beings, despite the difficulties noted previously, through conscious efforts and political leadership can create alternative forms of globalisation or capitalism, or more radically transform global capitalism to something else. A third alternative is presented by state-controlled economic formations located outside the core capitalist societies in the rising semi-core of states led by China.

Self-destructive tendencies, or a metamorphosis, in capitalism, have a long history. Friedrich Engels contended that 'The universality towards which [capitalism] is perpetually driving finds limitations in its own nature, which at a certain stage of its development will make it appear as itself the greatest barrier to this tendency, leading thus to its own self-destruction'.[7] This conclusion is shared, but for different reasons, by other twentieth-century critics. J.K. Galbraith and Joseph Schumpeter contended that the development of industrial society would lead to the rise of a technologically based class structure and the growth of the state thus diminishing the bourgeois class and its propensity for entrepreneurship. These approaches envisaged systemic developments, which would lead eventually to the disintegration of liberal capitalism and its replacement by statist forms of capitalism or a shift to a new mode of production, socialism.

Twentieth-century socialists, following Engels, saw the causes of capitalism's collapse arising not from developments in 'industrial society' but from the economic exploitation of labour which led, on the one side, to overproduction and a falling rate of profit[8] and, on the other side, to

---

[7] Karl Marx, Grundrisse, The rise and downfall of capitalism, in David McLellan (Ed), *Karl Marx, Selected Writings*. Oxford: Oxford University Press, 1977, p 364.

[8] This is demonstrated by writers in G. Carchedi and Michael Roberts, *World in Crisis*. London: Haymarket Books, 2018.

growing unemployment and poverty. The prospect of economic abundance given by the advanced form of technology would foment a revolution, and state planning would replace the anarchy of competition. Echoes of these positions currently are heard in the voices of Nick Srnicek and Alex Williams, who foresee a future industrial society with an abundance of production predicated on high-level technology and a post-industrial workforce. Sergei Bodrunov goes even further by suggesting that the higher levels of production will lead to the transcendence of market relations as economic abundance increases under conditions of a new industrial society.[9] The vision here is the advent of Fully Automated Luxury Communism (discussed in Chapter 11). These are optimistic approaches that envisage an emancipatory positive form of post-capitalist modernity. They are limited, however, to the advanced countries and will require political action to put them into effect.

A social autonomy approach, discussed in Chapter 12, is one reaction to the harmful tendencies of global neoliberalism. It involves a retreat from an urban-industrial social order, an exit from global capitalism, to self-sufficient communities. The proposal here is for the formation of autonomous economic and political formations and some advocate the creation of a new ecological civilisation. The autonomist prefigurative proposals (for the development of alternative networks of communities operating in parallel to, and gradually replacing, globalised capitalist society) remain a long-term strategy. Contemporary societies can certainly promote spaces for those who wish to live outside the capitalist market. Such proposals, however, do not amount to a replacement of the system of liberal capitalism – they form islands within it, and islands, surrounded by hostile seas, can easily become cut off from the mainland.

Socially autonomous economies can fill 'the cracks' in modern industrial and post-industrial societies, but they cannot displace them. The proposed autonomous economies are dependent on developed economies providing commodities (electricity, tools, materials) and services (healthcare, education, communications) without which life would be precarious. While they mitigate some of the malfunctions of modern society, they lack the technological base to service the kind of society that most people in the post-industrial societies expect. In the environmental sphere, allowing only subsistence emissions and curbing luxury ones would require a move to austerity policies in the advanced countries which would be widely resisted. Moreover, people in developing countries also aspire to the consumer society

---

[9]   S.D. Bodrunov, Prospects of transition to a new model for socioeconomic system organisation (noonomy). *Global Journal of Human-Social Sciences*, 19:11, Version 1.0 (2019), pp 1–11.

of the post-industrial stage. A non-growth world economy is not a viable political position.

Antonio Negri and Michael Hardt[10] move significantly away from the traditional Marxist class conflict framework. Their argument is predicated on what they consider to be the ways that post-industrial capitalism is creating 'forms of cooperation' that are emerging from the production process and establishing a 'new mode of production'. They advance the idea of the 'multitude' having the capacity of a 'political entrepreneur'[11] (see Chapter 11). They contend that social forces in the shape of the human 'multitude' are able to act as a real democracy. This is a heterogeneous formation containing modern elements as well as those of previous forms of production.[12] The approach is a return to the idea that capitalism is subject to an economic metamorphosis, rather than to the leadership of a socialist revolutionary or reformist political party. Any realistic and effective alternative, I contend, can only emerge through actions at a state level (either through singular governments or in concert with others). Changes in the level of productive forces create the conditions for a metamorphosis but collective human action is necessary to bring it about.

In contrast, state-controlled capitalism (epitomised by China discussed in Chapter 15) presents a viable economic alternative as a developmental model. It retains market forms of economic coordination on a nation state basis, and concurrently market relations are subject to state control under the hegemonic communist party. While the system of 'socialism with Chinese characteristics' has been effective for societies moving from pre-capitalist economies, it does not present itself and is not proposed as a model for present advanced neoliberal economies, which have different histories, political cultures, and structures. The model of state-controlled capitalism, however, could be adapted by many countries.

While the alternatives considered in this book have positive qualities, they all have shortcomings. My own proposal, outlined later, is that political and economic policy should move in the direction of regulated market socialism. I suggest a state led hybrid system of public and private ownership, combining the advantages of economic planning at the macro level with market relationships in the retail sectors. The objectives are to satisfy individual needs and public well-being through the promotion of full employment of capital and labour.

---

[10]   Hardt and Negri, *Empire* and *Assembly*.
[11]   Hardt and Negri, *Assembly*, p 280.
[12]   Hardt and Negri, *Assembly*, p 145, p 144.

Regulated market socialism

Regulated market socialism delivers a minimalist answer to the problem of the transition to socialism. Proposals for regulated market socialism entail the elimination of excessive unearned personal wealth. Twentieth-century advocates of public ownership, such as Oskar Lange, feared that nationalisation, in depriving some citizen of their private wealth, would fuel public discord, and he predicted consequences of 'financial panic and economic collapse'.[13] The October Revolution in Russia led to civil war and protracted internal civil conflict and repression, which have blighted the socialist cause. These adverse consequences have to be avoided and need not occur. A major objective of policies in the transitional period is to prevent civil war. Traditional revolution in the sense of violent state capture is ruled out. Unlike in the former communist systems and contemporary China, the competitive electoral system would not be dismantled; civil society would remain pluralistic. Forms of electoral competition would continue giving citizens the opportunity to modify, even reverse, the changes. As electoral democracy is not threatened, opposition to the installation of a 'totalitarianism' society would be disarmed. Practices of democratic participation could be widened to include employee participation in economic enterprises. Such proposals have the great advantage that a transition could take effect within the existing political framework, it would preserve economic and political stability and have immediate positive effects.

Unlike market socialist models discussed in Chapter 5, regulated market socialism would be predicated on a national state-led plan. Modern state economic planning should not be equated with earlier Soviet planning. The economic and social conditions of Soviet planning, the political framework that emerged from the October Revolution, are alien worlds to modern Western post-industrial societies. With the development of technology and artificial intelligence, one can envisage an economy of potential abundance with a short working day. Computers can simulate demand and reduce the detailed administrative calculations needed for the coordination of earlier state plans. Such conditions further a transition to socialism. Politically, a dominant stratum of the current capitalist class would lose its wealth creating assets. The property of large financial and non-financial corporations could be gradually transferred to collective ownership. Consequently, state control over the use of economic surplus would transform capitalism. Sectors of the economy formed by small and medium enterprises would continue in private hands. Any movement to socialism in the present hegemonic capitalist

---

[13]   O. Lange, On the economic theory of socialism: Part two. *The Review of Economic Studies*, 4:2 (February 1937), pp 123–42, quotation p 134.

countries would accept many of the norms which sustain capitalism – some 'capitalist characteristics' would have to be retained.

James Yunker[14] has by far the best worked out economic prospectus, which is closely attuned to conditions found currently in the advanced Western countries. It is important not to threaten citizens who have hard-earned savings or have built up (or intend to create) small- and medium-sized businesses; initiative and innovation have to be encouraged and rewarded. Nationalisation of property would be limited to assets that create illegitimate social privileges to the detriment of the great majority or to wealth that presents an obstacle to economic progress. The accumulated wealth of families derived from *lifetime labour* would be preserved. The objective is to create a political and social base of support for the transfer of ownership and control of corporate private property. It would allow, even encourage, the use of economic surplus which furthers economic development (for example, 'green' technology) but would limit and control levels of economic exploitation. Profits in the private sector would continue to be subject to taxation as they are under competitive capitalism. For companies that are transferred to public ownership, appropriate compensation could take the form of bonds, on which interest would be paid from future earnings of the company. The overwhelming majority of the population would not be under any threat of being dispossessed of their personal possessions. Corporations to be nationalised would have immediate benefit to the public. The structure of proposed Regulated Market Socialism is summarised in Appendix 16B.

Though most invention currently takes place in private or corporate institutions, a place remains for capitalist entrepreneurs, and earned income would not be threatened, though economic rents and gains from speculation would be severely curtailed. The petty-bourgeoisie – owners of small and medium business, the legal, health, accounting, theatre/sporting/music and teaching professions, and the clergy – would continue. Public ownership would be introduced gradually. Companies that fail the public and are clearly lacking in public responsibility would be taken into public ownership. Banking and currency exchange, energy, natural resources, armaments' industries, and public transport would be prime candidates for public ownership. In redistributing the wealth of the top stratum of the landed and capitalist classes, democracy is improved, its scope enlarged, and society is more equitable and participatory. Such a strategy is likely to appeal to the sentiments and dispositions of people who have been socialised into believing that democracy, creativity and self-improvement have

---

[14] See particularly James A. Yunker, *Socialism Revised and Modernized: The Case for Pragmatic Market Socialism*. New York: Praeger, 1992; James A. Yunker, *On the Political Economy of Market Socialism*, Aldershot: Ashgate, 2001.

merits. Inherited wealth, other than personal possessions, would be under threat. The British monarchy would lose its rights to inherited wealth,[15] though the ceremonial and representative functions could continue as paid employment – should this be required. The economic moral order of self-motivating individualism is retained and the political order of democracy is extended to include participation in work institutions (economic democracy). Socialist democracy would command the high moral ground.

A key to future development is the level and type of investment. Currently, investors often find it more profitable to speculate in money markets than to invest in the uncertainties and often lower returns of the real economy. The state would channel direct investment according to a long-term plan, taking account of social costs, technological and service developments, geographical location and the need to maintain a full employment economy. Re-industrialisation, if required, would receive government financial backing. Planning at the macro level linked to markets at the micro level leads to a hybrid form of economic coordination – regulated market socialism.

The form of regulated market socialism I have outlined is intended to move in the direction of socialism within capitalist market societies with established party-based electoral political systems. The objective would be to provide greater economic stability and sustainable development and to utilise production for public use, rather than private gain. However, the profit motivation for medium and small firms and concurrent economic rewards would coexist with policies to promote greater equality of income and life conditions. The social and moral order would be more collectivist and predicated on meeting human needs. Distribution of retail products and services (from the public and private sector) would be coordinated by the market. High levels of consumption would be driven by needs rather than artificially inflated wants. Opposition parties would continue and, as under current conditions, would function within the law. Economic strategy would be grounded on a coherent developmental policy, with economic democracy.

Re-evaluating the planning mechanism

In the late twentieth century, when the success of planned economies was in question, proposals for reform entailed a shift to free economic markets in the socialist countries. The tide has turned. In the twenty-first century, the

---

[15] Currently, the monarchy is not legally liable to pay income tax, capital gains tax or inheritance tax. The value of the crown's estate is estimated at £15.2 billion, and in 2021, the revenue received by the Queen is estimated at £22 million. Data cited by Daniel Boffey, *The Guardian* (London) 14 September 2022. The royal residences include Buckingham Palace, Windsor Castle, Sandringham, Balmoral (in Scotland), Highgrove and Llwynywermod (in Wales).

de-development experienced in the post-socialist societies, and the regular crises of liberal market capitalism have cast doubt on the efficacy of neoliberal market processes. The economics of the capitalist monetary system in the twenty-first century is grounded on speculation that has been exacerbated by the privatisation of public assets. Attention must turn to reconsider the critiques made earlier in this book of state planning.

The assertion that state planners are prone to corruption is not limited to socialist planning as levels of corruption and fraud exist in capitalist market societies where armies of accountants are required to check (not always successfully) company accounts. Private companies also engage in the promotion of economic rents (excessive profits), unjustifiably large executive salaries, and bribery to obtain contracts – deceiving shareholders and cheating consumers. Another impediment, levelled at state planning, is that bureaucratically managed enterprises will not promote invention; without private property there is an absence of a propensity to innovate. This view, however, is highly contested. The socialist states had relatively low quantitative budget levels for research, though planning enabled available funds to be channelled without undue duplication into priority investment areas. The USSR had some remarkable successes in military equipment production – tanks, rockets and fighter planes, as well as optics and sports' science, space exploration and nuclear engineering. The post-reform Chinese system has had notable successes with state sponsored innovation. Moreover, not all capitalist market economies are able to innovate. The UK, for example, in the late twentieth century, lost most of its capacity for manufacturing due to the uncompetitiveness of its products. The post-communist states, notably Russia and Ukraine, have had less investment and innovation under the market than they had under the planned Soviet system. Hence something more than private ownership and a free market is needed to explain the success and/or failure of states to innovate.

States even in market economies invest heavily in long-term high-risk projects which the private sector finds too risky to support. State bureaucracies under capitalism promote innovation (in universities and state sponsored companies, such as Airbus) and are major contributors to research. The image of the independent private entrepreneur–inventor, which informs much thinking of neoliberal writers has been replaced by highly organised research teams and corporations with huge research budgets. A socialist planned system has advantages.[16] There is no monopoly over inventions whereas, under capitalism, patenting accrues rights to owners who limit copying to maintain the source of profits. There is no disadvantage under

---

[16] For an overview see: David Kotz, Socialism and innovation. *Science and Society*, 66:1 (Spring 2002), pp 94–108.

socialism to pursue research to aid the development of public goods – rather than profitable market products. The absence of private monopolies enables a socialist planned system to make commodities (such as new medicines) universally available and cheap.

The widely accepted critique of state planning made by neoliberal economists is that the planning system could not possibly calculate prices and coordinate efficiently supply and demand. The conclusion they drawn is that, even if the positive points made about planned economies are true, it is practically impossible to plan a modern economy, and the results of such 'planning' will be faulty. While in the 1950s, this objection had substance, it is no longer valid. Critics of the feasibility of planning could not have been aware of the speed and accuracy of computers, which now can effectively calculate prices that equilibrate demand and supply, thus replacing the need for a market.[17] Advances in information technology have solved many of the technical problems involved in national planning.

The application of computers to solve the calculation of optimum prices has been developed by Paul Cockshott and Allin Cottrell.[18] They confront the pessimistic conclusions not only of Frederich von Hayek but also of Alec Nove (an economist specialising on the Soviet Union). Nove noted that the Soviet economy included 12 million distinct types of products which, he claimed, defied rational administrative calculation in a state plan. However, Cockshott and Cottrell point out that modern Fujitsu or Hitachi computers are capable of performing some 200 million arithmetic operations per second when working on large volumes of data. They consider that by using the approach of 'successive approximation' the problem raised by Nove could be solved 'in a few minutes' rather than in years as previously thought.[19] Edinburgh University, even in 1993, had a machine with a capacity of 10,000 million instructions per second. Leigh Phillips and Michal Rozworski have pointed out that Walmart, a company whose production is equal to the GDP of Sweden, is planned, efficient, and successful.[20] Such companies are islands of planning in a market economy ocean. They heed demand for their products and organise their internal processes to produce thousands of products and services at a definite time, based on estimated quantities and prices of components. Modern computing capacity, such as bar coding of commodities and universal bar codes, has transformed the practical operations

---

[17] See Sorg, Failing to plan is planning to fail.
[18] Cockshott and Cottrell, *Towards a New Socialism*; Mark Jablonowski, Markets on a (computer) chip? New perspectives on economic calculation. *Science and Society*, 75:3 (July 2011), pp 400–418.
[19] Cockshott and Cottrell, *Towards a New Socialism*. See p 55, pp 57–8.
[20] Phillips and Rozworski, *The People's Republic of Walmart*, p 29.

of economic planning.[21] With 1 million products, labour values could be revised (through bar coding and product codes) every 20 minutes.[22] Even greater speed and flexibility of later computational regimes are claimed by Mark Jablonowski, which enhance both 'feasibility and realism'.[23]

I am not suggesting that regulated market socialism should involve a detailed plan for all commodities and services. Planning could adopt more decentralised and indicative forms. In the state–owned sector, there could be a long-term plan that co-exists with market relationships. The combination of state ownership of strategic sectors and control over the economic mechanism regulate the amount of surplus and limit profit. The state, through the control of bank credit, determines the amount of and sectors for investment; it also monitors the levels of investment in the private sector. The state prioritises socialist objectives of services and products, the distribution between present and future needs and the balance between security and welfare, while the private sector satisfies the needs of a consumer society. High levels of household consumption would be maintained. A return to greater regional self-sufficiency for many supplies of non–capital goods and services (food, repairs, clothing, building materials, personal services) could inform government environmental policy. The objective of planning would be to provide a variety and dispersion of economic activities within national economic regions. Environmentally friendly policies could be built into the planning process.

Here is the challenge: the idea of a market socialist state must capture the public imagination. The image could move from a 'welfare state' to a 'social state' that supports the wider social needs of citizens: security in employment, a minimum income, as well as provision for happiness, health, old age and education. The expectations of people for the provision of ample goods and services have to be fulfilled and individualistic innovation in arts and business would be supported. The rising level of technology, the increasing abundance of output conjoined with decreasing demand for labour call for greater state regulation to reduce the length of the working day and the provision of a universal basic income. With the rise in gross national product (GNP), the objective would be to take goods and services out of the price system, to provide services free at the point of use. The production of use value would play a greater role in the economy and exchange value less: for example, the de-commodification of health and education, and local government authorities would be able to expand their provision of economic, cultural, sporting and leisure activities. Such a 'social state' would provide a vision

---

[21] See also Evgeny Morozov, Digital socialism?. *New Left Review*. 116–117 (2019), pp 33–67.

[22] Cockshott and Cottrell, *Towards a New Socialism*, p 59.

[23] Jablonowski, Markets on a (computer) chip?, p 403.

of a post-capitalist socialist political and moral order – without losing the gratifications of a consumer society.

Changing the structures and obligations of economic corporations

Not all economic enterprises would be publicly owned. Nationalisation would take place gradually. Moreover, private and state corporations would be required legally to fulfil social and economic obligations in addition to their objective of making a surplus. Regulated market socialism could promote reforms in the structures and obligations of companies. State-owned and private corporations could be required to fulfil obligations of social responsibility to all their stakeholders, rather than prioritising profits for shareholders. Such proposals have been articulated by the 'Better Business Act Campaign', which seeks to change the UK Companies' Act to define 'the purpose of a company ... to benefit its members as a whole, whilst operating in a manner that also ... benefits wider society and the environment'.[24]

Private and public corporations could be licensed and their roles defined in charters. Before the twentieth century, British companies were licensed to perform particular tasks and their charters initially had a limited duration (15 years for the East India Company of London) which, if fulfilled, could be renewed.[25] The articles of company charters would be revised to specify their economic and social obligations with regular review of their performance.[26] Laws would prescribe the wider responsibilities of companies including the recognition of social costs. Here I follow the criteria suggested by Will Hutton. Governments would recognise that public interest and shareholders' interests do not always coincide. The renewal of company charters would be subject to the realisation of their economic goals as well as to compliance with their public responsibilities. As Hutton points out, many of the regulations are currently in place, but not enforced by governments, consequently British industry and public well-being suffer.

In the private sector, the criteria for private mergers would be defined by stakeholders not by financial interests. Stake holders (national and local government bodies, employee representatives) would join shareholders and directors on the boards of large companies. In 2014, over 41 per cent of the shares of British companies were held overseas, 'typically by a global

---

[24] Reported in *Financial Times* (London), Moral Money, 23 April 2022.

[25] W. Dalrymple, *The Anarchy: The Relentless Rise of the East India Company*. London: Bloomsbury, 2019. In practice, they were renewed, the principle is important in giving effective control over corporations.

[26] Hutton, *How Good We Can Be*.

asset-management group ... [A] significant part of their shareholder base is held by global asset managers supported by a vast network of supportive intermediaries and agents all taking fees and commissions'.[27] Changes in company law enacted by a government working within a planning framework could promote companies as 'value creators rather than rent extractors'.[28] Some public companies could take the form of mutual associations. Major commercialised sports companies (previously known as clubs), for example, would be prime candidates for mutualisation involving participation on the boards by their employees, club members (supporters) and shareholders as well as local authorities where they are located. Such changes would have significant implications for the composition of national sports governing bodies and would reverse the excessive commercialisation of sport.

Obstacles to socialist measures

Significant reforms along the lines suggested in this chapter, if introduced at the right times, would require electoral support which would be essential if regulated market socialist policies are to be successfully instituted. The legitimacy of corporate capital is widely questioned and its unpopularity has been particularly evident in the aftermath of the financial crisis beginning in 2007 and during the energy prices crisis in 2022. Socialist reformers would look to support not only from the traditional constituency of the working class but also from the petty bourgeoisie and professional classes (particularly in state employment – the health services, social care and education). Securing public support is crucial and necessary to disarm those who propose that socialism involves dictatorship. One has to emphasise the point made by Karl Kautsky: you can have democracy without socialism, but you cannot have socialism without democracy.[29] Bureaucratic measures and negative attitudes by government officials are not without foundation and ways of extending effective democratic participation and control over bureaucratic management have to be implemented. Government officials have to consider themselves servants of citizens, not masters of the public.

The state remains a legitimate instrument to bring about significant system change. Unlike in polities (such as the EU and the USA) where the legislature is subject to legal constraints, the UK Parliament can legally bring private assets into public ownership. But such initiatives would undoubtedly

---

27 Hutton, *How Good We Can Be*, pp 138–9.
28 Hutton, *How Good We Can Be*, p 141.
29 Karl Kautsky, *The Dictatorship of the Proletariat*. Vienna: National Labour Press, 1918. Available at: https://rowlandpasaribu.files.wordpress.com/2013/09/karl-kautsky-the-dicta torship-of-the-proletariat.pdf

face legal and political hurdles. The division of powers and the rule of law are devised to prevent governments from carrying out 'populist' policies, even if they have electoral support. Nationalisation of property would be challenged as undermining individual property rights. Constraints operating through international agreements binding on states are a serious problem (for example, agreements such as The Transatlantic Trade and Investment Partnership, TTIP). Transnational and foreign ownership of economic corporations would pose a substantial hurdle. The 'rules based international order', however, even in capitalist countries, is subject to state intervention. During the Russian invasion of Ukraine, for example, the foreign assets of Russian owners were 'frozen' and some seized by Western states – even though there was no state of war – and their owners, 'oligarchs', were not charged with any criminal or financial offence. In the transition to state-controlled market socialism, assets would be legally transferred from private to state ownership.

A major obstacle to establish public ownership and to strengthen socialist coordinating powers of the state has been the influence of the media in the formation of public opinion. The corporately owned mass media, deeply embedded in established capitalist countries, socialise people to be critical of, even hostile to, moves for collective ownership. There has developed a deep-seated negative political immunity to socialist proposals and policies. Whereas people are positive about the collective provision of education and health services, in other areas, the state is often regarded as a negative oppressive political force. The proposals in this chapter promote collective control by stakeholders of media corporations which would act to promote the public interest.

Making the transition

In earlier chapters, we noted the significant decline of European socialist and social democratic parties. Despite the weakening of contemporary capitalism following the financial crisis of 2007, turning policy proposals, such as those discussed earlier, into an electoral political programme promoted by any major political party, would require major changes in political culture. The leaders of social democratic parties, fearing electoral defeat, have relied on personality politics and have neither proposed nor sought alternative policies even during capitalist crises (noted in Chapter 6). Prominent writers sympathetic to the socialist cause are pessimistic about the possibility of a move to socialism. David Schweickart opined that 'there is no evidence … of *any* movement to nationalise our established corporations'.[30] David

---

[30] Schweickart, *Against Capitalism*, p 323. Italics in original.

Miller acknowledged that owners and top managers would lose out[31] and he had doubts about the possibility of 'ballot box socialism'.[32] Such sentiments have continued into the twenty-first century. The economic crisis of 2007 and the energy price hikes in 2022, however, have led to widespread public criticism of institutions in the financial system that have privatised profits and socialised losses. The state became the saviour of capitalism – at great public cost. There was no public outcry in the USA and the UK against nationalisation, which saved corporations in the financial sector. The privatisation of transport, public utilities (in the UK – gas, electricity, railways, water, post and telecommunications) has led to higher prices and the subsequent diversion of revenue to profits. During the significant price rises of fuel in 2022, Michael Roberts has calculated that in the first six months of 2022, the top energy companies (Shell, ExxonMobil, Chevron and others) made a profit of $100 billion.[33] As Roberts points out, political discourse dwells on how to relieve, or to avoid, the price rises. In the UK, only the trade Union Congress proposed to nationalise the retail sector – but not the major energy companies.

While critics are correct to suggest that there is not a 'movement' in the UK and other European countries in support of collective ownership, there is ample public opinion survey data showing significant public backing for selective state ownership. A YouGov poll conducted in May 2017 asked a sample of British electors whether or not they approved of various British companies and economic sectors being 'nationalised and run in the public sector or being run by private companies'. The results are shown in Table 16.1.[34] The first column shows those positive towards public ownership.

The first column shows overwhelming support for the public sector running the National Health Service, the British Broadcasting Corporation, the Royal Mail, the railways, water companies and (though to a lesser degree) energy and bus companies. However, one must be cautious about the extent of public support for comprehensive public ownership. This is indicated by the considerable backing for privatised air travel, telephone and internet suppliers and banks. No doubt the positive effects of companies in air transport (such as Ryanair), with 68 per cent of respondents being in favour of private ownership, is due to cheap public travel. Even energy companies received the backing of 31 per cent of

---

[31] Miller, *Market, State and Community*, p 336. Management would not be subject to the personal wishes of owners, however.

[32] Miller, *Market, State and Community*, p 323.

[33] Energy, cost of living and recession – Michael Roberts Blog (wordpress.com)

[34] See also similar findings for 8–9 May 2014. Available at https://yougov.co.uk/topics/politics/survey-results

Table 16.1: Public opinion on private and public ownership, 2017

	Public sector	Private sector	Don't know
National			
Health service	84	5	10
Royal Mail	65	21	14
Railways	60	25	15
Energy companies	53	31	16
Telephone and internet	30	53	17
Airlines	14	68	16
Water	59	25	16
Bus companies	50	35	15
Banks	28	53	18
BBC	58	25	17
Schools	81	6	13

Question asked: 'Do you think the following should be nationalised and run in the public sector, or privatised and run by private companies?'

Note: Percentage of respondents favouring public or private ownership for the sector.

Source: YouGov Survey. Poll of 1936 Great Britain adults conducted on 17–18 May 2017.

the respondents, though this number dropped in 2022 as a consequence of excessive company profits. A UK poll by Survation conducted in July–August 2022, asking 'Do you think the following should be run in the private or public sector?' found overwhelming support for the public sector for the following: water 69 per cent, buses 65 per cent, railways 67 per cent, National Health Service 78 per cent, energy 66 per cent, Royal Mail 68 per cent.[35] These findings remind us that an alternative system could be set up with substantial and widely based social support for the measures proposed. The excessive executive salaries associated with market competition and the distortions caused by the enormous wealth of speculators have led to widespread public disapproval.

Nationalisation need not have significantly disruptive effects which might lead to electoral defeat. Public control can be extended initially to companies that fail due to mismanagement and to those that indulge in excessive profit making. In the UK, financial companies and public utilities could be taken into public ownership with wide public backing. It is during

---

[35] Survation (London). Available at: https://www.survation.com/new-poll-public-strongly-backing-public-ownership-of-energy-and-key-utilities

periods of economic failure or crisis that alternative policies are likely to find political support.

Writers who declare that the end of human civilisation looks more likely than the end of capitalism are unduly pessimistic. Socialism could, under the right circumstances, gather considerable appeal – even in the USA, where Gallup polls show that 'socialism' has been regarded 'positively' by 38 per cent and 40 per cent of respondents in 2010 and 2021 respectively. However, 'free enterprise' had a 'positive image' for 84 per cent of respondents. Bearing these figures in mind, any path to socialism must recognise the cultural and political context. In 2021, 65 per cent of respondents with Democratic Party (US) 'leanings' had a positive image of socialism.[36] 'Socialist' policies (such as public healthcare) are widely favoured. Selected nationalisation would not be an electoral liability. The success of the Scottish Nationalist Party in preserving welfare services in the face of austerity programmes gives confidence that such policies can rely on considerable electoral support.

Political parties as movers of socialism are not a lost cause. The appeal of Jeremy Corbyn's policies (in the 2017 election Labour won 40 per cent of votes cast – see Chapter 7) and the success of Bernie Sanders in the 2016 US presidential campaign is evidence of such backing. 'The greed, recklessness, and illegal behavior of major Wall Street firms plunged this country into the worst financial crisis since the 1930s', Sanders wrote in his Agenda for America (a set of 12 economic policies). He has supported the establishment of worker-owned cooperatives and proposed workers' self-management' and public ownership.[37] Sanders's presidential campaign and policy were reformist calling for significant reforms within the capitalist system. While Sanders might well espouse such views as a candidate, implementation is another question. Moving such proposals to Party Manifestos binding on leaders faces opposition even from Party supporters. However, without political organisation, sentiments will never turn into political achievements.

A more fundamental obstacle to socialism is the widespread belief that market rewards reflect what people believe they truly deserve – at least for

---

[36] https://news.gallup.com/poll/357755/socialism-capitalism-ratings-unchanged.aspxother

[37] 'I believe that, in the long run, major industries in this state and nation should be publicly owned and controlled by the workers themselves.' 'Democracy means public ownership of the major means of production, it means decentralization, it means involving people in their work. Rather than having bosses and workers it means having democratic control over the factories and shops to as great a degree as you can.' Bernie Sanders taken from entries in Wikipedia. Available at: /en.wikipedia.org/wiki/Political_positions_of_Bernie_Sanders#Employee_ownership

those who have earned (rather than inherited) them. However persuasive the arguments of writers such as Robert Dahl on the moral foundations of economic democracy,[38] nationalisation has been unable to command enduring support. My proposal is that 'market rewards', for those who really earn them, have to remain in place and, concurrently, socialists have to promote socialist policies to influence the public's consciousness. My conclusion is to retain much of the culture of consumerism. The form of socialism will bear the imprint of its origin: 'socialism with American or British characteristics'.

Regulated market socialism has many contradictions that stem from its hybrid economic forms. Autonomous enterprises in the private sector, competing through markets, seek profits to provide for investment and also as a 'reward for enterprise'. The danger is that the market components will stimulate the approval of capitalistic features that are antithetical to socialism. People become motivated to strive for mercenary ends – for accumulation and speculation. The market is a form of social control – it identifies the goods and services people have and should have. It generates the criteria for individual success and status. It defines the capitalist economic order as natural and moral. To prevent negative outcomes, competition and the market have to be contained within the regulatory framework of an economic plan. Regulated market socialism, if adopted, would be a positive achievement in terms of the reallocation and redistribution of assets and income. It would change for the better the nature of the moral and social order.

The international dimension

Any market socialist alternative has to be contextualised in the framework of a global economy and developments in international relations are outside the framework of this book. A potent criticism of a move to regulated market socialism is that even if endorsed democratically and adopted by a government, it will not happen because foreign interests will stop it. Transnational corporations, if confronted with nationalisation, would not meekly 'surrender' the ownership of their assets. Hegemonic states would intervene in support of corporations registered in their countries. Intervention in Cuba, Venezuela, Bolivia and Chile illustrate previous forms of opposition. Such interests are embedded in the international structures that limit states' abilities to serve their citizens. However, we are considering here a transition in the advanced capitalist states under conditions of electoral competition and compensation for shareholders. Contemporary capitalism

---

[38] Robert A. Dahl, *A Preface to Economic Democracy*. Berkeley: University of California Press, 1985.

lost the high moral ground of the sanctity of private property when the assets of Russian 'oligarchs' were 'frozen', forcibly sold and some were confiscated during the Russian invasion of Ukraine in 2022.[39] The effects of sanctions have significantly limited the free flow of information and stifled criticism of Western governments.

The Western core of capitalist countries led by the USA is no longer an unchallenged leader of a unipolar world. It is faced by a rising semi-core of states headed by China, as discussed earlier in Chapter 10. The One Belt One Road initiative and the rise of the Eurasian Economic Union and closer association of the BRICS present an alternative source of economic and political power distinct from the core Western powers led by the USA. Chinese corporations are significant players in the world economy. The Chinese-sponsored Developmental Bank already provides financial support related to its One Belt One Road programme.

Something like a 'Beijing consensus'[40] could replace the 'Washington consensus' and provide the basis for a more pluralist and multi-polar world. Under this scenario, an alternative 'capitalism with socialist characteristics' could not easily be suppressed by a hegemonic capitalist bloc.[41] The open globalisation of the early twenty-first century could be replaced by a more limited regionally based form of internationalisation. The idea of a 'developmental peace' which promotes economic and social development, irrespective of the political ideology and structure of states, is a possible alternative foreign policy option for countervailing powers. If adopted, it would avoid the negative consequences of Western democracy promotion. However, a word of caution. One must avoid substituting an Asian Eastphalian 'developmental peace' panacea for a Western 'democratic peace'. The rise of a competing bloc of states, formed from the BRICS, the Eurasian Economic Association and other states (such as Venezuela, Cuba) and led by China, might well exacerbate tensions with the capitalist economic core headed by the USA.

---

[39] The British (Conservative) government was considering the seizure of the assets of Russian oligarchs 'without the need to pay them compensation'. *Financial Times* (London) 3 March 2022. The application of sanctions on Russian firms and people in Western states made their businesses impossible to continue.

[40] This is not the policy position of the Chinese government, though some of its statements are in line with it. The ideas are attributed to Joshua Cooper Ramo, *The Beijing Consensus*. London: Foreign Policy Centre, 2004.

[41] This is not the policy position of the Chinese government, though some of its statements are in line with it. The ideas are attributed to Ramo, *The Beijing Consensus*.

Conclusion

The proposals in this chapter mark a path away from liberal capitalism. A democratically controlled socialist state could provide a hierarchical framework ordered by a national plan, within which economic markets operate. Christopher Pierson has contended that 'The market is indispensable ... as the least bad form of organisation under prevailing conditions'.[42] What were 'prevailing conditions' have changed, and many of the market's functions can be augmented or replaced by computer simulation. In a 'market society', market relations predominate to shape economic outcomes. It is quite a different matter to utilise economic markets to realise consumer preferences in the context of a national socialist plan. Market relations contained within a system of planning would have faults but, I contend, these are less than the faults currently in operation under neoliberal conditions.

The proposals here outline the steps towards regulated market socialism. Extreme levels of inequality would be curtailed by blockage of the sources of inherited wealth. Public ownership, taxation policies, the creation of a full employment economy and the provision of universal basic services would 'level up'. Public ownership would also 'level down' by eliminating the source of unearned income. One might agree with Pierson that the major claim for market socialism is that its feasibility outweighs the loss of the scope and purity of the idealistic socialist agenda.[43] And my proposals are more than what Will Hutton defines as 'stakeholder capitalism'.[44] The state would have a comprehensive purposive planning role and would be a major actor with considerable ownership of industrial and financial assets. The economic plan would define the parameters of the market. As wealth increases, so would the free supply of collective goods (health, education, pensions, economic welfare). As technology develops, the working day could be shortened. Such measures would result in a cumulative reduction in surplus value, of profit for private means. An emphasis would be put on sustainable economic development and social security – the provision of fundamental social services, environmental sustainability, poverty reduction, human development, and the expansion of local and regional industries. Consumer satisfaction would not be neglected and here the market would be important. A modern form of socialism would provide mechanisms to evaluate social costs, particularly ecological consequences of industrialisation.

---

[42] C. Pierson, *Socialism after Communism*. Cambridge: Polity, 1995, p 88.

[43] Pierson, *Socialism after Communism*, p 189.

[44] Hutton, *How Good We Can Be*, p 141.

Doubts remain about its sustainability. The values, norms and institutions formed under capitalism might overwhelm the socialistic forms that are suggested here. The corporate mass media present a considerable challenge. The media, however, would be subject to conditions laid down in the charters of broadcasting and print companies. Oligarchic control of the media would be weakened. There would also be stakeholder participation required by law, which would address and prevent the degeneration of the mass media to an instrument of proprietors and their backers. Even under benign developmental policies, countries will experience internal conflicts consequent on processes of domination, discrimination between social classes and between national elites and between elites and non-elites. My contention is a modest one: regulated market socialism will be better than anything else that has been tried.

Social Formations: Patterns of Coordination and Control

This appendix compares: self-sustaining communities, liberal capitalism, social democracy, state-capitalism, state-controlled capitalism, and state socialism. They are analysed according to three criteria: type of ownership of productive assets (private or collective, shown on top horizontal axis), form of coordination (market, state – left vertical axis), and of control of surplus product (minimally regulated by the state, partially regulated, and regulated – right vertical axis). These models are simplifications illustrating the major characteristics of economies. Real economic formations are in practice mixtures of these variables.

TYPE OF OWNERSHIP

COORDINATION	Private	Private/collective	Collective	SURPLUS PRODUCT
Collective			SELF-SUSTAINING COMMUNITIES	Minimal
Minimal state	LIBERAL CAPITALISM			Minimal regulation
Minimal state		SOCIAL DEMOCRACY		Partially regulated
State			STATE-CAPITALISM	Regulated
State (minimal market)		STATE-CONTROLLED CAPITALISM		Partially regulated
State			STATE SOCIALISM	Regulated

Regulated Market Socialism

Regulated market socialism is analysed into four major components: type of ownership, form of allocation of economic surplus, economic coordination and type of society. The top axis indicates the allocation of economic surplus by the private sector and the state plan. The bottom axis shows the form of ownership: private and state. The right-hand axis shows the form of economic coordination: market and state. The left-hand axis defines the type of civil society; unitary, one in which the state suppresses civil society; pluralist, one in which there are multiple groups. There are two economic sub-sectors, public and private. Both are coordinated by the market, but subject to a state plan, which effectively controls and allocates surplus product.

**ALLOCATION OF
ECONOMIC SURPLUS**

		Private/state	**State plan**		
	Unitary	–	–	**State**	
	Pluralist		PUBLIC	Market	
CIVIL SOCIETY			SECTOR		**FORM OF ECONOMIC**
	Pluralist	PRIVATE		Market	**COORDINATION**
		SECTOR			
		Private	Public/		
			state		

FORM OF OWNERSHIP

Index

Printed and bound by CPI Group (UK) Ltd, Croydon, CR0 4YY

13/04/2025

14656584-0005